POWER, PROFIT AND POETRY
TRADITIONAL SOCIETY IN KATHIAWAR, WESTERN INDIA

POWER, PROFIT AND POETRY

Traditional Society in Kathiawar, Western India

Harald Tambs-Lyche

MANOHAR
1997

First published 1997

ISBN 81-7304-176-8

Published by
Ajay Kumar Jain for
Manohar Publishers & Distributors
2/6 Ansari Road, Daryaganj
New Delhi 110 002

Typeset by
AJ Software Publishing Co. Pvt. Ltd.
305, Durga Chambers, 1333, D.B. Gupta Road
Karol Bagh, New Delhi 110 005

Printed at
Rajkamal Electric Press
B 35/9 G.T. Karnal Road Indl. Area
Delhi 110 033

Contents

Acknowledgments

I could hardly have finished this book without the encouragement of my wife, Marine Carrin. Fredrik Barth taught me anthropology, Reidar Grønhaug was my most critical and most inspiring colleague during 20 years at the University of Bergen, and Adrian Mayer offered constant friendship and encouragement over a number of years. In Saurashtra, there are much too many who have helped to include them all, but Jayant Meghani and Haribhai Patel have been outstanding friends as well as intellectual contacts. In Rajasthan, I have much to thank Inder Dan Detha for. This book represents but a small part of the investment all these and others have made in the project; I hope to satisfy more of their expectations in another volume.

This book is dedicated to the memory of my mother, who lived to see the thesis which provided the groundwork for the book. Through a long and heavy process of digesting the impressions Saurashtra made upon me, she stood firm in supporting the work, as she knew from her own painstaking study in entomology how slow can be the progress of scientific work.

Note on Language and Transcriptions

Names and terms from Saurashtra are here given the usual 'English' form, except in quoting other writers. For all-Indian concepts too, I have used the common form, thus Shiva and Shakti rather than Śiva and Śakti. In the same vein I have preferred Kathiawar to Kathiawad, and this has implied using the uncommon forms Jhalawar or Gohilwar for consistency, though these district names are more often transcribed by '-wad'. I have done so feeling that linguistic precision would add little to the purpose of this book. Wherever Gujarati terms differ from all-Indian forms, I have used the form least likely to cause confusion.

Introduction

Throughout history the ideal empire has been conceived of as the religiously constituted state. The resurgence of the Islamic states in Iran and Pakistan, and the attempt to bring about *Ram Rajya* in India[1] are the modern manifestations of this age-old dream. These attempts have also exposed the precariousness of the notion of a secular state in a democratically constituted society in which religion takes a back seat.

It is against this background that I present in this volume an analysis of tradition in Saurashtra, formerly known as Kathiawar, which forms the peninsular part of the state of Gujarat, on the west coast of India. As in Rajasthan, traditional political institutions were allowed to continue here even after independence. The princely states of Saurashtra are among the last extant examples, and thus most accessible to us, of traditional Hindu states.[2]

These states, I argue, did not constitute religious entities in the sense of Rama's mythical realm. They can be analysed only if power is taken as the central dimension in the construction of the state. Religion was important; indeed certain religious ideas were integral to the very conception of the kingdom and state. But these were not shared by all subjects. Religious opposition and conflict—within Hinduism, as well as with Jainism and Islam—called, on the part of the ruler, for a considerable degree of diplomacy and tolerance. If these states differed from the modern conception of 'secularism', being intrinsically bound to religious institutions, they nevertheless controlled societies where the right of minorities to their own religion, custom and law was recognized practice. In the separation of the affairs of the state from those of its constituent communities, they remain closer to the ideas behind the present constitution of India than to the image of Rama's legendary domain.

I stress, then, the plural character of society in traditional Kathiawar. While not denying the presence of hierarchy, as propounded by Dumont (1966), I re-locate it. Elsewhere, I have seen hierarchy as a factor guiding interaction in India, as well as structuring important cultural images of the whole.[3] In the present book, the image of a hierarchically ordered whole is not used to explain the integration of society, which, rather, is effected by power. Here I follow largely the analysis of Howard Spodek (1974, 1976) of society in Saurashtra though I deal with questions outside the scope of his work.[4] Concerned with rural-urban integration, he largely left the religious aspect aside. In my approach, religion appears not as the integrating factor but as a vehicle of cultural pluralism.

Hinduism in Saurashtra is not a unitary phenomenon. Its constituent elements may be interpreted to form a 'unity in diversity'—a view held particularly by Brahmins in the traditional set-up—but, on the regional level, Hinduism tends to dissolve into several mutually conflicting sub-systems. The chief opposition, here, parallels the structure of power and economic relations; it divides the merchants from most other communities. Thus there is a structural contradiction between rulers and merchants, parties which are nevertheless dependent on each other in forming traditional Saurashtrian society. Behind the rulers stand the rural, agricultural population, in an alliance known here as the *ter tansali* or 'thirteen castes'.[5] The opposition between merchants and rulers, then, is more than just a conflict between the elite; it integrates the rulers with 'the people' and isolates the merchants from them.[6] Later, sectarian Vaishnavism—especially the Swaminarayana movement—draw the masses away from the religion of their landlords towards the vegetarian and non-violent attitudes of the merchant groups.

This book, then, deals with a fundamental contradiction in regional Hinduism, but leads up to its transformation. Following independence, the merchant and Swaminarayana view came to stand for modernity as against tradition, enlightenment versus obscurantism, democracy and land reform as opposed to the old powers of the land. With the end of princely rule, the values and ideas of merchants—in effect, of the bourgeoisie—came to dominate modern Saurashtra. Yet perhaps the trend has turned, as elements of the traditional pattern are now used to legitimize the regional conception of the new fundamentalism.

Located between the Indian mainland and the Middle East, Saurashtra is close to major trade routes. But Barygaza (Broach) of the Greeks, Cambay in medieval times, Surat of the seventeenth and eighteenth centuries, Bombay today, are all ports located on the mainland. Those of Saurashtra have been of secondary importance, even before the arrival of the steamship made their shallow harbours unsuited to the mainstream of trade. While the history of the peninsula is replete with attempts to partake its profits, directly through commerce or indirectly through 'piracy' (smuggling, indeed, still looms large among the criminal activities of the area; Porbandar has become as notorious for it as Jamnagar once was), Saurashtra's relation to the main trade links may be qualified as 'peripheral'.

As regards agriculture, the peripheral position is even more marked. The alluvial soils of the mainland do not extend far into the peninsula, which is relatively rocky and has shallow soils. Until modern times, in fact, the peninsula was underpopulated,[7] and competition for people was as much a feature of traditional politics as was competition for land.

While mainland rulers seldom subjected the peninsula to outright conquest and direct taxation, they tried to control it indirectly, through vassalage. Military expeditions from the mainland, for subjection and taxation, are a recurring feature in Saurashtra's history, while for much of the time a measure of independence was maintained. This limited autonomy is important in explaining the extreme political fragmentation of the peninsula, which in British times numbered some two hundred 'states'.[8] Some such units contained but a single village; some were states of considerable size, with an army and a degree of bureaucratic administration. The political organization, as of 1800, could not be termed 'tribal'; yet by no means were all villages incorporated into 'states'. To an extent, therefore, the history of the area, from medieval times onward, may be seen as the emergence of states from a tribal background. But large cities and states were extant before medieval society brought reorganization as well as the introduction of new elements.

The peninsula is geologically distinct from the mainland; it is believed at some time in prehistory to have been an island. Culturally, it is equally well defined, and people define themselves as belonging to Kathiawar, rather than to Gujarat. Kathiawadi—the local dialect—differs from standard Gujarati and seems more closely to ressemble the dialects of western Rajasthan. Socially, though some groups span the border, Saurashtra has its own combination of castes. While stereotypes of Gujaratis relate to the image of a businessman, Kathiawadis are seen as the 'hill-billies' of the state. Material culture, too, differs from that of the mainland. Handicrafts are in some ways closer to those of Rajasthan, as is traditional dress. While women in Gujarat mostly wear saris, the skirt, blouse and shawl remain the traditional dress of Kathiawadi women.

Some of these differences may not be regional in origin, but rather indicate that Saurashtra, like Rajasthan, has retained a number of cultural traits which, in mainland Gujarat, have changed or disappeared. Centuries of Muslim rule, merchant cultural influence, and the regional dominance of such castes as the Anavil Brahmins of south Gujarat and the Patidars of Charottar[9] all affected mainland Gujarat, while Rajput culture remained dominant in Saurashtra and Rajasthan.

Important, too, is the influence of pastoralists on the traditional culture of the peninsula. Its stony and infertile soils, compared to mainland Gujarat, make for a less intensive pattern of land use, with more land available for grazing. This similarity to Rajasthan is, however, counteracted by the urban element, allowing for greater density of population. This, too, is a factor in the importance of the merchant castes, leading to the balanced influence of ruler and merchant in the small city-states.

For European readers, it may be illustrative that both the area and population of Saurashtra are comparable to those of Denmark—a considerable density when the quality of the soil is taken into account.

Rajput states covered much of the area before 1952. A typical feature of such states was the integration of kinship into the structure of the state. At the basis of the state was the segmentary lineage, belonging to a larger, named clan. These lineages were ranked, with the ruler's lineage at the top. *Bhayat* or junior relatives might hold their land in *jagir* from the ruler, while their relatives again held land from them. Thus a feudatory structure of landholding emerges which at once ranks the relatives and integrates the whole clan. Even a smallholder might be party to this structure, becoming a minor aristocrat. This set him apart from other peasants, and strengthened caste solidarity. Thus the Rajput state was built upon a particular form of caste dominance.

The Rajput chiefs of the peninsula belonged to four major clans. In the northwest were the Jadejas, who also ruled Kutch. East of them, and almost down to the Gulf of Cambay, were the Jhalas. South of them again, the Gohils were the last of the Rajput clans to establish themselves in the peninsula. The fourth clan, the Jethwas, ruled in Porbandar on the western coast. They were the oldest ruling house by British times; we shall later see that they are a rather special case. Other Rajput clans were confined, by 1800, to small and peripheral states, but some had once been powerful. There were also non-Rajput areas. Most important were the small states dominated by Kathis, at the centre of the peninsula, and the large Muslim state of Junagadh. Other peripheral areas were dominated by different castes, some of them, with mixed results, claiming Rajput status.

Political domination was effected by a combined control over fortresses—the Uparkot in Junagadh was the most formidable—and over agricultural land, from which most of the revenue came. War was an integral part of the political system.[10] In the towns, protected by fortresses, trade and manufacture formed an additional, and important, source of revenue.

Culturally, Rajputs shared with most of the rural population the worship of goddesses, with animal sacrifice as a central element. The traders, as an important minority, were opposed to these cults. Whether Jain or Vaishnavite, they were vegetarian followers of non-violence. But their presence was necessary for any chiefdom to become a state. Indeed, traders were well established in the area under the Vallabhi kingdom, which collapsed in the eighth century AD. Trade seems to have suffered from the unsettled conditions of early medieval times, until it picked up under the aegis of the later medieval rulers by the fifteenth to seventeenth centuries. Merchant influence on society and culture rose and fell with the fortunes of trade.

Different historical periods contribute to what is, today, the 'past in the present' in Saurashtra.[11] From the points of view of present-day Saurashtrians, there is not one past but at least two; while equally true or false, they define in each case the background to perspectives on the present and the future. There is the heroic history of Kathiawar, a land of noble warriors, the home of chivalry and honour. But there is also the history of towns and traders of Saurashtra, threatened in their non-violent pursuits by the instability of the political system. Both versions are post-hoc constructions; they correspond nevertheless to the opposition between landholding and merchant interest that we can follow, like a thread, through the history of the peninsula.

Our discussion begins with the emergence, in the beginning of the middle ages, of those traditions that, in due time, constitute the social structure of traditional Kathiawar. As such I am less concerned with history than with myth, though I shall of course try to place the myth in historical context. Thus it is not the events as such that interest me, but the pregnancy of myth as 'charter' (Malinowski 1954, 101) for traditional society.

I go on to describe this form of society, as it flourished from the sixteenth to the eighteenth century; a society clearly dominated by the martial Rajputs and their princely states that were populated mainly by Kheduts or peasants. But the dividing line between them and their Darbars or lords is often fluid. The Maldharis or the pastoral castes roam between villages, but sometimes play a role in the politics of land. In the towns, we find that community of merchants (Banias) which, as the counterpart of the Western bourgeoisie, rose gradually in importance until it became, by the eighteenth century, strong enough for a 'balance of power' to obtain between them and the rulers. The states, too, underwent a transformation in the eighteenth century, when the larger ones acquired bureaucratic administration and standing armies; changes that lead from traditional Kathiawar to modern Saurashtra. It will always be an open question how this modernizing process might have continued, if the British had not come. The transformation had, indeed, begun when the treaties of Colonel Walker tied Kathiawar into the system of British suzerainty. The effectiveness of this system increased gradually, and from 1858 politics in the peninsula had to relate to the frameworks of British control, freezing the boundaries between states. The rulers were now secure in their positions, free to look for alternatives to warfare in allocating funds and energy, and many of them took a very active part in developing the resources of their state.

But this brought conflict with the merchants, as both were now active in the economic field (Spodek 1976, 48-53). Trade initially profited from the Pax Britannica. But as the Gujarat mainland, under direct British rule, developed, it became clear to Saurashtra's merchants that political fragmentation, with the customs barriers and other restrictions it involved, was limiting their operations. Large numbers migrated to Bombay and other major cities, and the merchants came to spearhead the opposition against the rulers that grew, gradually, into the independence movement, led by the Congress. The alliance between rulers and peasants proved resilient, however, and the satyagrahas of Rajkot and Limbdi, in the thirties, showed how limited was the support for the independence movement in Saurashtra. With independence, Saurashtra, like Rajasthan, became a confederation of princely states led by a Rajpramukh elected from among the rulers. Junagadh tried to secede to Pakistan in 1947, and in the following years several members of the princely families were active in an insurrection against the new political order. It was only in 1952 that conditions allowed elections to be held, and Saurashtra to be incorporated as a state in the Indian Union. These elections were, surprisingly in view of what had gone before, a resounding victory for the Congress. Now merchants became the dominant political element in Saurashtra, and their culture an overwhelming influence. Many elements of the older Rajput-dominated order were swept aside, becoming folklore survivals. This was the situation when I did my first fieldwork in Saurashtra in 1973-4.

From 1947 the old name of the peninsula, 'Kathiawar', fell into disuse. It was too intimately connected with the old order. Instead, the even older, and scripturally sanctioned, term 'Saurashtra' was revived. Thus from ancient 'Saurashtra' we progress to medieval 'Kathiawar', while modernity sees the return of the name 'Saurashtra' in another guise. By the late 1980s, the dominance of merchant culture was being challenged, as the movements of the 'backward castes' and the fundamentalist revival called forth again, from near oblivion, some of the survivals of traditional Kathiawar.

This book aims at analysing the changing forms of society in the peninsula as a shifting balance of forces; the opposition between rulers and merchants, between town and country.[12] These oppositions involve a cultural discourse, a conflict of values, expressed largely through religion. I assume, then, that the values and religious forms of interest groups—'estates' as I shall call them—have, to a considerable degree, been continuous throughout history. This basically Weberian approach is used to analyse the caste system of Saurashtra, which emerges not as an ordered hierarchy, but as a scene for competition and discourse.

We may now return to the present. If caste is, indeed, less a 'system' in itself than a set of rules guiding interest groups in their cultural, economic and political competition, the idea of a 'return' to the ideal Hindu state should remain a dream. Politics in such a society should aim, rather, at creating as far as possible equitable rules of competition within a basically neutral—or, to use the current term—secular framework.

NOTES

1. According to the views of many Hindu fundamentalists, the Babri Masjid was constructed on the foundations of a Hindu temple, which marked the actual birthplace of Rama, the royal hero of the *Ramayana*. Following demonstrations

for its removal, a group of activists backed up by masses of demonstrators broke through police cordons and demolished the Masjid on 6 December, 1992. This action dramatized the present conflicts between secularism and fundamentalism in India.

2. In Saurashtra, these state formations lasted until 1952, when the first elections were held to the Legislative Assembly of the State of Saurashtra. They had, of course, lost much of their autonomy by then, first through British suzerainty, then by the establishment of independent India in 1947.
3. The hierarchical pattern of social interaction has been treated in Tambs-Lyche (1992a), but will be further analysed in a forthcoming book. As to 'hierarchical discourse', I discuss this concept more fully in a forthcoming book (b).
4. Pearson (1976), writing of sixteenth-century mainland Gujarat, paints a rather different picture, where the very considerable merchant activity remained, nevertheless, peripheral to the state.
5. Literally 'thirteen bowls', refers to the commensality of these castes.
6. For further discussion of this opposition, see Tambs-Lyche (1976a, 1982, 1992, 1996) and Spodek (1974 and 1976).
7. This is an important point in Spodek's analysis, and he notes the considerable migration that resulted from this competition for people or followers (1976, 27).
8. See, for example, Spodek (1976) or Wood (1978, 241-2). When Colonel Walker, in 1806-7, laboured to set up a system of treaties to ensure peaceful conditions, no less than 153 'states' were included. By 1924, when the Western India States Agency was formed, there were 225 of them. There were numerous changes during British dominance, notably under Keatinge in 1863, when seven classes of state were instituted according to the degree of jurisdiction; in 1925, when clusters of 'non-jurisdictional' states (or estates) were formed for administrative purposes; and finally the 'attachment schemes' of 1943, when the smallest units were merged with larger neighbours. Most of the reorganization concerned, however, only the very minor states.
9. The Anavil seem to have established their dominance under the Mughals, or possibly even earlier (Van der Veen 1972). The Patidars gained ascendancy over the local Rajputs as the Marathas took over from the Mughals in Central Gujarat (e.g. Shah 1964, Pocock 1972).
10. Spodek describes the peninsula as 'studded' with fortified towns. Colonel Walker identified 162 places as fortified; a survey of 1849 notes 921 towns containing fortified residences of the ruler (Records of the Bombay Government, 1856; cited by Spodek 1976, 6). When Pramar (1988, 52) discusses the different settlement patterns of Gujarat state, it is the village walls which set Saurashtra apart from the rest.
11. For a discussion of this concept, see Bloch (1977). I wish to underline here the element of interest that enters into any group's conceptualization of the past.
12. Much of this perspective is present in Spodek (1974, 1976) and in some of my earlier work (1976, 1982, 1992).

CHAPTER I

Twilight of Ancient Saurashtra
The End of an Empire, the Birth of a Goddess

A FORGOTTEN EMPIRE

Excavations at Lothal and elsewhere have established the presence of the Indus civilization in Saurashtra. Much later, that most famous of Mauryan rulers, Ashoka, had his edicts inscribed on a rock at Girnar. It was from this city, then known as Girinagara, that viceroys of the later Guptas held sway over Saurashtra. When Gupta rule declined towards AD 500, they became independent. Ghatarka, founder of the Maitraka dynasty, moved his capital around AD 470 to Vallabhipur, in what is now Bhavnagar district on the eastern side of the peninsula. It was a port then—the gulf of Cambay has since silted up—and was already established as a centre of trade and learning.[1]

Junagadh is a classic site for a fortress, but its position was never suited to trade.[2] Vallabhipur lay where the peninsula joins the mainland, close to other historic ports on the gulf of Cambay; it was well placed for trade, but difficult to defend. Thus Ghatarka's move indicates his desire to control trade, and shows that he did not fear an attack from the mainland. Indeed, the kingdom he founded—known as the Vallabhi or Maitraka empire—came to control considerable territories to the east.

Vallabhipur was a centre of Jainism. According to their accounts, the Shwetambara sect was established here around AD 80.[3] Important redactions of Jain religious works were made here, in AD 300 (or 313) and in AD 453 (or 466). The latter version became canonical for the Shwetambaras, and led to the definitive split between them and the Digambaras.[4] The city was also a Buddhist centre. In the fourth century AD, several important Buddhist treatises were produced from a nearby monastery.[5] And Vallabhi was enthusiastically described by the Chinese traveller Hiuan Tsang as a site of Buddhist learning. He claimed a hundred Buddhist monasteries, with six thousand devotees.

'All the families' of Vallabhi, he says, 'live in wealth. There are a hundred whose wealth amounts to a million. Merchandise from distant countries is found here in abundance....'[6] In short, this eyewitness account of around AD 640 describes a wealthy trading centre. The impression is strengthened if we assume, as Lamb (1959) does, that Buddhism and trade go together in this period, and that Jains, as ever since, were primarily merchants.

The rulers of Vallabhi were probably Shaivite, at least in the beginning (BDG, 48, Gadre, 63-4). But Dhruvasena (*c.* AD 520-40) professed to be a Bhagavata—a follower of Vishnu. His sister Dudda seems to have been a Buddhist. Dhruvasena is further credited with an important reform of Jainism: following a recital of the Kalpasutra to console him at the loss of a son, laymen were allowed to hear the text. Earlier, this had been a privilege of only monks and nuns. Thus Dhruvasena seems to have taken an interest in all the main religions of his day, whether for personal or political reasons. His successor, Dharapatta, calls himself a devotee of the Goddess Aditya. Guhasena, who followed him, declares himself, at different times, as a follower of Shiva and the Buddha. His grants were to Buddhist viharas, but Dharasena II, next in line, gave grants to Brahmins also. And while Shiladitya I, his successor, 'took keen interest in following the tenets of Buddhism', he granted land to Shiva and Aditya temples as well as to viharas (BDG, 49-50).[7]

A liberal attitude to religion seems, indeed, to be typical of the Maitraka rulers of Vallabhi. It is an attitude we recognize from other ancient empires in India; a later example would be the Gujarat of the Chalukyas in the twelfth and thirteenth centuries. A similar climate characterized the Gujarat sultanate in the following centuries, as is evident from the degree of freedom enjoyed by Jain and Hindu merchants in this Muslim state (Pearson 1976).

There is thus a certain continuity in the way rulers deal with urban society, in Gujarat and Saurashtra, from the Vallabhi period onwards. The continuity of this urban society is manifest in the merchant population. Everything points to present-day Jain Banias of the region as the descendants of the Jains of Vallabhi, while the guild organization among Gujarati merchants may be equally old.[8] What became of Vallabhi's Buddhist merchants is not clear, but an earlier guess that they came from communities which turned to Vaishnavism, to become the Vallabhacharyas of modern times, has at least not been countered by recent research.[9]

The reason for taking our story back to Vallabhi times is precisely this continuity of urban and merchant organization, in marked contrast to the changes taking place in the countryside. Saurashtra, a complex region, has not one tradition but many, and it is significant that merchant tradition relates not to the medieval and martial order of society, but to the perceived glory of ancient India. The name of the region, in this period, remains Saurashtra. In re-establishing this name, during the post-independence period, the merchant and urban elements of the population could make, of medieval Kathiawar, a historical parenthesis between ancient and modern India.

In ancient Vallabhi, as in post-independence Saurashtra, trade was important. We may assume the religious liberalism of Vallabhi's rulers to be due, at least partly, to the position of the trading communities.

What do we know of trade during the Vallabhi period? The 'golden age' of Greco-Roman trade was over. Trade with Egypt had declined under the Ptolemaic kings, and with the Greeks trade withered away in the third century AD (Maqbul Ahmad 1978, 79).[10] But trade improved again by the end of the sixth century, under the dominance of the Sassanians in Western Asia (op. cit., 81). This fits rather well with the rise of Vallabhi, especially as trade was now diverted eastwards, from the Red Sea to the Persian Gulf route.[11] Maqbul Ahmed sees the period from the seventh to the tenth century as the 'golden age' of Indo-Arab trade; the rise of Arab political power and the Arab conquest of Sindh were the main factors behind this improvement (op. cit., 83). Chaudhuri, too, sees a strong expansion of trade from the seventh century onwards (1985, 34ff). Yet some time during this expansion, the Vallabhi empire collapsed. These were unruly times in India, due to the wars of Harsha with Pulakesin II of South India. Indeed, Maqbul Ahmad registers a decline in trade, breaking the upward trend, from AD 622 to 722 (1978, 85). The suspicion that times were hard at Vallabhi is borne out by the comments on the reign of Kharagraha II (alias Dharmaditya) who ruled from *c.* AD 655-60. He is said to have renewed the grants confiscated by earlier kings (BDG, 52). The decline in trade and in grants to religious institutions coincide, fairly well, in time.

The Maitraka dynasty of Vallabhi ended with Shiladitya VII (from *c.* AD 760), or possibly with his general or younger brother Kaladitya. The fall of the city of Vallabhipura, it is now more or less agreed, was in the Vikrama year 845 or AD 788 (BDG, 52-5). And a few centuries later, at the end of Maqbul Ahmad's 'golden age', it was to Cambay and Broach that the Arab traders came (Maqbul Ahmad 1978, 83-4).

END OF EMPIRE

The fall of Vallabhi has made a considerable impression on the traditions of Saurashtra, as well it might, as I shall argue that the end of this empire is also the beginning of the middle ages in the region. But the very importance of the event has led to a multiplicity of traditions, each ascribing the fall of Vallabhi to a different cause. One of them, the myth of the Goddess Khodiyar, will be considered more fully here. But we may first note some of the others.

The destruction of the city has been ascribed to Muslims from Sindh, who made frequent raids at the time. Thus, in AD 766, Abdul Malik led a fleet against Vallabhi. Apparently it fell to the invaders but they in turn were stricken by illness and had to retire. The Gazetteer takes this Arab invasion to be instrumental in destroying Vallabhi, though it fell two decades years later (BDG, 54).

The Jain Prabandhas tell a different story. The merchant Kaku (*alias* Ranka) was offended by king Shiladitya, who had taken the 'rare covetable comb' of Kaku's daughter. The merchant, who came from Marwar, had gained enormous wealth by his supernatural powers; now he went to Mleccha-mandala, the town of the Mlecchas, and bribed their lord with 'crores of coins' to invade Vallabhi. This he did, and Vallabhi was destroyed (BDG, 54-5; Burgess 1882, 20). We may take it that the Mlecchas here were again the Muslims of Sindh. Yet the Jain trader must have regretted his move, for

> when the fall of Valabhi was anticipated, the principal Jain images left Valabhi for different places of Safety. The Image of Chandraprabha shifted to Devpattana (Prabhas Pathan) along with those of Amba and the Ksetrapala; the image of Vardhamana Mahavira shifted to Srimali (Bhinmal in Rajasthan)... that of Adideva to Kasahrada (Kasandra, 12 miles south-west of Ahmedabad), that of Parsvanatha to Harija (Mehsana district) and that of Valabhinatha to Shatrunjaya. (BDG, 55)

The images leave in all directions. The danger seems to stem not from an invading, conquering force with a defined territorial boundary: it is rather as if, the centre having collapsed, the images are brought to provincial locations, possibly protected by former vassals of Vallabhi, or, in the case of the mountain of Shatrunjaya, to a location thought impregnable. We may perhaps assume that the Jain community itself spread out in a similar fashion to their images, as if conditions no longer permitted the concentration of wealth in a single place. Indeed, while we know little about Jains in Rajasthan before this event, they became important there in the following centuries. Some of them may well have come from Vallabhi. Thus ended a period of relative peace, and of strength for the merchant community in Saurashtra. We may note that yet another tradition has the state conquered by the Gurjara-Pratiharas (BDG, 55). This is perhaps more likely. But leaving the search for historical truth to the historians, we turn, instead, to local Hindu tradition.

To the north of the present city of Bhavnagar, facing east towards the sea, we find the temple of the Goddess Ruwapari. One version of the story of the Goddess, told by a visiting Shaivite sadhu, runs as follows:

'The sadhu Tundlinath once came to Vallabhipura in the course of his travels. He had a young boy with him, and as he himself set about meditating, for some six-seven months, or perhaps for a year, he said to the boy: "Go and beg from the people, and get your food." But nobody gave. When the boy came to them, they said: "You should do some work, and maintain yourself." So the boy went to cut trees for firewood, to sell; he was carrying all these branches on his head. He lost his hair, and he got spots on his back, for wear. When Tundlinath awoke from his meditation, he saw the spots on the boy's back, and burst out in anger: "What is this?" The boy told him: "People are not giving anything, so I had to do this hard labour." Tundlinath was enraged.

'There was an old lady who was cooking for the boy. Tundlinath said to the boy: "Now, get out of town, and take the old lady with you; I will bust this town. And, tell the woman that if she turns around (to see the destruction), she will turn to stone. The boy and the woman did as they were told. But when the old lady came to this very spot (he points to the *murti* of Ruwapari) she turned around, and she became the statue that you see."

'The old sadhu was careful to explain: "That is the story of Ruwapari. This is not the story of the powers of Tundlinath." And he continued: 'Tundlinath burnt Vallabhipura, the town near Bhavnagar, by mantra. But then, all the Siddhas (holy men) of Girnar, the Naonath sadhus of the surrounding area, scolded Tundlinath: "What you have done is not good." Then they came here, and all the siddhi people gave their own *siddhas* (powers) to the old lady, so now she is a great goddess due to the siddhas of all these people.'

Here the destruction of Vallabhipura is the work of an enraged sadhu—but more fundamentally, the result of the irreligiosity of its inhabitants. The latter motive is recurrent in myth concerning the fall of kingdoms; but this very story is told by Nath sadhus claiming responsibility for the destruction of a number of Indian cities, thus, for example, of Anhilwada Patan, capital of the Chalukyas, in north Gujarat.[12]

KHODIYAR: THE BIRTH OF THE FIRST MEDIEVAL GODDESS

Ruwapari, the Goddess herself, does not take part in this act of destruction. But in another myth, which we shall deal with more fully, the end of empire is precisely the work of a goddess. And, with the arrival of this goddess, Khodiyar, we enter into a whole set of religious and social phenomena which mark the middle ages of the peninsula, turning it into Kathiawar.

'Almost twelve hundred years ago', the chronicler tells us, 'in the village Roisala, which is today in the region of Gohilwad in Saurashtra, in the taluka of Botad-Pariyad, there lived a Maldhari of the Charan community'[13] (Mehta 1978, 9). He was happy and lived well, but for one thing: he had no children, and so his wife was sad. He tried to comfort her, saying the Goddess Jagdamba, having provided so well for them in other ways, would surely also give them offspring.

The herdsman, Mamodiya Gadhavi,[14] was devoted to Shiva, and learned in religious matters. He was also a great poet. Indeed, as court poet he was the favourite of Shiladitya, the king of Vallabhipura, and every day he rode to the king's court. Here, the king and the bard took Kasumba—opium drink—together, and the bard informed the king of events in his kingdom. They discussed political and religious matters, but, states our author, the bard never interfered in state affairs. Yet jealousy arose among the ministers and the business community. 'When any matter of importance was to be discussed, the Darbar[15] was summoned. Besides the ministers and administrators, the merchant community (*shresti*) was also invited.'

Deciding to put an end to the influence of the bard at court, the ministers and merchants got together. They sent for the Rajpurohit;[16]

if he would help in their plan, he would be given as much wealth as he could wish. The priest was jealous of the bard. 'Though I am the Rajpurohit and a good scholar ...', he thought, 'the king pays more respect to the Gadhavi (than to me), on hearing his false poetry of praise.' So the priest mounted his plot. 'It was in the pious month of Shravan.' Every day the Rajpurohit recited from the Shastras. And, on the eleventh of the month, came the day of fasting to get male offspring.

'One who has no son cannot be happy, neither in this world nor the next ...' recited the priest. Then he told how the king Mahijit had instituted fasting on the eleventh, finally to be blessed with a son. Then he recited another verse, including the word *apraj*, and explained: 'O queen! Apraj means one who has no offspring ... the Shastras state that one who looks at the face of a barren person, will be faced with some unforeseen calamity....' With a show of extreme concern, even regret, he continued: 'Mamodiya Gadhavi has no offspring. Therefore nobody should see his face....' The queen, much disturbed, asked her husband to keep the bard away from the palace. Next morning, as the Gadhavi arrived, the king said: 'To have children is in the hands of destiny. But to see the face of a barren person, is a sin [*pap*].[17] You may go; and please do not come any more.'

Sadly the bard returned to his village, realizing, however, that the king had opened his eyes; his wife had been unhappy because of their childlessness. 'I have no alternative but to ask the blessing of Umapati Shankarbhagwan (Shiva).'[18] To his wife he declares: 'Either I will return with his blessing to have a child, or sacrifice myself to him.' 'May Jagdamba,[19] the goddess, help you', says she, and the bard leaves for Shiva's temple in the jungle. Bathing and fasting, he enters into trance[20] for eight days, without having the sight of the God. Only when, in despair, he prepares to sacrifice himself by cutting his head off,[21] does Shiva appear to him, asking him to name his favour.

Having listened to the bard's request for a child, Shiva says: 'O dear Bhakta (devotee)! Not for one but for fully eight days have you been doing austerities,[22] and so you will become father of eight children; and those children will brighten your name by their good deeds.' Thus the bard becomes the father of seven daughters and a son. The youngest girl is limping, and so is called Khodiyar.[23]

The first medieval goddess of Kathiawar is born; her role is to be the destruction of ancient Saurashtra's last empire.

THE GODDESS' VENGEANCE

'Happiness had come to Mamodiya Gadhavi's household. But as time passed, there were sudden changes in the way of life of the daughters, for which both the Gadhavi and his wife became worried. The seven sisters had understood from the talk of their parents that they were the gifts of Mahadev, but now they awoke to an unforeseen inspiration that they were different incarnations of the sixty-four joginis,[24] which form part and parcel of the Goddess Parvati's power. They lost their appetite for ghee, milk and other cereals [*sic*!]. Instead they wanted to have the blood of animals....' The sisters begin to steal and kill the cattle of neighbouring Maldharis, such as the Ahirs and Bharwads. There is a panic, and the herdsmen complain to king Shiladitya. But his efforts at keeping order are all in vain.

The sisters now prepare to kill the king's favourite bull,[25] 'in order to take revenge of the insult done to their father, and to make the king understand the matter'. The bull is kept well guarded, but one night 'at midnight, there was some uncanny commotion. The bull started to bellow with such ferocity that it would have suppressed the roar of a lion—as if he was fighting with something—or somebody....' The guards saw nothing—or nobody, as if the bull was dragged away by 'some unearthly power'—and when the sentries tried to follow, they lost their way.[26] But finally, 'when they reached the outskirts of Roisala, they saw that the seven sisters, along with other joginis, were already enjoying the feast of beef and blood by ripping the slain bull open'.

When the enraged king Shiladitya reaches the place, the joginis have parted, and only the seven daughters of Mamodiya Gadhavi are left. The king orders that they be burned alive. But the girls make themselves invisible—while at the same time cursing the king: 'You insulted our father for his barrenness, and so your own family line will come to an end.' The king now remembers the bard he has chased from court; he has heard rumours, too, that the bard has been blessed with children by Shiva himself. 'O jogmayas!...' he is asking their forgiveness, 'please... free me from my curse!'

Gadhavi's daughters spoke: 'As you are repenting of your sinful acts, we pity you. Your children will bear children, provided they give up their caste and mingle with other castes. In this way, the family line will continue. But if they remain in their own community,[27] they will not produce any offspring....'

Subsequently, Khodiyar becomes a goddess, and the royal line of the Maitrakas of Vallabhi becomes extinct.

The narrative sequence is clear: the king chases the bard from court, accusing him of barrenness. The latter goes to the jungle, and offers himself in sacrifice to Shiva, who accepts his devotion and grants him children. They, in turn, avenge the wrongs against their father, culminating in the malediction which charges the king's line with the sterility of which the bard was originally accused. This structure is constructed from a set of oppositions. We depart from a friendship between king and bard, a relationship which is to become central in the constitution of the later Rajput states. However, this friendship is broken by the intrigues of 'ministers and merchants', for whom the Rajpurohit acts as an agent. The conflict between priest and bard, rivals for the favours of the king, becomes a feature of court life in later times. Here, they equally represent a religious opposition: the scriptural Shaivism of the priest confronts the bard, who represents popular devotion: but Shiva himself intervenes to make the bard father the goddess who will dominate the religion of the region in medieval times.

The conflict, here, clearly stands for a broader set of oppositions; between merchants and pastoralists, or town and country. The myth thus introduces the opposition between rulers and merchants.

The Brahmin preaches at the urban court, but Shiva answers him from the jungle, with the countryside, home of the pastoralist bard, as mediator between urbanity and wilderness.[28] Ultimately, it is not even Shiva who answers, but Shakti, the essence from which goddesses are made. The bard is presented to us as a devotee of Shiva, but the latter is identified as Umapati Shankarbhagwan—the consort of the goddess. The seven sisters see themselves as joginis; incarnations of the Shakti[29] of the goddess. And, when Khodiyar, towards the end of the myth, offers herself in sacrifice to the Goddess Jagdamba,[30] it is the latter, giving to Khodiyar part of her own shakti, who elevates the jogini to a goddess in her own right (Mehta 1978).

Starting with the conflict between bard and priest, there is a confrontation of sanskritic Shaivism, by implication sterile, with the fertility of the goddess, the very essence of Shaktism. The myth claims an absolute victory for the latter. Implicit is a victory of countryside over town, of tribe over state, of the subjects over the king. When the king breaks the relationship—through the bard—which links him to the countryside, the social order breaks down, symbolized by the murder of the cattle. We may assume that the unorthodox marriages imposed by the representatives of Shakti on the king's family, stand for a re-establishment of these ties.[31] The myth also stresses the king's need of the Goddess' blessing, a theme we shall return to later. When the king ignores her cult, his line is terminated. And we note, here, what is to become another essential feature of medieval society in the region; the bard and the Goddess come from the same caste. The bard, then, becomes an intermediary between the Goddess and the king.[32]

Finally, the myth is seen to introduce, or re-establish, the buffalo sacrifice. The description of the bullfights in which Shiladitya took part may be a later reconstruction, though bullfights apparently did exist in ancient India.[33] But in the myth, the seven sisters as incarnations of Shakti demand buffalo blood, and their 'theft' of the king's favourite buffalo is acting out what was to become, in traditional Kathiawar, the main sacrificial institution of kingship; the buffalo sacrifice to the goddess at the Navratri festival.[34]

Thus the myth of the Goddess Khodiyar, who remains to this day the most popular of Saurashtra's goddesses, may be seen as a 'charter', in Malinowski's sense, of the social order of medieval Kathiawar.[35] This order, rooted in the countryside, is established in contrast to the preceding one, represented by urban merchant tradition, which it will dominate, but not destroy. The fall of Vallabhi implies a change in the nature of the state, and we shall turn, now, to the form of state that establishes itself in the former Vallabhi dominions of Saurashtra.[36]

NOTES

1. I rely mainly, here, on the Bhavnagar District Gazetteer, hereafter BDG, pp. 47-8.
2. See, e.g. Spodek (1976, 13).
3. Vikrama era 136, Vira 609, i.e. AD 79-80 or 82-83 respectively (BDG, 48).
4. Vikrama or Vira era respectively. The famous Jain saint Nagarjuna Suri presided over the first of these councils; Devarddhigani Kshama Sramana over the second (BDG, 48).
5. These treatises were by Acharya, Sthiramati and Gunamurti (BDG, 48).
6. Cited by Wilberforce-Bell (1916, 41) from Julien (1857).
7. The important work of M. Njammasch is becoming known to me as I finalize this text. Though she stresses that Vallabhi flourished during a period of urban decline in India, as well as in Kathiawar (1992b, 27-8; 1993, 36-7), most of the land grants made by the Maitraka kings were to Brahmins (1992a, 31), apparently of urban origin, who might hold land in several villages (1992b). Among these may have been the ancestors of the Nagars. But there were also

farmers (kutumbin), who both held their own land and rented land from the king, from monasteries and temples, and from Brahmins (1992a). She sees a movement towards increasing alienation of crown lands from the second half of the sixth century, when the grants become more standardized in form (1992b, 57). Throughout, she stresses the importance of urbanism and the market in the Vallabhi empire, in spite of the general decline.

8. Guilds were present in ancient India, e.g. Lamb (1959), and so probably in Vallabhi. We know them well from the sixteenth century onwards, but have little information regarding the period from AD 750 to 1500. Even so Pearson concludes his discussion: 'Such has been the general pattern of *mahajans* in Gujarat for at least the past two millennia. Their power and composition have varied from time to time, in accordance with the strength of the government, the religion of the rulers, and the creation of new merchant groups, most notably that of several Muslim communities. The continuous existence of such bodies over this long period is clear, and their basic character seems to have changed little until the twentieth century' (Pearson 1976, 124).
9. The best recent work here is by F. Mallison (1983, 1994). We may also note that the merchant Suleman, in AD 851, states that Buddhism is the chief religion of Gujarat. Al-Idrisi, in the eleventh century, describes the inhabitants of Cambay as Buddhists; though he may have confused them with Jains (Gadre, 64-5). Wilberforce-Bell says of Vallabhi that 'Buddhism was nowhere in a more flourishing condition, and it is most probable that the fall of Walabhi sounded its death-knell'(1916, 42). Perhaps Buddhism, trade and Vallabhi all declined and fell together, and for the same complex of reasons.
10. Maqbul Ahmad puts this 'golden age' at 31 BC to AD 96. Chaudhuri, however, warns us against assuming too dramatic a decline in trade during the ensuing period (1985, 36).
11. Sailing from Malabar or the Konkan to the Red Sea, there is no reason to go by Gujarat. The Gulf route, however, would make Vallabhi a natural entrepot for these areas, as well as for the trade to Upper India.
12. Personal information; David White (University of Virginia) who has close knowledge of the Nath sadhus.
13. A Maldhari is a 'milkman', by extension a member of the pastoral castes (see Ch. VI). The Charan community are pastoralists as well as bards; the majority of the regional goddesses are deified Charanis (see Ch. VII). Khodiyar is probably the oldest of the Charani goddesses in Saurashtra. The presentation of Khodiyar's story here follows Mehta (1978), from whom all direct quotations are translated.
14. Gadhavi is synonymous with Charan; it is also Mamodiya's surname, and a common one within the caste.
15. The word 'Darbar' may mean several things. Here it is the assembly of the king or chief. It may also refer to the chief himself, especially in his official role, or to the government of a princely state. Finally, it is used generically, in Saurashtra, for any member of a landowning or dominant caste. We shall return to this latter use of the term.
16. The Rajpurohit is the priest of the royal household, and is always a Brahmin.
17. The word *pap* may loosely be translated as 'sin', but one should keep in mind that it refers rather to committing a fault, a mistake, a break of the moral order (*dharma*). It is not related to conscience in the Western sense.

18. The term Umapati Shankarbhagwan identifies Shiva as the husband of Uma, the mountain goddess, herself usually identified with Sati or even Parvati. Uma is her oldest name (Wilkins 1975, 285). Wilkins adds 'that although Uma is called the wife of Siva, it is understood that she represents the energy or active power of that deity; she assumed a body in order that she might be united to him in due form ...' (op. cit., 289).
19. Jagdamba's main temple is in the Girnar mountains, near Junagadh. She is sometimes called Girnar Mata. Little is known about her, but she is not among the deified Charanis and there is no tradition of her having had a human existence. She is clearly older than Khodiyar and other medieval goddesses. Burgess seems to equate her with Ambika Mata or Ambaji, and gives her a role in relation to the Jain temples of Girnar similar to that occupied by Ambaji in relation to the Abu temples (note to Amarji 1882, 29). It was the goddess, according to myth, who ordered these temples to be built. Ambika is one of the earliest goddesses we come across in the Hindu scriptures, as the sister of Rudra (Wilkins 1975, 285-6; Dowson 1982, 12).
20. 'Trance' here means *samadhi*, which has a number of other meanings. Thus the death of a saint is often referred to as his samadhi, indicating that for him, death is just another form of meditation.
21. Self-sacrifice by cutting off one's own head with a curved sword, is the classical form of *traga*, the ritual suicide traditionally practised by Charans. More on this institution later.
22. *Tapas*, the word commonly used for the ascetic exercises of the Yogi.
23. According to the traditional etymology; *khodvun*, to limp, *khodel* or *khodiyar*—the limping one. I plan to deal more fully with this aspect of Khodiyar elsewhere.
24. The joginis, here, are seen as minor incarnations of Shakti in her terrible form. In some parts of India, the term denotes a kind of female ghost; thus in Bengal women who die during childbirth become joginis. In all cases the term is assimilated to female powers of fertility, though the connotation may be positive or negative according to region and sectarian views.
25. Mehta gives an interesting description of the function of this bull: '(Shiladitya)... had a whim to arrange fights between bulls, and he often staged such contests. He used to invite Ahirs, Bharwads and Charans to bring their animals, betting that, if any of their bulls won, they would be provided with gifts of land (jagirs). If, on the other hand, the king won (the contest), they had to stay his subjects even if they were under some other ruler. The king's bull was always victorious, and Shiladitya used to feel that, by defeating the bulls from other kingdoms, he had triumphed over the kingdom itself' (Mehta 1978).
26. It is explained in the text that 'they remained wandering aimlessly; such was the influence of the multiple *shakti* of the seven sisters'. For the concept of Shakti, see below.
27. The word used here is *kom,* by far the most common term for caste or jati in Gujarat, but which may also have other connotations of 'community'.
28. Both Jagdamba and Khodiyar, like many other goddesses of the region, have their temples in the 'jungle', often on the top of a mountain or a hill (cf. Beck 1972, 24-5 and 25n).
29. The concept of Shakti is complex, and we shall return to it frequently. Here, we may understand it as power, of essentially female nature, present in all females,

but particularly in the goddess. Charan women, having more Shakti than others, are seen as potential goddesses.

30. Khodiyar's offer of self-sacrifice is quite analogous to that of her father, and similarly evokes the Charan practice of *traga* (self-sacrifice).
31. There is, indeed, a tradition of Shiladitya's successor marrying a Kathi woman, which would have effected such a re-integration (Mehta 1978). The tradition that the Vala Kathis descend from the Vala Rajputs (e.g. Amarji 1882, 81) may have the same origin.
32. I shall return to this theme. Suffice it to say here that the twin ties that bind the bards to the Goddess, as her fathers and brothers (since all medieval goddesses are deified Charanis) and as the singers of her praise, make them a central element in the medieval social order.
33. Probably the best discussion of this question remains Alsdorf (1962).
34. We shall return to these themes. While such sacrifice, in southern India, seems to have been a community affair (Biardeau 1976, 149), among Rajputs it was the responsibility of the king. But there are cases in our area where the relationship to power is not obvious, as in the buffalo sacrifice of Gir forest Charans studied by Westphal-Hellbosch (1976, 179-80).
35. True, the term Kathiawar was introduced much later. But we may note an inscription from Baroda, dated AD 812, stating that Saurashtra had 'lost its appellation of Saurajya from the ruin that had fallen upon it' (cited by Burgess 1882, 20).
36. There is no space here to deal with the Chalukya kingdom of Gujarat, which succeeded to Vallabhi's regional dominance. We shall later note its frequent inroads into the peninsula.

CHAPTER II

Saurasthra to Kathiawar
Emergence of Traditional Society

THE SAINDHAVAS OF GHUMLI

While the Maitrakas held sway at Vallabhi, their vassals, the Garulakas, ruled the north-western corner of the peninsula. But around AD 740 one Pusyena (or Pusyadeva) established himself there. His line became known as the Saindhavas—from Sindh; he is likely to have been the scion of a chiefly line, and may have been driven south by the Arab conquest of that country in AD 712. We hear of him in the context of Arab raids on the coast around AD 735; he lost a battle to them in 738. Saindhava seals have been found at Vallabhi, and the Gazetteer surmises that Pusyena may have been welcomed by the Maitraka ruler, Shiladitya V or VI, as a chief capable of defending the frontier. The Saindhavas may have become vassals of the crumbling empire, or just allies. We hear no more of the Garulakas (JMG, 59-63).

Pusyena built his capital Ghumli in the Barda Hills, 'a fortification wall from which one could watch the movements of any invader by the Arabian sea'. This would need good eyes, but the Saindhavas may, indeed, have been a sea power, as witness their epithet 'masters of the Western sea'. It is believed that they had a port at or near modern Porbandar, and a navy. They dominated north-western Saurashtra from around AD 740 to 920 (JMG, 61). The situation of Ghumli, its fortifications, as well as the fact of separation of headquarters from the port, indicate troubled times. Yet Saindhava land grants give long lists of state officers—a trait shared with the Maitraka kingdom—and show their liberal attitude to religion. They used an elaborate Sanskrit in these grants, and used the Vallabhi era for dating them. From this and other evidence, it has been inferred that Saindhava rule 'gave a further lease to modified Gupta culture for 200 years after the disappearance of the Maitrakas from Saurashtra' (JMG, 68). It would seem, then, that Pusyena took over the form of state administration as he found it; the Saindhavas thus represent the end, rather than the beginning, of an era.

THE CHUDASAMAS OF JUNAGADH

Further south, the province of Sorath, with Junagadh (Girinagara) as its centre, saw the emergence of another kingdom. Under the Maitrakas, Sorath seems to have been dependent on them.

Hsiuan Tsang, who also visited Girinagara, makes a statement to this effect. He describes the city as wealthy, but the soil of the land as 'impregnated with salt ... its flowers and fruits are few'. 'As this realm is on the way to the Western sea', he adds, 'all the inhabitants profit by the advantages the sea affords, and give themselves to trade and barter.' It seems clear, however, that Girinagara was no rival for Vallabhi in this respect. The trade described by the Chinese traveller evidently depended on a port, possibly Prabhas Pathan near Somnath. As in Vallabhi, Buddhism[1] seems to have held a strong position, and there were a number of convents, one of them on mount Girnar itself. Clearly, the mountain was important as a sacred place even then (Burgess, 1882, 34, see also Julien 1857, 448).

According to a legend, Girinagara was deserted for some time. Thus in the ninth century, the former governors of Vallabhi ruled at Vamansthali (presently Vanthali), about eight miles away. About AD 875 their line died out, and the last of the family, Wala Ram, was followed by Ra Chuda, the son of his sister, who had been married to a Sama chief of Sindh. Thus he became the founder of the Chudasama dynasty. They became the most powerful rulers of Saurashtra for several centuries; an inscription from Dhandhusar tells us that they were paramount to other rulers of the area (Wilberforce-Bell 1916, 54-5).

Legend has it that Uparkot fort at Junagadh, was re-discovered and rebuilt under Graharipu or Grahario I, who is said to have died in AD 982. A woodcutter had cut his way through the thickets then surrounding the area, to find stone walls and a gate. A holy man told the woodcutter that the name of the ruined fort (*gadh*) was *juna* , 'old', and so, Junagadh it became (Wilberforce-Bell 1916, 55-6). The existence of this stronghold, formidable in its day, certainly contributed greatly to the strength of the Chudasama rulers.

In some ways, Sorath is the part of the peninsula for which we have the best documentation; this is due to Ranchodji Amarji, the son of

Junagadh's most famous dewan. In the early nineteenth century, he wrote the *Tarikh-i-Sorath,* a history of the Chudasamas and their Muslim successors at Junagadh. Here he states that the Nagar Brahmins and the Brahmakhatris were brought there by the Chudasama kings. He adds:

> In this country have been settled from time immemorial—Girnara Brahmans, Ahers, Khants, Kolis, Parmar Rajputs, Vaghelas, Vala Rajputs, Chudasama Rajputs, Sarasvati and Soratha Brahmans, as well as Surthi people. There are also Lohanas and Bhatias, whom king Naughan brought from Sindh. The governors and Naibs of the Ahmedabad and Dihli Sultans maintained Sayyids, Baluchis, Lodis and Afghans in various offices, paying them salaries and pensions; but the cultivating classes immigrated from Gujarat. (Amarji 1882; 27)[2]

Certainly the Ahirs were important to the Chudasamas. They were called, in bardic accounts, Ahereranas (Enthoven 1920, 25)[3] and their close relationship with the Ahirs will be illustrated below. With the Chudasamas, the goddess enters into the constitution of royalty in Saurashtra.[4]

THE GODDESS AND THE KING IN HINDU JUNAGADH

Ra Dayas was the king of Sorath, but though successful in every other way, he had no children. Through her favourite maidservant, Queen Samaldi hears about the Goddess Khodiyar, and by devotion to her, the couple is finally blessed with a son, Naughan.

Ra Dayas also asks for the hand, in marriage, of the sister of Durlabsen, the Solanki king of Anhilwada Pattan. But the latter refuses,[5] and when his queen later comes on pilgrimage to the Girnar, Ra Dayas denies her access to the Damodar Kund, a sacred bathing-place. Furious, Durlabsen attacks Sorath. Dayas is killed, his wife commits sati,[6] and a viceroy or Subedar is installed at Girinagara.

But the maidservant escapes with the prince, and takes him to a village near Kodinar, in the south, leaving him in the custody of an Ahir chief. He, too, is a devotee of Khodiyar. When the *Subedar* comes to know, he demands that the prince be given up to him, but the Ahir brings his own son instead, and publicly beheads him in the market-place. Satisfied with this show of submission, the Subedar puts his trust in the Ahir chief, who continues to visit him regularly.

In secret, however, the chief is training the prince to fill the royal position to which he has been born. He ensures the support of the Ahir community, but as Naughan reaches the age of fifteen, one difficulty remains: to find the necessary money to arm his supporters.

> The Devait (chief) thought intensively and prayed often to Khodiyar Ma: "O Mother! Naughan is given by You". And so Khodiyar Ma appeared in his dreams, saying: 'You have sacrificed your son in place of Naughan. Devait, you are no less than divine. In the middle of a field amongst the land held by you there is a treasure hidden under a tree. I bless you that your desire may be fulfilled. (Solanki, n.d.)[7]

The Devait finds the treasure and arms his followers. He invites them all to the marriage of his daughter Jasal, who has been brought up side-by-side with the prince. And, not only does he decide to celebrate the marriage at Junagadh, but he invites the Subedar and all his men.

> Then, according to a pre-arranged signal, when the Subahdar reached the marriage grounds, he was immediately beheaded. The Ahirs attacked the army and massacred them. Getting possession of Junagadh, he (the devait) immediately put Naughan on the throne. Instead of putting a vermilion tilak on the forehead of Naughan, Jasal put a tilak of blood by cutting her small finger, on Naughan's forehead—(the prince) with whom she had been brought up, as brother and sister'. (Solanki, n.d.)[8]

The event is said to have taken place in AD 1025.[9] Khodiyar's importance for the Chudasamas is taken further in another story, which we shall tell presently.

KING AND GODDESS: THE RESCUE OF A SISTER

Having, so to speak, received his throne from the Goddess Khodiyar, King Naughan decides to seek her *darshan* at Galadhara. There he sees a chariot running, without horse or driver, across the water; a miraculously beautiful woman is seated in it. When the chariot starts climbing the precipitous rock of Khodiyar's temple, Naughan realizes that the woman is none other than the goddess herself. Saluting her, he receives her blessing (Mehta 1978, 33-4).

But some time later, a terrible famine strikes his country.[10] The Ahirs, taking their cattle, go to Ṣindh, and Naughan's step-sister Jasal, who had married the Ahir Sansatiyo, goes with them. In Sindh, the ruler Hamir Sumra[11] catches a glimpse of the beautiful Jasal. 'Like a sudden stroke of lightning, the appearance of Jasal enchanted his mind. He told Sansatiyo to "send Jasal to the palace"—to join his harem. The frightened husband could do nothing, but, placing her trust in Khodiyar, Jasal told the king: "Maharaj, it must be the good fortune written in my fate that I shall become a Queen. Maybe that is why we have had the fortune to come to your kingdom. It must be a sign of divine will. Therefore, it must be the will of fate that I shall be made the Chief Queen. Thus I shall be happy to come to the palace. But I shall have to send for some beloved friends and relatives, as well as some of my belongings, from my country. My beauty, as well as these arrangements, will make for a lot of splendour." These sweet promises made Hamir Sumra happy, and giving a turban to the chief of the nes[12] he went to his capital.'

But Jasal sent a masterpiece of a letter—full of double meanings—to her step-brother. Naughan understood, and reciting the name of Khodiyar, immediately got his army together. He set out for Sindh. Meanwhile, Hamir, impatient, took Jasal to his palace by force. But Jasal resisted his advances, saying that she was fasting in honour of her ancestors. Thus she got a respite of six months (Solanki, n.d., 87-90).

On his way to Sindh, Naughan came to the banks of the river Macchu, in north-eastern Saurashtra. Here, there was a settlement of Charans. There lived a girl of twelve, Varudi, who was already getting known for the miracles she performed by the aid of Khodiyar. Now she was aiming for greater deeds, hoping that the king of Sorath would come her way. 'Thus, as she was grazing the cattle in the wilderness Varudi caught sight of the army of Naughan. She went to stand in his way and said...: "Raja, it will not please us Charans that your army should only skirt the precincts of our village; come and rest, we will feed your army."'

The king does not take her seriously at first. But finally he is convinced that the Goddess Khodiyar is acting through the little girl. And indeed, performing miracles with the aid of the Goddess, who herself appears, the girl manages to feed the whole army. The king, acknowledging the child as a manifestation of Adishakti,[13] asks her benediction for the task he has set himself, the rescue of his sister (Solanki, n.d., 89-93).

And the child, with the aid of the Goddess, then performs another miracle, well remembered in the lore of Saurashtra. The waters of the Rann of Kutch are made to divide, opening a passage through which the army of Naughan passes dryshod to Sindh. Thus he catches Hamir Sumra by surprise, routs his forces and kills him in battle. Jasal is liberated.

On his return, Naughan builds a temple for Varudi, thus establishing her as a goddess. But meanwhile, in the Sumra's palace, he comes across yet another divinity: this is the Goddess Shikotar. Greeting the goddess, Naughan hears her speak:

'Naughan, I am pleased with you. I gave the kingdom of Sindh to Hamir Sumra but later he became wicked, arrogant, and mad with passion. He did not respect my words. Therefore I stopped giving him assistance. Thus he was destroyed. I want to come to Sorath'. Naughan, therefore, takes the goddess, in the form of water in a golden vessel, back with him (Solanki, n.d, 94-9).

Thus both kings need the support of a goddess. Yet even if Hamir is said to have propitiated Shikotar daily and correctly, this is not enough. The Goddess is the arbiter of the king's fate, and if he fails in his duty to uphold Dharma—the moral order—she will desert him; just as she will perform miracles if necessary for a just cause. The story establishes the relationship between goddess and king that is to become a central feature of kingship in traditional Kathiawar.[14]

THE JETHWAS OF GHUMLI

Meanwhile, in the north-western corner of the peninsula, the Saindhavas were followed by the Jethwas, who ruled until 1952, lately from Porbandar.[15] They thus claim a continuous rule of close to a millennium, and were by far the oldest ruling family, and oldest of the ruling Rajput clans, in Saurashtra in British times.

The Jethwas, and possibly the Saindhavas, have been seen as a 'clan monarchy' in Irfan Habib's terms, where the kinship foundation of the ruling group was the patrilineal segmentary lineage (1974, 284). He associates this system, of which the Gurjara-Pratiharas were the first representatives, with the Rajput castes. Kulke and Rothermund go even further in assuming that this empire was based 'on the integration of the various Rajput tribes and clans into the imperial system' (1990, 117).

Other scholars have identified the Gurjara rulers with the present-day Ahir or Gujar community (Munshi 1954; Enthoven 1920, 23-4). We shall see, later, that these theories of caste origins may not really be contradictory. The Gurjara-Pratiharas established their empire in the wake of the collapse following Harsha's death in AD 647 (Kulke and Rothermund 1990, 116, 109). There is little doubt that its social form grew from migrations. The Saindhava kingdom, then, may have been of a similar type (Tambs-Lyche 1992, 42-5).

To Kulke and Rothermund, the basics of Rajput polity were established by the seventh or eighth century. But there is a problem here, with regard to the Saindhavas and Jethwas. In the typical Rajput state, the dominant agricultural caste in much of the territory is the Rajput clan of the rulers. It is precisely this link of kinship that is typical of Rajput state formations.[16] In Porbandar, however, the dominant caste of most of the state was the Mers, who have no such connection to the ruling house (Trivedi 1961). Instead, the connection is constructed as a marriage alliance:

> A Jethva prince, Randhirji, married a Mer woman named Pabi, who received the village of Khandagad as a gift from her father, Nagarjan Keshwara.[17] Her children were also known as Khunti, probably a corrupt form of Khandagad. Her husband was forced to give up his claim to the Jethva throne for having married her, and so a new royal branch, called the *rajashakha*, came into existence. This breaking away of Randhirji from the royal line was marked by the fact that he himself enthroned his younger brother by putting a 'mark of royalty' (*rajatilaka*), with the blood from his little finger, on the forehead of the latter. This age-old event is symbolically repeated when a new prince ascends the throne. On such an occasion, a descendant of Randhirji's lineage puts the auspicious forehead-mark on with the blood of his little finger.[18] (Trivedi 1961, 106)

Amarji has a different story to explain the alliance between the Mers and the royal house. According to him, when the Jethwa king was fleeing from the army of Jam Raval (of Navanagar), he took refuge with the Mers. But this would have been in the sixteenth century (Amarji 1882, 83). We may note, however, another statement by Amarji, that Nagar Brahmins were entrusted with a number of villages by the Jethwas in early days (op.cit., 84). We shall return to this point later.

As for Vallabhi, a number of myths relate to the fall of Ghumli.[19] Historically, it is probable that the Jam Jadejas, the later lords of Navanagar (Jamnagar), were responsible for its destruction (JMG, 70). But the myths, to which we shall return below, make the Muslims of Sindh responsible for the destruction of the city.

CENTURIES OF IMMIGRATION

The period from the ninth to the twelfth century marks a transition. The last vestiges of ancient Saurashtra disappear with the Saindhavas, and the states which appear do not yet show the traits of the Rajput political system. This is an age when immigrants came, mainly from the north and north-east, to people the countryside of Saurashtra. They included pastoralists, but also—as far as we can separate the two—communities looking for agricultural land. Kosambi stresses the 'great increase in the number of village communities, and the need to create a class who could concentrate enough of the surplus in their hands to assure the trade of steady customers and supplies' (1975, 296). To Kosambi, the increasing population seems to be the prerequisite for the transformation from feudalism 'from above' to feudalism 'from below'.

It seems logical, then, to presume that an increase in rural population would precede the establishment of rural-based feudalism. Indeed, this seems to be the case; for the full-fledged Rajput state of the later medieval period is preceded by an alliance between tribe and king. Here, the pastoral communities are particularly important in our area.

The Ahirs, on whose support the Chudasama kingdom was founded, have been identified with the Abhiras of Sanskrit sources. But let us note Enthoven's view that the term Abhira only came to be associated with pastoralists—as the Ahirs undoubtedly were—from around AD 500 (Enthoven 1920, 20).[20] For our purposes, this is early enough. Enthoven cites references to Abhiras in western India, concluding that they 'must have held sway over Khandesh, Nasik, Kathiawar, Palanpur and Cutch. With regard to the latter provinces, this will be seen from the fact that, when the Kathis arrived in Gujarat, in the eighth century, they found the greater part of the country in possession of the Ahirs' (1920, 23-4).

In short, everything points to the Ahirs as present in Saurashtra before the fall of Vallabhi and the foundation of the Chudasama kingdom. Of pastoral communities in Junagadh, only the Ahirs are identified by Amarji as having been there frome 'time immemorial'. The other pastoral castes seem to have arrived during the early medieval period. The Charans, richer than most in mythical tradition, are particularly difficult to place.[21] If, indeed, Charans were present on the outskirts of the crumbling Vallabhi empire, as the Khodiyar myth would have it, they are likely to have been newcomers to the area. The Bharwads[22] and Rabaris[23] seem to have arrived somewhat later.

Of present-day agricultural communities, Amarji includes the Kolis in his list. We shall return to this enigmatic community later. Let us only note here that Koli is a large and badly known set of agricultural communities with lower-than-middle status in the hierarchy, and that some Koli groups have been seen, at various times and by various people, as Hinduized tribals. Amarji is probably right when he considers that they were there before the foundation of the Chudasama state. They may have been part of the labour force of the estates owned by the citizens of Vallabhi; they may also have formed the bulk of the free peasantry Njammasch describes.

At the time of Amarji, most Ahirs had become farmers, as they still are. Other castes he notes are either Rajputs or Brahmins, or they are of little present-day importance. The Kathis may have been there from the ninth century, but Amarji does not mention them.[24] The presently important Kanbis are clearly among the later immigrants he notes; many, in fact, came in the nineteenth century. The early Rajput communities mentioned by Amarji, are all small groups today,[25] as are the Brahmins mentioned by him. The latter are traditionally connected to such places of pilgrimage as Girnar and Prabhas Pathan (Somnath). Both groups may indeed have been landowners when the Chudasamas established themselves, but they cannot have formed a broad base of cultivators.

Nagars, Brahmakhatris, Lohanas and Bhatias are all said to have come to Junagadh under the auspices of the Chudasamas. Lohana and Bhatia traders are regarded as coming from Sindh; their arrival may indicate that trade was improving, since many Lohanas, at least, remained in Sindh in spite of the introduction there of Islam—there cannot have been a general exodus of Lohana 'refugees' at the time.

The Nagars were to play an important role in traditional Kathiawar. In British times, they were known as bureaucrats and administrators.[26] Amarji, himself a Nagar and son of a minister, informs us about villages held by them. They were then important as landowners resident in the city, a pattern which may well go back to Vallabhi times. Enthoven traces three of their surnames to Vallabhi inscriptions, and finds that surnames in existence among them in the early thirteenth century are still in use today.[27] It is quite likely that some of them moved to Junagadh, where they are still numerous, when Vallabhi fell.

What emerges quite clearly from the available information, then, albeit scanty and imprecise, is the considerable immigration into the peninsula between the eighth and twelfth centuries. These were unruly times, and are seen as such by Wilberforce-Bell: from the fall of Vallabhi, he holds (1916, 47), may be said to have begun

> that influx of foreigners who established themselves in various parts of the Kathiawad peninsula, carving out for themselves those various divisions which

nowadays form the many states into which the country is divided. The process of formation of these states has been necessarily gradual, and it was not until some time after the fall of Walabhi that their founders began their incursions.

A CHANGE OF SOCIAL STRUCTURE

With the fall of Vallabhi we enter the middle ages of Saurashtra's history. But the early medieval period, as characterized by the states of the Jethwas and the Chudasamas, must be distinguished from the later period of full-fledged Rajput states.[28] The most striking element of social structure in these early medieval states is the alliance between the king and a particular, ethnically distinct community. The Jethwa state was conceived as a marriage alliance between the ruling house and the Mers; and we have seen above how the link between the Chudasamas and the Ahirs was constructed. Here, the latter are represented as foster-father and half-sister of the king. Wilberforce-Bell noted the similarity of these alliances. 'The Ahirs', he says, 'had become the hereditary soldiers in the service of the Chudasamas, and were, indeed, to them what the Mers were to the Jethwas' (op. cit., 58).

The form of alliance recalls the 'marriage to a local princess' that legitimized the royal house in Tehri Garhwal (Galey 1989). In this frontier area, too, this constructed alliance furnishes the state with a popular base in the absence of a large, dominant Rajput clan. There is a similar 'tika ceremony' in Mewar (Udaipur), Rajasthan, where a representative of the Bhil tribe marks the king's forehead with his blood (Stern 1986). The Mewar dynasty was, according to tradition, founded at Chittor in AD 728.[29] Though the ceremony might be of a later date, Tod's story of its origin underlines our sociological point. According to him, a queen from Saurashtra was returning from pilgrimage, when she learnt of the conquest and destruction of her husband's kingdom. Highly pregnant, she took refuge in a cave to give birth to her son, who was accordingly named Guha (cave).[30] He became the ancestor of the Guhils or Gohils, rulers of Mewar, and, as we shall see later, of Bhavnagar and other states in Saurashtra. Harlan (1991, 27-8) tells the significant part of the story thus: 'Guha grew up in a forested area populated by members of the Bhil tribe. Enormously popular, he was eventually elected king of the Bhils at Idar (also in Gujarat). He was officially invested with royal authority when a Bhil cut his own finger and with his blood applied to Guha's brow the red mark (tika) of sovereignty.'[31]

The origins of the ceremony, which is found in other Rajput states also, are not important for us here; what is significant, is how it marks an alliance between a distinct, subject population and a ruling house.

Usually in later Rajput states, it was the chief vassals of the ruler who marked his forehead with the *tikka*: such was the case when Tod was present at the enthronement of the ruler of Bundi in 1821. On that occasion, Tod himself put the first mark, symbolizing the acceptance of the succession by the paramount power (Tod II, 749-52). We may assume that a representative of the Mughals may, at other times in the Rajput world, have played a similar role. The placing of the *tikka*, in all cases, serves as a sign of loyalty or alliance.

But in the Jethwa and Chudasama case this alliance effectively forms the basis of the state formation. It corresponds functionally to the dominance of the Rajput clan, as an agricultural caste, in the later states, and sets these earlier formations apart. The locally dominant position was occupied by a separate caste, and its alliance to the rulers was marked ritually by the *tikka* of blood placed on the king's forehead by a representative of this sector of the population.

The ceremony, then, symbolizes a direct link between a 'tribal' population and the king—clearly so in the Mewar case, whereas the Ahirs of Junagadh are pastoralists. As to the Mers, we only know that they are ethnically distinct from the surrounding populations. In Porbandar, by the way, the pastoral Rabaris later claimed a similar, and parallel, link to the rulers, which came about through their service as soldiers for the state (Westphal-Hellbosch 1974; Village Monograph No. 1).

The direct link to the ruler avoids the 'feudal' intermediary, who receives a share in the peasants' harvest and gives part of his share to the king. Such absence of an intermediary distinguished the position of the Bhils in Mewar, and the Mers of Porbandar; we may suppose that the same observation is valid for the Ahir subjects of the Chudasamas. What is indicated, therefore, is a change in the economic base of society from the early to the later medieval period. While the latter is characterized by the importance of revenue from peasant agriculture, passing through several intermediaries from cultivator to king, such revenue seems to have been less important in the earlier period.[32]

It may now be clear why I see no contradiction, for the Gurjara-Pratihara state, between its identification with the early Rajputs and with the large Ahir/Gujar caste. Its rulers may, as Munshi (1954) and also Enthoven (1920) imply, have been a 'Rajput' elite recruited from the Ahirs, or they may have been 'foreigners' basing their state on alliance with this large caste, as the Chudasamas seem to have done. In both cases, both the rulers and their allied subjects would have been relative newcomers to the area. This immigration might be expected to produce a change in the exploitation of agricultural resources, to which question I shall now turn.

DEVELOPMENTS IN AGRICULTURE

It is clear that important changes in agriculture took place during the early medieval period, but historians differ as to the nature and importance of these developments. Thus Irfan Habib states that the general prevalence of peasant cultivation, consolidated during the earlier period, was little modified during medieval times (1974, 282). But he admits the introduction of serfdom, which Sharma regards as established from the eighth century onwards (1965, 57-60). Moreover, Jain holds that the ruling classes were 'falling back on the land' during this period (1976, 344). 'In essence', adds Irfan Habib, 'what happened during these five centuries (seventh to twelfth) may be called the ruralization of the ruling class.' He relates this to a marked decline in commerce, as indicated by the paucity of coins (1974, 283).

This seems to contradict Maqbul Ahmad's view, that the seventh to tenth centuries were the 'golden age' of Indo-Arab trade (1978, 82), but fits our idea of developments in Saurashtra after the fall of Vallabhi as well as the decline in trade from the tenth century onwards (op. cit., 87). From this period we see considerable technical improvements in agriculture. Thus in AD 1042 a large tank was built, near Sirohi on the boundary of Rajasthan and Gujarat, by the sister of the king of Abu. Three enormous tanks were excavated near Anhilwada Pattan, in North Gujarat, during Chalukya rule, from the twelfth century onwards (Jain 1976, 121-2). Though Jain maintains that such works were exceptions to, and contradictory to, a general rule of oppression (op. cit., 105-8), they do indicate an interest in agriculture by the rulers.

Kosambi, too, stresses the oppression of the peasant during this period and sees in the 'failure of indigenous feudalism "from above" to develop new techniques ... a basic contrast with the medieval European achievement' (1975, 355). But technological development and increased oppression may well go together in a quest for augmenting land revenues. The Persian wheel was introduced to India during the same period, and became important to agriculture in Rajasthan and north India. In Gujarat, we find instead the step-wells called *vao,* several of them dating from this period. Irfan Habib, conceding the worsening lot of the peasant (1974, 286), points out that owners of Persian wheels appropriated part of the crop. Such owners might be 'landlords', employing 'cultivators, workers and servants' (op. cit., 282-3). If Persian wheels could bring revenue in this way, tanks and step-wells, too, may have been built to increase the revenue of the ruling house. Thus, in the period stretching from the fall of Vallabhi to that of Ghumli, there is indeed a marked development in Indian agriculture. It seems that new groups became interested in it, or that older dominant groups —perhaps due to the decline in trade—now 'fell back on the land'.

These technological developments do not follow directly upon the fall of Vallabhi. Rather, it is from the eleventh century onwards we see such signs of more intensive agriculture. The eighth to the tenth century, then, is the intermediate stage, the period of immigration which sees the forging of the king-tribe alliance marked by the *tikka* ceremony. The subsequent developments follow the establishment of a strong state, building tanks and step-wells, in north Gujarat. And the next state-formation we hear of in the peninsula, that of the Jhalas, are precisely the frontier vassals of this state. The technological developments in agriculture seem to indicate the interest in land and its revenue that announces the true Rajput state.

THE JHALAS OF NORTH-WESTERN SAURASHTRA

Indeed, one of the oldest and most beautiful step-wells in the peninsula is said to have been built at this time, near Dhrangadhra in north-western Saurashtra, at the instigation of Shakti Devi, whose story deserves to be told.

Young Harpal, a refugee from Sindh—where his father and brothers have been slain fighting the ubiquitous Hamir Sumra—is in the service of the Solanki Raja of Gujarat, when one day a young woman, possessed by a *bhoot,* jumps into a well.[33] Harpal, a Makwana Rajput, jumps after her, and drags her out. Subsequently, he tries to find a way to exorcise the *bhoot.*

Pondering the question, he takes a walk through the cremation grounds[34] when, suddenly, he meets a wonderfully beautiful woman. He asks her twice for water, but she remains silent. Irritated, he pulls her skirt. The woman, laughing at him, grows 'as high as the sky'. Harpal, undaunted, beats her feet with his stick. They fight furiously.

She is, in effect, the Goddess Shakti Mata, attendant of Ambabhavani, who has descended on earth to find a human husband. Impressed by Harpal's courage, and having at last found a real Rajput, she agrees to marry him, but nobody must ever know her real identity as a goddess. She helps Harpal to drive out the bhoot, and the Solanki raja, much pleased, grants Harpal a boon.

He gives the young Rajput the right to all the villages on whose gate he can tie a garland in one single night. Helped by the supernatural powers of his wife, and by the defeated bhoot, he thus marks two thousand villages. Most respectably, he returns five hundred to the Solanki queen in honour of her friendship;[35] then he and his queen go off to found their dynasty ruling the remaining villages from their capital at Patdi[36] (Mayne 1921, 25-7). Thus is founded the first state of the Jhala clan, soon to get its name from another miracle of Shakti Mata:

> In Patdi the Makwano built many a palace. The Rani sat at the window, no one knew that she was a Shakti. The King's elephant broke loose, she saw, from a distance, the princes playing. Shedo, Mangoo and Shekuro, extending her hand she laid hold upon, she gave them the title of Jhala. (op. cit., 27)

Jhala is here given the etymology of that which is grasped or snatched. Sometimes the word is turned into its active sense, one who grasps, takes, conquers. The latter sense well illustrates the image that Jhalas like to present of themselves.

We have seen that the Goddess Khodiyar is using her shakti—for the good of the Chudasama king, to whom she becomes his lineage goddess or kuldevi. Another source of shakti, for the king, is his queen, just as the goddess is the shakti of the male gods and every woman is the shakti of her husband. But Shakti Mata of the Jhalas is unique in being queen and goddess in one and the same person.

It is to the same queen, say the villagers, that we owe the beautiful Matavao step-well mentioned above, said to be built in the queen's own village, Kankavadi.[37] She died, according to the story, in AD 1115; the style of the well fits that date. This royal interest in agriculture—which parallels the construction work in Gujarat at this period—is perhaps underlined by another point in the myth. This is the stress laid on the control of villages.

Moreover, and more to the point: at Harpal's death his territory was divided between his three sons, Shedo, Mangoo and Shekuro. Shedo is the ancestor of the senior line at Dhrangadhra. From Mangoo descends the Limbdi royal house. Shekuro got Sachana, in the present-day Viramgam district, this area was 'subsequently annexed to the crown-lands, but his descendants still held 'wantas' there in British times, 'being styled Wantadars' (Mayne 1921, 28). Thus from the start, the Jhala clan segments into several states, as all subsequent Rajput states have done in Saurashtra. Such segmentation was not a feature of the Saindhava or Jethwa state, nor of Junagadh. In the latter case villages were, as we have seen, given to Nagar Brahmins, in one version of the Khodiyar myth we are told that the Devaiyat, who helped Naughan win back his throne, was rewarded with a number of villages. Such gifts took place at a later date, in other states, but the primary ties of vassalage were to junior members of the ruling Rajput clan.

With the Jhalas, therefore, we see a shift to a new base of power. The alliance between tribe and king has gone, to be replaced with statewide dominance by the ruling Rajput clan. This would seem, indeed, to presuppose that land revenue was becoming the main base of the state. The ruling class was, indeed, 'falling back upon the land'.

THE FALL OF GHUMLI

We may now turn westwards again. At the foot of the Barda Hills, north-east of Porbandar, may be seen the ruins of Ghumli, ancient capital of the Saindhavas and the Jethwas. The fall of Ghumli is as steeped in myth as that of Vallabhi. 'Nothing definite is known...', says the Gazetteer, 'Ghumli was destroyed in the fifteenth century, probably by the Jams from Sind...' (JMG, 70). The same source credits Jam Bamanioji, of the Jadeja clan, with the conquest of Ghumli (op. cit., 90-1).

Around AD 1300, this clan had established a small chiefdom in what is today Jamnagar district. They, like the Chudasamas and the Bhattis of Jaisalmer, belong ultimately to the Yadava branch of Rajputs, said to have been Krishna's own people. According to tradition, the Jadejas, whose line includes the rulers of Kutch, came from Sindh, where their title Jam was used by a Muslim ruler of the fifteenth century.[38]

As the Jethwa power declined, the resulting power vacuum seems to have been filled by the Jadejas. Jam Bamanioji died in 1535; his son

Raval was the founder of the city of Jamnagar—then Navanagar—and may be regarded as the founder of the state. Like the Jhalas, the Jadejas then divided their domain between the sons of Raval; we have entered the period of Rajput polity. The foundation of Navanagar may serve, then, as the starting point for our treatment of traditional Kathiawar society.

But let us first see how the fall of Ghumli appears in myth. Tod tells us about Salamun, the son of Seoji, son of Bhanji; in the reign of the latter Muhammad Ghori was in Saurashtra.[39]

> In a neighbouring state, the daughter of a Chohan chieftain had the gift of poesy, and her productions were the theme of universal admiration: nor did she put her light under a bushel, but, with that freedom granted to the Rajpoot fair in those chivalrous days (prior to the Islamite coming against them), she used to circulate her incomplete couplets, challenging the princely Komars around to fill them up. One of these poetic circulars reached Goomli, and in full durbar was placed by the itinerant bard of the Chohans in the hands of Salamun, who in an instant improvised a completion of the couplet, and in due time received the promised reward—the hand of this Sappho of the Chohans. But the king of the Jaitwas, instead of feeling pride in his son's successful talent, visited it with a jealous wrath, sentencing him to *desvati*, or banishment. Salamun, with his bride, sought shelter in Sinde, from whose prince he received the lands of Doba and Dharaja for his support. There he remained, and had numerous progeny, who, with himself, became converts to Islam, and, according to tradition, it was his son who brought an army from Sinde, and overturned Goomli. (Tod 1971, 414-15)

We see how the myth blames the destruction of Ghumli on the Muslims, while at the same time implying that the valour necessary for their success stems from their Rajput blood. The bardic tradition, here, is taken for granted, the practice of Parda and the elaborate arrangement of later Rajput marriages is not—unless we see the appearance of these two elements as the real subject of the myth, present through the opposition of Seoji to his son's marriage.[40]

Another myth, reported by Tod, implies 'that the overthrow of thrones is ... ascribed to some act of impiety':

> The rape of the brazier's daughter, and its consequences, drove the princes of Goomli from the throne, and in lieu of being lords of almost all of the Western peninsula, not a tithe of their ancient possessions was left them. The brazier's daughter was virtuous, and we may suppose beautiful, she rejected with indignation the base overtures of her sovereign, and feeling insecure against his power, sought the protection of the altar. But the mad passion of the prince

rendered him blind to all consequences, he demanded that she should be delivered up, and this being refused, violated the sanctuary, and dragged his victim forth among the curses of the priests, who, impregnating vengeance on him and his race, slew themselves before the altar of the god. Soon after came the invader from Sinde, when Goomli was infested, and defended for six months.[41] (Tod 1971, 415-16)

Ghumli was taken, Seoji, with his kindred and friends, were massacred. Tod points to the identification of the Asuras of this myth with Muslims, they have beards.... He places the event at AD 1053 (op. cit., 416), which is certainly too early. 'The Ghori', in fact, invaded Gujarat in AD 1178 and again after 1193 (Kulke and Rothermund 1986, 167-8). This would place the above events in the first half of the thirteenth century.

These stories, then, do not fit the conquest of Ghumli by Jam Bamanioji, at least a century later. They are more notable for their stress on female honour and the divine vengeance which awaits the lascivious or ungenerous king. In this, they closely parallel the group of myths surrounding Khodiyar. Historically, we may perhaps suppose that Ghumli may have been weakened by Muslim attacks from Sindh before finally succumbing to the Jadejas.

AN EARLY EXAMPLE OF SATI

Tod speaks, in regard to the stories above, of female vengeance, of the vengeful powers of women. This leads us to the phenomenon of sati, another central element in the traditions of medieval Kathiawar. We have seen that the mother of prince Naughan, who re-established the Chudasama dynasty with the aid of the Goddess Khodiyar, committed sati. But the most famous early example of this institution relates to the story of a later queen of the same dynasty, Ranik Devi.[42]

In Sindh, a certain king had a daughter born under the inauspicious 'mul' constellation. Whoever married such a girl, said his astrologer, would lose his throne. Accordingly, the girl was sent into the jungle, where a potter found her and brought her up as his daughter. She was so beautiful that the chief, Lakha Pholanee,[43] asked her hand in marriage, and threatened the potter with violence if he refused. The potter fled to Saurashtra, where ruled the Chudasama, King Khengar II.

Now, four of the household bards of king Siddha Raja of Gujarat, on a voyage in the west, saw the girl. They reported on her beauty to the king, who was eager to marry her. Returning to the potter, they found he now kept his step-daughter concealed in an underground chamber, as he feared that her beauty would sooner or later create problems. 'I have no daughter', he told the bards, but they of course knew better, and by a mixture of promises and threats they prevailed upon him to perform the ceremony of betrothal for his daughter, to the king of Gujarat.

But then the nephews of King Khengar also came to visit the potter's village, and saw the girl. Learning that she had been betrothed to the king of Gujarat, they returned to their uncle, saying: 'If the Puttun Raja take such a maiden out of our country, what reputation will remain to us?' (Forbes 1878, 122-4).

The king orders them to go back and marry the maiden to his sword.[44] The potter protests, and prophesies war and destruction if Siddha Raja's betrothed is taken away to Khengar, but the nephews of Khengar do not heed his warnings. Ranik Devi, as the girl is now called, is brought to Khengar's palace in Junagadh, but as she is about to enter, hurts her foot against a stone—another bad omen.

The marriage takes place, but a group of Vaghris,[45] invited to the feast, carry the news to Siddha Raja at Anhilwada Pattan. The king of Gujarat sets out for Junagadh with an army. The war is said to have lasted twelve years, but finally Siddha Raja is victorious, Khengar is slain, and Ranik Devi is taken prisoner (Forbes 1878, 124-7).

The bardic poetry relating the grief of Ranik Devi, her love for her husband, and, when taken to Gujarat, her longing for 'the land of Sorath', is movingly beautiful.[46] The latter passages are interesting in that they indicate regional patriotism at a time when, usually, we tend to think of boundaries as fluid and indefinite. Yet at Ranik Devi's time, 'Sorath' had been a state under the Chudasamas for almost two hundred years. It is true, of course, that the poetry is likely to have been composed at a later date (see also Tambs-Lyche, 1995).

Refusing consolation, Ranik Devi is at last allowed by her captor to return to Wadhwan—which seems then to have marked the boundary between Sorath and Gujarat. Here, she prepares her funeral pyre. As soon as she kneels down upon it, flames arise by themselves (Forbes 1878, 127-30). To Siddha Raja, to the spectators as well as to later commentators, this spontaneous ignition is proof that she is a real sati, one who reveals her truth (*sat*) by the manner of her death.[47]

According to Forbes, Siddha Raja ruled from AD 1094 to 1143 (1878, 138). Ranik Devi, then, was a near contemporary of Shakti

Mata of the Jhalas. While there are earlier references to sati in Saurashtra, it is fair to say that the fame of Ranik Devi gives her a central role in subsequent tradition and serves to strengthen the ideals of the sati in Kathiawar.

DEVELOPMENTS IN OVERSEAS TRADE

By the tenth century large communities of Arab merchants were found along the coasts of India. Among the important ports were Broach and Cambay on the Gujarat mainland (Maqbul Ahmad 1978, 83). The Saindhavas were posed alongside, but not on, the main trade routes. Whether they used this position for trade or piracy, we do not know.

Much trade centred on the Chalukya empire of Gujarat, and Cambay flourished as its main port when Al-Idrisi visited the kingdom. Maqbul Ahmad identifies the 'Balhara' of his account with Jayasinha Siddharaja who, according to him, ruled at Anhilwada from AD 1096 to 1143; we met him in the story of Ranik Devi. 'These Gurjara rulers', says Ahmad, 'also welcomed the Arabs and gave them all trade facilities' (op. cit., 83-4). Al-Idrisi also went to Broach, where he found 'the inhabitants ... rich and engaged in trade and they freely enter upon speculations and distant expeditions. It is a port for vessels coming from China as it is also for those of Sind' (cited by Majumdar 1956, 268).

Maqbul Ahmad speaks of Arab trade to India. What was the position of Indian merchants in this trade? A traditional view sees Indian shipping as 'peculiarly inefficient', due to the 'inability to trade in the goods they produced' (Kosambi 1975, 360-1). Kosambi relates this inability to the growth of a rural, village-based economy at the cost of towns and cities. Trade, according to him, became concentrated in certain ports, often administered by Muslim governors (op. cit., 361-2). Basham, similarly, assumes a decline in Indian seafaring by the middle ages, which was further accelerated by the Muslim invasions (1963, 233).

Marco Polo, however, speaks of the Gujarati pirates as 'the worst in the world'—clearly somebody, in Gujarat, went to sea at least (cited in Majumdar 1956, 268). During Chalukya rule in Gujarat, trade was directed eastwards as well as westwards; Java and Sumatra were well known to Gujarati writers of the period (Majumdar op. cit., 265). And even in the West, Muslim traders do not seem to be monopolizing the trade:

Abu Zayd Hasan of Siraf, who completed the Travels of Sulaiman in AD 916, states that when the Indian merchants of Siraf were invited by one of the principal merchants of the place, the latter out of regard for the susceptibility of the Hindus served them food in separate plates. Abu Zayd states that on these occasions there would be about 100 guests, and probably they would be all Indians, from which we can form a rough idea of the total number of Indian merchants residing in the coastal towns of Persia. (Majumdar 1956, 267)

In the *Jagaducharita*, the merchant Jagadu trades regularly with Persia using his own ships, and his agent at Hormuz was an Indian. Later, Muhammad Ufi (AD 1211) tells us of a Gujarati trader at Ghazni; in spite of his defeat by the Gujarati army Mu'izz ud-Din bin Sam refused to seize this merchant's property, as an act contrary to justice (ibid.). In spite of armed conflict between Hindu and Muslim rulers, then, merchants were allowed to go on trading. This distinction between trade and politics remained valid in the sixteenth century, as analysed by Pearson (1976).

The traditional view, that Indian seafaring declined in the medieval period, has recently been criticized. Specifically, Pearson and others are highly sceptical to the importance of the 'taboo on sea travel' invoked to explain this decline (Pearson 1981, 133-8). Though he admits to a Muslim dominance in seaborne trade around 1500, Pearson (1981, 120-1) stresses that Hindu merchants, too, went to sea. As for Gujarat, the 'numerous Portuguese descriptions make it clear that by 1500 foreign Muslim merchants were less dominant than previously, and that Hindus and Muslims both traded extensively.'

In the preceding century Mahmud Begada, ruling Gujarat from 1459 to 1509, had followed an expansive policy, taking Junagadh in 1470. According to Chaube, one important motive for this and other annexations was precisely to control ports and trade routes (Chaube 1975, 39-66). The flourishing state of Gujarat and its cities during the years of the independent kingdom (1407-1573) must be attributed at least partly to the importance of its trade.

The Vaghers,[48] then as later, were pirates, plundering the pilgrim ships bound for Mecca. The ship of Maulana Mahmud Samarqandi, a merchant, was taken by them and they 'also detained his wife and property and allowed only Maulana Mahmud to go with his two small children who were so tender in age that they could not walk on foot ... with great difficulty he carried one to a distance and having left him there, fetched the other....' (Chaube 1975, 67-8)

Safe at last in Gujarat, the Maulana appealed to the king. Having settled the trader comfortably in Ahmedabad the sultan set out on a punitive expedition, taking Dwarka and the Bet[49] in AD 1473 (Chaube 1975, 66-72). Clearly, Mahmud acted here to protect shipping. He also fought Malabari pirates off his coast, and strengthened the defence of Gogha, Cambay and other ports. For these purposes, and for the conquest of the Bet, he created a small navy (op. cit., 72).

In the following century, Jain and Hindu Bania participation in trade tended further to increase, as the Muslim traders were opposed by the Portuguese, while Gujarati Banias accommodated to them. This was nowhere more evident than in Diu (Pearson1981, 124-31).

GUILDS AND TRADERS OF THE MEDIEVAL PERIOD

We know little about the organization of the merchant community of Saurashtra from the fall of Vallabhi to the foundation of Navanagar. But in Jain literature, there is considerable information regarding mainland Gujarat under the Chalukyas. Majumdar gives a list of thirty trades or professions—mainly artisans—mentioned in the literature of the period. Hemachandra, in the *Trishastisalakapurushacharita* mentions eighteen guilds, but does not name them. A list of eighteen named guilds is found in the *Jambudvipaprajnapti*, and Majumdar thinks they may have existed under the Chalukyas (1956, 262-4). But this list refers again to crafts rather than trades, only the cloth-printer, among them, has today become a Bania.

The world for guild—*shreni*—was applied to these groups of craftsmen. Did merchants, too, have guilds at this period? No definite answer can be given, but Pearson and others certainly feel that they had been in existence before the medieval period. Majumdar cites evidence to show that several specialists, such as smiths, braziers and ship-owners 'took part in the deliberations of a city council, and most probably they were members of their respective guilds.' He holds that 'trade guilds existed in Gujarat from early days ...' and notes that the Chalukya administration included a special department, the *shreni-karana*, to look after them (op.cit., 263).

Merchants were certainly a presence in Chalukya times, and some were very rich indeed. A special flag, called *kotidhvaja*, might be seen over the houses of these 'multi-millionaires' (Majumdar 1956, 284). Majumdar cites a story by the learned Jain monk Merutunga,[50] in which a merchant wanted to participate in the expenses of digging the Sahasralinga tank. But king Siddharaja (*c.* AD 1094–1144) refused his offer, and Merutunga concludes that the king wanted to keep the religious merit of his works to himself. Now, when Siddharaja was away on his campaign in Malwa, the merchant accused his own son of stealing the ear-rings of a rich lady, and then promptly paid a fine of 'three lakhs' into the state coffers. This sum corresponded to what was needed to complete the tank—work had been halted from lack of funds. But when Siddharaja came to know about the stratagem, he immediately returned the money. Majumdar's conclusion (1956, 284) differs from Merutunga's. The story shows that 'Siddharaja was unwilling to associate with a merchant in a joint undertaking or venture ... the reason might be that the great emperor wanted to keep a free hand in dealing with all classes of his subjects, and felt that if he took money for his pet project from any one of his subjects, he would not be able to maintain his dignity and impartiality'.

This impartial practice recalls our impressions of Vallabhi. But, notes Majumdar, the practice was to change later; when Siddharaja's successor Kumarapala was installed, he was probably helped by the Bania Udayana and his sons. Udayana had himself been a merchant, and according to Merutunga it was

> due to his fabulous wealth that people came to call Udayana a minister. It is possible that Udayana was a junior minister with no influence during the reign of Siddharaja just as Vastupala and Tejahpala had been junior officials in the administration of Bhima II before the two brothers' rise to political power. It is a peculiar fact hard to explain that these great captains of commerce and industry should ever come to occupy minor offices in the administration. However, to continue the story of Udayana, soon after Kumarapala's accession he and his sons rose to fame. Part of their influence might have been due to Hemachandra's ascendancy over the king, for the great monk had been since his childhood associated with the family of Udayana. (op. cit., 285)

Vastupala and Tejahpala, brothers, were not only the leading merchants of their time in Gujarat, but became 'the chief officers of state during part of the reigns of Bhima II and Viradhivala' (ibid.). Bhima II ruled from about AD 1179 to 1242, and Viradhivala and his father Lavanaprasada were his contemporaries, sharing his power in a way that still seems difficult to establish (Majumdar, 1956, 162-7, 170).

Thus during the second half of the twelfth century and the first half of the thirteenth, merchants played an important role in the politics of the Chaulukya state. They were clearly supported by Jain monks, who in their turn wrote eulogies of such merchants as Vastupala and

Tejahpala. The strong position of the merchant community was clearly related to the control of such centres of trade as Cambay and Broach. It does not follow that merchants in Saurashtra had similar influence over their rulers. But the strength of merchants on the mainland must have been known to their caste-fellows in the peninsula. The cultural continuity here is indicated by Merutunga's residence at Wadhwan.

Let us just note that Somnath, too, is mentioned as an important port by Alberuni, Abulfida and Marco Polo. It was 'controlled' by the Chalukyas since the days of Karna I, who ruled from AD 1066–7 (Majumdar 1956, 265, 56). It is not unlikely that this port was the outlet of Junagadh's trade in Vallabhi times, as we have noted above. There is no reason to believe that trade there stopped entirely at any time between the end of Vallabhi and the conquests of Mahmud Begada.

JAIN LITERATURE; CRITICISM OF KSHATRIYA VALUES

And if trade continued, even at a reduced scale, merchants must have remained a minority element in regional society and culture. The evidence here is mainly from Jain literature. If Jainism in Saurashtra suffered a setback when Vallabhi fell, Jains of the region continued to write. They were part of a tradition which, we may now safely say, had its roots in Vallabhi.

Writing of non-canonical Shwetambara Jain literature, Chatterjee takes us back to the first century AD. Vimala's *Paumachariyam*, the Jain Ramayana, is notable for making the Rakshasas not only vegetarians, but Jains—which rather alters the moral of the story. It is clearly conceived as an ideological counter-point to Valmiki's original epos,[51] where the heroes are Kshatriyas (Chatterjee 1978, 273-8). Jains clearly formed a core of opposition to martial Hindu values even then.

The *Vasudevahindi*, probably written during the Gupta period, likewise imitates and re-works a Hindu text, in this case the *Brhatkatha* by Gunadhya. This work has several references to Saurashtra. The subject of its first story—the merchant Dhammila—is a city man, with urban enjoyments, including a 'passion for prostitutes'. The author knows intimately several places in Western India, Kalyana, Bharukaccha (Broach), Girinagara (Junagadh) and Yavana-visaya—the land of the Yavanas. Part of the work may be seen as a Jain version of the Vaishnava Puranas, dealing with Krishna at Dwarka. The text also refers to foreign countries such as China, Sumatra and Java (op. cit., 278-80). The conditions under which the work was composed, cannot have been very different from those obtaining at Vallabhi.

In the opinion of Chatterjee, the original *Satrunjaya-mahatmya*, no longer extant, was written in Vallabhi under one of the Shiladityas. It was reworked, by one Nandisena, into the *Ajitasantithaya* before the ninth century (op. cit., 289-90). Haribhadra and Udyotanasuri, in the eighth century, wrote from Rajasthan (Chittor and Jalor, respectively). Haribhadra describes the 'corrupt city life' at this time of Jain exodus from Vallabhi (op. cit., 280-4). Jayasimha, too, lived in Rajasthan, at Nagaur, where he composed his *Dharmopadesamala* in AD 867. But originally he may have come from Vasanthapura (Vasantgadh) near Sirohi, on the borders of Gujarat. He refers to the Sakunikavihara of Broach, which Chatterjee thinks must have been built 'several centuries earlier', and to the sacred hill of Shatrunjaya (Palitana) in Saurashtra (op. cit., 286-7).

Several other works attest to the strength of Jain literature during this period. The Jain presence at the Solanki court is well known. Thus, though Vallabhi was destroyed and its Jain community dispersed, Jain writers continued to criticize the dominant values of kings and Kshatriyas. There is a strong continuity, here, with Merutunga's critique of Hindu ideas of kingship in the fourteenth century.

At a time when trade had not yet become a major component in the Rajput states of Saurashtra, the intellectual vanguard of the Jain community was already on the offensive, formulating an ideological opposition to the hegemony of the landlords.

BANIA VIEWS OF KINGSHIP: A VIEW FROM THE FOURTEENTH CENTURY

The presence of Jain scholars at the Chalukya court indicates that they had re-established themselves by the twelfth century. The opposition of merchants to Rajput hegemony certainly did not depend on their position in the peninsula, and the writings of Merutunga, the fourteenth century Jain monk, may have been addressed to the more centralized society on the mainland. Here, Jain merchants were an important element in the population. But Merutunga wrote from Wadhwan in Saurashtra, the town where Ranik Devi had performed her sati.

With Merutunga, the Jain opposition gains a more overtly political form, as he criticizes Hindu ideals of kingship to advance a Jain alternative view. We know of no Jain kings in Saurashtra, though they were found in the Deccan.[52] Even so the *Prabandhacintamani*, written by Merutunga at Wadhwan in AD 1304, gives us a good idea of Jain views of the ideal king. These have been analysed by Arai (1978).

The *Prabandhacintamani* is a collection of stories arranged to show the contrast between Hindu and Jain conceptions of kingship, stressing the superiority of the latter. The ideal qualities of a king are shown through the legendary Vikramaditya. The next ruler Satavahana, in contrast, incarnates the Hindu ideals. Last of these legendary kings, Bhuyaraja combines both sets of ideals, and by renouncing his throne demonstrates their incompatibility. He also prepares the setting for the subsequent stories, when he gives Malwa to the Paramaras for the protection of the Mahakala (Hindu) temple. This creates two kingdoms, Malwa and Gujarat. The latter is then seen to represent Jain values, as opposed to the Hindu values of the Malwa kings. All this certainly differs from our historical information, which indicates that the kings of Anhilwada Patan were actually Shaivite (op. cit., 77-8).

Merutunga maintains the superiority of Jain over Hindu values, but does not denigrate the latter.[53] The differences between Hindu and Jain conceptions of kingship, then

> are subtle, a matter of emphasis rather than negation of each other. This means that ... when a king with Jaina quality loses interest in self-elevation and begins to enjoy keeping the *status quo*, he becomes a Hindu type of king. On the other hand, when a Hindu type of king abstains from worldly pleasures and attempts to conquer inner and outer evils, he becomes a Jaina king, regardless of his religious affiliation. (ibid.)

Thus, in negation of meekness, the Hindu king shows military strength, while the Jain king is daring; the Hindu may oppose learning to self-conceit, but the Jain works for constant self-elevation; while arrogance, as a negative quality, is opposed to the gallantry of the Hindu king, the ideal Jain king shows humility; and the absolute generosity of the latter is superior to the relative generosity of the former in its opposition to hypocrisy (op. cit., 100). The superiority of the Jain king is not in religion *per se*, it is a matter of religious superiority on the individual level. 'Courage-and-wisdom' results from such moral strength. Jainism is superior to Hinduism in creating better men, so also better kings (op. cit., 102). Jain kingship

> is identical with perfect manhood, the Jaina king must be a perfect person. On

the other hand, Hindu kingship is exclusively for those who can afford the cultivation of literature poetry and martial arts and those who are wealthy enough to promote learning. By stressing the personal quality of kings, the Jainas have succeeded in encompassing Hindu values within their value hierarchy. (op. cit., 101)

The Jain individualist bias is underlined when Merutunga shows Hindu kings delegating more power and functions to their ministers: '...for the Hindus, statecraft is a collective affair to be exercised by the king and his ministers jointly' (Arai, op. cit, 101).

Another difference is the importance given to royal descent: 'Hindu *prabandhas* manage to attach royal descent to all the kings while the Jaina sources emphasize royal qualities and obscure the origins of some of the major kings' (ibid.).

What is opposed, here, is position and individual, social competence versus individual qualities. Merutunga's bias is towards achievement rather than ascription, in Parsons' terms (1936). Since the qualities of the Jain king are equal to ideal manhood, we have here a conception of the individual. Stressing religious achievement, this view clearly reflects the influence of ascetic ideals. We are reminded of Weber's and Dumont's writings on the emergence of the individual in Western society (Weber 1930, Dumont 1965, 1971, 1988). Nevaskar's view of Jains as a parallel to Western protestants seems to be supported by these images of the ideal Jain king (1971).

Or does the emergence of ascetic ideals result from, rather than initiate, a conception of the individual inherent in the contractual nature of trading relationships? If, indeed, trade is associated with Buddhism and Jainism from very early times, the question is surely worth asking.

We can see the advantage of such a view of kingship for people who, at that time and place, had no hope of putting up kings who were themselves Jain. The standards claimed for the king become, at least in principle, independent of religious affiliation, even of the Hindu-Muslim controversy. Indeed, in later times, there is little to indicate that Jains suffered particularly from Muslim rulers. The views quoted here would serve to create a certain distance, mingled with superiority, towards the powers-that-be in traditional Kathiawar.

Certainly, while the Rajput polity is establishing its dominance in the peninsula, the voice of dissent is already making itself heard. The opposition between rulers and merchants is, indeed, present from the very beginning of the medieval period.

NOTES

1. In Junagadh, interestingly, these were of the Mahayana sect (ibid.).
2. Hemachandra, in the Dyashraya-Kavya, describe the prince Grahasipu, ruling at Vanthali near Junagadh, as an Abhira and a Yadava (Krishna's legendary tribe) (Enthoven 1920, 25).
3. We may, of course, doubt these statements made nearly a thousand years after the event. Amarji is often wrong about specific events, particularly their dates. But it is my impression that his 'sociology' is often better than his history, in the strict sense of the term. Certainly, his view represents tradition as it had come down to the Junagadh of his time.
4. The following account is from Solanki (n.d.).
5. It is tempting to associate this refusal, ending in war, with the idea of hypergamous marriage. The Gujarat king had insulted the Chudasama's claim to higher or 'at least equal' status. If so, it runs counter to Kolff's view that hypergamy was established only by the 'new Rajput great tradition' in the early seventeenth century (1990, 72-3).
6. This is our first reference to sati in Saurashtra, understood as a wife's burning herself with her husband. A fuller example is Ranik Devi (below). In Saurashtra, I found a tendency to extend the term to other forms of heroic death by women, as in Mewar (Harlan 1991).
7. Kolff remarks: 'There is indeed a political quality about Indian hoarded wealth and treasure trove as is testified by Indian folklore. Riches in Indian stories are often miraculously unearthed ... and states immediately spring into existence. A hidden treasure is a hidden kingdom and its rediscovery was enough for the rays of royalty to shine again in the world...' (1990, 68). Here we note the goddess' role in revealing the treasure, consistent with her role as creator of Maya, the world illusion, to which such riches surely belong.
8. This story corresponds with the 'foundation myths' of Rajput kuldevis (Harlan 1991, 54ff). Such myths of the goddess also deal with the foundation of a royal house.
9. Amarji tells the story with some differences; he leaves out the goddess (Amarji 1882, 102-5). Wilberforce-Bell follows Amarji here (1916, 58-9).
10. The story is analysed more fully in Tambs-Lyche (1991, and in 1992a, 476-89).
11. There are many references to Hamir Sumra in Saurashtra folklore. They span several hundred years, and cannot refer to a single person. It seems that Hamir is a title used for all the Sumras, quite possibly a corruption of Amir.
12. A *nes* is a settlement of tribals or pastoralists. The gift of a turban would mean that the Ahir chief is acknowledged as a vassal of the Sumra king.
13. Adishakti—the essential shakti, common to all females that incarnate shakti.
14. The best recent treatment of this theme is in Harlan (1991). See also Tambs-Lyche (1991), and Carrin and Tambs-Lyche (1993).
15. Whether the Jethwas were the senior (*jyestha*) branch of the Saindhavas, or came from a separate family, is not clear. For a discussion of this problem, see JMG (67-8). But from the tenth century the rulers of Ghumli were known as Jethwas, where they continued to rule until the thirteenth century or the fall of Ghumli, in the fifteenth century. The ruins of the city are described by Burgess (1971, 178-86).
16. There are numerous accounts of this system, beginning with Tod (1829). Of

modern studies by historians, we may mention Sharma (1977). For an attempt to build an anthropological model, see Fox (1971). See Ch. III below.

17. The Keshwara lineage of Mers is still proud of this royal connection. Cf. Trivedi (1961).
18. A.C. Mayer comments that the use of the little finger is highly unlikely. I cite Trivedi here, without further comment.
19. Some of these stories will be related later.
20. The derivation of (prakrit) Ahir from (sanskrit) Abhira is often accepted, but there is no proof that the terms refer to the same people. Sanskrit sources—such as Manu, the Brahma Purana, and the Bhagavata Purana—give no indication of their presence in Saurashtra, unless we accept the Ahir's own claims to be Krishna's people. Enthoven saw this as a 'later invention' and I concur (Enthoven 1920, 20-3). In Rajasthan, Ahir and Gujar pastoralists claim to be one community. Abhiras and Gurjaras turn up at roughly the same time in the same parts of India, suggesting that the terms are interchangeable or refer to communities which were close. The Ahirs may have been of the same stock as the Gurjara-Pratiharas, as Enthoven thought (ibid.). Westphal-Hellbosch agrees that Ahirs came to this part of India before the Jats, Bharwads or Rabaris (1968, 1974, and 1976). A summary of this discussion is given in Tambs-Lyche (1992a, 173-9).
21. I shall say more of Charans later. Tod takes them back to AD 714 (I: 77), while Westphal-Hellbosch (1976, 104) accords them a history of about one thousand years. Their mythical origins take them back to the gods, See Ch. VII, also Westphal-Hellbosch (1976), and Tambs-Lyche (1992a, 193-204).
22. The Bharwads tend to regard North Gujarat as their ancestral home. According to legend, they were powerful enough there to shelter Rajputs from nine different clans, seeking refuge from the Muslims. This event is put at AD 961. Westphal-Hellbosch thinks they came to Saurashtra somewhat later (1976, 18-19) See Ch. VI, also Westphal-Hellbosch (1976), and Tambs-Lyche (1992a, 185-93).
23. The Rabaris were regarded by Enthoven as an immigrant tribe (1922, 252), and Westphal-Hellbosch holds the same view. According to the myths she cites, they came from Jaisalmer. These myths cannot go back further than 500-800 years, so that she dates their immigration to Saurashtra between AD 1100 and 1400 (1974, 40-1). See Ch. VI, also Westphal-Hellbosch (1974), and Tambs-Lyche (1992a, 179-85).
24. There are traditions of two Kathi migrations to Saurashtra. The first, according to which they came in the eighth or ninth century, is hazy and not accepted by all historians. The second took place around AD 1400 (Enthoven 1921, 165-6). In the intervening period they are said to have lived in Kutch, but it is not clear whether some remained in Saurashtra during these centuries, if indeed they had already come.
25. An account of the early Rajputs is found in Wilberforce-Bell (1916, 50-3).
26. See Spodek (1976, 16-17) and Tambs-Lyche (1992a, 123-7).
27. Enthoven (1920, 234-5): we return to this question in Ch. VIII.
28. Of the contemporary Chaoras we know much less (cf. Wilberforce-Bell 1916, 48ff).
29. The date given by Mehta and Mehta (1896, 145). Tod (I, 71, 188) and the Udaipur palace records give the date as mid-eighth century, marked by the deposition, by Bappa Rawal, of the Mori ruler of Chittor. Bappa Rawal thus

became the founder of the Mewar dynasty (Ziegler 1973, 115). Harlan also cites Somani as accepting this date. The Udaipur family belongs to the Sisodia branch, and inherited Chittor after its sack by Ala-ud-din in the early fourteenth century (Tod I, 216, D. Sharma (ed) 1966, 672-3, Harlan 1991, 30 and n.)

30. Tod (1829, 71). The lost kingdom here is sometimes identified with Vallabhi (Wilberforce-Bell 1916, 52-3).
31. Tod and the genealogical records of the Udaipur palace place this event in the sixth century, a date supported by Somani, and accepted by Harlan (1991, 28).
32. This corresponds broadly to what some scholars have called the proto-Rajput stage. While I have used that term tentatively in earlier work (1992, 42-5) I have avoided its use here, to underline the specific criteria I use for my definition of its state formations.
33. A common form of suicide in Gujarat and Saurashtra. The wells then become inhabited by a *bhoot*, the ghost of the deceased. Sometimes, suicide 'by water' serves as an alternative to death by fire, associating the deceased to the category of sati (Carrin and Tambs-Lyche 1993).
34. Such visits to the cremation ground (especially at night) are widely associated with tantric practice. Shakti Mata's appearance here is, therefore, an indication of her powers.
35. I understand here that they have performed the rite of *raksha-bandhan*, making the queen the 'ritual sister' of Harpal.
36. Patdi is on the mainland, but close to the Saurashtra border and to the present Jhalawar.
37. Kankavati is some ten miles west of Dhrangadhra. It is the inhabitants who claim the village as 'the home of Shakti Mata'. It is not clear how they relate this claim to her descent from heaven and her appearance in the cremation grounds.
38. Mavelanji, author of the Yadavamsa-Prakasa, makes the Jadejas' ancestors one-time rulers of Egypt, migrating via Syria, Iran and Afghanistan to their present area (JMG, 72).
39. Tod tells us that the Ghori had become the 'adopted brother' of Bhanji's queen. Probably (see n. 35) she had performed *raksha-bandhan* to him, making him 'like a brother' to her.
40. Tod's remark 'the freedom granted to the Rajput fair in those chivalrous days ...' suggests, perhaps, that he had such an interpretation in mind.
41. Tod calls this woman a sati, perhaps extending this term too far (see n. 11). We note, however—keeping in mind the Khodiyar myth—the importance of a woman's vengeance, even posthumous (Carrin and Tambs-Lyche 1993). The mode of self-sacrifice here, by—supposedly Brahmin—priests, interestingly conforms to the later Charan custom of Traga.
42. The sati of Naughan's mother may be a later interpolation. But the story of Ranik Devi builds up to the sati as its climax and it cannot thus have been added. Though the poets may have added details—her inauspicious birth, the verses she pronounces on leaving Sorath—the historical references are rather precise and likely to be substantially correct. My account follows Forbes, who obviously based his on bardic sources.
43. Lakha Pholanee was king of Kutch. He turns up in Charan myth, too, and seem to be an important starting point for much of medieval Rajput and Charan tradition. This myth places him in the late eleventh or early twelfth century, which fits rather well with other sources.

44. Substituting the sword for an absent groom was a well-known usage in western India.
45. Vaghris are untouchables and suffer heavy discrimination. In Praj they still had to wear their hair in a pigtail in 1973-4, and were not allowed new or well-kept clothes. They are often seen as ex-hunters, and so 'ex-tribals'. Their present connection with the forest is restricted to gathering and sale of *neem* sticks for cleaning the teeth. See P.G. Shah (1967).
46. This expression of patriotism sounds anachronistic, and the poetry may have been composed later. We only know it was 'old' when Forbes heard it in the mid-nineteenth century. Yet it shows the feeling of regional identity which, by then, had become part of tradition.
47. One derivation of sati is from *satya* (truth, purity) or *sat* (virtuous, wise) (Mallison 1973, 27). Here this etymology is used consciously. Harlan confirms the derivation of sati from *sat*, a quality inherent in the woman, which may manifest in the performance of sati, but only if the woman possesses that quality (1991). In Muktananda's Sati-Gita (Mallison, op. cit. 27n) the sati is the true wife; he uses the word *suri* for the woman who burns with her husband. Muktananda, however, holds such a practice unworthy of the real sati.
48. The Vaghers retained their reputation for piracy into the nineteenth century, and are still associated by others with smuggling. They remain a good recruiting-ground for seamen. Later, they were alone in Saurashtra in taking part in the insurrection of 1857-8.
49. The famous pilgrimage centre of Dwarka, Krishna's holy city, is in the extreme north-west of the peninsula, dominated by the Vaghers. Bet is an island off the tip of the peninsula.
50. Merutunga lived in the late thirteenth and early fourteenth century at Wadhwan, on the boundary between Saurashtra and the mainland. The *Prabandhacintamani*, an 'historical' account of edifying stories showing the superiority of Jain philosophy, was written in AD 1304.
51. I do not discuss, here, the age of the Ramayana or the dates of Valmiki, I simply assume as, e.g. Ghurye does (1962, 184), that the epic 'in its main portion must be pre-Christian'.
52. Especially in Karnataka, which was well known to Gujaratis through trade links. For these kingdoms, see, e.g. Saletore (1938), Stein (1978) and Gururaja Bhatt (1975).
53. Arai shows how this is done: 'Episode 65 ... is exclusively concerned with the benevolence of the Hindu deities, Surya and Candika, by whose grace the poets Bana and Mayura are cured from diseases and granted beautiful figures ... in Episode 66, the Jaina teacher Manatungacarya is asked by hostile Hindu courtiers to prove the superiority of Jaina deities. (He) says, 'What is the sense of superiority here for our gods who are liberated? Even so, I shall show some world-astonishing power of the lesser deities *(sura)* who are their servants.' He has his body bound with 44 iron chains.... As he recites one stanza after another praising the Jaina god, the chains are broken one by one. This ... implies that the Hindu deities who grant favour in response to devotion are inferior to Jaina gods who are absolute and beyond subject-object dichotomy. The sequence of these two episodes also effectively emphasizes Jaina superiority' (1978, 97). This is a typical example of what I have elsewhere called hierarchizing discourse (Tambs-Lyche, forthcoming b).

CHAPTER III

Traditional Kathiawar Rajput State Formation

THE GRADUAL GROWTH OF RAJPUTHOOD

We are moving towards the social institution most conspicuous to medieval Kathiawar: the Rajput state. Much has been written about it, but here I stress its gradual growth.

It might be tempting to follow Kolff (1990) in distinguishing between early 'soldiering' groups, who gradually come to occupy landholding and ruling positions, and the cultural elaboration of a 'Rajput Great Tradition' from the seventeenth century onwards—the tradition embraced and reified by writers such as Tod (1829ff) and Forbes (1878). I shall bypass this two-fold distinction, however, to stress the gradual growth of the order that came to dominate traditional Kathiawar.

The founders of the 'clan dynasties' of the early medieval period—the Gurjara-Pratiharas or, in Saurashtra, the Saindhavas and Chudasamas—may be identified with lines we now call Rajputs. But their kingdoms were built differently from the later Rajput states. Only from the late eleventh century do the Jhalas introduce, to Saurashtra, the typical Rajput polity, based on the clan's dominance at village level. Later, the Jadejas, and then the Gohils establish themselves; we shall follow these two clans to their establishment of full-fledged Rajput states.

It is not the state-building process alone that is gradual; other traits central to Rajputhood appear one by one. With the myth of Khodiyar emerges, under the Chudasamas, a special relationship between king and goddess. The Jhalas then give it a slightly different form in merging queen and goddess in their Shakti Mata. This combination remains exceptional, however. We shall see how Khodiyar herself, after the fall of the Chudasamas, is taken over by the Gohils. As their protectress, she finally becomes associated with a Rajput clan—a kuldevi in the classic sense of the term.

Early references to the sati ritual may be spurious. But with Ranik Devi's death in the twelfth century sati appears as we know it from later times, closely associated with fundamental Rajput values. Only by the seventeenth century does the rite reach its zenith in Saurashtra to become accepted practice. Untill then, female participation in politics does not seem to revolve around the sati phenomenon.

The queen's role in traditional Kathiawar shows the fundamental importance of marriage alliance in Rajput polity. This role, too, changes, but the idea of patriliny is certainly as fundamental to the marriage alliance as the latter is to the constitution of the clan. The idea of Rajputhood, as it emerges, involves a complementarity of male and female, of brotherhood and alliance. But by the eighteenth century, the queen fades from politics in the more advanced states, as the army and the bureaucracy increase in importance, pushing the kinship nexus into the background.

In this kinship nexus, the place of the kuldevi or clan goddess is central; linking her to the king are her brothers, the bards, from whose caste the goddess herself is recruited. We have met such a bard in the guise of Khodiyar's father, but the position that the Charan caste—'the children of the goddess'—comes to occupy, seems to develop only during the twelfth to thirteenth century. Later, every royal clan depended on a line of bards for its recognition.

Parallel to the growth of Rajput polity in the countryside, the world of towns and merchants, surviving the change from classical to medieval times, continues to exist. Only by tapping this source of revenue and finance, could the Rajput state emerge from rural chieftainship. The merchants, though culturally distinct from, and ideologically opposed to, the kinship-political nexus of the state, were a necessary condition for its growth.

THE SECONDARY NATURE OF THE RAJPUT STATE

From the rise of the Jhalas in the eleventh century the kinship-political nexus remains central to the structure of the state. We are concerned, thus, with the formation of states from a base of clan dominance. Among the considerable literature on this theme, the analysis by Fox, though criticized, will form a convenient framework, to be modified and extended as we proceed.

Fox's point of departure is the 'secondary' nature of the Rajput state (Fried 1967, 240ff). Typical of the founders of Rajput lineages in Uttar Pradesh, he writes, 'was their political and military pioneering on the margins of state authority' (Fox 1971, 69). This secondary nature is inherent in Rajput tradition itself, for the Brahmin Parashurama—the sixth *avatar* of Vishnu—destroyed all the Kshatriyas (warriors) twenty-one times (Dowson 1982, 230-1). Only much later were they re-created, to become Rajputs, from the great fire-sacrifice (Agnihotra) near Mount Abu (Tod 1829, 77, Forbes 1878, 536).[1] Rajputs, then, acknowledge the 'recent' origin of the caste, compared to Brahmins.

Fox sees their origin in freebooter bands, organized as segmentary lineages, and establishing themselves on the fringes of existing states. Kolff (1990) prefers to talk about the rise of the Rajput from a 'soldiering' tradition. But in the earlier period, it is hard to distinguish between a soldier and a freebooter acknowledged as such by an overlord, since such martial activities were often paid for in booty alone. Fox appears to be closer to Kolff's views than the latter acknowledges. The main difference is their view of the lineage, to which I return below. Certainly, these early bands are known by clan names. They may not have been lineages; but they do seem to have identified themselves as such.

As noted, Saurashtra itself may be seen as a marginal area. It also contains areas marginal to its centres. Thus Jam Bamanioji, the Jadeja, appears as a marauding adventurer on the margins of the foundering Jethwa state. Harpal the Jhala, similarly, was creating his domain on the outskirts of, and as a vassal of, Gujarat itself. These figures correspond to the 'lineage ancestor/ adventurer' at the first stage in Fox's 'development cycle' of the Rajput lineage. The adventurer might act on his own behalf, as Bamanioji apparently did, or he might be backed by a neighbouring power, like Harpal. In the latter case, states Fox, 'the adventurer had to validate the patent of the central authority with his own courage and strength' (1971, 69).

PROTECTION AND SUBJUGATION

The adventurer and his companions were, of course, subjecting peasants to their rule. But we must assume they were, then as later, protectors as well. Kolff shows well how widespread a feature 'soldiering'—which its implication of pillaging and looting—was of medieval Indian society. A village would need defence. To allot a certain surplus to an armed brotherhood of men might be a price worth paying for a minimum of security.

At first the lineage adventurer is the only intermediary between cultivator and state (Fox 1971, 69-70). There is not yet a complete 'feudal' hierarchy. Indeed, in Saurashtra, the first of these adventurers break into the stage of 'tribe-state' alliance, and they precede the later pattern of vassalage.[2] We may suppose that the surplus taken from the cultivator was not yet as high as it would become later.[3]

Not only peasants had an interest in protection. The Rathods of Marwar started their rise to power by protecting the Brahmins of Pali, who held their lands on grants from the ruler of Mewar. But he was far away; their immediate protectors had been the Kanha Mers.[4] They were surrounded by a number of small 'Rajput' principalities, such as Khed and Ranthambhor. 'It seems', says G.D. Sharma (1977, 1-2), that as long as these rulers were strong, 'the Paliwal Brahmins could live peacefully with the Mers. But, with the decline of these Rajput rulers, the leaders of the Mer tribe started asserting more and more.... Such was the situation that no one dared to camp outside the city or outside the village even for a night due to the fear of the Mers'.

Rich but vulnerable, the Paliwal Brahmins[5] were clearly in need of protection, and found it in the Rathod band led by Asthan.[6] They constructed a mansion for him and his brothers in Pali, paid them 45.5 taka a day for protection, and gave their Rathod followers land in the surrounding area (op. cit., 2). Clearly, even a rich and powerful community was willing to pay well for protection. We may imagine that ordinary peasants would be in an inferior bargaining position relative to the Paliwals.[7]

Asthan became a chief, his brothers closely associated with him, while their followers became farmers; since they were spread over a wide area, it is said that Asthan thus came to control 50-60 villages around Pali (op. cit., 3). The geographical distribution of the 'clan' thus ensures regional dominance, while a degree of stratification between the chief and his men appears in the war-band.

At this stage, such distinction apparently did not threaten solidarity. Later, as with Harpal's sons and heritors, or Navanagar in its early years, feudatory relationships between senior and junior kin were used to consolidate the chiefdom, with cadet lines assigned villages on the edge of the chief's area of influence. Thus segmentary kinship, grown from the chief's band of followers, by taking on the hierarchical aspect so peculiarly Rajput, comes to integrate wider groupings than before.

THE LINEAGE BASE OF RAJPUTDOM

It is at this point that the question of this following arises. Were the 'kinsmen' really 'kin'? Kolff's view, clearly, is that they were not. But we know from other cases of segmentary lineage organization, that there is nothing particular in non-kin agglomorating around a core of kin, using the idiom of brotherhood (*bhai-band*) for their integration.[8] This is the mode of recruitment that we must assume for early 'Rajput' bands, identified as they are by clan names. As in many such cases, followers may in fact have been tied to the core in rather spurious relationships.

What makes such an assumption likely is the expansion in clan population which follows the successful establishment of such chiefdoms. We are often told that members of the clan were given land in conquered territory, as was the case with Asthan's men. Were there enough kinsmen to distribute among 50-60 villages? And their number increased as the chiefdom expanded.

Certainly, clan members might migrate to the area, following the successful establishment of one of their members as chief there. But it is doubtful whether this can account for the necessary increase in clan population. It must have been tempting, for the chief, to accept into his fold adventurers from other origins willing to contribute to the clan's fortune—probably providing they possessed some common qualities.

In this sense, we may accept Kolff's view that the country saw numbers of 'soldiers of fortune' and that kinship in a strict sense was not necessary for their integration into groups. Yet all sources use kin terms for such bands, and we assume that kinship served as the idiom for their integration. This is the most likely genesis of the 'Rajput clan' as we know it.

It is my reading of Fox that he assumes such processes, widely acknowledged by anthropologists dealing with segmentary lineage systems.[9] Kolff, perhaps, thinks of kinship as literal 'blood links' rather than a mode of categorization. That the specific stress on 'pure' blood is a later development and part of the consolidation of Rajputs as an 'aristocracy', is surely a point where Kolff (1990, 72-3) is likely to be right. We shall return to it later.

The model of the segmentary lineage, on which Fox based his analysis, has become rather unfashionable. Yet for a long time it seemed central to political anthropology, generating a vast literature, beginning with Evans-Pritchard's classic monograph on the Nuer of the southern Sudan (1940). Here, in the absence of chiefdoms, solidarity was seen to be based on segmentary kinship. At the widest field of relevance, all Nuer are 'brothers', but according to kinship distance, some are more so than others. Alliances—for cattle raids, mainly—tended to form around closely related patrilineal groups.

Similar patterns were found elsewhere, in Africa, the Middle East and northern India.[10] For Sahlins (1961), 'segmentary solidarity' produces a 'massing effect', making the segmentary lineage an 'organization of predatory expansion' at the cost of neighbouring societies—unless these be powerfully defended states. In real life, the solidarity of such lineages was found to be substantially affected by other factors, notably marriage alliance.[11]

In a particularly interesting case, Barth showed how segmentary solidarity among Pathans of the Swat Valley (1959a and b) is inverted; close kin becoming enemies rather than allies. Two factors contribute to this inversion. First, the limited area of the valley leaves no room for expansion, which otherwise ranges kin against non-kin. Secondly, each Pathan chief depends for support not on kin but on followers, who show solidarity by frequenting his men's house. Thus, for Swat Pathan chiefs expansion can only be at the cost of close kin, who according to segmentary logic occupy adjoining areas. This creates moral stress, since 'brothers' are supposed to show solidarity (Tambs-Lyche 1992b).

In the case of Kathiawar Rajputs, we see clan solidarity[12] manifest itself at what Fox terms the first stage, when land is conquered from non-Rajputs or from distant clans—as in the case of Asthan's Rathods. Subsequently, when descendants of each 'brother' holds his own principality, rivalry and conflict between them alternates with support against common enemies.

At this stage, marriage alliances create ties that lead sometimes to solidarity, sometimes to conflict; and notably, this choice is tied to internal politics in each state. Thus Jadejas (Navanagar) and Jhalas (Halvad, later Dhrangadhra) were sometimes allies, sometimes rivals, for several centuries; while taking wives from each other. The choice between alliance and conflict, here, does not seem to follow from structural contingency but has to be analysed in each case.

The possibility of expansion remains important for the clan's solidarity, however. The Jhalas, hemmed in between the rulers of mainland Gujarat and strong Rajput states in the peninsula, acquired the reputation of being at once the most courageous and the most divisive of Rajput clans in Saurashtra. The Gohils to the south fought each other mainly at the later stage, when further expansion against Kathis and Kolis became difficult. The Jadejas were generally united against the Jethwas of Porbandar, while conflicts with the Jhalas, to whom so many marriages were made, often divided the two clans equally.

Stage two in Fox's cycle—'the rise of the Raja'—grows from stage one as, between cultivator and king, 'the powerful and autocratic lineage elite', close to the chief, imposes itself over 'the large body of his subordinate and often oppressed kinsmen' at village level (Fox 1971, 75).[13] Such internal stratification within the dominant group takes time to develop, however. Among the Rathods, who came to Pali early in the thirteenth century, conflicts due to this stratification appear only after the death of Rao Jodha, eleventh in line from Asthan, towards the beginning of the sixteenth century (Sharma 1977, 1-8). By this time, the chiefdom was well on its way to becoming a small state.

THE RAJPUT CHIEFDOM AND STATE

Encroachment on the autonomy of subject lineages by the chief, then, is one factor behind the transition to stage two. The other factor is the growth of more formal arrangements of revenue collection. The whole process is accelerated wherever a central power holds some degree of control over the area (Fox 1971, 75).

With revenue collection the distance between the levels of the hierarchy increase, elevating the raja over and above his subordinate kinsmen. In short, the typical Rajput state, central to our subsequent discourse, has been brought into being. Kinship, chiefdoms and the state form a continuous series of political forms among Rajputs; but as we go from one form to another there is a change in scale (Grønhaug 1978).

The very nature of kinship is affected by this change. 'The close-knit family-based lineages of stage one (within a confederacy)', says Fox, 'individually began to develop into the impersonal, 'feudal' kin bodies that comprise the most common literary stereotype of Rajput clans' (op. cit., 76). Even if the early bands were not as kin-bound as Fox seems to suppose here, the main point is not affected, for what must have integrated non-kin with the early bands were surely loyalties of a personal or small-scale nature.

Stage three, too, seems largely to be a function of increasing scale. 'Intrusion by the state', as Fox calls this stage, is marked by a change in delegation of power at the local level. The state may replace local lineage leaders by junior members of the senior lineage; alternatively, local leaders are separated from their kinship base, creating a new intermediary level between ruler and cultivator. Such re-organization may be combined with delegation of revenue collection from the centre to the new local leaders (Fox 1971, 97-9). In general, only the larger states in Saurashtra reached this stage before the British came.

In practice, the new local leaders were often adventurers sponsored by the centre, while the original leaders, reduced to the status of their kin, took to the jungle as adventurers in their own right. In both cases, there is a structural reversion to stage one (op. cit., 101-2). Local leaders may then re-assert themselves, supported by their lineage, or be replaced by 'tax-farmers' installed by the centre (Fox 1971, 108-13). The latter development has been of minor importance in Saurashtra, except for Junagadh and other Muslim states.

The other possibility discussed by Fox for stage four is the decline of the local kinship-based leaders to yeoman-peasantry. 'The absence of a frontier', he writes, 'requires the lineage to proliferate steadily in a fixed area. Ancestral lands become progressively more divided, and the lineage population are forced to take over increasing amounts of land under direct cultivation...' (op. cit., 114). This, we have seen, is a logical consequence when the segmentary lineage faces closed frontiers; it happened to some Kathiawar lineages, among them the descendants of the Chudasamas. But, till the coming of the British, there was always a frontier; outlaws frequently operated all over the peninsula.

One Rajput role served to keep the frontier alive: the 'younger brother' setting out as an adventurer to carve his own dominion, often seeking service with a ruler to promote his career. He is an important figure in Kolff's work (1990); he is central to the foundation of Rajput power in Bundelkhand (Jain 1975), and the subject of a number of stories from Gujarat (Forbes 1878, e.g. 90-118). He turns up frequently in Kathiawar, too, and is not restricted to the early period, though his scope for enterprise diminishes from the sixteenth century onwards. The 'return to stage one' of Fox' scheme seems, in fact, to have been an ever-present factor in Rajput politics until a very late date.

Stage five in Fox' cycle returns to this stage through 'descent into anarchy' (op. cit., 124). Such conditions marked the periphery of declining states throughout Saurashtra's medieval history, but no important state collapsed completely. Junagadh had its ups and downs; yet from the ninth to the nineteenth century it remained a centre of power. The Jethwa state of the Porbandar area endured the changing fortunes of a millennium. The senior Jhala state Halvad (Dhrangadhra from 1730) was a constant factor in peninsular politics, as Navanagar (Jamnagar) became from the sixteenth century. Conversely, the southeastern corner of the peninsula saw no state of regional importance from the fall of Vallabhi to the rise of Bhavnagar in the early eighteenth century. The 'cycle' of Fox, then, seldom turned full circle in traditional Kathiawar; complete 'decline into anarchy' was reserved for the minor states.

Fox's model has been severely criticized, notably for stressing patrilineal kinship to the exclusion of matrimonial alliance (Stern 1973, Galey 1973). For traditional Kathiawar, however, elements of it provide a useful framework to understand the dynamics of states. We shall discuss the alliance problem later. Quite another factor prevented the completion of Fox's development 'cycle': the relationship between power and trade, between rulers and merchants.

MERCHANTS AND RULERS

A simple illustration of this relationship is found in the story of the formation of Chital state. One of the minor states ruled by Kathis, it was situated in a frontier area—the peninsular centre, where the interests of Junagadh, Navanagar (Jamnagar) and Bhavnagar were to clash.

When Amreli had been plundered by the Nawab of Junagadh in or just before 1735, a rich merchant, having lost his property, fled to Chital. He offered its Kathi chiefs half his property if they could recover it for him. They raided Amreli, and brought back the merchant's goods. They then wanted to kill the merchant to get the rest of his property. But one of their women intervened, and 'they decided instead to give their share to the merchant. He, in turn, rewarded their generosity by settling permanently at Chital, and, as this became known, he was followed by others. The neighbouring landowners also placed themselves under the protection of the Chital Kathis' (ADG, 59-60).

Later, Chital formed part of a Kathi confederacy attacking Bhavnagar. Bhavnagar won the war, but Wakhatsinhji, its ruler, restored Chital to its former owners in 1793 (ibid.). By this act Wakhatsinhji evidently recognized the legitimacy of its Kathi rulers. In effect, Chital had become a state. In 1735, the Chital Kathis still seem to have been seen by outsiders as simple robbers. The story of the merchant, whether myth or history, may be seen as the turning point in effecting this transformation. The Rathods of Marwar similarly began their rise to statehood by protecting the Brahmin traders at Pali (Tod II; 14-15, Sharma 1977, 2-3).

But let us turn to Navanagar, the state which was to supplant the Jethwas of Ghumli as the main power of north-western Saurashtra. We left Jam Bamanioji, the adventurer of the Jadeja clan, as the possible conqueror who laid Ghumli waste. His son, Jam Raval, founded the city of Navanagar—now Jamnagar—in AD 1540 (JMG, 73).

It seems safe to assume that the port was established to encourage trade and raise revenue. Raval may have taken Porbandar as his model. If, indeed, he wanted to build a competing trade centre, he was successful; Navanagar became the main port of north-western Saurashtra, though Porbandar remained a rival throughout the history of Navanagar state.

The rise of this new regional power was related to the 'power vacuum' left by the decline of the Jethwa state as well as weak control from the mainland. With the foundation of Navanagar, we pass from stage one of Fox's model to his second stage. But the city introduces an element foreign to his analysis. Promoting stability, the control of trade disproves the view of Rajput states as intrinsically unstable entities. Yet we have seen how closely the establishment of a city follows the creation of the state of the Jams.

The Portuguese attempts at control may have helped Jamnagar become an alternative outlet for the trade of Gujarat. A Portuguese fleet had sacked and burnt Gogha, Surat, Mangrol, Somnath, Bassein and some smaller ports in 1531-3, but did not attack ports north of Mangrol (Pearson 1976, 75, 95). The Portuguese gained control of Bassein in 1534, Diu fort in 1537-8, the island and town of Diu in 1554-5, and Daman in 1557-9. Settled at Daman and Diu, they were able to control effectively all trade to the Gulf of Cambay (op. cit., 67-83).

By the 1530s the traders of Gujarat had, in general, given up their defiance of the Portuguese and tried instead to accommodate to their conditions. Thus by 1540, when Jam Raval founded his city, the Portuguese presence did not hinder trade; but the Portuguese passes (cartazes) of course had to be paid for.

Who were the traders of the new port, and where did they trade?

Among the several merchant communities found in Jamnagar, the Bhatias are by far the most typical and famous. According to Pocock (1973, 117) they had their origins as humble fishermen and coastal traders in Kutch and its Gulf,[14] but by the nineteenth century they had become very prominent traders indeed. We know little about Bhatia trade networks on the Indian Ocean before British times, but it seems that they rose to prominence with the port of Jamnagar, that they were always a main factor in its trade, and that Pocock (op. cit.) is right in thinking that their conversion to the Vallabhacharya sect is related to their rising position. Always among the main supporters of the sect, it is likely that they were early converts. The sect became important in Gujarat from the late sixteenth century (Mallison 1983, 1994). One source supposes that the conversion of the Bhatias mainly took place during that century (Tripathi and Mehta 1984, 156).[15] This may be a little early.

The trade route from Gujarat to East Africa was well established by 1500, but then Cambay, Surat and Rander were the main ports; those west of Diu were of minor importance in international trade (Pearson 1976, 10-11). Hormuz, at the entrance to the Persian Gulf, was an important destination for ships from Gujarat, but its trade was dominated by Muslims. Aden controlled trade to the Red Sea, but this, too, was in Muslim hands (op. cit., 14). At a later date at least, the Vora community of Gujarat were important there, trading in perfumes.[16]

This leaves Oman, where the Portuguese had dominated the coast, but by the seventeenth century British and Dutch presence reduced their control, and they were thrown out by 1651 (Kumar 1965, 18). This may have provided an opening for the Bhatias. Oman rose to regional importance during this and the next century, and came to rule Zanzibar. It is likely that the growing Oman-Zanzibar trade played a part in the rise of the Bhatias, and that they in turn were a factor in the Omani expansion. The proximity of Jamnagar to Oman would have been an enabling factor. My hypothesis, then, is that Bhatia trade through Oman to Zanzibar and East Africa picked up considerably in the seventeenth century, and that this was the period when the newly-rich Bhatias improved their status by adopting the Vallabhacharya sect.

By the1850s, when Richard Burton visited Zanzibar, Bhatias were prominent traders there (Pocock 1973, 117). In 1873, Sir Bartle Frere referred to the commerce of Maskat and Oman as 'exclusively Indian' (Kumar 1965, 66). Bhatias were, and still are, important in Oman

(Barth 1983), and probably formed the bulk of its Indian merchants.

In 1856 the British established a de facto protectorate over both Oman and Zanzibar, and incidentally separated the colony from the mainland (Kumar 1965, 24-33). This separation hardly affected the Bhatias, by now well established and trading under British protection.

THE GROWTH OF NAVANAGAR STATE

With the establishment of Navanagar, the new state was to become the dominant power of Halar, the northern coast of Saurashtra. Jam Raval's conquests, however, did not take place without fighting. The Jethwa and Vala Rajputs, the Kathis and the Vadhels joined their forces against him (JMG, 73). Clearly, if there was a 'power vacuum' in the sense that neighbouring states were weak, this did not mean that the field was lacking in contestants for power. But at the battle of Mithoi near Khambhalia Raval defeated this alliance, driving the Jethwas out of Halar, the Kathis south of the river Bhadar, the Dedas eastwards across the river Macchu, and the Vadhels across the Okha Rann. Bakota pargana was taken, and Jadeja territory was extended southwards as far as Kandorna (JMG, 73).

True to their kinship obligations, Raval's younger brothers had assisted him (Fox's second stage). They got their shares of the spoils, forming a cluster of Jadeja states. Modji got Khandhera, Hardholji got Dhrol, and Ravoji got Khambhalia.

As a result of the conquests, and the foundation of his port city, Raval's chiefdom was well on the way to statehood. But the territory was still expanding, and there was room for further cadet lines. Thus not only did Raval's brothers get their own chiefdoms, his sons, too, got their shares. By the time of Jam Sataji, however (1569-1608) further expansion became impossible. Akbar had conquered Gujarat in 1573, and his Viceroy made the presence of a central power felt; Navanagar's claims to independence were thwarted. There was no more land for allotment to the cadets of the clan.

The Jam supported the Gujarat sultan in his efforts to regain independence from Delhi. The resulting conflict ended in the battle—still remembered in Saurashtra—of Bhuchar Mori in 1591. Here, the confederacy led by the Jam was beaten, and Navanagar became tributary to the Mughals. (JMG, 74-6).

The seventeenth century, therefore, represents a new phase in the history of the state. Conflict with the Mughals, and scattered attempts at regaining independence, alternate with alliance through marriage to the Mughal's representatives. It was a period of internal conflict at the court, not unconnected with the state's dependence on the centre.

We have noted that Fox neglected affinity; the Rani's family ties certainly become a major factor of internal politics in Navanagar at this period. The *bhayats*, junior relatives of the king, remained a force in palace politics. Kinship was thus still paramount; the bureaucratic element remained weak. Only once do we come across a Nagar—apparently in a 'bureaucratic' capacity—in state politics. The state had not yet entered stage three of Fox' cycle. The strains and stresses of the power struggle still indicate an inherently unstable state.

This was even more so in neighbouring Jhalawad. Chandrasinhji, whose wily sister we will soon meet, was attacked by Navanagar and at one time held prisoner by his rival. Afterwards, his three sons gave him trouble. Askaranji and Amarsinhji, the younger ones, managed to have the Viceroy at Ahmedabad imprisoned and later killed their elder brother Prathiraj. In 1628 Askaranji succeeded to the throne of Halwad, but was in his turn killed by Amarsinhji six years later. But he was faced with Prathiraj's son Sultanji, who founded the state of Wankaner by the help of Navanagar. Prathiraj's other son, Rajoji, managed to wrest Wadhwan from Askaranji, and this state, too, became independent. Adding to the division of the domain, Rajoji's grandson Abhyesinhji later occupied and kept Chuda, while another Abhyesinhji, the fourth son of Chandrasinhji, had been given Lakhtar (Wilberforce-Bell 1916, 112-13).

Thus while dynastic strife split up the Jhala lands, Navanagar remained intact—but the problem of maintaining brotherhood within the ruling family was clearly common to both. These stresses and strains, with the need to define more closely who really had a stake in the kinship core of the state, go a long way towards explaining what Kolff calls the 'new Great Rajput Tradition' from the early seventeenth century onwards in the Rajput world (1990, 72-3).

In Jamnagar, at least, the rulers had gained ascendancy over their 'kinsmen', and they surely meant to keep it. Stricter rules of intermarriage, a greater stress on purity of blood, eulogizing the Rajputs as the real Kshatriya caste—all this must have been highly useful ideological tools in the period now starting.

NAVANAGAR STATE: POLITICS OF THE ZENANA

In principle, primogeniture prevailed in Navanagar. In fact, only in seven out of nineteen cases of succession, from 1535 to 1743, did the eldest son ascend the throne.[17]

There were two cases in which the succession went to a younger son of the ruler. In three cases, the king was succeeded by his brother. But equally, in three other cases, a brother's son succeeded to the throne. In one case, the next ruler was a son of the king, but by a concubine rather than one of his queens. There was one case of an adopted son, and one of an adopted son of the ruler's father. Finally, one successor is held to have been a pretender son, i.e. a boy adopted secretly by the queen in order to claim, for her, a legitimate candidate to the throne.

This short list gives some idea of the field of heir-apparents potentially available although it includes only the successful ones. To be more precise, we shall give some examples.

Jam Raval's grandson Sataji lost the battle of Bhuchar Mori to the Mughal forces in 1591. His eldest son was killed there, but Jasoji, his second son, succeeded him. Bharoji, the youngest son of Jam Raval, is said to have been given an apanage rather than control of a defined area. Otherwise, Jasoji's brother Vibhoji was the last to be given his own lands; fighting his way south from there, he became the founder of Rajkot state. We are told that Navanagar helped in these conquests (JMG, 76). We do not know who the vanquished were: perhaps they were Kathis.

Jasoji, Vibhoji's father, ruled Navanagar from 1608 to 1624. His death provides us with an interesting case of palace politics:

> Jam Jasoji married the sister of Raj Chandrasinghji of Halvad. One day he and the Jhali Rani[18] were playing chess ... he took her knight.... The Rani losing her temper said: 'It is no great thing for you to take a horse from a woman, but if you can take a horse from my brother, then you are indeed a raja.' Jasoji rose up displeased and remembering her taunt, sent men to Halvad ... and contrived to capture (Chandrasinhji) by a stratagem and carry him to Navanagar. But he released him afterwards at the intercession of a Nagar Brahmin....[19] On this occasion he taunted the Jhali Rani at her brother being a captive, and she treasuring up this grudge against him, contrived some years after to administer poison to him, of which he died in 1624. (JMG, 76)

The Rani evidently identifies herself with her natal family and the Jhala clan, rather than with her husband's. The story may be apocryphal. This does not really matter; we have here an important element in the patrilineal kinship of the region. Women were, and to some extent still are, not simply 'transferred on marriage' from one clan to another. Rather, they remained members of both clans for different purposes.

Doranne Jacobson has pointed to a similar situation among women in rural Maharashtra (Jacobson 1977) while similar double allegiances for women are described with regard to the Muslim Marris of Baluchistan (Pehrsson 1966) and the Basseri nomads of Iran (Barth 1964). Closer to us is Harlan's description (1991) of Rajput women in Mewar.[20] Here, much attention is given to the kuldevi. Usually the wife officially adopts her husband's kuldevi on marriage. Yet, as Harlan points out, this is not easy nor an automatic process.

Sometimes, in fact, the girl takes her own kuldevi with her and continues to propitiate her in a minor capacity (1991, 92-101). But in a few cases the affinal kuldevi has replaced the patrilineal one, or come to occupy a prominent place beside her. Harlan cites two such cases. In Jaipur an unusual situation prevailed. The 'official' kuldevi of the Kachvaha royal line was Jamvai Mata. But the state buffalo sacrifice at Navratri was dedicated to another goddess, Shila Devi, whose temple is found at the entrance to the old fort and palace at Amber. Shila Devi is identified with Kali, and according to myth, she came from Bengal. The ruler of Amber, Man Singh, was serving the Mughals as a general there, and defeated the local king. According to one version of the myth, he bestowed his daughter upon Man Singh, and 'at the marriage ceremonies he presented ... the image of the goddess Jessoreshvari, who came to be known as Shila Devi' (Harlan 1991, 103). Shila Devi thus came to Amber as the kuldevi of the Bengali queen.

The kuldevi of the rulers of Mewar, Ban Mata, likewise joined them through marriage. At Chittor, their old capital, one may still see the image of Kalika Mata, said to have been the old kuldevi. But later, when the king conquered Gujarat,

> he demanded a Gujarati princess in marriage. That princess had always wanted to marry the Sisodia king. She had even sent him a letter telling him that, her kuldevi, Ban Mata, had determined to help her accomplish this aim. After the conquest, the marriage occurred. When the princess left for her new home, Ban Mata came with her in the form of a pendant. That is how Ban Mata left Girnar (though there is still a temple for her there) and came here.... (Harlan 1991, 57)

The two stories show a number of similarities, especially the link between marriage and conquest. Indeed, we have seen how king

Khengar brought the kuldevi of Hamir Sumra back with him to Sorath.[21]

If we relate the murder of Jasoji by his queen to these acquisitions of a kuldevi by marriage, we must suppose that at this period (fifteenth-seventeenth century), the queen remained more firmly bound, ritually as well as socially, to her natal lineage than is the case of Rajput women today. Here, too, we might see a tightening of patriliny with the new 'Rajput Great Tradition' mentioned by Kolff. This loss of the queen's independence fits well with developments in palace politics, which gradually come to accord more importance to the Dewan as representative of state bureaucracy, and less to kinship and alliance. For Navanagar, that stage is definitely reached with Meraman Khawas, who was Dewan from 1743.

The political role of the Rani did not end with the Jhala Rani's murder of her husband, however. Jasoji's brother's son, Lakhaji, was succeded by his son Ranmalji. Before dying, in 1661, Ranmalji wished his brother to succeed him. But his Rani, a Rathod from the Jodhpur royal house, had other plans. According to the story, she tried to introduce an outside child as heir, pretending he was her son. In this, she had the support of her brother. During the funeral, however, Raisinghji, the brother of the deceased, introduced his men to the darbar disguised as women. They massacred the garrison and expelled the Rani, her brother and her pretended son. But the Rathod lady sought the support of her family; Jaswatsinghji of Jodhpur was then Subedar of Gujarat. He was absent in the Deccan, so it was his proxy, the Mughal fouzdar of Sorath, who invaded Navanagar. Raisinghji was killed, and the fouzdar took the city, renamed it Islamnagar, and annexed it to the Mughal dominions in 1664. The Rani thus succeeded in her revenge, but the prize was lost.

Tamachi, Raisinghji's son, fled to Kutch; he was still a minor. From there, he raided Navanagar territories. But Jaswantsinghji of Jodhpur now intervened on his behalf, and the state was restored to Tamachi. Navanagar itself, however, remained in Mughal hands; Tamachi reigned from Khambalia. He remained subsidiary to the Mughals. (JMG, 77-8).

Conversely, when Jaswantsinghji Jhala succeeded to the throne of Halvad in 1673, his sister, married to Ajitsinghji Rathod of Jodhpur, brought the Viceroy's army against her brother. Jaswantsinghji was expelled, and Halwad, renamed Mahomed-nagar, was given to a Muslim. Chandrasinhji Jhala of Wankaner took Halvad in 1679, and

Jaswantsinhji finally regained his dominions in 1682 (Wilberforce-Bell 1916, 119-20).

While in this example, the sister of the prince sides with her affinal clan, the case confirms the importance of the affinal alliance, and of female actors, in palace politics.

Tamachi's grandson Raisinghji regained Navanagar, but had to fight the Rathod Ajitsinghji, now Viceroy of Gujarat. He was forced to pay a handsome tribute, but Navanagar remained with him. Then, in 1718, Raisinghji was killed by his younger brother Hardholji. Here again, the women enter the story:

> A slave girl of Raisinghji's, concealing his young son Tamachi in a box, fled with him to Kutch, where she implored the aid of his aunt Bai Ratnaji of Bhuj, who warmly espoused her nephew's cause. She wrote to her brother Raj Pratapsinghji to give his daughter in marriage to Mubariz-ul-Mulk Sarbuland Khan, the Subahdar of Gujarat, and also to marry the daughter of one of his cousins to Salabat Muhammad Khan Babi, the commander of the imperial forces in Gujarat. The Raj did so, and by their aid seated Jam Tamachi on the throne of his ancestors. (JMG, 78)

Tamachi fought the Mughals to escape paying tribute, but more remarkably, he sent his *bhayats* back to their villages, thus eliminating a major source of intrigue at court. Reacting against this move, one of them, Halaji, sent a relative by marriage, Karsansingh Jhala, to kill the ruler. He succeeded, in 1743, but Tamachi's daughter, Rajkunwarbai, astutely

> dressed up her father as though he were alive, and placing him at a lofty window of the palace showed him to the people, who believing he was alive, pursued Karansingh. In the meantime as Tamachi had no son, Rajkunwarbai counselled his two Ranis to each of them adopt a son secretly, and pretend that they had given birth to sons. The Ranis did so, and the eldest of the boys was named Lakhaji and the younger Ajoji, and Lakhaji was proclaimed Jam in place of his father.... (JMG, 79)

The women of the *zenana*, then, were as active politically as the men. This gave particular importance to affinal relations, so the analysis of Rajput politics as a segmentary lineage system, based on relations between men, needs considerable modification. In the period under review these marriage connections are heavily intertwined with the vassalage relationships to the Mughals and their representatives, making hypergamous marriage a particularly important political tool. An allusion to this was made by Jam Sataji of Navanagar, on paying tribute to Muzaffar Khan of Gujarat. Producing one of his coins, he said, 'Just as the dignity of Rajas is increased by the gift of their daughters to the Sultan their overlord, so I marry my coin as a 'Kunwari' to this rupee of yours ...' (Wilberforce-Bell 1916, 115).

Thus the idiomatic overtones of hypergamous marriage had been established in the area at least since the turn of the sixteenth to the seventeenth century. The Jamnagar coins, incidentally, were later known as *kori*, said to be a contraction of Kunwari (ibid.)

From 1743 we enter another phase of Navanagar's history. Lakhaji was married to Bai Jawuba of Halvad—another Jhala lady. She brought to Navanagar the 'slave' Meraman Khawas, who was to become one of the great dewans in the history of Saurashtra. The age of the Great Dewans, however, forms part of the development that led medieval Kathiawar towards modernity, and will be dealt with later.

THE GOHILS ESTABLISH THEIR CHIEFDOMS

From the Jhalas and Jadejas, we now turn to the third clan of 'classical' Rajputs—organized on the segmentary lineage model—to establish themselves in Saurashtra. The Gohils are the last representatives of this political form to gain a powerful position in the peninsula. They founded Bhavnagar state, where they continued to be the 'state-bearing' group. This was true at the centre, and formed the basis of state ideology, though Garasia Rajputs—'rajputized' from local groups rather than immigrants—probably formed the majority of landowners in the state. Garasias are said to have been Kolis originally, though this term, imprecise as it is, does not tell us very much. The Garasias, however, never came to occupy the kind of position allotted to the Mers of Porbandar or the Ahirs of Junagadh at the time of the Chudasamas. They were attached to the Gohils by conquest, not by alliance.

The Gohils of Saurashtra claim descent from king Shalivahan, who lived in AD 78. This distinguishes them from the Gohils of Mewar, who claim to stem from the solar dynasty of Ayodhya. This early period is steeped in myth, and sometimes the Saurashtra Gohils link themselves with the dynasty of Vallabhi, through Guha, said to have been the son of Shiladitya VII. This is the Guha that we met above, the first ruler of Mewar to receive the *tilak* from a Bhil. This accounts for the connection between the Gohils and the Mewar dynasty. Anyway, the Saurashtra branch is said to have come from Khergadh, on the river

Luni in Marwar. According to legend they left there in AD 1260, led by Sejakji, the chief of Khergadh (BDG, 58).[22]

This was a time of decline for the Gujarat kingdom. The Jhalas were already established in the north-eastern part of the peninsula. Ghumli had just fallen, probably to the Jadejas, but the Chudasamas were still lords of Junagadh. They seem to have been the strongest power in the peninsula at the time. Outside their dominion prevailed, probably, the kind of unsettled situation that Fox describes as stage one of his cycle (Fox 1971, 67-74). Sejakji, in fact, sought the protection of Ra Khengar III of Sorath, and cemented the alliance by marrying his daughter to him (Wilberforce-Bell 1916, 71). This is one of the first clearly hypergamous marriages we hear of in Saurashtra.

In return, Sejakji was granted Shahpur in Panchal district, with twelve other villages. Here, at the Jhalawar frontier in north-eastern Saurashtra, at the opposite end of the peninsula from Sorath, Sejakji founded a new village, Sejakpur (Wilberforce-Bell 1916, 71-2). The Gohil settlement must have represented an extension of the Chudasamas' domains at the time. We do not hear, here, of the Jhalas, but it may well have been against them that Khengar's protection was sought. Sejakji, however, soon added to his grant (op. cit., 72).

The power of the Turks was on the rise in western India. In 1298, they overthrew the last of the Vaghela kings of Gujarat and established their dominion over the mainland. The Rathods, driven from the mainland by them, in their turn drove the Gohils from Jhalawar.[23] Under Sejakji's son Ranoji the latter began to spread out southwards, both to south Gujarat and to the more southerly parts of Saurashtra. While the Turks were now firmly established at Patan, Ranoji founded a new capital at Ranpur. He died in 1309 defending the capital.

Ranoji's daughter Valam again was married to a Khengar of Junagadh; hypergamy would seem to grow into an established practice. His two step-brothers, Sarangji and Shaki, were given fiefs by the Chudasama ruler, establishing the lines of the smaller Gohil chiefdoms of Palitana and Lathi respectively. Ranoji's line was to become the founders of the house of Bhavnagar (BDG, 58).

Ranoji was followed by his son Mokhdaji, who made Umrala his capital and captured Gogha and the island Piram. While the latter was taken from the Kolis, the conquest of Gogha from Muslim Kasbatis led to war with the Sultan Muhammad Tughlaq. Mokhdaji is said to have levied a toll on all ships passing up the Gulf of Cambay; the Sultan's action against him as a 'pirate' shows the interest taken in sea trade by the rulers of the time. Killed fighting the Sultan in 1347, Mokhdaji was succeeded by his elder son Dungarji. His younger son, escaping to Rajpipla on the mainland, went on to succeed his maternal grandfather there. Thus Rajpipla too became a Gohil state (BDG, 59)

Dungarji was able to re-establish the chiefdom as the Sultan left, but it remained a minor state. The Gohils, then, had established three minor chiefdoms of south-eastern Saurashtra by AD 1400. Since even Junagadh paid tribute to the Sultan from 1414 onwards, we may assume that the small Gohil chiefdoms were tributary as well. In 1420 the brother of the next ruler, Kanoji, tried to succeed him by surrendering Kanoji's son, Sarangji, in lieu of tribute. But Sarangji escaped to regain his throne, helped by Rawal Patai of Champaner, as well as his kinsmen at Lathi and Gariadhar. Recognizing the assistance of the Rawal, Sarangji, too, assumed this title (BDG, 59).

The Gohils now spread out in a number of collateral branches, one as far as Bhuj, while enjoying a certain freedom at the periphery of the Sultan's sphere of influence. The power of Junagadh was waning; it fell to Mahmoud Begada in 1470. During the rule of Jetaji (1470-1505), Ranpur, too, was attacked by the Sultan. According to Bardic lore, the conflict was due to the refusal of the Gohil's wife to eat with her sister, married to the Sultan—and thus defiled by marrying a Muslim. More likely, Ranpur was too close to Ahmedabad to be left alone; it lay in the present-day Ahmedabad district, just across the border from Bhavnagar.

Jetaji's successor Ramdasji was killed defending Chittor, then capital of Mewar, from an attack by Bahadur Shah of Gujarat. It is said that Ramdasji was killed wearing his wedding clothes; he had just returned from a pilgrimage to Benares and had married a princess from Mewar on his way back. Chittor fell on 8 March 1535 (BDG, 60). The next rulers saw the decline and fall of the Gujarat sultanate with Akbar's conquest of Gujarat in 1572-3. At the battle of Bhuchar Mori in 1591, Mughal dominance over the peninsula became firmly established. Visoji (1570-1600) achieved, however, the conquest of Sihor and made it his capital, making use of internal strife in the city. He was opposed in this by his kin from Gariadhar. 'Visoji and his principality' do not seem to have been much affected by the events stirring the mainland and the northern parts of the peninsula' (BDG, 60).

Mughal dominance may have weakened the main powers of the peninsula, but in doing so probably opened an opportunity for smaller chiefdoms to expand. The Gohils as well as the Jadejas—at their southern flank—benefited from this. Their expansion was at the cost of the Kathis, who occupied the central part of Saurashtra. The results of these fights were not a foregone conclusion, however. Gariadhar was taken by the Kathis, and Visoji's successor Dhuniji (1600-19) died in this fight. His successor Ratanji, too, fought the Kathis till he was killed in 1620. His son Harbhamji died in 1622, leaving only an infant son. The child was brought to Kutch, to escape from his uncle who had usurped the throne in 1622 (Wilberforce-Bell 1916, 115-16).

Harbhamji's brother Govindji ceded Gogha to the Mughal deputy at Junagadh in 1636, in order to retain the power he had usurped. He died in that year, and Akheraji, Harbhamji's son, regained the throne, supported by the Kathis. Akheraji then helped his kinsmen to recover Gariadhar from them. He died in 1660.

Ratanji, Akheraji's son, then reigned peacefully till 1703. While the period 1591-1703 had seen some expansion for the Gohils, their chiefdoms remained small during Mughal dominance in Saurashtra. By the time of Ratanji's death, however, Mughal power was declining. This 'power vacuum', a new 'stage one' in Fox's terms (1971, 67-74) was the opportunity for Ratanji's son Bhavsinhji to expand his chiefdom into a state of regional importance. It was Bhavsinhji who founded the city of Bhavnagar, in 1723, and moved his capital there.

KHODIYAR BECOMES THE GODDESS OF THE GOHIL KINGS

We left Khodiyar in charge of the fortunes of the Chudasama kings. That dynasty came to an end in 1470, when Junagadh fell to Mahmoud Begada of Gujarat. But Khodiyar was to find support from another royal line; now she became the protectress of the house of Bhavnagar.

'Shadulsingh, the Thakore Saheb of Sihor, was a devout follower of the Goddess. In his own house he had built a temple to Adishakti Ambika, and was doing puja to the Mata. His devotion was such that Bhagatbapu's religiosity was known all over Sorath (Saurashtra)...' (Solanki, n.d., 107). Bhagatbapu—'father devotee'—is the ruler's nickname. Then one day Premdan Gadhavi came to the Raja of Sihor. Seeing Bhagatbapu, the true devotee of Devi, he chanted:

> Lion of Sihor, Shadul; Jogini Mata Ambika;
> Having ascended the Pavagadh mountains from Chotila,
> seen the blessings of the Girnar;

Having seen the 68 tirthas, with mother giving darshan;
She remains the gift-giver, the one that takes away,
Joy, shelter, riches—the Jogini![24]

The Charan affirms that 'Mata Ambika-Bhavani's appearance in Mamoddev's house is fully a miracle', then eulogizes Khodiyar:

Khodel Khod-Hari is capable of mercy,
She is fully a miracle, caring and giving joy;
The intermediary of God, the Mother, Jogini of the World,
Jogini of the world bestowing children, Mata Khodiyar,
Caring and giving Joy.[25]

Impatient, Shadulsinhji set out for Roisala the next day. And there, people understood his purpose. He asked for the house of Mamoddev. He strongly desired the darshan of the Goddess.

'His soul had strength. The likeness of a woman, a hundred years old, appeared at the end of the street and came in front of Bhagatbapu. She said: "From what village, brother, have you come? And of which kingdom are you king? To which house are you going?" But Bhagatbapu had no pride in his status of king.... He said, very modestly: "Maji, maji, I have come for the darshan of Khodel. That is, the darshan of the Jogini of the world of worlds, to make death and suffering go far away, by the power of Ma."

'The old woman answered: "But king, I am no Jogini. This is only a hamlet of Charans. Why are you talking such nonsense? Good, be on your way, Bap!" But seeing the old woman smiling.... Bhagatbapu said: "Yes, I know that this whole village is of Charans. And Charans commonly respect God. That too, I know; also that in the lap of Mamoddev and Devalabai a true appearance of Shakti has manifested herself. This, too, I know. Thus you do not deceive me!"

'Hearing such a statement of affection Khodiyar appeared in her real (original) form. On seeing this wonder Bhagatbapu, falling on his knees, started to beseech her: "My Mother, O Khodel! You have deceived me but ... now I have your darshan and I cannot ask for more. I want your darshan every day ... therefore come to Sihor with me!"

'The Goddess said smilingly: "Devotee, your wish shall be fulfilled; by the source on the mountain you shall find a *thapa* (mark of the hand) of kumkum, and there you shall build my temple" (Solanki, op. cit., 108-10).

'Bhagatbapu returned to Sihor in a happy state. A short time later Navratri came and Bhagatbapu got all his people together. In the main square a mandap was built and the praises of Khodiyar were sung. Everybody present received her darshan. Bhagatbapu found the thapa and built a temple, instituting the worship there' (Solanki, op. cit., 110). There is still, in fact, a temple to Khodiyar in the old palace at Sihor.

The king was impressed sufficiently by Khodiyar's darshan to choose her as his main Goddess. She might then, strictly speaking, be an ishtadevata, a chosen deity; but she was to become the kuldevi (lineage goddess) of the future kings of Sihor and Bhavnagar.

The story may be myth. It illustrates, however, the mutual respect between the Charan and the king; both are devibhaktas—followers of the goddess. She, incidentally, is both 'benevolent' and 'malevolent' at the same time; a common feature of Saurashtra's goddesses.[26] She is the giver of shelter, a concept discussed by Wadley (1975).

Ambika was, indeed, the kuldevi of the Gohils, and her main temple, still an important place of pilgrimage, is not far from Chittor, which fortress plays an important role in the history of the clan. It fell to the Muslims, as we have seen, in 1535.

For devotees of Khodiyar, the experience of her darshan is reason enough for the change of goddess. The choice was made and the change of goddess effected; this tells us a great deal about the relationship between king and goddess. But let us investigate some possible social and historical factors which might have contributed to the change.

The historical circumstances are confusing, however, for I have found no Shadulsingh in the historical sources available to me. The reference to Sihor points to Visoji or his successors, and would place their adoption of Khodiyar as kuldevi between 1570 and 1723, when Bhavnagar was founded. But what is now the main Khodiyar temple is not at Sihor, and the reference to Sihor may be a later interpolation. Yet the Gohils cannot have adopted Khodiyar before 1300, when they came to this part of Saurashtra, and hardly before 1400, when they finally settled down as chiefs in the area.

They had been tributary to the Chudasamas since their arrival in Saurashtra. Could they have adopted the kuldevi of their superiors? Tributary chiefs are not known to have done so in the ordinary run of things. Sejakji's daughter was married to Khengar III, and the daughter of Ranoji, who died in 1309, was also married to a king of Junagadh. Might not her new kuldevi 'by marriage' become the goddess of her natal clan? Kuldevis may, as we have seen, be adopted by marriage. But in such cases it is the daughter of a prestigious clan who brings her kuldevi to the house of her in-laws (Harlan 1991, 93-104).

A kuldevi might be adopted by conquest, in which the prestige of the goddess was among the spoils of victory: the two types of adoption merge, as the conquered often gave his daughter in marriage to the conqueror (ibid.). The logic of rank in the transfer is such that the transfer of kuldevi follows the asymmetry of hypergamous marriage, but with the quirk that only a very prestigious devi would be so adopted. The typical situation seems to be that of a famous clan with a prestigious goddess being forced to give a daughter in marriage to a house superior in strength but inferior in ancestral rank.

This cannot have happened in the early stages of the Gohil chiefdoms in Saurashtra, for it was they who gave daughters to the prestigious Chudasamas. In spite of Kolff's assumption (1990, 72-3, 198) that Rajput alliance partners were not yet ranked systematically in a hypergamous series, the Gohil-Chudasama alliance was certainly hypergamous even at this date. The transfer of the Chudasama kuldevi to the Gohils by marriage, therefore, must be subsequent to the fall of Junagadh in 1470. A marriage then fits the structural prerequisites for such transfer, but there is no record of such an alliance. After the fall of Junagadh, however, this well-known and prestigious goddess had no royal protector. She was, so to speak, 'free'.

The Gohils, too, lost their ancestral fortress in 1535. Their lines in Mewar and Saurashtra had separated, but they had the same goddess till the Saurashtra branch adopted Khodiyar. The fall of Chittor must have made quite an impression in the peninsula, since Ramdasji fell there. Mother Ambika had failed to protect Chittor, and the Sisodia Gohils of Mewar also changed their kuldevi subsequently (Harlan 1991, 57-60). Was Ambaji's reputation hurt by the fall of Chittor? It is not impossible. Moreover, the Gohils of Saurashtra were now establishing themselves permanently in the region. Here, they found a Goddess, Khodiyar, who was popular with the people. To adopt her would be a move to 'indigenize' the Gohils, to give them local roots. Jain (1975) has shown the importance of such means of 'indigenization' in Bundelkhand.

Between 1535 and 1600, the Gohil chiefs would have been faced with the weakening prestige of their own kuldevi and the availability of a well-known Goddess, close to their seat, who was free from other dynastic connections.[27]

The reference to Sihor omits any allusion to its conquest. Probably, then, either the chiefs adopted Khodiyar before Visoji took Sihor, or the story is correct in its reference to the city, and the mysterious Shadulsinhji is Visoji himself. It is not unusual, in Saurashtra as generally in India, that a king is known by several names.

THE ESTABLISHMENT OF THE CULT OF RAMA

We have seen how the cult of the goddess becomes an integral part of the Rajput conception of kingship. But there is another deity, closely associated with the Rajput state; this is Rama, the god-king. Temples to Rama are found in most Rajput villages of Saurashtra, as also in the capitals of the old states. In Dhrangadhra, typically, not only is there a large temple to Rama opposite the City Palace, but the blazon of the state is prominently exhibited on its front.

Rajputs are widely held once to have been followers of Shiva.[28] Their best-known bureaucrats in Saurashtra, the Nagar Brahmins, still are. Today, however, Shiva plays only a minor role in the religion of Saurashtra's Rajputs. Apart from the goddess, Rama has become their main deity. We must ask, then, how he came to occupy this position.

Asking precisely this question, Ghurye believes the Rama cult 'began to gather strength about the 11th century in the Eastern part of the former Central Provinces and Orissa' (1962, 190). It became a major cult, he thinks, only when Islamic pressure became important in north India (op. cit., 193). Its main sponsor was the ascetic Ramananda, commonly believed to have been born in AD 1300 (ibid.). Under Islamic pressure, the cult spread; in the third quarter of the sixteenth century, it received 'a great fillip in Northern India but for which in all probability Krishnaism would have overwhelmed it'. Among the important protagonists of Rama who took part in this process was the ascetic Ramadasa, and Sridhara, the author of the Ramavijaya (op. cit., 195). Eck seems to concur in talking of Rama being popular 'at least since late medieval times' (1991, 49).

These dates go well with the growth to real statehood of the Rajput domains, as opposed to the petty chiefdoms from which they grew. Ghurye's view supports the thesis that Rama's importance lay in 'sanskritizing' the emerging chiefdoms to a form of Vaishnavism, through Rama as an avatar of Vishnu (Ghurye 1962, 182-209). This process coincides with the birth of what Kolff calls the 'new Rajput Great Tradition' (1990, 72-3), of which it became a central element.

The idea that Rajputs originally worshipped Shiva, may have some foundation in fact, for Ghurye hints at the replacement of Shiva temples by those dedicated to Rama. The latter are more common in Saurashtra and Rajastan than in mainland Gujarat or Maharashtra. In other words, Rama is strong where Rajputs are dominant; where other castes predominate, Shiva has kept his position.[29] Thus in Rajkot, Ghurye notes, the four most important Rama shrines are all in the precincts of Shiva temples (op. cit., 198-9).

This analysis fits the distribution of the cult, and its timing accords with the rise of the 'classical' Rajput state in Saurashtra from the late sixteenth century onwards. Saurashtra's Rajputs have probably worshipped Rama since the early seventeenth century.[30]

Rama represents the traditional Kshatriya ideal. Leaving Ayodhya for the jungle, in accordance with the wishes of his father the king, he symbolizes obedience to authority. His exile stems from intrigue at the palace; the king is misled by his favourite wife, who wants her own son to succeed. In numerous adventures Rama proves his valour and martial skill, remaining true to the code of honour. Indeed, he won his wife Sita by his precision with the bow. In Valmiki's version of the epic, Sita must prove her chastity, having been abducted by the demon Ravana; true to his duty to his subjects as guardian of dharma, Rama orders her to burn herself, the only act which can save her honour. So pure is Sita, however, that the fire-god Agni refuses to touch her,[31] and her purity allows her to return with Rama to glory and happiness at Ayodhya (e.g. Rajagopalachari 1968, 308). The story provides a variation on the theme of the king who departs for the jungle—and for war—in order to return with a degree of sacredness that sets him apart from his subjects.

In other versions of the story, Sita does, however, burn at the pyre. Some writers have seen here the origin—or the legitimation—of sati. But as we have seen, this institution seems to be older than the Rama cult in Saurashtra.[32]

In spite of recent upheavals about Ayodhya, it is Nasik which, in Gujarat, was traditionally regarded as Rama's birthplace. Nasik was the seat of the Gurjara-Pratiharas, whom Kulke and Rothermund think were Rajputs.[33] Placing Rama's birthplace at Nasik brings him even closer to the antecedents of western Indian Rajputs.

The cult of Rama has not supplanted the worship of goddesses. In Saurashtra, the religion of the Rajputs is goddess worship with the cult of Rama added as a separate, more 'sanskritic', element. This points to a continuing role for certain deities in group formation and maintenance. From that concern, we are led in two directions; the importance of such deities for socially enacted identities of groups, and the moulding of such deities according to the demands that such a function makes upon their ritual and symbolic representations.

Rather than ask, as did early writers on caste, about the 'origins' of certain ethnic groups, we may ask to what status group—or 'estate' in Weber's terms—a certain deity would appeal. Taking the deity to represent, metonymically, a certain ideology, we may then follow the history of that ideology to identify the emergence, rise and fall of the estate concerned. This is the idea that underlies Ghurye's essay on 'Gods and Men' (1962) and what I present here, follow his inspiration.

THE 'RAJPUTIZATION' OF THE RAJPUTS

Ghurye's views about the origin and function of the Rama cult should be related to his view of Rajputs as a category created from various populations through a process of 'Rajputization'. This view has had many followers. One of them is Fox, who writes:

> 'Rajput' is a status title which local groups assumed as a part of their claim to social position or higher rank on a regional level. The title required of its claimants an ideological and a minimal behavioral commitment to a life style defined as Rajput. In the course of Indian history and often within geographical proximity to Rajput groups, other locally dominant status categories emerged such as Jats, Bhuinhars, or various Muslims. At times, such 'ethnically' homogeneous groups arise from a common, tribal migration. However, they also come about through the assumption by diverse local groups of a single identity and title. (1971, 17)

Kolff (1990) holds a similar view. The Rajputs, then are not a single ethnic group, continuous through history, but a status category to which a number of groups have assimilated themselves. But when did this 'Rajputization' take place? Like the establishment of the elements which were to become central to 'Rajput culture', this must have been a gradual process.

We may, however, start by the term itself. The well-known Rajput clan names are certainly much older than the title of 'Rajput'. But the systematic categorization of them as Rajputs may date from as late as the twelfth century.[34] The title itself seems to have been used from the eleventh century onwards, while in an inscription from 1230 the connection between the known clan names and the title is first made in writing (Qanungo 1969, 96-7). But still, in the middle ages the word 'Rajput' usually meant 'a trooper in the service of a chief or a free-lance captain, and sometimes was applied in applause even to a brigand of desperate courage' (op. cit., 99).

And as late as the last quarter of the seventeenth century the Rajput historian Nainsi used the word 'in more than one sense'. When used to designate a warrior, 'the word is invariably qualified in his *khyat* by some adjective such as bada, bahut accha, banka, balavan or vikat (grim)' (op. cit., 98).

Qanungo adds that a Rajput asked for his caste would answer by his clan name (ibid.). Clearly, Kolff (1990) is right when he holds the use of 'Rajput' as a caste name to be a late development. But the process of identifying certain clans with the caste seems to have been a gradual one; there is nothing strange, in India, in using the same term both for an occupation (warrior or soldier) and for a caste. This double sense of 'Rajput' was current, then, from the twelfth century, when the clans were first listed in bardic poetry, to the late seventeenth century, when Rajputs had, quite definitely, become a 'caste'.

The narrowing down of the term's field of reference may have coincided with the change from relatively open recruitment of outsiders to the early lineage, to the stress on genealogical purity in later days. We have seen that these changes may again be correlated with the gradual growth from 'tribal' lineage society, through chiefdoms, to the classical Rajput state formation—the age of Kolff's 'Rajput great tradition'.

Yet access to Rajputhood was never completely closed. There is ample evidence of recent 'rajputization', both in Saurashtra and elsewhere.[35] We assume, then, 'rajputization' as the origin of the Rajput category, and accept Ghurye's theories on the growth of the Rama cult as related to this process. The Rajputs as a group did not precede their institutions; as clans and goddess worship, the bardic lore, sati and the heroic dimension of warfare grew, the term Rajput gradually came to include all of these, as the 'Rajput great tradition' found its main expression through a particular form of the state.

THE FIELD OF POLITICS AND KINSHIP

The Rajput states of traditional Kathiawar emerged gradually from an early stage of tribal conquest into the pattern that characterized a state like Navanagar by the sixteenth or seventeenth century. Throughout this period, the kinship base of the state remains predominant, but the content of kinship concepts such as lineage and brotherhood changes, as the lineage chief becomes a king, and his chiefdom grows into a state.

At first, the lineage remains open to recruitment of outside members; these, of course, would have to be 'Rajputs' in the sense of acknowledged warriors. At stage two of Fox's cycle, the chief would still need such recruits to cover his domain with allies. Later, as subordinate kin became a problem for the central power, the lineage became more exclusive, and the rules of access to Rajput aristocracy closely defined. The queen's role, and the importance of the marriage alliance, show that kin and state interests remain indissolubly connected. Developments in kinship influence state and interstate politics, and vice versa.

Fox's model of the Rajput system offers a logically consistent model of the segmentary lineage, its aptitude for conquest, its adjustment to conquest and its role in the fabric of the Rajput state. But he places too much stress on this single factor. Two modifications are necessary.

First, as Stern and Galey (both 1973) have pointed out, any exogamous lineage implies a network of marriage alliances. But among Rajputs the idiom of marriage is made to go far beyond its literal sense. Thus marriage to the 'daughters of the soil'—or, indeed, to the soil itself personified as a goddess (Galey 1989, Jain 1973)—may be central to the constitution of a state. Through such a marriage the relationship between the localized lineage and its conquest is cemented, and the land becomes involved with the kinship network. At the same time, however, some of the flexibility inherent in segmentation is lost.

Marriage tied the lineage to other Rajput lines, cementing their solidarity beyond lineage level. While it did not always produce lasting political alliances, marriage did serve to establish Rajputs as a 'caste', and hypergamy came to build a more or less orderly ranking within it. Thus, the founder of a ruling house might marry a 'daughter of the soil' to establish his base, while giving his sister to an acknowledged Rajput royal family to secure his rank and caste membership (Galey 1989). In Bundelkhand the conquerors married the soil herself, in the form of the local goddess (Jain 1973). The local and the clan goddess was, however, not always one and the same. Thus the relationship to the soil constitutes an element distinct in principle from that of the lineage.

While the 'proper dynamics' of the segmentary lineage remains an important factor in understanding Rajput polity, the establishment of the state adds new factors. Localization is one; but as we have seen in the king–tribe alliance, as well as in marrying a 'daughter of the soil', this element of localization may itself be expressed in a kinship idiom. This idiom must, however, be that of marriage alliance, for it seems a general rule that Rajput ruling houses are never autochthonous. They—and their clan of kinsmen—all came from the outside;[36] they are seen as conquerors, ruling a territory won by the sword. The king has always 'come from elsewhere' (Carrin-Bouez 1991). Marriage is a fitting idiom, for a recurrent theme in Rajput stories is the marriage of the vanquished ruler's daughter to the conqueror. In the hypergamous mode, such an arrangement at once establishes both a bond and a rank difference between the conqueror and the conquered. Conquest and marriage, then, are bound inextricably together.

As the state developed, the hierarchy between senior and junior kinsmen evolved into relations of vassalage. Marriage could not serve to mark ranking here, as the vassal's daughter was of the clan of his lord. But between lineages, the rank of the partners within their lineage determined, to a large extent, marriageability to members of the other line. Thus, when the Jam humiliates his wife's brother, the Jhala chief of Halvad, he is trying to force the hierarchy implicit in marriage on a ruler who is ostensibly his equal in other terms. Such implicit contradictions between equality and hierarchy are important to understand strategies of establishing and managing alliance within the hypergamous mode.

A similar contradiction existed in the relationship between 'lineage brothers'. Born of the same stock, they were graded only by seniority. At the early stage, juniors got their own estates—which might then grow, by conquest, to rival the senior state. Such segmentation could not continue for it would have made the formation of sizeable states impossible.

Thus, as the main state grew, the younger brothers had to contend with smaller shares, until rivalry for succession replaced segmentation of the state as a vehicle for the division of power between brothers. Members of bhayats, having already inherited their estates, remained a presence which the senior state's ruler tried, with the growth into statehood, to suppress. But the means to do so effectively only became available with the standing army and the growing bureaucracy that were to characterize the eighteenth century.

The segmentary structure of Rajput kinship in Saurashtra should therefore be seen, not as a single factor producing a certain pattern of alliances, but as a field of relations which, though structured in a certain way, left room for a number of alternative modes of action.

In Grønhaug's terms, kinship and state formation form a single *field* of interrelated social and cultural phenomena. To analyse such a conglomerate of traits and activities as a 'field', action within the field must have implications for other activities in the same field. These effects, of a causal or implicative nature, should be distinguishable from other sets of cause and effect; we may then talk of the 'proper dynamics' of the field. These 'proper dynamics', spelt out in their interrelations, define the extent of the empirical phenomena to be included in the field. Once defined, these dynamics can be used to simulate events in the empirical world, and the results of simulation can be tested against our observations (Grønhaug 1974, 3ff; 1978). Such interconnection is, of course, the basis for Fox's model.

The developments of the seventeenth and eighteenth centuries broke into these connections, as a bureaucratic state apparatus and a standing army made the king's position less dependent on kinship. As a result, important state dynamics were taken away from the kinship field. Yet the bond between kinship and state was not broken completely. The field remained intact, characterized by its own 'proper dynamics', even if it had less effect on the state. Its dynamics were simply counteracted or even annulled by the influence of other fields.

In other words this field consists of the kinship and lineage politics of Rajputs. It includes the foundation of chiefdoms, and their rise towards statehood until bureaucracy and a standing army reduce kinship to a secondary role. Kinship continues to influence the state in this secondary role, however, insofar as even the highly developed states at the time of British ascendancy in Saurashtra continued to practise strategic marriage alliances and to arbitrate their differences through intermediaries recruited by kinship.

The kinship-political field is at the roots of 'aristocracy' and rural class formation; it underlay central relations of authority in traditional Kathiawar society. Authority is mediated through the Rajput—or Darbar—monopoly on carrying weapons and using the horse, (important elements in the martial culture), with emphasis on strength and courage. These, in turn, are seen to derive from shakti, giving the male warrior role a basis in the conception, intrinsically female, of power. Thus male and female roles become complementary; the protection of women by men, and the protection of men by women, produce important implications for family, marriage and sexuality within the group—prototypically Rajputs—that dominate the field (cf. Harlan 1991).

Such complementarity works well between brother and sister, and the ritual of *raksha-bandhan* could therefore serve as a way of cementing political alliance. Marriage, however, entails a dilemma, for as a sister and daughter of her natal clan, the wife remains a potential enemy within the camp constituted by 'brotherhood'. The celebration of the faithful wife, which reaches an apotheosis in the sati rite, serves to counteract this important structural problem. It is the counterpart of the examples of wives poisoning their husbands or making secret alliances with the enemy. The saying, common in Saurashtra as elsewhere in India, that women split the unity of brothers, is a faithful rendering of this underlying reality, and Bernier, the French seventeenth-century traveller, was told that the sad lot of widows was due to the fear of wives poisoning their men (Bernier 1916, 310-11).

This, in short, is the 'patrilineal dilemma' that corresponds to the matrilineal dilemma of so many anthropologists. When marriage partners are potential enemies, the alliance must be fraught with danger. But this very polyvalence makes marriage a central idiom for other dangerous alliances; the king is married to the throne (*gaddi*) as well as to his queen. Certainly, when he acceeds to the throne he also acquires rivals and enemies. We have seen how the ruler's relation to the people or the land may be couched in the idiom of marriage.

If mortal women, then, have a dual nature[37]—the true sister and the ambiguous wife—the kuldevi is a refuge. For she, representing the female source of all power, is the protector of the king and his clan. Yet her character, too, is twofold; she can work miracles on the clan's behalf, but is also capable of its destruction. This makes her the protector of dharma, and the archetypal breach of dharma in this context becomes, not the crimes against cows and brahmins mentioned in scriptures, but violence against women. We have seen several examples of this in the myths centering on Khodiyar.[38]

While the king receives his strength from the goddess and is protected by his sister, his marriage implies the conflicts inherent in a segmentary, patrilineal system. To survive in this world, he must not only be an able warrior—for which he needs the help of his kuldevi—he must also choose his marriage alliances carefully.

At the early stage of the developing Rajput polity, he gains support by making brothers of his followers; but, as he tries to gain ascendancy over them at a later stage, brotherhood too becomes a treacherous matter. He therefore has to restrict and graduate it, so that only his nearest kin partake of the ruling brotherhood. In this ascendancy he needs Rama, sanctifying kingship over kinship. He also needs material resources, to recruit his own men to suppress troublesome kin. These men must, quite expressly, be excluded from his lineage. This is also true of the dewan, who, in the eighteenth century, becomes both a necessary helper and a formidable opponent at court.[39]

While these factors grow from the state created by the kinship–political field, they are best seen as extrinsic to it, as is the Rama cult. The problem of women, marriage, and the Goddess, are not. Bound to the dynamics of the segmentary lineage, they form a single field, where events concerning one have necessary implications for the other. The kinship–political field forms the core of the Rajput state, but cannot be reduced to the lineage; gender and religion form intrinsic parts of it.

NOTES

1. In view of present acceptance of the Varna scheme, it is interesting that Forbes could write: 'The Rajpoot tribes still maintain that they are true Kshatriyas, though the Brahmins deny that the warrior caste has any longer an existence.' The reason given by the latter is Rajput non-vegetarianism and intermarriage with Muslims. Forbes notes, for Gujarat, that Banias now occupy second rank in the hierarchy and that 'Brahmin-Bania' has become the synonym of the 'high castes' (Forbes 1878, 536-7).
2. Thus Jam Bamanioji. Pusyena the Saindhava might be an earlier example, but we know little of how he established himself, and whether or not he was followed by his 'clan'.
3. If only because the proportion of population benefiting from the surplus was still small.
4. These Mers are not the Mers of Porbandar. They take their name from Mer—a hill, and were known as 'bold licentious marauders' to Tod. Only 355 were left in Marwar in 1894, concentrated in the hills of Merwara (M.H.Singh 1990, 50-1).
5. Paliwal Brahmins are both traders/bankers, and farmers. According to one myth, Pali was taken by 'Ghori Shah', who massacred them. The survivors who left the town by the west gate became cultivators, while those who left by the eastern gate became merchants. Most Paliwals of Marwar are cultivators, while the traders are chiefly found outside Marwar (M.H. Singh1990, 90-1). The 'Brahmin' cultivators near Praj, in Saurashtra, call themselves Paliwals, but their ties to the Marwar group are as spurious as their Brahminhood.
6. Note the parallel with the story of Chital told later. Here, a band of Rajputs

accede directly to rule merchants, without prior control of agricultural revenue.

7. Tod tells a different story: The Rathod leader, Siaji, was invited to defend the Paliwals against the Minas of Aravalli, and the lions. 'Siaji relieved them of both, but the opportunity to acquire land was too good to be lost, and on the festival of Holi, he put the leading Brahmans to death and took possession of Pali' (cited by M.H. Singh, 1990, 91).
8. Literally, 'bond of brothers'. Usually, of course, patrilineal kin is indicated by the term, which is also found in Saurashtra. As men acquired 'sisters' by the rite of *raksha-bandhan*, so it is likely they might acquire 'brothers'. The expression is used both in the literature and today, but I know of no ritual to establish such brotherhood, except through the sister.
9. See notes 10 and 11: specifically, see L. Bohannan (1952) and Newcomer (1972).
10. See, e.g. for Africa, Fortes and Evans-Pritchard (eds) (1940), Middleton and Tait (eds) (1958), Bohannan (1958), Sahlins (1961), the Middle East, Evans-Pritchard (1949), Barth (1954, 1959, 1964), Pehrsson (1966), Peters (1967), northern India, Mayer (1958), Pradhan (1966), and Tambs-Lyche (1992b).
11. See Peters (1967), Barth (1964), Pehrsson (1966), and for Rajputs, Stern (1973) and Galey (1973).
12. From here on, I use the term 'clan' for the Rajput patrilineal unit, since it may contain members who are not strictly patrilineal kin. 'Lineage' is used in contexts where an attested genealogy is central. Thus royal lines become 'lineages' from a certain point in time, whereas junior lines may belong to the royal clan but not to the lineage. Thus all Jadejas or Gohils are clansmen, whereas there are chiefly lineages within each clan.
13. Fox calls the latter zamindars. In Saurashtra, the term is little used, and for general purposes may be replaced by jagirdar. There were several other, more or less specific or local, terms, of which girasdar was probably the most common. The wantadars of some Jhala estates have been mentioned. For a general understanding of the system, jagirdar is used here.
14. One may doubt Pocock's conclusions here. If the Bhatias, as Amarji maintains, came to Junagadh (Girinagara) with king Naughan, it was hardly as fishermen.
15. This is probably too early; judging from Mallison the seventeenth century is more likely. Tripathi and Mehta also think the Bhatias settled in the 'Kutch-Kathiawar area' in the fourteenth century. This is at odds with Amarji's statement that they came to Junagadh in Naughan's time.
16. Information from interviews with Gujarat Voras and Indian traders from the Sudan.
17. For genealogical information, see JDG; (90-1). See also Tambs-Lyche (1992a, 58-64).
18. One of many cases where a queen is identified by the feminine form of the name of her natal clan. Such designation was a common practice, and shows that marriages were seen as alliances between clans, and the queen herself seen as a representative of her clan of origin.
19. One of the first references to a Nagar involved in Rajput state activity. In another story, the same Shankardas is credited with the capture of the Jhala ruler.
20. For Rajput marriage alliances, see also Stern (1973).
21. For a story where the kuldevi is herself the main prize of conquest, see Jain 1973.

22. Wilberforce-Bell (1916, 71) has AD 1240, adding that the Gohils were driven from Marwar by the Rathods. The area to which the Rathods came was formally under Mewar, and the Rathods from Pali overthrew the ruler of Kher, who was a Gohil (G.D. Sharma 1977, 3).
23. A Rathod chief is supposed to have taken Wanthali from the Chudasamas in about AD 1261 and to have ruled there for over a hundred years (Wilberforce-Bell 1916, 72).
24. Ambaji or Ambika temples are found in several places, the best known being near Mount Abu and Chittor in Rajasthan. Here the bard refers to the temple near Chotila, between Rajkot and Wadhwan, centrally located in Saurashtra. For the term jogini, see also note 25.
25. 'Jogini of the world' and 'God, the mother' refer to religious ideas, once 'widely diffused in brahminical society throughout India', while they 'subsumed many local cults of mother goddesses', as they do here. S. Gupta regards this theology of shakti as tantric. 'The cosmic functions of God, ... common to the Indian monotheistic religions are here assigned to Sakti. This accounts for the oppositions in her character; she is both benign and terrible... in fact, she is God's grace' (1992, 205-6). One with creation, she is largely synonymous with Maya (Gupta 1992, Tambs-Lyche 1994a). In this tradition, the feminine ascetic is called a yogini. In Gujarati, jogini/yogini, or jogi/yogi, are synonymous, alternative forms. Thus 'Jogini of the world' may refer both to shakti in general, as the Goddess, and to her incarnation in the world, that is, Khodiyar as a human, saintly woman of the Charan caste.
26. The goddesses in Saurashtra, therefore, do not fit the classification of Babb (1975) into dark, malevolent ones and benevolent, light ones. See note 25 above.
27. Khodiyar may, of course, have been adopted later; under Dhuniji, Ratanji, or Harbhamji (d. 1622). But Akheraji and Bhavsinhji are too well known, I think, to have been given a different name in our story. Under Bhavsinhji, of course, Sihor ceased to be the capital.
28. This is often stated by informants. The Chalukyas of Gujarat were Shaivite, and Shiva is 'tutelary deity' of Mewar, whose kings are seen as 'regents' of the God (Stern 1986, Kolff 1990, 81-2). Kolff believes in the 'common identity of the ancient Rajput and the Saivite warrior-ascetic', which may be going too far. But these two warrior figures are often compared by bards (1990, 74-85, Forbes 1878.) Further, Rama himself is closely associated with Shiva, and is sometimes seen as worshipping him (Eck 1991).
29. Thus the present Rama cult is not identified with Rajputs; 'he belongs to everybody' and is rather seen as guardian of Hindu dharma in general. But many Rajputs support the cult.
30. Rama's rival as 'God of kings' is Krishna. While stories of Krishna as king are common in Saurashtra (e.g. Mallison 1980), state or dominant caste temples were dedicated to Rama.
31. There are many versions of the Ramayana, and Sita's destiny is a point where variants differ greatly. I here follow Rajagopalachari (1968) who was of course opposed to sati.
32. Sita's story might of course later have served to legitimate sati.
33. Enthoven, we have noted, thinks they were Ahirs. Nasik's role as Rama's

birthplace is, of course, changing now, in the wake of the revived Rama cult and the role Ayodhya plays in it. Even in 1973-4, most informants talked of Ayodhya, and only a few of Nasik, as Rama's birthplace.

34. B.N. Sharma thinks the Kshatriyas 'multiplied into a number of clans by the end of the 12th century AD' citing the *Prithviraja Raso*, the *Kanhadadeprabandha*, and the *Visaladeva Raso*. (1972, 20) These sources systematize the clans, and are at the origin of the '36 clans' of Rajput lore. But many of the clan-names are themselves much older, as we have seen.
35. We shall see some examples of this later.
36. This recalls Heesterman's view of kingship in general: the king must always be both an insider and an outsider (1985, 143).
37. Leslie underlines the contrasting images of women, to the extent that 'Better still, in orthodox eyes, the concept of 'woman' should be suppressed altogether ...' (1992, 189-90).
38. For further examples of female honour and vengeance, see Carrin and Tambs-Lyche (1993).
39. Qanungo expressly states that no Rajput chief would ever choose a Rajput for his dewan. The reasons she gives are basically those I have given here (1969, 50-1).

CHAPTER IV

Traditional Kathiawar
The Darbars

KINSHIP, POWER AND LANDHOLDING

From the eighth to the seventeenth century Rajputs gradually became the dominant force behind most states of traditional Kathiawar. A strong patrilineal ideology, segmentary lineage organization, goddess worship, and a martial tradition were, and are, features of their culture.

In the beginning they left cultivation to others, forming tribe–king alliances with them. Later, the ruler's community became the dominant caste, holding land as well as power in the countryside. This pattern emerges with the first Jhala states in the eleventh century. Their country and that of the Jadejas remain the most typical Rajput areas in Saurashtra. The Gohils gained control of non-Rajput lands as late as the eighteenth century, and the southern part of Bhavnagar state is still marked by the recent admission of its landholders to Rajput status. In the more exclusive mode of Rajput kinship then prevailing, they were not admitted to the ruler's clan. Before Bhavnagar conquered them, they were still known as Kolis.

Traditional Kathiawar was dominated by Rajput culture.[1] Their model for 'sanskritization' of lower castes, imitating Rajput behaviour, had much stronger 'pull' here than in mainland Gujarat, where the Bania (merchant) model remained dominant.[2] Only with modernity has the Bania model come to rival the Rajput one in Saurashtra.

When speaking of this dominant Rajput category, local people tend to use the term Darbar. We have noted several references for this term, which is best translated as those in power, those exercising control. In most current usage, it is not landownership as such which is indicated, but membership of a social category. As such the term is still used, while the prince who was once 'the Darbar', or his court or council, known by the same term, have disappeared.

The Rajputs of Saurashtra differ in status from those of mainland

Gujarat. While the Gujarat Kshatriya Sabha—a Rajput caste organization—became a vehicle of smallholders' interests, the similar organizations in Saurashtra were founded on the interests of Rajputs as important landowners. Only in 1961 did the two regional groups combine to form the Gujarat Swatantra Party—widely regarded as the party of the old landlords (Kothari and Maru 1970).[3]

Villagers in Praj, where I spent some months, used the term Darbar for Rajputs—the caste which, indeed, may be seen as the prototype of the Darbar category. Kathis, too, are called Darbars wherever they are dominant, while the Ahirs of Junagadh district, in spite of their historical importance and still strong position, are not so designated. People do, however, use the term for the Mer landholders of former Porbandar state. The difference between Mers and Ahirs, so close with regard to the historical genesis of their position, is probably due to Junagadh being a Muslim state from 1470 to 1947. Revenue was collected by zamindars rather than allocated through jagirs; the zamindars were not supported, as were local Rajputs, by a localized section of their own community. Ahirs were excluded from dominance; thus they were not Darbars.

Darbar, then, refers to that particular combination of numbers, political power and ownership of land which anthropologists call a dominant caste.[4] This pattern of landholding, where land is held by the military force of the caste itself, is common in western India. When the dominant caste extends all the way to the top, forming the base for state-formation, we are dealing with 'Indian feudalism', or, to follow Kosambi, 'feudalism from below'.[5]

In the last two centuries, Kanbis, assuming the title of Patidars, (cf. Pocock 1972) have become dominant in many places. They are not called Darbars. Many Kanbis were, in fact, invited to settle in villages by the rulers, supported by the power of the state rather than by their own strength. The same is true for those Kanbis—who are numerous—who gained their position through recent land reforms. Finally, there were once many chiefs from the Koli communities. It seems likely that the chief would have been called a Darbar while his caste were not, but nothing definite can be said about the matter.

Rajputs, then, remain the prototypical Darbars. They hold land won by force, and are ready to defend it by force. This may be thought irrelevant today and correctly so, in a strictly juridical sense; but force remains part of popular categorization and stereotypes.

THE MARTIAL ASPECT OF DARBAR CULTURE

Stereotypes of Darbars centre on their fierceness and martial nature. This disposition is thought of as running in the blood—both by Darbars themselves and by their surroundings. The exercise of bravery, facing death if necessary, implies, for Rajputs, devoted service to those they should protect (Harlan 1991; 168-9). Bravery is thus a disposition for sacrifice (op.cit., 204), living and dying for one's subjects. A Rajput, and, by implication, a Darbar, should always be ready to fight if necessary.

Thus, even today, Saurashtra Rajputs carry their *kuvadi* (battle axe) with them in most situations.[6] It is strange to see this cumbersome weapon, about six feet long, carried on to a bus. One Rajput, asked what the axe was for, answered promptly: '*marva mate*', for killing. Metonymically, then, the axe stands for the right to use violence if necessary. It is a sign to all that the bearer is a Darbar—a person of rank and authority, unlikely to tolerate any nonsense.[7]

Such fierceness extends to modern daily life, as noted by a Charan friend. 'You have to recognize the caste of those around you', he said. 'Say you are in a cinema queue. If the man in front of you is a Bania, you may try to pass him—he may be angry, but he will do nothing. But if he is a Rajput, you should never try anything like that. He may kill you!'

The Rajputs of Praj, a large village south of Bhavnagar, were conspicuous for their natural sense of authority. In speech and manners, they seemed unusually sure of themselves. There was nothing submissive or domineering about them, as perfect politeness merged with a strong sense of their own worth. These peasants were indeed 'men of the world', who would not be out of place anywhere, court or cottage. Such natural authority does not however exist in a social vacuum. I had an impressive demonstration as I was walking through the village soon after arrival, followed by some fifty children shouting and making a nuisance of themselves. Suddenly three boys appeared, aged ten to fifteen. They scolded the other children, who disappeared swiftly, and gave no more trouble that day. Then we met some female labourers returning from the fields with vegetables, apparently for their own use. Without a word the three boys served me from the women's baskets. There was no protest. These three boys were the sons of the village *pramukh* (headman), a Rajput of substance.

The role of the battle-axe is not merely symbolic. Violence against low-caste people, who try to improve their lot through demonstration and protest, is common in Saurashtra. Newspapers reported several cases of organized attack on low-caste hamlets, house burning and rape during 1973-4. This, admittedly, was a year of unrest in Gujarat. While the *kuvadi* was the common weapon for Rajputs, one farmer showed me the pistol[8] he kept to guard his fields against thieves. These arms are old-fashioned, but effective enough. The axe remains the monopoly of Darbars, and nobody else is likely to possess a gun.[9] While violence in the village is not frequent, local Rajputs still have the potential to use force against lower castes.[10] At village level, this potential coercion is certainly more important than the presence, in Praj, of a couple of policemen and a police station. In fact, regarding the massacres in low-caste hamlets, I was told later that police intervened only during the 'emergency' rule of Indira Gandhi in the seventies.[11]

THE CULTURAL IMPORTANCE OF THE HORSE

Another traditional monopoly of Darbars is the horse. It was important in the old days as the only means of fast communication in the peninsula. Motor cycles, still unusual in the seventies, are now taking its place, and buses, trains and bicycles have democratized transport. In 1973-4, the ownership of a horse remained a status symbol, though only two Rajputs of Praj still had one. They were regarded by others as old-fashioned, and the horses were kept mainly for sentimental reasons. But Praj had good communications; there was a narrow-gauge railway (now closed), and the buses were numerous. In other villages, far from the main road, the horse might still be a useful means of transport. Now, of course, it is exclusively a luxury item. Darbars at the time kept the monopoly of horse ownership alive. Gadhavi (n.d.) mentions a case where this issue provoked conflict, in a village dominated by Kathis in the former state of Limbdi. A lower-caste man bought a horse, but was thoroughly beaten up by the Kathis, and forced to give up the animal. The event took place around 1970.

My attempt, in 1973-4, to find a horse for field work helped make contact with Rajputs, even as lack of familiarity with the reins provided some entertainment. As one horse was described as difficult, I abstained from trying it, while the other, an old mare, proved to be no faster than myself! Had I been a good horseman, however, I would have gained considerable prestige and easy access to the Rajput milieu.

The horse may have lost its practical value, but remains central to Darbar tradition and folklore. On memorial stones *(palios),* the fallen hero is always shown riding. Folk songs celebrate, not only the warrior or outlaw, but equally his horse. The latter are praised for their speed, beauty, and fearlessness in battle. In style and content, such ballads are similar to those about human heroes, and reflect the same martial values (Kincaid 1905).[12] All Darbars of the peninsula share this veneration for the horse, though the latter is known as the 'Kathi' horse.

In Saurashtra, never under direct rule, the British sometimes seem almost forgotten. But one Rajput of Praj gave them excellent testimony. 'I remember the British', he said. 'They were good horsemen!'

REMEMBERING THE HEROES: *PALIOS*

Outside most Saurashtra villages, usually to the south or east, we find long lines of *palios*, the memorial stones erected to the memory of fallen heroes. On these flat slabs of stone, raised to lean slightly backwards, the warrior—whether he fell on horseback or not—is shown riding, swinging his sword or his *kuvadi.*[13]

Typically, in Praj they are placed near the *talao* or tank southeast of the village, overlooked by the house of the Pramukh's family. The palios are found south-west, east, and north-east of the tank. Those to the east belong to the Kanbis; the others all celebrate Rajput heroes. The north-eastern location is under a holy tree close to a Shiva temple. Around, there are numerous tridents *(trishuls)* assigned to the goddess. This symbol, of course, is also associated with Shiva.[14] The proximity of temple, tridents, and palios seem to indicate that they form a single complex of ideas. We can easily believe that Rajputs were Shaivite before the cult of Rama gained ascendancy among them.

The palios are not worshipped equally by all members of the village. First, most Praj palios are erected for Rajput heroes, and seen as belonging to that caste. Those east of the tank similarly belong to the Kanbis; people agree that their use of such memorials is a relatively recent phenomenon, and typical of the time, now largely past, when Kanbis imitated Rajputs in an effort to raise their status as a caste. Secondly, palios are seen as belonging, first and foremost, to the members of the hero's paternal line. It is this quality which makes Fischer and Shah speak of 'ancestor worship' (1971, 39ff). The palios, thus, form part of the cultural complex that underline the importance of the lineage among Rajputs.[15]

Fischer and Shah also note the separate location of palios of different castes in Ratadi, near Porbandar (1971, 39). They found memorials not only to the dominant Mers, but also to Rabari pastoralists and Lohana traders. The use of palios by these castes, too, must be seen as an imitation of a Rajput custom.

According to Narottam Pallan of Porbandar, an active member of the Sorath Archaeological Society, palios were unknown in Saurashtra until the rise of the Rajputs. Thus, in Ghumli, palios appear with the first Rajput invasions (personal information), and may thus belong to the Jadejas, but not to the Jethwa rulers. This would date the first palios to the thirteenth century: these typically Rajput memorials would be roughly coeval with the institution of sati, with the first known use of the term 'Rajput', and with the oldest bardic poetry we know today.[16]

While some informants—notably townspeople—told me that palios are relics of a distant past, I found them still revered by the Rajputs and Kanbis of Praj. Fischer and Shah also indicate their continued use. Some of the recent palios may, however, deviate from traditional patterns of hero worship; one recent palio of Praj was said to be erected for a man who was killed when the roof of his house collapsed on him.[17]

HOST–GUEST: THE ARISTOCRATIC CULTURE

Everyday Rajput behaviour, like the tradition, point to valour and honour as central values. Hospitality forms part of the same complex. 'These are your fields' *(a kheterapna)*, the Praj Rajputs told me as they showed me their lands. The expression is the counterpart of the ideal Western host's 'what is mine is also yours'. Such hospitality is central to Rajputs, as it is to other martial castes of South Asia. It is no coincidence that the term *jajman*, which refers to the holder of a sacrifice as well as the traditional employer in what anthropologists once called 'the *jajmani* system', also means simply 'host'.

Barth has shown how in the Swat Valley hospitality in the men's house is fraught with political implications. To accept hospitality in the men's house, on a recurring basis, amounts to accepting the political leadership of the host; the men's house becomes the centre of local politics (Barth 1959; 79-81). This is not quite the case in the north Indian plains, nor in Saurashtra. But the men's house survives as an important Rajput institution, the *chora*, where the Rajputs of the village meet and discuss political matters.[18] Here 'guests of the village' were received and entertained. Today this function has partly been taken over by the Panchayat office and, in less formal cases, by the tea-shops. One guest, however, who was received in the chora of Praj, was the Barot. He came there on his annual visit as genealogist of the village Rajputs, inquiring about recent births, marriages and deaths. He also told stories of old times and entertained with songs and poetry, and though brief his visit was compared to those of 'old times'.[19] As an entertainer, he was certainly not enjoying the popularity accorded to Barots in the past, but the small gathering, mainly older men, enjoyed his performance.

While political authority in a Rajput state stayed with the chief's court, and the court of the village jagirdar has been replaced by the panchayat office, the *chora* remains a centre of social and cultural activity. Some tea-shops, however, have become important alternative centres in Praj. Thus it was in one particular shop near the bus-stop, locals told me, that village politicians were made or unmade.[20]

The *darbar* of a chief was not just a political assembly, but also a node of cultural and social life. Guests were constantly received, and bards—Barots and Charans—came to recite genealogies and chant poetry. In fact, the ruler in court may be seen as the prototypical jajman or host (Tambs-Lyche 1992b). Moreover, while visits did not carry the same political meaning as in Swat, the visitor might place himself under the host's protection; any threat to the guest's security thus became a matter of honour to the chief. The history of Saurashtra is replete with stories of refugees who, seeking shelter with a chief, forced him to defend his honour as a host through armed conflict.

These are not the only contexts where the host-guest relationship is central. On my arrival in Praj I found the notables of the village vying to have me as their guest. I was the first Western guest in living memory; people still remembered the one who had visited the taluka headquarters, some twenty kilometres distant, some years earlier.

When I accepted an invitation to dine in a certain house it was seen as an affirmation of that family's rank in the village. I had no means of returning the hospitality; I soon learned that this would have been out of place. The host-guest relationship is hierarchical, as the overlap in meaning between 'host', 'jajman', and 'patron' indicate. This, of course, underlines the importance of what Raheja (1988, 1989) calls 'centrality' for the dominant caste in Indian villages. She stresses the right to give, as against the obligation to receive, gifts. While hospitality, is spoken of as a 'duty', people actively compete to host any noted visitor. Raheja's analysis follows Marriott (1976, 1989), who endeavours to define, through a number of contexts, the more general concept of 'hierarchizing transactions'.[21]

Marriott distinguishes between maximal and minimal transactors. The first exploit the transaction to gain rank; the second avoid it to escape being outranked. While the Bania, avoiding contact to escape impurity, is an example of the latter, the king or dominant caste exemplifies the former. Thus an aristocrat, and consequently a Rajput, should appear as a donor in as many situations as possible.

Thus while the indication that the Rajputs' fields were 'mine' was an expression of politeness, of being the perfect host, it was also an assertion of rank and authority on the part of the speaker.

MARRIAGE: A RANKING TRANSACTION

Hospitality is a ranking transaction; the host outranks the guest. So is Rajput marriage; among traditional Hindu marriage forms, the gift of a daughter—accompanied by other gifts—is the highest form (Van der Veen 1972; Fruzzetti 1990). But here, apparently, the receiver of the gift outranks the donor; the groom's family outranks that of the bride. We must therefore assume that the acceptance of the 'virgin' constitutes the real gift. According to Inden, the wife-giving family comes to share in the prestigious 'coded substance'[22] of the groom's line (Inden 1976, 20-2, 108ff). Yet in the cases where the bride's kuldevi is adopted by the groom's clan, there is clearly some transfer of 'coded substance' in the other direction too. Classical Rajput marriage, like that of most high-caste Hindus, is a highly asymmetric affair; yet the degree of rank difference, as well as the elements that were considered in deciding rank, may have varied both by historical period and due to individual circumstances.

Hypergamy was to become an important feature of Rajput polity. It is hard to say when marriage alliances first came to be systematized in terms of rank, but the Gohils gave daughters to the prestigious Chudasamas of Junagadh by the second half of the thirteenth century, and repeated the alliance early in the fourteenth. This was clearly a case of the vassal's daughter marrying the overlord. Earlier cases are less clear, and several later marriages cannot be classed as hypergamous in any obvious sense. Yet by the turn of the sixteenth to the seventeenth century, the gift of a daughter to a superior ruler seems to be common practice, as witnessed by Sataji's remark on marrying his *kunwari* (princess) coin to the Mughal rupee. Probably, like so many other traits of Rajput culture, the practice grew only gradually, the asymmetry of marriage alliances becoming more pronounced with the establishment of the 'Rajput Great Tradition' in the sixteenth-seventeenth century.

The unequal status of marriage partners is common in the region. Terms of affinity, in Gujarati, are asymmetric. The sister's husband may visit his wife's brother; on such visits he is to be treated 'like a king'. If the wife's brother visits his in-laws, on the other hand, he is treated 'like a servant'. As Pocock puts it, writing of the Patidars of mainland Gujarat, whose elite practice highly hypergamous unions, 'The sister is the one form whom nothing is to be received and to whom things must be given. This is in accordance with the whole spirit of hypergamy; she is given as a gift and if anything is received from her it is returned with excess' (Pocock 1972, 97).

It is important to realize, with Pocock, that the asymmetry of marriage stems from the brother-sister relation, and ultimately from the very conception of male and female. In this cultural universe, gender difference is fundamental. We have seen how, in the Khodiyar myths and in Tod's stories about the fall of Ghumli, the defence of woman, of her honour, is central. Thus men protect women. But this protection is matched by the protection that women afford men.

MALE AND FEMALE RAJPUTS: THE COMPLEMENTARITY OF GENDER

This complementarity is fundamental to Rajputhood itself. Rajput status 'is understood to connote ideal manliness as well as ideal femaleness' (Harlan, 1991, 169). We have noted above how Rajputs and other Darbars see bravery as a willingness to sacrifice their lives for their subjects—an integral element of the code of honour. This too, is a gender-specific duty: 'The Rajput male performing his duty as a soldier is idealized in the warrior-turned-ascetic[23] who sacrifices his life in the *saka*[24] in order to preserve the realm. The Rajput woman performing her duty as a *pativrata*[25] is idealized in the sati, who sacrifices her life on the pyre to preserve her husband's honor by showing her devotion' (Harlan 1991, 179-80).

In Rajput culture, the man's role as a warrior and the woman's role as a mother and wife is clearly complementary. The institution of *purdah* underlines this complementarity. Rajput women of Mewar, interviewed by Harlan, see *purdah* as the most characteristic aspect of a Rajput woman's identity. *Purdah* kept Mewari Rajput women from worshipping in local temples, though they might of course go on pilgrimage. In the latter case, they were strictly veiled and chaperoned (op. cit, 37-8). Tod thought Rajput women of early medieval times went about much more freely; some of Forbes' stories suggest the same interpretation. Tod, of course, assumes *purdah* to result from Muslim influence.[26] But *purdah* is not just a means of male dominance. For aristocratic women, it provided an arena outside the control of men.

'A man's entry into the *zanana* commences a visit. The male is a guest who comes for a specific reason, food and drink, the attentions of his wife, or the companionship of his mothers and sisters. Once his needs are fulfilled, he is expected to return to male quarters and male company' (Harlan, op. cit., 169).

It would be wrong, then, to see the female role as imposed solely by the power of men. In the present state of affairs, it is true, Bania women have a much better chance of obtaining education and aspiring to the 'freedom' of modern womanhood. But it is by no means clear that this leads to a higher status for them. Rajputs—men and women—tend to see the women of the merchant castes in a negative light, and this viewpoint extends to the castes that are today imitating Bania culture. 'A Bania or Patidar girl will sleep with anyone', said an informant from a Rajput-allied caste. Briefly, such women lack honour.

We may rather see the differing roles of women in different castes relative to a scale concerning the sacredness, in Durkheim's sense, of womanhood. The chastity of women must be protected by men, but from this purity of womanhood stems the female force that, on a different level, protect men (Harlan 1991; 166). In this sense, Rajput women are sacred; this is much less so in merchant castes. Such sacredness confers status and power, but the possession of these qualities also places restrictions on female behaviour.

What is mutually protected, in the Rajput paradigm of male–female relations, is not, primarily, physical existence but honour; the duty of the ideal wife is to support 'male duty but not necessarily male desires' (op. cit., 168). Thus, in one of Harlan's stories, a warrior returns from battle to see his wife but she locks the door on him, forcing him to return to his duty. In another story, the wife cooks for her returned husband but in doing so, bangs her cooking pots together; the husband's mother then intervenes: 'You mustn't frighten my son', she says—'How the sound of clanging iron terrifies my timid little son!' Faced with such a terrible insult, the husband at once gets up and returns to battle (op. cit., 158-9). If the husband proves cowardly, says Harlan's informants, the wife breaks her bangles, given to her at the time of marriage, as do widows at their husband's death (op. cit., 164).

In 1564, Raisinhji Jhala succeeeded to the throne of Halvad. He fought with Jasoji Jadeja of Dhrol, his maternal uncle. The latter was mortally wounded, but lived long enough to send a Charan to ask Sahebji, brother of the Jadeja ruler of Kutch, to avenge him.

> Sahebji crossed the Rann, and a fierce engagement took place near Malia, where the Jadeja was killed and Raisinhji left for dead on the battlefield. The Jhala chief recovered, however, and as soon as he was strong enough to undertake the journey he went to Delhi. Meanwhile Khan Khanan had been ordered to march against Sultan Muzafar Khan of Gujarat, and Raisinhji met him on the way, and laid his case before him, pointing out that he had been left for dead and would not be recognized if he returned to Jhalawad. The General, however, advised returning and declaring himself, which advice was followed with complete success, only marred, however, by all his wives but one refusing to return to him, saying they regarded him as dead. (Wilberforce-Bell 1916, 103)

Clearly, his return was dishonorable, even if he won the battle.

A wife whose chastity is doubted destroys the man's honour; a coward on the battlefield destroys the honour of his wife (Harlan 1991, 166). If the husband dies in battle and his scalp is taken by his enemies, the honour of both is similarly destroyed, for scalping carries the connotation of castration (Ziegler 1973, 79-80). This implication that castration of the man implies a violation of the wife points to an important element in the Rajput—and more generally, north Indian—idea of chastity, for it is not associated with virginity as such but with the preservation of female powers for their proper purpose, i.e. marriage. The 'virgin' goddess, then, is not primarily a woman untouched by man but one who has kept her powers intact, and who is thus able to divert them to the purpose of her choice.

FEMALE FIGHTERS

While defending woman's honour and chastity is the task of men, some heroines were fully capable of defending themselves.

When the Parmar hero Jug Dev came to Anhilwada Pattan (Forbes 1878, 101ff), he had to leave his young wife—a Chaora Rajputni—behind. Waiting near the tank, she was tricked by the matron of a dubious establishment and locked up. Here, the son of one of the king's officers comes to enjoy her; but as he is stoned with opium, she kills him and throws the bundle through the window and into the road. The father sends armed men to revenge his son; they enter through a window large enough only for one man at a time. As the first one tries to enter, head first, 'the Chowree struck him with her sword—his head fell into the room, and his trunk outside; in the same way she slew five or six men; but no one was able to kill her' (Forbes 1878, 108).

In the end Jug Dev returns, and the honour of both is saved. But this is only one example of the fighting Rajput heroine; she represents an important part of the cultural heritage. The most famous of all these female fighters is the queen Padmini, who liberates her husband, held captive by Alauddin Khilji; then leaves him to his desperate fight against the Muslims and returns to Chittor to perform *johar*—collective suicide—with the other women of the castle. Thus she becomes both a female warrior and a sati (Harlan 1991, 183-4).

Iconographically, the image of the Rajputni, sword in hand, is assimilated to that of the kuldevi, 'the lone protectress who fights among men in the battlefield' (op. cit., 72). It is an image of a fierce female, a woman possessing both powers and her own strong will. On the subject of Rajput women, in a more practical sense, Jacob (1894, 34) said, 'The wives of the Rajpoots have generally more to do with the management of their estates than their lords; these are sunk into sloth and debauchery whilst their ladies, whose intellect the use of opium has not clouded, hold, either directly, or indirectly the reins of government'.

It has also been said of them, that they married the land, not the man (Westphal-Hellbosch 1974, 33; MacMurdo 1894; 226-7). Jacob should know: he spent years in the service of the British agency in Rajkot. In 'Western India' (1872), he makes several references to the role of his wife. Without her help, he could not have had access to the politics of the zenana, and it is clear how he feels that this would have severely restricted him in the performance of his duties.

Ideally, the wife should support the husband, not manipulate him for her own ends, as some of the Ranis of Navanagar certainly did. Such examples of court intrigue are seen, in retrospect, rather as the negative side of the coin; but evidently the woman's reputation for posterity depends on whether her designs were, ultimately, successful (Harlan 1991, 168).

SHAKTI OR SAT: THE FORCES OF WOMEN

Earlier, we have been discussing the role of the queen in state affairs. We have also met, in the example of the queen Ranik Devi, the institution of sati.[27]

Near the palios in Praj, we also find stones erected in memory of satis.[28] But instead of the rider the image is that of a standing woman, with her right hand raised towards the onlooker, the fingers turned upwards. There are only a few of them, as compared to the many *palios* erected for male heroes, but the place chosen for their memorials and the similarity with the *palios* point to a symbolic equivalence between *vira* (hero) and sati.[29]

The puranic figure of Sati parallels the story of Savitri.[30] This aspect of womanhood is often seen in polar opposition to that of shakti. In Saurashtra, however, the two concepts are closely associated, even confounded. Elsewhere, too, it is shakti, the elemental force in woman, which, unleashed by the act of sati, emerges as highly dangerous and destructive (Weinberger-Thomas 1990).

In Mewar, the women speak of sat rather than shakti:

> The enabling function of women's *sat* is somewhat like the motivational aspect of *shakti*, the female power discussed widely in literature on women and goddesses in India. My Rajput informants did not invoke *shakti* in discussions of *satis* or heroines. They describe the Goddess or a kuldevi as being Shakti... or having *shakti*, but they overwhelmingly speak of *satis*, heroines, and ordinary women as having and seeking *sat*, understood as substantive virtue and power. Informants understood what I meant when I spoke of *shakti* but themselves employed the term *sat* when talking about women's duties, powers, and goals. *Sat* is the term they employ when they describe themselves and their motivations in admiring and worshipping *kuldevis*, *satimatas*, heroines.... (Harlan 1991, 185n)

It is shakti that is used in the goddess myths of Saurashtra, such as those relating to Khodiyar. But I did not have access to Rajput women as Harlan, herself a woman, gained for herself. Thus I cannot say whether Rajput women of Saurashtra use sat or shakti in their discourse on these themes. The men, with whom I mainly spoke, used the term shakti.

This may indicate that men and women view these matters differently. From an article by Jacobson (1981) emerges an aspect that Harlan continually stresses; intention and will-power are important elements in performing according to *sat*. *Shakti*, however, is seen as an impersonal force, a force of 'nature'. Sexuality is clearly implicit in shakti, while sat is concerned rather with the control of sexual powers. This duality is, of course, a recurring theme in Indian religion and mythology, notably as regards Shiva (O'Flaherty 1973).

If men see femininity as a primeval force, to be respected and propitiated but difficult to control, while women see it as an aspect of their personality to be integrated and controlled through the power of will and intention, we need not be surprised. It would parallel the many instances where men seem to assimilate femininity to 'nature', while women do not (Ardener 1972). In the Indian context, 'nature' is not the neutral factor that it has become in Western thought; it is the home of forces such as shakti beyond the control of man (Marriott 1976, 1989).

Shakti worship is found among male Rajputs of Praj; 'the worship of power' as one devotee called it. They see themselves as going beyond the ordinary goddess cults, to their very essence; the power common to all gods and goddesses, on which depends the vital force of men. Such forces fascinate women too. Fire—which in India surely is not 'natural' but a sacred force—engenders such fascination. A Mewar woman says 'there is something about fire that still attracts Rajput women ... they still cannot but gaze into the fire and feel an urge to join it' (Harlan 1991, 203).

This means, says Harlan, that women still have *sat*, even if they no longer immolate themseves. They are closer to this primeval force than men; they do not fear it. A Rajput nobleman recited to Harlan a *doha*[31]

> about a spectator who sees a lion (Rajput) drawn to a fire but fearfully skirting around it and then sees a Rajput woman drawn to the fire and fearlessly mingling with it... The narrator used this verse to back up his point that Rajput women are actually braver, more heroic, more virtuous than their men. He then recited one of the stories in which a woman shames her man into battle (the story of 'the sound of clanging iron'...) and concluded, even today, 'Whatever we (men) do, it is our women who make us do it'. (op. cit., 203)

SATI

The figure of the *sati* known in Western sources—the faithful wife entering the pyre in self-sacrifice on the death of her husband—certainly forms part of Kathiawadi tradition (e.g. Jacob 1872). But the term sati is also used in a number of other ways. Thus in Junagadh, the legend of the Adi Chadi well concerns a Hindu woman who, to escape marriage to the Muslim king, kills herself by leaping into the well. In spite of the fact that she was unmarried and died in a quite different way, people sometimes speak of her as a sati.

Another example is Jamboo Ma, maid-servant of the ruler of the village of Pacham (in Limbdi state, then Shiani), who cut off her breasts in protest against the annexation of her lord's village to the state of Limbdi. Dying, she puts the mark of her hand—the sign of the sati—on the walls of Shiani fort. She may or may not be seen as a sati; but she is certainly placed with them in a common context of female heroism.[32]

Satis are honoured by palios, and such memorials are not confined to satis in the strict sense. They instead celebrate the female heroic self-sacrifice. Thus palios show male and female heroism equally, though memorials to men are in a clear majority. The similar symbols indicate that the honour of both sexes is seen as being fundamentally of the same kind, or at least intrinsically comparable.

A similar situation obtains in Mewar. Hari Rani had just been married when her husband had to leave for war. But he, greatly in love, hesitated to leave her. Finally he starts off, but

> when he reached the palace gates, he sent word back to Hari Rani that she should send him some souvenir to take to war with him so that he could feel she was by his side. Without hesitating, the devoted wife drew a sword and sliced off her head so that he could take that with him. When a maidservant delivered the head to him, he affixed it to his saddle and, inspired by his wife's example of devotion, rode off to do his duty as a soldier. (Harlan 1991, 160)

Hari Rani is not a sati in the narrow sense of the term. But she 'is called Sati Hari Rani and is invoked in discussions on *satis* because her death is seen as a direct manifestation of her *sat*' (ibid.). Another extension of the term in Mewar is the recent phenomenon of the 'living satimata'; these are women wanting to become satis, who have abandoned their project in the face of modern opposition to the rite. Their eagerness for sacrifice earns them a sacred status, and women come to them for blessings and advice (Harlan 1991, 180). In this they resemble the sacred Charanis of the past, with which we deal below.

RAJPUT RELIGION

Rajput religion, we have seen, is intimately connected with the martial culture of the community. We have noted the importance of the kuldevi, and the sacredness of women. The importance of the goddess can hardly be overstated. She is not only the power behind the foundation of each Rajput lineage; she is the very source of power itself. As Shakti she represents power in all its forms; the forces of fertility as well as the strength for political enterprise. Naturally, she demands the most 'powerful' or 'hot' among offerings; meat, alcohol and opium. If the allusion to human sacrifice, often made by informants, is not supported by concrete evidence, it does underline the logic of her cult. For the martial culture of the Rajputs, she is indispensable.

But while the goddess is important, she is not exclusive to the caste. Even the kuldevis of royal houses were often popular with large sections of the population. And while the goddess cult is related, as we shall see, to the 'sacred' genealogies maintained by Charans, and thus to the very essence of Rajputhood, the books of the genealogists form but one part of the 'argument' for Rajput supremacy.

This supremacy, which implies a claim to Kshatriya status, is legitimated by the cult of Rama. In Saurashtra, the Rama temple has a central place in villages dominated by Rajputs, and is also found attached to the palace in the capital. We have mentioned the temple in Dhrangadhra, which bears the blazon of the royal family prominently over its entrance. This and other royal temples have since, generally speaking, become public property, but their link to the ruling house remains clear.

Rama, the ideal ruler, adds the element of *dharma* to legitimation by descent and heroism represented, jointly, by the goddess and the Charan bard. While goddess temples may or may not be served by Brahmin priests, for the service of Rama Brahmins are indispensable. His cult symbolizes the claim of the Rajput king to rule justly and by moral law; the Brahmins underline this point by offering their service to the ruler.

The good king is, above all, a protector. In his kingdom there will be justice and prosperity; both will suffer from a bad ruler. And, as we have seen in the myths of Khodiyar, the protection of women is metonymic of a good ruler's qualities (Harlan 1991; 36). The Rama temples, then, may be seen as part of the positive stereotype which Rajputs try to build around themselves. It represents a counterpart to the realities of power and descent, whereby the kingship remains but the succesful apex of a continuous rise from robber or petty chief, even if that success has the sanction of the king's kuldevi.

TER TANSALI—THE 'THIRTEEN CASTES'

The influence of Rajput cultural ideals is not confined to the landholding castes. They are central to a 'cluster' of castes, referred to in Saurashtra as the *ter tansali*—the thirteen 'plates'. 'Plates' here, refer to the commensality of the groups—each 'plate' representing a caste. This cluster seems to ressemble the kind of grouping that Mayer calls 'allied castes':

> We see that the Rajputs are part of a cluster of roughly equal castes, which are separated essentially by endogamy alone; for they are reciprocally commensal, and their occupations are mainly agricultural, save for the two craft castes of Nai and Kumhar (potter). Since the Rajputs are the most eminent of the allied castes, we may ask whether they do not dominate the political life of nearly all villages, either at first hand *or* through their allies. I am not saying that the Rajputs are the universally dominant caste in that they *explicitly* link up with their allies to form a caste 'bloc'; but I suggest that the 'Rajput-allied' caste is dominant in the sense that a section of the population with common values and friendly equality is dominant. The votes allied castes now give to Rajput candidates in local elections supports this argument.... (Mayer 1958, 418-19)

His analysis further suggests that, where a single caste 'does not control all or even a majority of the villages of the region, these other villages will tend to be under the authority of castes which are sympathetic to it, and which adopts its ways in order to identify themselves with it, and then become its commensal equals and allies...' (op. cit., 419).

The concept of 'allied castes', then, is clearly similar to the 'thirteen castes' of Saurashtra. The latter, however, differ by their occupational diversity; for they include not only agriculturists and craftsmen, but also pastoralists and traders. The 'thirteen castes' do indeed accept each other as near-equals; they freely eat, drink and smoke together. In some cases, even intermarriage is deemed possible, in certain areas and among certain pairs of castes within the group.

Rajputs are, of course, the most prominent among these castes. Others mentioned by informants include: Charan and Barot (the bardic castes); Ahir, Bharwad, and Rabari (pastoralists); Kathi, Mer, Babria, Parajia (agricultural castes, sometimes regionally dominant); Lohanas (traders); Lohar, Mistri, Kumbhar (artisans). Kolis and Kanbis were sometimes included, but sometimes definitely and absolutely excluded.

None of my informants offered a full complement of thirteen castes, and their lists differed considerably. Obviously, there is no 'definitive' list serving as a reference point. But all agree in excluding certain castes, such as Banias, most Brahmins, and all untouchables. The concept of *ter tansali,* then, does not depend on precise enumeration. Rather, there is a general idea of such a cluster, with a willingness to admit that differing conditions, in parts of the peninsula, lead to variation in the actual castes admitted to the fold. Probably, the actual grouping would seldom reach the full number of thirteen.

The important point here is that both Rajputs and a number of other castes recognize relative equality with certain others—according to circumstances. Such recognition implies a certain cultural homogeneity, as is evident from the examples of castes never admitted to the group.

This grouping presents thus the central cluster of castes in any Darbar-dominated village of Saurashtra. They are the groups stereotyped by outsiders as 'Kathiawadis', they are the main speakers of Kathiawadi dialect, and share a great deal of similarity in dress, manners, lineage organization, and religion. Thus while only Darbars (especially Rajputs) are truly martial castes, all groups among the thirteen share a religion influenced by the martial aspect of Darbar culture. They are all, except when converted to certain sects, goddess worshippers.

THE KATHIS

I include Kathis among the Darbars, since they are seen as such by informants. Though their often minuscule chiefdoms were often ravaged or even conquered by their stronger neighbours, particularly in the eighteenth century, they never lost their Darbar status. Yet many of them are simply peasants, and they certainly represent a borderline case. It is by cultural, rather than economic, criteria that they are included. While their traditions relate them to Rajputs, they differ significantly from the peasant Kanbis. Thus the British classed them as a 'criminal caste', in complete contrast to the Kanbis, who had the reputation of being hard-working and law-abiding—excellent subjects for revenue purposes. The Kathis, on their part, exemplify, with their martial tradition, the continuum between warrior and robber as well as that between landlord and peasant.

Enthoven cites a myth which, in this regard, is not without interest. It tells of how they came to Gujarat with the Pandavas, who were pledged to wandering after losing the game of dice.[33] They took refuge in Virat—modern Dholka—but

Dyryodhan, the head of the Kauravs, got scent of this and marched upon Virat with a large army. But he could not get into the walls of the town, much less discover the Pandavs. Karan, his minister, suggested the course of driving off the cattle of the ruler, which would bring out the true Rajputs as protectors of the cattle. It was, however, considered disgraceful for a Rajput to stoop to cattle-lifting; so Karan struck his staff on the ground and produced a newly created man who was called *Kath*, i.e. stick, and who, in return for his carrying off the cattle, was to be granted immunity to commit theft, especially of cattle, in all future time. The Kathis claim to be the descendants of this *kath* and give this legend as a proof of their right to commit robbery. (Enthoven 1921, 164-5)

The stereotype of Kathis as robbers, strong in British times, was certainly shared by Enthoven. But many of their 'criminal' acts were related to encroachment on Kathi lands by surrounding states, notably Bhavnagar. This led many Kathi chiefs into *baharvatia* or becoming outlaws.

All accounts seem to agree on the foreign origin of the Kathis. The theories, sometimes rather fantastic, of their origin need not detain us. One tradition, more reasonably, places their origin at Pawar, between Sindh and Kutch. From there they came to Than in central Saurashtra, whence they drove the Babarias to the southern region, known as Babriawar, where the latter are still dominant (Enthoven 1921, 165). Another tradition stresses their closeness to the Rajputs:

The true original Kathis are called Avartias, while the descendants of Dhan Vala of Dhank, a Rajput who married the daughter of Umro Patgar a Kathi, are called Sakhayats and fall under three branches—(1) Vala, (2) Khuman, and (3) Khachar—who are said to have been the three sons of Dhan Vala and his Kathi wife. Dhan Vala was of course put out of caste by the Vala Rajputs of Dhank and banished the territory. This took place about the year 1400 AD. according to the Kathi tradition. Dhan led his Kathis back to Kutch from where they had come. From Cutch, however, they were afterwards driven forth on account of quarrels with the ruling chief who was said to have dishonoured one of their women and whom they murdered, and were consequently banished by his successor. There was a pitched battle at Than, in which the Kathis won. Finding the country quite good and agreeable grazing ground for their cattle, they settled there and built a temple in honour of the sun, who is an object of worship among the Kathis to this day and whose symbol is used on all their deeds. Vala the first son of Dhan occupied Jetpur, Khuman the second son took Chotila, and Khachar settled at Mithiali. (Enthoven 1921, 165-6)

This migration to Kutch and back has generally been accepted as fact in the literature. The marriage between the Rajput and his Kathi wife may be assumed hypergamous, indicating the superior status of the Rajput. Yet the Kathis beat them in battle. The descendants of Dhan are, in effect, half Rajputs by blood, and so may be seen to have inherited some of the martial qualities of that caste.

We see here the ambiguity of the Kathi position. Unlike some Koli groups, they do not claim to be Rajputs, and apparently never did so. The assertion made in this myth is rather that of being equal or 'almost equal' to them. Indeed, 'Kathis believe their original occupation to be that of soldiers', says Enthoven (1921, 169), who continues with a version of the Chital incident noted above, in which a wise Kathi woman advises her brethren to protect, rather than to rob, a wealthy merchant. Taken together, the two stories support the claim of Kathis to be real chiefs—darbars—and not just peasants or robbers.

The reference to sun-worship among the Kathis is interesting, but we know very little about it,[34] though the memory both of the worship and the temple is very much alive. Another strange, but badly known, element of Kathi culture is the kinship system. Unusually for northern India, Kathis practise cross-cousin marriage, and there have been suggestions that they have moieties.

Even if badly known, these traits set the Kathis apart from Kanbis, Rajputs and Mers. Like Rajputs, Mers are strongly patrilineal, and each village tends to be dominated by a single clan. Kathis are non-vegetarian by tradition, they used to employ Charan bards, and in general, they resemble Rajputs; 'in dress, manners, food, superstitions, and modes (of) thinking, they are one', says Tod, 'a shade, a name only divides them' (1971, 316). A major difference, however, has been their willingness to till their own lands; in this they again resemble the Mers. Rajputs traditionally tried to stay aloof from manual work.

The Kathis are always included among the the 'thirteen' castes of traditional Kathiawar. This name, evidently, identifies the peninsula as 'the land of the Kathis', though the name has also been used for its central parts, the Kathi area proper.

DARBARS AS AN 'ESTATE'

I have tried here to make two points. First, the category of Darbar includes several other dominant castes as well as Rajputs. Secondly, the latter, most typical of Darbars, show a number of traits intimately connected with this position of dominance. On this basis I propose to treat the Darbars as an 'estate' in Weber's terms, i.e. social grouping whose cultural distinctness is closely related to its interest in maintaining a particular position in society.

We have seen how Rajput kinship, with its segmentary lineage form, relates to the state-building activities of the community. We saw, too, how kinship itself was moulded and modified by the state-building process; the hierarchically ordered aristocracy of later days differed from the much looser segmentary idiom of an early stage. Marriage and alliance were heavily influenced by politics, too; in this chapter we have seen how the perceived role of the Rajput in society moulds gender relations and ties in with the worship of the Goddess. The institution of hospitality, which forms such an important aspect of Rajput demeanor, also relates to dominance and control over others. Horses and memorial stones also derive their importance from the martial tradition that helped make Rajputs dominant.

In these matters, Mers and especially Kathis differ to some extent from Rajputs. Most succinctly, the moiety-based marriage alliance among Kathis must be seen as counteracting the hierarchical tendency so strongly in evidence among Rajputs; it may, indeed, be one main reason why the Kathi polity had difficulty in evolving into stable states. Similarly, the lack of primogeniture made succession troubles inimical to their political organization—but then, such disputes were not exactly scarce among Rajputs either.

Certain other differences—such as the sun-worship of the Kathis—do not seem to have had any great influence on the political role played by the caste. But for a large set of cultural practices, the relationship to the exercise of dominance is clear. It is in this sense that we may speak of a Darbar culture, and look at Darbars as one social grouping.

This is, above all, consistent with the way people in Saurashtra themselves look at these groups. Everybody, of course, knows that Darbars are not a *jati* or a *kom* in the strict sense usually translated as 'caste'. And yet, in a number of contexts, it is the category 'Darbar' that is used for reference, rather than the caste name. And in other contexts, the term 'Rajput' is used in a sense where it refers less to the particular clan involved than to a general 'cluster of statuses', which are those associated with Darbars or—by anthropologists—with one kind of dominant caste.

The category Darbar, then, is neither an 'ethnic' entity nor a unit in a 'caste system'; it is a social position. It is defined by a set of common interests, notably those tied to control over land and people, to the exercise of power, as the etymology of Darbar—'power-holder'—makes clear. Such a community of interest is at the base of Weber's concept of 'estate' (1948, 81-4). Such 'status groups'—an alternative translation of 'ständer'—share not only a position in society but also play a demonstrable historical role. In the Weberian view of history, estates become the main actors; and as such they become powerful culture-bearing elements. They are not simply a community of interest.

For the Darbars, historically, these common interests do not preclude internal conflict; they rather imply such conflict as a matter of course. To exercise power over land and people means defending one's claims against others, or to extend one's interests at their expense. But, and that is the central point, those against whom one fights this kind of zero-sum game become partners in the game. They become people like oneself. They, too, then, are Darbars.

Recognition of a partner in this game clearly does not constitute solidarity. In a critique of Barth's work on Swat, Talal Asad notes that the internal conflict among the power-holders, in effect, serves to strengthen their position; the feuds of Swat create for the rest of the population just those conditions that make protection indispensable (Asad 1970). In the Marxian terms of Asad's work at the time, the power-holders constituted a class-in-itself but not a class-for-itself.

So it was in Saurashtra at the heyday of the Rajput states. Conflict, real or potential, was indispensable to dominance. Thus the zero-sum 'power game' that maintained a certain equilibrium among Darbars inspired a stress on war, courage, honour and other elements of a martial life-world. At the same time this game maintained the role of the 'protector' and the submission of the 'protected' population.

But the equilibrium was never more than relative. As chiefdoms grew into states, they acquired the resources necessary to eliminate their smaller neighbours. The larger states became able to field armies that were not recruited from Darbars. Gradually, then, caste dominance was encompassed by state control, and the descendants of adventurers who had become Darbars were now able to control fighting men who would never have access to such status. The martial caste became, in short, an aristocracy. But the category as it exists today extends all the way from the ex-rulers of important states to the farmer struggling to maintain a minimal difference from the ordinary peasant.

This underlines the character of the Darbar category; it has long since ceased to be a class, if it was ever so. Instead, it refers, today, to shared traditions rather than shared interest; and these traditions concern the role of the estate in forming traditional Kathiawar through a long historical process.

Let us now examine other categories at a similar level. By viewing them as 'estates' in Weber's sense, we may clarify our understanding of the structure of traditional society in Saurashtra.

NOTES

1. The concept of dominant caste was first introduced by Srinivas (1952), who has later elaborated it. Its use here follows its precision by Mayer (1958).
2. This is a recurrent theme in literature on mainland Gujarat. Classics are Malabari (1884), Thoothi (1935) and Munshi (1954). A more anthropological discussion is found in Shah and Shroff (1958), Pocock (1957, 1972) and Tambs-Lyche (1980a, 1982).
3. This characterization is supported by the long-standing association of the Jaipur royal family with the party (Gayatri Devi and Rau 1983, 251ff).
4. Sharpe used the term in this sense—member of a dominant caste—as early as 1931.
5. The term 'feudalism' is highly contested for the Indian case. Tod, of course, regarded Rajput polity as 'feudal' (1829; 1: 153 and 1829-32 *passim*), while later British critics, such as Lyall, characterized the Rajput states as 'tribal', albeit with some 'feudal growth' (Inden, op. cit., 172-8; R.W. Stern 1988; 23-62). Such characterizations should be seen, first and foremost, in opposition to ideas centering on 'oriental despotism' (Inden, op. cit., 164). In Tod's case, his characterization also served to defend his Rajputs from the 'contempt for all that is Asiatic (which too often marks our countrymen in the East)' (1, 155).
   This discourse should be kept separate from that about the term feudalism itself, and its usefulness outside the European context. R. Stern discusses this problem thoroughly. While the majority of European scholars regard feudalism as a phenomenon peculiar to Europe, Ganshof (1961) distinguished between feudalism in the 'narrow sense' and what Marc Bloch (1975) called 'feudal society'. Bloch thought that the fundamental notions of feudalism might well have existed outside Europe. Pointing to a 'striking ressemblance' between Bloch's 'fundamental notions' of feudal society and the British interpretation of Rajput polity as grounded in Tod (1988, 37), the conclusion to Stern's excellent comparative work is perhaps best stated in the title of his chapter 'Something very like feudalism'—a phrase borrowed from Lyall. Wherever the term 'feudalism' is used in this book, then, the reader should interpret it in Bloch's wider sense, or as a statement regarding comparative similarity in social systems. I do not wish to enter into the argument as to the proper use of the term.
6. This was quite striking in 1973; it is somewhat less common today.
7. In earlier days Rajputs as well as other warriors carried swords. It is not clear why

the *kuvadi* is still carried, while the sword has disappeared. I suspect that the law, in establishing the illegality of carrying weapons, has failed to take note of the *kuvadi's* existence.

8. A muzzle-loader, this gun was a true museum piece, and must have been more than a hundred years old, even assuming that local gunsmiths were late in picking up technical developments. The owner assured me, however, that it worked well enough.
9. Guns may have become more common recently, with increasing conflict between Rajputs and Kanbis. Through the smuggling link to the Gulf, it should not be too difficult to obtain them. In fact, during a conflict related to a Lohana marriage near Dhrangadhra in 1992, I was advised to stay away from the celebrations in case the injured party should turn up with a gun.
10. I have referred to more serious cases above. Though I observed no such incidents, I assume that the more usual way of keeping low-caste people 'in their place' was simply to beat them up—as was the case in a friend's home village in northern Gujarat.
11. The informant, here, was a left-wing Congressman and supporter of Indira Gandhi, though he had his doubts about the wisdom of her emergency rule.
12. Some of these songs are reproduced in Village Monograph No.16. The geographical range of these horses, as described in the songs, coincide with the peninsula and the points mentioned help us define the conceptualization of the region (see Tambs-Lyche 1994b).
13. Two Praj *palios* are illustrated in Tambs-Lyche (1992, 138). The figure of the rider-hero is, of course, central. Above it, most show a vertical line surrounded by two circular figures, one on each side. Similar dots are often inscribed in the trident of the goddess when drawn, e.g. on a stone or on a tree. In both cases two explanations are given: sometimes the dots are identified as 'eyes' or 'eyes of the Mata'; sometimes as 'sun' and 'moon'. When, on some *palios*, one dot is crescent-shaped, the latter identification seems obvious. Rolf Lunheim tells me that during recent fieldwork in Bikaner district, he noted the same dots on palios. There, they were identified as 'sun and moon'. This pattern is absent from the palios illustrated by Fischer and Shah from Ratadi, a Mer village in former Porbandar state. Perhaps the dots refer to Rajputs as descendants of sun and moon, which would explain their absence in Ratadi, where the heroes are Mers. Kanbi palios in Praj carry the same dots as the Rajput ones, but Kanbis were of course imitating local Rajputs in erecting them.
14. The same symbol is used for both deities, but in Saurashtra, the *trishul* is primarily associated with the goddess. When with Shiva, it is explicitly identified with his shakti—his primeval power, intrinsically female. It is natural that the fallen heroes should be associated with the goddess, but the Matas found here are nameless ones, not the kuldevi of the clan. Such Matas might once have been living Charanis, sacred enough to be honoured yet not important enough to be remembered by name. But nobody offered this explanation. They were not satis; in that case, a 'sati stone' would have been erected, as they were found in the same location.
15. And, of course, among Mers, who are also strongly patrilineal.
16. See the discussion in Ch. III.

17. I never found out why this man's death was deemed worthy of such a memorial. The house may have collapsed during some fight, but if so, my informants did not tell.
18. For a comparison of such institutions in the northwestern part of the subcontinent, see Tambs-Lyche (1992b).
19. In view of the common statement that such visits are a thing of the past, however, its persistence in Praj as late as 1974 is not without interest.
20. In 1973-4, the Congress was in control in Praj. Other factions would have met elsewhere.
21. Marriott's work on such transactions are of long standing. Among the first such contributions is his article on food transactions from 1968. A more general treatment is found in Marriott (1976), being greatly expanded in the 1989 articke. Tambs-Lyche (1976b and forthcoming b) are also dedicated to this theme.
22. By this term is meant, by Marriott and Inden (1977), that 'code' and 'substance' merge; the medium in which a message is carried becomes part of the message itself. Thus the ranking of a family cannot be distinguished from its heritage, and the latter is itself the result of ranking transactions—in Inden's case of Kulina Brahmins and Kayasthas of Bengal, the rank of a family is created by its preceding marriages (Inden 1976).
23. In bardic poetry, renunciation and death in battle are often compared or equated. Warriors certain of death were imitating the vow of renunciation (Olivelle 1978) and wore saffron clothes, like those of the renouncer (Harlan 1991, 179-80). Bards speak of an army going to war like a host of renouncers (Forbes 1878; 175). See also Tambs-Lyche, 1995.
24. *Saka* is the word used for the final battle of a warrior, in which death is a foregone conclusion. Such battle is seen as a sacrifice (Harlan 1991, e.g. 179-80).
25. The *pativrata*, the vow of wifehood, denotes the perfect wife. See Harlan (1991, e.g. 167-8), but particularly Mallison (1973 and 1979).
26. Tod's view is widely shared, but this conclusion is by no means obvious.
27. See also Tambs-Lyche 1992a: 515-23 and 1995.
28. Here, too, the 'dots' identified as 'sun and moon' are seen.
29. In the north of the peninsula, the sati stones are different from those in Praj. Here, only the hand is sculpted on the flat raised stone slab. The 'sun' and the 'moon' are still there. The raised hand is the standard symbol of the sati, in the form of the *thapa* or imprint made by the woman's hand on walls etc. Normally, the fingers are always turned upwards, and the mark should be made with *kumkum* (cinnabar).
30. See e.g. O'Flaherty (1978, 30-1), Weinberger-Thomas (1990), Mallison (1973), Harlan (1991), and, for Savitri, Babb (1975, 140-1).
31. A verse form used in bardic poetry.
32. Jamboo Ma's story is told in Sharpe (1931, 1-3), and discussed in Tambs-Lyche (1992a, 517-18).
33. A well-known episode of the Mahabharata, leading up to the great war.
34. The once famous sun-temple near Than was no longer in use when Enthoven wrote (1921; 165), and Burgess thought it fell into disuse when the Kathis were driven from Than by the Jhalas about AD 1690 (1971, 89).

CHAPTER V

Traditional Kathiawar
The Kheduts

KHEDUTS: THE PEASANTS OF SAURASHTRA

The common term for a peasant in Saurashtra is *khedut*, from *kheter* — field. The term is as well known and widespread as Darbar. But if everybody knows what a peasant is, it is less clear whether the category should be seen as an 'estate'. In economic terms, we can certainly draw a line between 'landowner' and 'peasant'. It is less obvious how we are to distinguish kheduts from Darbars in cultural terms. As an interest group, they opposed the Banias who bought their produce and lent them money, rather than the landowners.

The cultural continuity between landlord and peasant becomes apparent when we study the two largest peasant communities, Kanbi and Koli. The Kanbis reached, as 'Patidars', a status approaching landlords on the mainland. The model of this upwardly mobile sector of the caste, from the area known as Charottar (which largely coincides with Kaira district south of Ahmedabad) has had profound effects among the Kanbis of Saurashtra, too. As for the Kolis, we have to consider, rather, a downward mobility; we shall see that they have a martial background, and that their reduction to peasants has been a gradual process. Like the Kathis, their resistance to downward mobility earned them the name of a 'criminal caste' in British days.

PEASANTS IN THE REGIONAL ECONOMY

The peasants formed the economic base of the power system of traditional Kathiawar. This is true even for the merchants, since a great deal of the trade of the peninsula dealt with their produce.

If the village is seen in isolation, the opposition between landlord and peasant must surely remain in focus. But the isolated, self-reliant village is largely a myth in India, as indeed elsewhere.[1] We shall mainly concern ourselves here with the way in which the village realizes and expresses aspects of wider-ranging power relations.[2] These relations mediate between the peasant and the power-holder; the former is not simply the submissive source of the latter's revenue.

It is here that the market and the merchant enter our view of the village. While we may assume a general trend from a state where peasants gave part of their crop in kind to the landlord, to the present cash-cropping economy, it would seem that cash-cropping has existed, subsidiary to the 'feudal' order, for centuries. The development of towns, with their concentration of craftsmen, indicates a market for agricultural commodities, at least in mainland Gujarat, by the sixteenth century (Gopal 1975, 146). Gopal sees a further development towards cash-cropping on the mainland in the early seventeenth century; this was accompanied by migration to the towns, where weaving, especially, absorbed the immigrants.[3] Early examples of cash-cropping included the Parsi agriculturalists of south Gujarat (Guha 1984, 114).

Gujarat is invariably described as more prosperous than its neighbours—town and country alike—in this period (Gopal, op. cit., 222-3). We have no such information on Saurashtra, which may have retained a more inward-looking agricultural economy. But Dholka, on the very edge of Saurashtra, was a weaving centre of importance. Part of its work force may have come from the peninsula, as did, probably, some of its food supply. We also know that merchants, at least by the eighteenth century, acted as middlemen in the conversion into cash of agricultural revenue paid in kind for the state coffers. This has been shown for Baroda and the kingdom of the Peshwas (Subramanian 1992), but we may assume the practice to be older and more general. The position of merchants at the court of the Gujarat kingdom (Majumdar 1956, 162-7) leads me to suppose that they were important for the conversion of revenue since the agricultural improvements of the eleventh-twelfth centuries. While this cannot be proved at the present state of knowledge, certainly the role of merchants had brought merchants into a structural opposition to peasants by the end of our 'traditional' period.

This opposition between peasant and moneylender does not arise from first principles; it is obvious however, from our material, that the relationship between peasants and landlords was strong enough and sufficiently imbued with loyalties to make of the Bania a 'stranger' to the village community.[4] And, from what we know of the village communities it is clear that we cannot assume 'jajmani relationships' to have been an institution strong enough or well enough documented to be given explanatory value in this regard.[5]

Three other factors must instead have been important. First, the institution of the 'thirteen castes' made of the Rajputs and their allies an 'imagined community', stressing a certain amount of egalitarianism as well as loyalty. The inclusion of peasants with their lords in this alliance would have served to exclude the Banias. Secondly, common cultural values are expressed through religion—and particularly through Goddess worship. It is closeness between Darbar and Khedut religion that ties the two groups together. We shall see that one effect of 'modernity', in Saurashtra, is the breaking of this bond.[6] Finally, tillers of the soil had a community of interest with the landholders in defending the village against outsiders. This common interest, however, was of varying strength, for land was generally available elsewhere, and there was considerable migration; peasants could and sometimes did leave an oppressive landlord (Spodek 1976, 26).

With these factors in mind we shall look at the main castes that constitute the peasant population in Saurashtra.

KANBIS AND PATIDARS

Kanbis are a large caste found all over Gujarat, as also in neighbouring areas of Maharashtra and Rajasthan. They have been settled in this area for centuries, though their origins are by no means clear. Enthoven, noting that the term Kanbi refers simply to a cultivator, makes a clear distinction between the Gujarat Kanbis and the Maratha Kunbis; while he claims a probable 'Gujar' origin for the former, the latter are said to be 'of common stock with the Marathas' (1921, 134). While Kanbis may have been in Saurashtra for a long time, most who live there today descend from relatively recent immigrants: in the nineteenth century many Kanbis settled in the area, now more peaceful than before.[7]

Only in north and central Gujarat, on the mainland, were Kanbis dominant by 1947; in Saurashtra, they became so only with recent land reforms. Pocock has shown (1955, 1957a and b, 1972, 1973) how Kanbis of Charottar in central Gujarat rose to dominance. The story has also been told by several other scholars.[8] In the wars between Marathas and Mughals, they were supported by the former against their Rajput landlords, who sided with the Mughals. Thus the

Gaekwar of Baroda gave to some of them—styled Patidars—taxation rights in the land. This led the Patidar families to assume a leading position in the caste.

Indigo cultivation became a profitable enterprise to Kanbi/ Patidar farmers, making them favoured by the British and Baroda authorities as particularly capable and progressive farmers. When the famine of 1899 struck Gujarat, it was perhaps their cash-cropping experience that led many members of the caste to try their luck in East Africa. There, they became the backbone of the 'Asian' community of small traders. As Pocock shows (1957b), this new calling had repercussions in Gujarat itself, and was at the core of their gradual rise to a trading community. Through the agency of the Swaminarayana sect, the upper layers of the caste underwent a 'sanskritization' process.[9] In Baroda state, the alliance between the Kanbis and the state remained important for a very long time (Hardiman 1978).

Gradually, this development led to an extended hierarchy within the caste, to a point where 'Patidar' and 'Kanbi' came to represent poles of a continuum sometimes conceptualized as one, sometimes as two 'castes' (Pocock 1972). 'Patidarization' gradually spread downwards in the caste as well as outwards from Charottar, and has today reached Saurashtra.

KANBIS IN SAURASHTRA

Here, too, the Kanbis were favoured by the Gaekwar of Baroda (S. Gadhavi, personal information), who controlled what is now Amreli district, an area largely dominated by Kathis. Here, they were invited to settle largely in order to counter the influence of this somewhat unruly community. But Kanbis became popular with other states, too; thus the ruler of Gondal invited them to settle in village Chichod—near the Junagadh-Gondal boundary—where the rebellious Mahias represented a problem for the state administration. Bhavnagar, too, invited Kanbis to settle, in the new villages established in the saline Bhal area northeast of the capital.

It may be remembered that Amarji, listing the people of Junagadh state, speaks of the 'agriculturalists' as immigrants, by which he almost certainly means the Kanbis. In Saurashtra, the Kanbis established themselves as tenants or farm labourers. In the Bhal, as in Chichod, they got their own land from the start. Where Rajputs were dominant, they were largely given tenancies. With the Kathis, who preferred to till their own lands, they often started as farm labour (Tod 1971, 303ff; S. Gadhavi, personal information). Gradually, through the nineteenth and twentieth century, their status improved, and they are now locally dominant in many places. But they were never a martial caste in Saurashtra, and are not called Darbars. The Kanbi stereotype, here, is still marked by sturdiness and a willingness for hard work, with little of the aristocratic flavour of the Rajput nor the urban elegance of the Bania.

More than any other caste, they have taken advantage of the modern economy. Since 1952 land reforms have made many Kanbi tenants into owner-cultivators, and they have added to their position in the countryside a prominence as traders and industrialists. Thus the timber market in Bhavnagar is dominated by Kanbis; they control the light engineering industry of Rajkot; and among the flourishing small industries of other Saurashtrian towns, many are owned by Kanbis.

In 1973 the term 'Patidar' was seldom used in Saurashtra, except to denote Patidars from Charottar; by 1980 'Kanbi' was still the common term for the caste, while 'Patidar' was used for its industrialists and traders. By 1990-1, 'Patidar' had become common usage in town, though peasants of the caste were still mostly called 'Kanbis' in Saurashtra. The leading Patidars of Charottar give dowries—sometimes extremely large—at marriage, and this practice is fast gaining ground among urban Patidars of Saurashtra. In north Gujarat, marriage by brother-sister exchange was earlier the rule, but in Saurashtra I have not found any reference to it. The Kanbis of Praj still paid bridewealth in 1973 and in 1980, and this remained the common practice in towns also. These variations in marriage form indicate rank or 'standing' within the caste; Saurashtra Kanbis still, generally speaking, rank below those of the mainland, and are seen as less 'sanskritized'.[10]

Charottar Patidars and other leading groups within the caste today imitate the merchant castes in their efforts at 'sanskritization'. They have been successful to the extent that it is now reasonable to include the upper layers of the caste, even in Saurashtra, among the merchants. This 'merchantization' of their culture contrasts with earlier 'rajputization'. Initially, in their rise to higher status, it was the Darbars whom they imitated.[11] We have seen an example in the case of the palios of Praj, where Kanbis have followed Rajputs in raising memorials for heroes of their own caste. While clearly a case of imitation, this points to the continuity that exists, on the level of cultural and religious forms, between the two castes.

Such 'rajputization' is common in Saurashtra, where the Rajput or Kshatriya 'model' continued to dominate until independence. The contrast to the mainland of Gujarat, with its dominance by the 'merchant model', is marked.[12] In style of dress, manners, language, etc., the Kanbis of Praj and other Saurashtra villages are rather similar to Rajputs—as well as to other members of the 'thirteen castes'—but they do not carry the kuvadi, nor do they own or ride horses.

They still rank below Rajputs, though the difference was much clearer in the seventies than it is today. In areas dominated by Kathis, their claim to equality is strongly resisted by the latter caste (Gadhavi, n.d.), as it is by Rajputs elsewhere. In Junagadh district, which lacked a clear-cut dominant caste due to the prevalence of zamindari tenure, they had not, by 1980, reached equality with the Ahirs. In spite of numbers, they were never referred to as dominant. Typically, in a village I visited near Junagadh, the headman remained an Ahir in spite of the numerical preponderance of the Kanbis.

But these observations of rank must be seen as highly relative to time and place. Today, there is a strong rivalry, sometimes leading to violent conflict, between Kanbis and Rajputs, to the extent that the opposition between these two castes has become a major factor in the local and regional politics of Saurashtra. The opposition should be seen in the context of the 'backward castes movement', where castes who have till recently lost out in terms of education and urban employment now try to revindicate their position. The Rajputs, who have remained conservative in this respect, oppose the Patidars, who have gained more than other castes from modernity. The loss of Rajput land to Patidars during the land reforms of the fifties is an underlying factor here.

I have not been able to gain a clear picture of present party affiliations of the two castes. To some, the BJP[13] stood (in 1991-2) as the champion of the 'backward castes'. Several of my Rajput informants, and members of other castes among the 'thirteen', have been active in, and enthusiastic about, the party. Yet some of my best informants are of a different view; according to them, the BJP's best supporters are the rising Kanbis, while Rajputs tend to support Congress. This is true of part of the old Rajput elite, including some of the former ruling families. Thus the question of party affiliation is not simple, and demands a separate study.

Gangs of Rajput and Patidar youth currently fight each other, beat up members of the other caste and destroy property of its members.

The violent character of this rivalry indicates that caste dominance still depends on physical force at the local level, and has not been completely replaced by parliamentary politics. But the present opposition between Kanbis and Rajputs must be seen against a background of a high degree of cultural continuity, evident, above all, in the traditional religion of the two groups.

KANBI RELIGION

At the regular Sunday evening sessions in honour of Mataji (the goddess), held by a Kanbi of Praj at his small shop in the market, Rajputs were present and took an active part. In contrast the Banias and Brahmins of the village were as a rule missing on these occasions. Their absence was even more conspicuous as even a couple of Muslims were seen there—though not taking an active part in the singing. On these occasions, Rajputs and Kanbis, as well as some other groups, were united in their devotion to Mataji. Thus, while Rajputs may prefer to honour better-known goddesses such as Khodiyar, there is no clear dividing line between the worship of simple Matas by lower castes such as Kanbis, and the goddess worship of Darbars.

Another trait common to Darbars and Kheduts is the fact that they are all, at least traditionally, non-vegetarians. Even if today, most Praj Rajputs claim in certain contexts to be vegetarian, this is by no means the whole truth—or at least it was not so in 1973-4. Whether or not an individual claims to be vegetarian seems, among the Rajputs of Bhavnagar district, to be a matter of context, depending on whom he is speaking to and the impression he seeks to create.[14] An exception here is, of course, members of the Swaminarayana sect, who are now found both among Darbars and Kheduts. In these cases, vegetarianism is a product of recent 'sanskritization'.

And so, we may add, is the vegetarianism of the Goddess. Most goddesses of Saurashtra quite recently required and got animal sacrifices, and there are informants who imply that some of them once took human sacrifice also. The vegetarianism is in fact largely a post-independence phenomenon (Tambs-Lyche 1982).

Today, the Swaminarayana sect holds a preeminent position among the Patidars of central Gujarat, while it is strong among Kanbis in Saurashtra too. Indeed, both the sect and the caste are central to the political and cultural life of Gujarat state. And sectarian affiliation among Kanbis is nothing new. 'As a class', says Enthoven, 'Kanbis are very religious .... Unlike Banias and other high classes, the Kanbis belong to many sects. Bijmargis, Dadupanthis, Kabirpanthis, Madhavgarnis, Pranamis, Ramanandis, Shaivs, Swaminarayans, and Vallabhacharyas. A few are Jains' (1921, 141).

Enthoven's statement about Banias, here, is less relevant today; but Srinivas has written (1953) that caste and sect form a crisscrossing pattern in Gujarat, corroborating Enthoven's statements.

In Pocock's work (1973), recent sanskritization is seen as a shift to vegetarianism, and away from the use of liquor. Yet Enthoven described the caste as vegetarian and teetotaller, with the exception of those he calls Anjnas (Enthoven, op. cit.). There is no reason to doubt Pocock's view, which fits my own observations. Informants stressed non-vegetarianism and the use of alcohol when talking about 'the old days'.

Possibly Enthoven's informants wanted to show their caste to advantage. Several of the sects he mentions would, however, have insisted on vegetarianism, and we may conclude that sanskritization is nothing new to the Kanbis: the Swaminarayanas have not been alone in making such efforts. And, since vegetarianism and its concomitant practices are today, in the case of Kanbis, mostly associated with the Swaminarayanas, some of their following may have been gained at the cost of other Bhakti sects as well as from among the non-vegetarians.

But it may well be that goddess worship regained some lost ground during the first half of this century, which seems to have seen stagnation or even decay for the Swaminarayana sect (Williams 1984, 34-6; Tambs-Lyche 1992a, 622). Certainly, the rulers and Rajputs, supporters of the goddess, remained strong until the middle of this century. Since then, a new branch of Swaminarayanas, the Yogijipanth, has quickly gained ground (Tambs-Lyche, op. cit.; 627; Williams 1984, 47-51).

THE KOLIS; WHO ARE THEY?

The term Koli, which is the origin of the Anglo-Indian word 'coolie', is widely used in Saurashtra. Ostensibly, it designates a 'caste'. Yet, it remains 'a term of vague meaning covering a number of tribes of inferior status which have little in common beyond a position inferior to the Kanbi or cultivating caste' (Enthoven 1921, 243) .

Koli as a category includes an unknown number of communities. Some, like the Mahias[15] have succeeded in becoming Rajputs—and in the process, have been recognized by others as a community by themselves. As for the communities still known as Kolis, we know very little about them.

Thus, several informants assured me there were two kinds of Kolis in Saurashtra, the pure and the impure. These, they say, belong to at least two different castes, respectively above and below the pollution line. Yet, David Hardiman tells me he has never heard of such a division in south Gujarat, nor of untouchable Kolis anywhere. In Praj, the Kolis were all above the pollution line; maybe no untouchable Kolis exist.

We may note, equally, that some Saurashtra informants saw 'little difference' between 'pure' Kolis and Kanbis, who seem to live in the same general area of many Saurashtra villages without any distinct geographical dividing line between them. Such was the case in Praj. This confusion regarding Kolis is noted by Shah. 'Unfortunately, although the Kolis are an important element in Gujarat's population, their earlier ethnography is confusing, and there is hardly any modern systematic, anthropological, sociological or historical study, so that the confusion continues to persist' (in Shah and Desai 1988, 13).

While some of our ignorance—and that of our informants—may be ascribed to the customary lack of interest among superiors for the internal affairs of their inferiors, Kolis may also have preferred to give little information[16]—they were still regarded as a 'criminal class' (though not officially listed as a 'criminal caste') in Enthoven's time.

Also, most Kolis prefer to be called by other names, indicating that the category does not correspond to their own classifications. The Kolis I have met have been willing and happy to stress their belonging to a particular community within the Koli category. Thus, I suggest, there is no one 'Koli' community but a number of different groups, all preferring their own names. It is because we know them so badly that most modern writers prefer to treat the term 'Koli' as generic.

No other low-caste or untouchable community allows such ignorance to persist. Thus nobody would call a Vaghri—an untouchable community associated with the forest—by any other name. Nor could the Mochi—shoemaker—be confused with another caste. Such communities are quite distinct and seen as such. Thus there may be some reason beyond lack of knowledge for the absence of distinction among Kolis. Could it be that their communities, in spite of separate names, do not maintain the strict boundaries that we associate with 'caste'?

That there are significant rank differences—as well as considerable cultural diversity—among 'Kolis' is clear from Enthoven:

The highest families in the social sense prohibit widow remarriage in imitation of the Rajputs, and the same is true of the Khant and Baria Kolis of the North and of the Patelias or Patelia Kolis of the Panch Mahals and the Rewa Kantha. These high caste Kolis [*sic*!] have given brides to Rajputs, and, failing Rajput husbands, to Molesalams[17] or converted Rajputs. They never give their daughters to the lower Kolis such as Pagis, Kotwads and Patanwadias. There are several general terms in use among Kolis such as Dharala and Talabda, and while in some areas these terms have a definite significance, in others they have none, and even where there is a definite significance this will vary from district to district. In Kaira, where Kolis are most numerous, all except the Kolis proper or Patanwadias are known as Dharalas, a term which includes the Khant, Baria and Talabda Kolis, the latter being further subdivided into Vaghelas, Pagis, Kotwals and Barias. Thus a Baria Koli is totally distinct from a Talabda Baria and a Rajput clan name like Vaghela or Parmar may or may not give some indication of a Koli's marriage group. Over the border in Ahmedabad district, the term Dharala is never used, and the Koli aristocracy is represented by the Koli Patelia or Talabda, while the Thakarda or Pagi, holding a distinctly inferior position and proclaiming his baser blood in every line of his features, intermarries with the numerous lower class Dharalas of Kaira. To add to this confusion, in the Gujarat districts of Broach and Surat, Talabda denotes precisely the better class Koli; while Thakarda is the title assumed by the higher families among the Chunvalia Kolis of Viramgam, who are said to be the common Kolis of Cutch and to be found in Palanpur and in the Maha Kantha. (Enthoven 1921, 245-6)

The districts mentioned here are all on or towards the mainland; little information is given by Enthoven regarding the Kolis of Saurashtra. But here, too, I found considerable variation in the use of terms.

EXAMPLES FROM SAURASHTRA

In and around Dhrangadhra, local Kolis speak of two different communities, Chunvalia, pronounced Chunalia—clearly the group from Viramgam mentioned by Enthoven—and Tarabda, which may be the Talabda of Enthoven. Talapada (Tarabda), according to Shah, means 'indigenous' (Shah and Desai 1988, 13). He holds that most areas of Gujarat had two hypergamous Koli divisions; one considered indigenous, the other 'foreign' (op.cit. 6-7, 10, 14-15) The word *pardeshi* ('foreigner') is indeed sometimes used to describe the latter.

In Dhrangadhra the Chunvalias rank above the Tarabdas and would, they stress, never marry them. Chunvalias claim to be prevalent among the Kolis of this area, while the Tarabdas, they say, are more important farther west, around Halvad.

The Gazetteer of Jamnagar district, farther again to the west, includes the Chunvalia Kolis among the 'backward classes'. The name, it explains, comes from Chunval, an area of north Gujarat, where the same group is also found (cf. Enthoven, above). The name is said to be derived from *chumalis* or forty-four villages, perhaps indicating places originally controlled by them.[18] The gazetteer states that their 21 exogamous subdivisions marry only within the Chunvalia group. 'In the past', continues the Gazetteer, 'Chunvalia Kolis were a body of organised robbers. For years, they have settled as cultivators and labourers. They generally take vegetarian diet though some also take non-vegetarian food' (JMG, 119). They must, however, have formed a considerable proportion of the agricultural population of the old Dhrangadhra state.

The Chunvalias today use the term Thakor (another epithet, regionally, for Rajput)[19] while the Tarabda are called Patel (like the Kanbis). Both terms are presented as 'modern', in other words they are chosen to avoid the negative associations of 'Koli'. Nothing indicates, however, that the terms Chunvalia and Tarabda are of recent origin.

In village Kankavati—Shakti Mata's old village, they say—the Chunvalias are today effectively dominant, since the Jhala Rajput landlords left after 1952. This dominance is also possible since the Kanbis, who came later, have formed another, adjacent village rather than live under the Rajputs and among the Kolis. It seems that the Kanbis have in fact taken up new lands, to the north-west of those farmed in the original village of Kankavati. Thus, the Kanbis, whose village has some 1100-1200 inhabitants, have avoided living under Koli dominance—Kankavati is a large village, with a population of some 5000.

The Chunvalias of Kankavati know about the Kolis around Ghela Somnath, a temple in the centre of the peninsula. They also know that these Kolis, like themselves, are now locally dominant as their Darbars have disappeared from the area. They were Parmar Rajputs, a clan which had lost most of its political position in Saurashtra by British times. The Ghela Somnath area is typical of such enclaves where a group otherwise ousted from power could hold its own.

The Kankavati Kolis know that those at Ghela Somnath belong to a different community, but were unable to give the name of that group. Nor did I get that information when I asked Ghela Somnath Kolis directly; I also got no indication that the area has more than one Koli community. It is not strange that Kolis should have kept their land and position here. Ghela Somnath is a very out-of-the way place, and the lands must be quite poor. Clearly, though the Parmar Rajputs were able to maintain their position there, it was an area of retreat which invited little immigration. There seem to be no Kanbis there, for example.

In Praj, south of Bhavnagar, Kanbis and Kolis lived together in the same quarter of this Rajput-dominated village. People of other castes seemed to make little of the differences between them, though whenever rank was discussed, Kolis were always placed below Kanbis. This was in spite of the fact that the area had once been dominated by Kolis, and that, by all accounts, the Rajputs of the village were of Koli origin. I was never able to get a more specific name for the Koli group or groups here. This is also the case of the Kolis of Velavadar north of Bhavnagar, where they again seem close to the Kanbis.

In Chichod, between Gondal and Junagadh, however, the Mahia Rajputs who once were Kolis are clearly distinguished from Kanbis. The two groups have been traditionally opposed to each other in this village, where Mahias once were dominant. This opposition seems lacking in Velavadar, where both groups were invited to settle by the rulers of Bhavnagar state. In the latter case, then, the two castes share the same structural position; in Chichod they do not. In Praj, finally, the sector of Kolis that has become Rajputs seem to have retained no particular ties to the Koli peasants—leaving the latter in a position parallel to Kanbis. Whether the ex-Koli Darbars and the Koli Kheduts originally belonged to the same community, or whether they were separate from the start, is a question that cannot be answered at present.

KINSHIP AND RELIGION AMONG KOLIS

The lack of correspondence in community terms between adjacent areas indicates that the geographical range of social categories is more restricted among Kolis than among most other communities. In other words, to the extent the categories imply organizational entities, these seem to have limited geographical extension. This observation was also made by Enthoven, who stressed the lack of inter-village kin ties among Kolis. Thus, kinship organization is not based, in practice, on the exogamous lineage or clan.[20] Asked for their kuldevi, my Koli informants from Dhrangadhra answered Bahucharaji, then added: 'Strictly speaking she is our jati-devi—our caste goddess; we have no kuls (lineages).[21] Only the village, then, is strictly exogamous, as with

Kanbis. And the asymmetrical village alliances are strongly reminiscent of what Pocock (1972) found among the Kaira Patidars, where in some cases 'a regular cycle of villages has been found to exist, brides being given from village A to village B, from village B to village C, and so on' (Enthoven 1921, 246-7).

Such asymmetrical marriage patterns, in India, can only mean hypergamy. And, while Enthoven was able to distinguish endogamous groups (op.cit., 247-8), he also points out:

> The Kanbi or Patidar caste of North Gujarat are very short of women. Brokers therefore obtain Koli girls and palm them off on bachelor or widower Kanbis as of their own caste. The practice is so common that there is no real deception. The Kanbi marries the girl, and all goes well unless some one from spite makes the girl's origins public. Then the husband has to clear himself by prosecuting the brokers for cheating and convictions are often obtained. Competent observers say that of the wives of Patidars in Ahmedabad city quite a large proportion are really Kolis. The Intercaste Marriage Bill so much discussed in 1918-19 would, if passed into law, regularize the practice; and it is noteworthy that the introducer of the bill is himself a Patidar. (Enthoven 1921, 245ff)

This is the pattern that Pocock describes from Kaira—where Koli brides are brought to their Patidar husbands from Saurashtra (1957a; 1972). To him, this is a logical extension of the hypergamous marriages running through the Kanbi/Patidar caste. At the other end, Patidar girls are given to Anavil Brahmins (ibid., also Tambs-Lyche 1980, 42-3).

We have seen that Kanbis are not the only recipients of Koli wives; Enthoven mentions Rajputs and Muslim Rajputs. Thus, marriage of girls across the upper boundary of the 'Koli' community would seem to be even more common than Pocock has suggested from his study of Kanbi/ Patidars. Since Enthoven found similar hypergamous marriage circles among Kolis it seems that a continuous stream of marriage alliances run well down into the 'Koli' caste, or even through it. Thus Shah writes:

> . . . as we go down the hierarchy, we encounter more and more debates regarding the claim of particular lineages to being Rajput, so much so that we lose sight of any boundary and the Rajput division merges imperceptibly into some other division. In most parts of Gujarat it merged into the various second-order divisions of the Koli division and possibly also into the widespread tribe of Bhils. (Shah in Shah and Desai 1988, 12)

This is what Srinivas deduces from Shah's work, citing the Bhils as a parallel case to the Kolis (in Shah and Desai 1988; xi).

The Goddess of the Chunvalias of Kankavati is Meldi Mata. She is mainly a low-caste Goddess, as the brief description of her by Pocock (1973, 64) indicates. He regards her as the archetypal 'unclean' Goddess of Charottar, demanding animal sacrifice. The name is said to be derived from filth (*mel*). Bahucharaji, too, is a goddess of this type; she has become mildly famous for the eunuchs that serve in her temple.[22]

The elderly wife of a Chunvalia farmer—the chairman of the village panchayat of Kankavati—serves Meldi Mata as a medium during the Navaratri festival. Thus she is her oracle, an interesting case, since that role is usually reserved for men. The role is, in her case, not just seasonal. I saw her receiving clients for divination, taking a handful of grains and counting them. The answer to a particular question, as communicated by her from the Goddess herself, depends on whether the number of grains are equal or inequal.

In general, the mode of Goddess worship practised by Kolis is less sanskritized that that of most other castes. While it is undistinguishable from the Goddess worship at the lower end of the Kanbi-Patidar scale, it seems seldom to approach the vegetarian form practised by Patidars.

A COMMUNITY OF CRIMINALS?

The 'criminal record' of the Kolis informs us not only about their position, but of power relations in traditional Kathiawar—and in modern Saurashtra. This 'criminal record' is rich, and Kennedy includes a chapter on Kolis in his work on 'Criminal Classes' (1908). But the picture of Koli crime is changing with the times. Thus Enthoven wrote:

> The earliest records of Koli exploits are mainly the deeds of the coast dwellers of the Gulf of Cambay. In AD 1535 they pillaged the baggage and books of the emperor Humayun.[23] In 1705 they captured Baroda. Probably many of the pirates of the Gulf were Kolis. These gave much trouble to the English, who in 1734 and 1771 sent expeditions against them, and on the second occasion occupied their strongholds at Sultanpur and Tulaja.[24] (1921, 248)

Remembering that the founders of Rajput states were little more than robber chieftains to begin with, we must conclude that the Kolis, here, are behaving like a martial caste. At this time they still had their own fortresses, and were capable of taking a city like Baroda—which admittedly became more important later. The story of Chital, told above, indicates how transformation from robbery to rule could be effected. The cases Enthoven notes, then, are less suited to mark the Kolis as 'criminals' than to pinpoint the floating distinction, in this area, between those who rule and those who do not.

But by the beginning of the British period Kolis had lost most of their forts and territories. Much of Bhavnagar state—including Praj—were lands taken from Kolis during the eighteenth century. In the 1820s to 1840s, says Enthoven, they 'came into prominence' more than at any other period; but their 'crimes' then bear little relation to those of the sixteenth century. 'At that time the regions of North Gujarat were particularly unsettled. There was no strong central power; the authority of the Gaekwar in Mahi Kantha was nominal only, and the petty Rajput and Koli chieftains were constantly fighting. The early writers of the 19th century described the Kolis as "bloody and untameable plunderers, uncivilized and filthy"' (1921, 248).

It seems that by then the Kolis were a dispossessed and disenchanted community. His account of the unsettled state of the country at that time fits other descriptions, such as those that chronicle the life of Swami Narayana.[25] Enthoven goes on to cite cases from 1812, 1819, and 1825, underlining the plundering activities of the Kolis (1921, 248-9). Among the sources Enthoven used was Bishop Heber's account, interesting here for the writer's belief in a close kinship between Kolis and Bhils.[26] Heber goes on to relate their relationship to Rajputs:

> They themselves pretend to be descended from the Rajputs, but this is a claim continually made by wild and warlike tribes all over India, and that the coolies themselves do not believe their claim, is apparent from the fact that they neither wear the silver badge, nor the red turban. Be that as it may, they are acknowledged by the Hindus as their kindred which the Bhils never are; and though their claim of being children of the sun is not allowed by the Rajputs who live among them, there have been instances in which intermarriages have taken place between Mahrattas of high rank and the families of some of their most powerful chieftains. (Heber 1828, 25ff, quoted by Enthoven 1921, 249)

How should we interpret this statement? If Kolis were claiming Rajput status, they should have adopted some of the outward signs too, as some Koli groups have, indeed, done. That does not seem to be the case here. Rather, I suggest, they were claiming equality with Rajputs for the exercise of power—as we have seen the Kathis doing above.

While intermarriage with Maratha chiefs represents an instance from the Konkan or the Maratha highlands, rather than from our area, the political position of Koli chiefs there appears to have overridden caste difference in the question of marriage. We have noted that Kolis in north Gujarat married their daughters to Rajputs. In short, we have here a situation reminiscent of the earlier medieval period, before marriage hierarchy among the Rajput aristocracy assumed its later, fixed form.

Heber describes the relationship between the Koli as a farmer and his criminal activities:

> Their ostensible, and, indeed, their chief employment is agriculture, and they are said to be industrious farmers and labourers, and, while kindly treated, to pay their rent to Government as well, at least, as their Rajput neighbours. They live, however, under their own Thakoors, whose authority alone they willingly acknowledge, and pay little respect to the laws, unless it suits their interests, or they are constrained by the presence of an armed force. In other respects they are one of the most turbulent and predatory tribes in India, and, with the Bhils, make our tenure of Gujarat more disturbed, and the maintenance of our authority more expensive there, than in any other district of the Eastern empire.... (Heber 1828, 25ff; cited by Enthoven 1921, 249)

Thus the 'turbulent and predatory' Kolis could be tamed by the simple expedient of being 'kindly treated'. In other words, they are freedom-loving people who do not tolerate subjugation.

Heber also notes, however, that they still had, and were obedient to, their own chiefs. Whether these were simple caste headmen or territorial chiefs is not clear, but in some areas, such as around the temple of Bahucharaji on the boundary between Saurashtra and the mainland, Koli chiefs still exercised territorial powers in the pre-1947 period. South of Bhavnagar state, Koli chiefs were still independent—though described as 'pirates'[27]—in the eighteenth century.

Heber relates the trouble taken to pacify the country. Force is necessary, and used by the British, since the gentry is 'addicted to acts of violence and bloodshed'.[28] It is not clear whether the Kolis are included among the gentry or excluded from it. But he stresses that they are no more cruel than other brigands.[29] Certainly, their violence forms part of the general pattern. The acts of the Kolis cannot be judged singly: they form part of an overall struggle—we may assume for power—where the Kolis are but one of the parties playing for gains.[30]

To Heber's account we may add that of Forbes. They, he says

> were independent in spirit, and although professed robbers, were said to be remarkably faithful when trusted, and were certainly never sanguinary. They were averse to regular industry, exceedingly addicted to drunkenness, and very quarrelsome when intoxicated. Their delight was plunder, and nothing was so welcome to them as a general disturbance in the country. The numbers of the Kolees would have rendered them formidable had they been capable of union, but though they had a strong fellow-feeling for each other, they never regarded themselves as a nation, nor ever made common cause against an external enemy. (1878, 442)

We now begin to get a picture of Koli 'criminality'. In the sixteenth century, when we first hear of them, they seem little different from other martial communities beyond the effective control of the Mughal empire. Their subsequent history recalls the banditry of peasant communities analysed by Hobsbawm (1969). So does the whole institution of *baharvatiya,* outlawry, in traditional Kathiawar (Spodek 1976, 8). At Heber's time Koli crime still retains its quality of banditry:

> In their marauding expeditions, they often use great secrecy, collecting in the night at the will of some popular chieftain, communicating generally by the circulation of a certain token, known only to those concerned, like the fiery cross of the Scottish Highlanders. They frequently leave their families in complete ignorance as to where they are going; and the only way in which, should one of their number fall in battle, the survivors communicate his loss to his widow or parents, is by throwing before his door some sprigs of the peepul, plucked and disposed in a particular form. (Heber 1828, 25ff; quoted by Enthoven 1921, 250)

Forbes, fifty years later, similarly stresses the aptitude of Kolis for 'night attacks, surprises and ambuscades. Their arms and habits rendered them unfit to stand in the open field....' (1878, 442). There is no mention of the special tokens mentioned by Heber. And in Kennedy's account from 1908, we are dealing with very ordinary crime. Kolis 'do not as a rule travel far from their villages in pursuit of crime', and he continues:

> They have no fixed season for criminal expeditions, nor do they embark on regular tours. They bide their time so to say, sallying forth when a favourable opportunity offers, returning home after their object has been accomplished. Away from their villages, unless temporarily settled in towns, they are not encumbered by families and either put up with friends, in out-of-the-way dharamsalas or temples or in the open some distance from villages under trees, passing themselves off as wayfarers. (Kennedy 1908, 98)

Kennedy, a police officer, specifies their kind of crime:

> Though brought to their bearings under British rule their hereditary love of plunder is by no means extinct. At present they are, as a class, addicted to highway and house dacoity and robbery, housebreaking and thefts, cattle lifting, thefts of standing crops and field produce, mischief by fire, thefts from running goods trains ... and acts of violence and bloodshed, in order to take revenge or terrorize (Kennedy 1908, 102).

If we add the use of blackmail 'for the restoration of lifted cattle', said to be prevalent in Kathiawar, and theft 'after administering some stupefying drug' (ibid.), it is clear that most crime attributed to Kolis by 1908 was committed in the interest of material gain.

LANDLORD AND PEASANT: THE FIELD OF LAND, POWER AND DOMINANCE

The position of the 'criminal' Kolis at the turn of the twentieth century is clearly different from their raids and their piracy of the sixteenth, when they were acting rather like other martial communities. Later, they were like other *baharvatiyos* or outlaws, recently chased from their land. A lot of land held by Kolis was lost in the eighteenth century.

The memory of these times is still present when Heber writes, and a lore of heroic banditry persists. Yet when he specifies, we are talking of a much simpler level of crime. Finally, with Kennedy and the early twentieth century, their main crime is theft and robbery in various forms.

Such a mode of action clearly has no need for what Sahlins calls the 'massing effect' of the segmentary lineage system. Thus Forbes saw no sign of the social cohesion that must have been present at an earlier period. As we have seen, the scant indications we have of their kinship system—from Enthoven onwards—points in a very different direction; an asymmetrical marriage alliance pattern reminiscent of the Patidars.

We may visualize, then, the history of the area as characterized by a continual struggle for land. On this scene of war and conquest, outlawry and criminality, there are different actors. Some, well organized and solidary within the group, succeed in becoming dominant, holding the land. Others are not so lucky, and have to go for the lesser spoils of movable property, by this action making dominance difficult or even impossible.

As the tactics of a regular army and of guerilla insurgents are different, so the tactics of the dispossessed Kolis differ from those of the successful Rajputs. The latter gain solidarity from their descent line, forming a segmentary lineage system. If we are to believe Sahlins (1961) and Fox (1971) this form of organization accounts, partly at least, for their success.

It is certainly too simplistic to state that the segmentary lineage system is the reason for Rajput dominance, and the lack of it why Kanbis and Kolis become peasants. Nor can we assume the opposite, viz., that rulers—more or less automatically—develop a kinship organization leading to mass mobilization, while the ruled do not. If so, Kathis should have developed such a system long ago. And yet, we cannot discount a certain adaptive interrelation between political position and kinship organization. We have seen that the Rajput lineage is itself a result of gradual development. It may not be for prestige alone that clan organization has been a feature of the 'rajputization' process of several groups.

The segmentary lineage is not the only form of kinship lending itself to a political purpose. As Hardiman has shown, the marriage circles of Patidars were also made to serve a political purpose during the independence struggle in Gujarat (1989).

Kolis are said to be law-abiding when 'well treated'; they then settle down, and make good tax-payers. In short, they become very like Kanbis. On the other hand, Rajputs become outlaws when robbed of their land. They, too, are threatened, almost by definition, by land-hungry rivals. The Kolis were among these rivals, but by early British times they had lost out. The Kathis were saved, just in time, from the final destruction of their power by the arrival of the British. Keeping in mind the myth Kathis quote in support of their right to cattle-lifting, we conclude that 'robbery' on a petty scale and 'conquest' on a large scale are but ends of the same continuum. They differ in scale, rather than in moral or martial content. There is continuity, then, between the conqueror and the conquered, between landlord and peasant, a continuity which underlies the shared fundamental values of Darbar and Khedut.

But what about the honest, hard-working, law-abiding Kanbis? In our period, they were the in-betweens; to get their share of the crops, they preferred to be loyal subjects protected by their lords. As such, they had no need to be martial or criminal. But was it always, or will it remain, so? In north Gujarat, they gained dominance, as they did in Charottar when supported by the Marathas against their Rajput lords.

Having gained from the reforms of the fifties of this century, they are now the ascendant caste in Saurashtra's villages, and their quest for dominance involves violent conflict with the Rajputs.

In short, we must establish, for the whole field concerning land, power and dominance, a framework which transcends the category of caste. It was natural for the British to imply an intrinsic relationship between the categories of people they tried to rule, and the qualities of each group. Essentialism, as we now call it, was the order of the day. But in view of the continuity in culture, rank and power position, it becomes necessary to separate the position each 'caste' occupies from the group itself. Elements of a group's 'culture' may be acquired or lost; and one central factor in this process must surely be the position, within the larger system, that the group has come to occupy. With this in mind, let me turn to the question of caste among Kheduts.

CASTE AMONG KHEDUTS

It is to Pocock we owe the observation that castes may be virtually open-ended categories. His case was the Patidars; the Kolis now seem to be a similar, large category whose boundaries are uncertain. We might consider, as a parallel case, the several communities, stretching across northern India, which form the large Ahir-Gujar category.

It should now be clear that the dividing line between 'Kanbi' and 'Koli' is as fuzzy as that that between 'Koli' and 'Rajput'—the latter line having been crossed several times in recent history by the 'rajputization' of Koli groups. Equally, the dividing line between the different Koli 'communities' is rather blurred. It would seem that these dividing lines between 'castes' of Kheduts follow the logic of 'exclusion' and 'inclusion' pointed out by Pocock (1957b); in other words, the divisions are created by the exclusion of inferiors but blurred by the latters' attempts at inclusion. This would explain what emerges from Enthoven's discussion; that the groups we can most readily identify are those of relatively high status. Thus while some chiefs married across caste lines, the 'real' Rajputs of the 'Rajput great tradition' (Kolff 1990) were able to insist on exclusiveness.[31]

While this interpretation disturbs any neat, general definition of 'caste', it follows the logic of hierarchically structured competition. The 'hierarchizing transactions' of Marriott (1976, 1989) may, indeed, be seen as a generalized form of the processes Pocock termed 'exclusion' and 'inclusion'. Such a logic would produce well defined, exclusive groups at the top of the system, where the stakes are high, but blur the distinctions in the middle, where differences matter less and are harder to maintain.

What is indicated here is the importance of common 'property', of 'estate' in Radcliffe-Brown's sense (1952, 34-5) for the cementing of a community into the corporation usually meant by the term 'caste' (cf. Sinha 1967). This, incidentally, would also explain why castes of craftsmen and other specialists do not merge with the peasant groups. At the bottom, of course, specifically stigmatized groups would be well demarcated and excluded from above. Thus, distinct low-caste communities remain separated from the Kolis, either by occupation (Mochis) or by a quite separate ethnic identity, assumed or ascribed (Vaghris).

Such a logic cannot explain all distinctions within the 'caste system' of Saurashtra, nor elsewhere. The Kathis, we have seen, remain distinct from Rajputs in spite of—or perhaps because of—claiming near-equal status with them; they differ here from the Kolis who have undertaken 'Rajputization'. So do the Mers. Still, the continuity and lack of distinction among the Koli/Kanbi categories indicates a place for caste among peasants different from that among members of higher or lower castes. Kheduts, then, do not make strong caste distinctions because their separate estates, unlike those of dominant, landowning castes, of specialists guarding an occupational monopoly, or of merchants monopolizing a particular trade or credit network, are not well demarcated one against the other. The demarcation of their main resource, land, is made not by them but by the Darbars. We may quote Enthoven again when he says the Kolis have become '... clearly a very mixed race, with too little pride in their descent to trace distant relationships or form large and distinct marriage groups' (1921, 248).

In other words, Kolis, and by implication other peasant castes, have little use for the kind of exclusiveness that distinguishes any form of 'aristocracy' from the commoners. Thus the presence of an 'estate' of importance—in Radcliffe-Browns terms—is the crucial element in constituting an 'estate'—in the Weberian sense. The Kheduts cannot be a Weberian 'estate' in the same sense as the Darbars.

ESTATE AND CASTE: DARBARS AND KHEDUTS

The distinction between Darbar and Khedut seems simple: those are landlords who are capable of holding the land. Those who live at the mercy of such power-holders are peasants. The transformation from one to the other is essentially a matter of power, sometimes helped by conflicts between rulers—as was the case with the Kaira Patidars, whose gain was due to the victory of the Marathas over the Mughals.

Sometimes castes on the rise are helped by a 'power vacuum'—as at Fox's first stage. Examples here are the Jadejas at the time of the fall of Ghumli, the Jhalas on the boundaries of old Gujarat, and the Mahias taking possession of their empty village between Gondal and Junagadh.[32] Sometimes too, peasants have risen to landlords through a soldiering career, individually or as a community—a process which forms the essence of Kolff's argument (1990).

But once such ascendancy is gained, the problem of transmission of status from one generation to the next implies a preoccupation with descent. Thus the significant breaks in Rajput lineages are identified with the conquerors of new territory, who thereby form a new branch of the line. Conquest, or ascent to present status, becomes the point from which present exclusiveness is legitimated.

Common descent from such an ancestor becomes a shared value, an 'estate' in Radcliffe-Brown's sense, and possession of such shared value must influence the way in which kinship is seen. Thus it is only logical that Rajputs and other Darbars should calculate kinship differently, and ascribe a different value to it, than what is the case among Kheduts.

Similarly, the kuldevi becomes first and foremost a Darbar phenomenon; it was she who aided the lineage founder in his enterprise, and so she becomes, for subsequent generations, synonymous with his success and with the continuing privilege of the group. Kuldevis, therefore, must as such be exclusive to the group; for the goddesses of Kolis, such exclusivity is not predicated. The Goddess becomes for the different Koli communities their jatidevi rather than their kuldevi.

But what about caste with regard to the distinction between Darbars and Kheduts? The Kanbis of Kaira, on becoming the dominant caste of the area, imitated Rajput custom (Shah and Shroff 1958); they became like Rajputs, but they did not become Rajputs. In parts of North Gujarat, the Kanbi/Patidar caste is dominant—but, as Pocock shows, while the ties to poorer caste members have been stretched, they have not been broken (Pocock 1972). The caste straddles the socio-economic boundary between landowners and peasants, as indeed it does for Kathis and Rajputs, even if these latter groups are recognized as Darbars.

Several Koli groups have 'become' Rajputs; the Mahias kept this 'title' even after losing dominance to Kanbis. They are 'Darbars' in name but not in fact, as many Kathis and Rajputs are. In short, as Beteille points out (1965), caste is not class; the two are mediated by status, which has an important place in the identities known as 'caste'.

THE FIELD OF AGRICULTURAL PRODUCTION

What binds the Darbar and Khedut, the conqueror and the conquered, together, is their interest in the produce of a common resource, land. Peasants stand for production, but in traditional society this activitiy must be protected by force, and this is the task of the typical Darbar community. In claiming their share of the produce, the Darbars have interests both in common with, and divergent from, the Kheduts. The relationship is basically transactional; the Darbars are converting their political control into agricultural produce through their dominance over the Kheduts, who, on their part, secure protection of their conversion of labour into a share of the same produce. This basic transaction, established through power and dominance, forms the basis for the field of agricultural production.

This field, then, constitutes a relationship between two interest groups of different status, two 'classes' in the Weberian sense. But as we have seen, the relationship does not lead to a clear cultural opposition between Darbar and Khedut. In fact, the institution of *ter tansali*—the regional form of 'allied castes' in Mayer's terms (1960)—serves to negate any such difference. Instead, they both oppose a third party, the Bania, who progressively, in course of time, comes to take care of the agricultural produce of both. It is this relationship which sets the field of agricultural production apart from that of power and dominance, making for village solidarity in spite of the inherent class difference. Thus the early stage of Rajputdom and the small to medium scale does not allow for the formation of a separate peasant 'estate' in Saurashtra. And when the opposition between state and peasant becomes clear at the later period or larger-scale level, the reduction of Darbar-caste agriculturalists to a peasant class position still serves to veil any such clear-cut cultural distinction between landowner and peasant, Khedut and Darbar. Only when rajputization yields to merchantization, when the political order of which the Darbar is the living representative crumbles away, can a 'peasant' culture and estate rise in its own right. And yet, as we shall see, rural solidarity persists well into the twentieth century.

To these basic relationships we may add others, which in their turn link the Darbar-Khedut node to other social groups. Thus, for agricultural production, a number of specialized services are necessary, linking craftsmen and other specialists to the village community. Finally, an exchange of agricultural and pastoral produce—where the village receives manure and milk products—constitute what may be seen as a 'symbiotic'[33] link to the pastoral communities.

NOTES

1. There is vast literature on this theme; for a recent overview, see Inden (1990, 131-61).
2. In a sequence to this book, I shall deal with different types of local settlement in Saurashtra, as the community frames local interaction.
3. Gopal's argument here is simple: in dealing with cities, we must imply some redistribution of agricultural produce from village to town. The degree of redistribution may differ, as also the medium of transaction. But markets where townspeople could acquire food must have been a feature of society, in Saurashtra, as elsewhere in India, from early days.
4. The merchant is the prime subject of robbery, while the robbers, as we shall see, are often peasants. The opposition comes out clearly in the immediate pre-independence period.
5. For a recent critique of the literature on 'jajmani systems', see Fuller (1989).
6. We shall return to this point later, particularly as regards the Swaminarayana sect.
7. See, for example, our later treatment of the villages of Chichod and Velavadar (p. 132).
8. The theme has indeed been extensively treated. See Shah (1964), Shah and Shroff (1958), H.G. Patel (1961, 1966a, 1966b, 1973), Hardiman (1981) and Tambs-Lyche (1980a and b).
9. Again, there is abundant literature, e.g. Shah and Shroff (1958), Pocock (1973), Williams (1984) and Tambs-Lyche (1980 a and b, 1992a).
10. For hypergamy, variation in marriage forms, and 'standing' within the caste, see Pocock (1955 and 1972). For marriage by exchange in North Gujarat, see H.G. Patel (1961 and 1966b). My observations here have been greatly enriched by discussions with H.G. Patel over a number of years.
11. See Shah and Shroff (1958), Pocock (1972 and 1973) and Tambs-Lyche (1980a and b, 1982a).
12. See, e.g. Munshi (1954), Toothi (1935) and Tambs-Lyche (1980a and b, 1982a).
13. The Bharatiya Janata Party, often characterized as 'fundamentalist'. It is certainly Hindu, traditionalist, and nationalist, and sometimes strongly anti-Muslim. But its social and ideological base differs from one region to another. In Saurashtra, it seems to get much of its support from reaction against the merchant dominance of Congress rule in the first 35 years of independence. Thus it is related to a revival of Rajput and Kathiawadi tradition as against Bania and

mainland influence. At the same time, it seems to receive support from the reformed wing (the Yogijipanth) of the Swaminarayana sect, which otherwise represents modernity. This double attachment—the first supported by Rajputs and their allies, the second by Kanbi/Patidars—makes it difficult to characterize the role of the party accurately, and may well reflect a possible division within the regional branch of the party.

14. This observation may be compared with that of Berreman (1962) from the lower Himalayan region.
15. We shall return to the Mahias in Ch. XI. We may note, here, that Forbes, writing of the Koli chiefs of Chunwal, the district surrounding Bahucharaji's temple, refers to them once as 'Kolee chiefs' (1878; 429) and, in a note on the same page, as 'Rajpoot chiefs, heading tribes of aboriginal descent'. In the latter context, he implies that the chiefs of the Chunwal Kolis were 'foreigners'.
16. Enthoven comments: 'Gujarat Kolis present numerous difficulties in classification, mainly owing to the varying nomenclature employed in different areas and the extreme vagueness of our Koli informants' (1921, 245).
17. The Molesalams, also called Molesalam Garasias or Behlims, are a community of Muslim Rajputs in north Gujarat. In spite of the conversion, they have retained many Rajput customs, but have generally been excluded from marrying other Rajputs (see e.g. Enthoven 1921; Misra 1964, 14, 81-2; 153,163). Misra points to considerable islamization of this community since Enthoven wrote, a trend that is likely to have continued since. This might, of course, have put an end to the practice of taking Koli wives.
18. Forbes gives the same etymology for the name 'Choonwal', the district surrounding the temple of Bahucharaji, just across from Dhrangadhra on the mainland (1878; 429).
19. The Koli chiefs of Chunwal were in fact known as 'Thakurras' or Thakors, according to Forbes. These chiefs are reported to have sacrificed thirteen buffalo calves annually at Navratri—thus following established Rajput custom—and there was a myth that they were in fact descended from a branch of the Solanki royal family of Gujarat (1878, 429).
20. 'Exogamous groups have been reported from Palanpur and the Mahi Kantha, but it is very doubtful whether marriages are regulated in practice by a consideration of these clan or family names, and careful inquiry has disclosed that the important group with almost all Kolis of the present day is the village' (Enthoven 1921, 246).
21. Bahucharaji does, however, seem to have been the kuldevi of the Koli chiefs of Chunwal. Forbes tells a story of this relationship which recalls several elements of other, such stories : The Koli chief Kanji had been slighted by the headman of village Detroj. 'At this time a Charun came to Kanjee's lodging, and when he had sung a song, he begged ... for a silk scarf. This Kanjee had it not in his power to give ... (he) resolved with himself that he would go and sacrfice his life before the Mata at Detroj (Bahucharaji).... In the night the Mata appeared to him in a dream....' The goddess announces that he will find a buffalo calf outside the village, which must be sacrificed to her. Then he must plunder the Patel's house; she also gives him a silk scarf for the Charan. Kanji finally attacks Detroj and kills the Patel, but then has to contend with the Mughal forces. Finally Kanji is reconciled with the Mughal's representative, and 'it is even said that the padshah

conferred upon him royal insignia, a drum, bearers of silver rods, and a state umbrella' (1878, 431-2).

22. Not much is known about them. A brief account of Bahucharaji's story is found in Forbes (1878, 426-9), while Westphal-Hellbosch (1976, 58-61) adds an account of the role of eunuchs in Bharwad marriage ritual. H.G. Patel has interviewed eunuchs and indicates that, in spite of the propagated and common belief that they are born as eunuchs, many have in fact been castrated (1983, 1988).
23. This story comes from the Mirat-i-Ahmadi. We may note, additionally, that when Muhammad Latif Khan decided, in 1545, to 'resume' the lands held by Hindu chiefs under Gujarat, these included Koli chiefs (Forbes 1878, 296-7).
24. Tulaja is Talaja; see the account of the growth of Bhavnagar state (ch. III).
25. See Parekh (1936), Dave (1967) and Williams (1984).
26. A belief shared by Wilson, whom Enthoven also quotes (1921, 243-4).
27. See, e.g., the first quote from Enthoven on p. 135 above (1921, 248).
28. The full quote goes: 'Yet in no country are the roads so insecure—and in none are forays and plundering of every kind more frequent; or a greater proportion of, what would be called in Europe, the gentry and landed proprietors addicted to acts of violence and bloodshed' (Heber 1846; cited by Enthoven, 1921, 250).
29. Ibid.
30. Ray (1992), who has investigated closely the unrest in the hinterland of the port of Cambay in the eighteenth century, clearly sees the Kolis as but one of the parties to the power game. In his article, their activities go a long way towards exonerating the Mahrattas from the blame of creating unrest in the area, but they are not seen as more 'criminal' than other contenders for power.
31. Even this is, of course, not true, since they married their daughters to Muslims.
32. See chapter XI.
33. See Barth 1956 and 1964b, as well as chapter VI in this volume.

CHAPTER VI

The Maldharis
The Pastoralists of Saurashtra

PASTORALISTS IN THE INDIAN SETTING

In agricultural India, several pockets of pastoralists survive. In the dry western regions, they have been important ecologically, economically and culturally. In Saurashtra, the herdsmen are seen as representing traditional culture and certain aspects of traditional religion. Krishna was one of them; but they themselves are prominent worshippers of the goddess in her many forms. The bardic Charan caste, which became so central to the Rajput state, was originally a pastoral community.

We shall mainly see these communities as a part of the regional society, but some general remarks on Indian pastoralism may be useful.[1] Sopher has studied the distribution of pastoral castes to understand their role in the general adaptational pattern of South Asia (1975). The pastoral castes do not form an extraordinary proportion of Saurashtra's population, compared to other areas of north India. Nor is the number of cows, sheep and goats exceptional. Both are higher, however, in the north of the peninsula than in the south (op. cit., 187-91). In Junagadh district, there are relatively more pastoral caste members than pastoralists by occupation. This may be due to the agricultural Ahirs being seen as a 'pastoral caste' (op. cit., 202). There has been a decline in the number of pastoralists relative to the total population.

Such specialist castes would, says Sopher, 'be generated where the Indian cultural ecology of caste society and an intense livestock-human symbiosis was fully developed' (op. cit., 205). This may explain why the proportion of pastoral castes in the plains of mainland Gujarat are higher than is the case in Saurashtra and Rajasthan. The symbiotic relationship between pastoralists and the settled population, alluded to here, is described by Pocock (1972) for the mainland, and recalls the analysis by Barth of similar patterns of north-east Baluchistan (1964). In Baluchistan, however, the clear-cut division between dry grazing land and irrigated agricultural areas differ from the close admixture of grazing grounds and agricultural lands in Saurashtra. It is this latter type of situation that Sopher is dealing with. As he notes, the Gangetic plain is lacking in grazing land due to intensive agriculture, but 'it was not always so' (Sopher, op.cit., 205).

He assumes that conditions were better for pastoralists in northern India at an earlier date, which might explain the mythical migrations of such castes southwards and westwards, reported by earlier writers. But Sopher holds that the distribution of pastoral castes does not indicate immigration from 'the drier lands to the west' as earlier writers usually believed. Neither does he find evidence of nomads shifting to a sedentary adaptation, another early theory (ibid.).

CASTE AND THE PASTORAL ADAPTATION

Another point made by Sopher is that the large communities, 'jati-clusters', characteristic of the nomadic castes, is due to 'the wider radius of their operations and contacts compared to that of most village folk'. He refers here to the clusters of Gujar and Ahir/Goala, in the western and eastern parts of northern India respectively (op. cit., 207). Indeed, this community may be even larger. Gujar and Ahir of Rajasthan draw no line between the two categories, while the Goalas I met in Birbhum, Bengal, claimed to be Ahirs. Yet Indian pastoralists include much smaller communities, such as Jat, Bharwad and Rabari, not to speak of the ubiquitous Charan—we shall deal with the latter three below. Sopher's view of the pastoral castes as an occupational specialization, followed by a tendency for pastoralists of different origin to merge into a single community, is perhaps less solidly based when viewed at a lower level of scale.

In terms of the caste system, the position of the pastoralists is ambiguous. British writers wondered whether they were 'castes' or 'tribes'; in a sense, they are both inside and outside the caste system. In Saurashtra, they are known as Maldharis, 'milkmen', and regarded with the mixture of suspicion and exotic appreciation that Europeans reserve for Gypsies.[2] Some of this ambivalence stems from the variation in pastoral adaptations. Some are long-distance nomads, travelling as far as a thousand kilometres. Migrating with flocks of a hundred animals or more, several families together, they stay out of villages.

During the dry season they graze their animals on the stubble of the barren fields: in summer they retire into desert or semi-desert areas. They specialize in camels or bovines, in both cases keeping a few camels for transporting their tents and other gear.

But there are also families of village herdsmen, settled for generations, herding the animals of other castes along with their own, and forming part of the local caste system. They herd sheep, goats or bovines. Only occasionally do they specialize in camels, raising the animals for sale. There is a particular caste, the Raval, who deal in transport by camel-carts, exploiting a niche between the truckers and the locally important oxcart.

Then there are semi-nomads, living in a village of farmers or in their own hamlets, but leaving during the wet season to find grazing elsewhere. Like the long-distance nomads, they enter into a variety of contractual agreements with farmers as to grazing and manure. Some shepherds, in fact, travel over long distances. But unlike the other long-distance travellers, they wander in small groups, often a couple of brothers or a father and a son, with smaller flocks. They are mostly sheep- and goatherds, though some keep cows.

In certain areas, hamlets of pastoralists cover pockets where no farmers live. Here we find the most traditional of all pastoral groups, who may well be regarded as 'tribal'; their only contact with other sectors of the population is when they visit villages to sell ghee and other durable milk products.[3]

Some of the pastoralist castes of Saurashtra have taken to agriculture. Most prominent here are the Ahirs, who form the main farming caste of much of the former Junagadh state. They, in effect, have become an agricultural caste in Saurashtra, though still identified with their original occupation. In their own hamlets, even Rabaris may have some land, and there are individual Maldharis, of all the castes, who have bought land, often in addition to their flocks.

Finally, there are urban Maldharis, living on the outskirts of the towns. They subsist by selling milk to townsmen, feeding their animals from grazing on unoccupied land (including parks and streets) as well as fodder bought in the market. This adaptation has become more important during the last generations. I describe such a household—of Bharwads—later; Salzman (1989) also gives some examples.

Salzman presents a case—from Surat—of Bharwads forming a concentrated, urban community and selling to the dairies. The Bharwads of Surat district belong to the same subgroup as those of

Bhavnagar district, and intermarry with them. Salzman's informants came originally from Dhandhuka taluka, in Saurashtra. Some Maldharis have—lately—become businessmen, buying milk on the outskirts of town and selling it in their own milkyshops.[4] Salzman stresses the capacity of Maldharis for adaptive innovation (1989, 44).

The variation in adaptation, then, allows both for tradition and modernity. The range varies, however, according to caste. And while the long-distance camel-herders occupy pride of place in the hierarchy as viewed by the pastoralists themselves—a view which seems also to have been traditional—modern sedentary people view these groups as less civilized than the urban or village dwellers to whom they are more accustomed. These, however, represented the bottom of the pastoral hierarchy in traditional terms. To the ambiguity inherent in the traditional relationship between settled and nomadic groups, then, are added the implications of differential responses to modernization.

Whenever I asked for the rank of pastoralists in the hierarchy, informants agreed in placing them in the middle. Nobody claimed for them equality with Rajputs; equally there were no hints at untouchability. In general, they are the equals of 'pure' peasants and craftsmen, and are always included among the *ter tansali*.[5]

CASTES OF PASTORALISTS

The chief pastoral castes of Saurashtra are the Rabari, Bharwad and Charan. These three castes have been the subject of two recent monographs by Westphal-Hellbosch, rather in the old German ethnographic tradition (1974, 1976). For the general history of pastoralism in the region, her book on the Muslim Jats is also relevant (1968).

The ethos of all these groups is rather similar. Their women are said to enjoy a relatively high degree of freedom and to hold considerable power in the family. The various castes are all regarded as unafraid, self-sufficient and proud. The jokingly independent Krishna is to an extent expressive of the ethos of these groups.

In Rajasthan, as well as in south Gujarat, we have to add another caste, variously known as Ahir or Gujar, traditionally regarded as Krishna's own people. No modern work on them is available, and we must turn to Enthoven (1920) for background information. Both the Ahir/Gujar and the Charan have settled, in various regions, as agriculturalists. Thus in Saurashtra, the Ahir are today agriculturalists, important in the area of the former Junagadh state. Charans dominate several villages of western Rajasthan, but in Saurashtra they are generally scattered, though in two pockets they are still concentrated as pastoralists. This is around the Nal, a lake on the mainland boundary of Saurashtra, and in the Gir forest.

In Kutch, even some Rabaris have become farmers, and wherever pastoralists have fixed hamlets or villages, they may cultivate some land in addition to their main occupation.[6]

I shall describe the Charans separately, for their particular sacred position is at the centre of the cultural and political traditions of Saurashtra and Rajasthan. But their status lends prestige and a degree of sacredness to the pastoral adaptation more generally.

THE AHIRS

The Ahir/Gujar group is the largest pastoral community in India, and thus difficult to describe briefly. Members of the caste have, sometimes for centuries, been settled as agriculturalists. Their status varies according to adaptation and region, but typically, they herd cows rather than sheep or goats, and thus occupied a position between Rabaris and Bharwads in the traditional hierarchy of Saurashtra's pastoralists.

Ahirs are found practically all over Saurashtra. It is in the south and southwest, however, mainly within the boundaries of the former Junagadh state, that they are most strongly represented. We have already noted their importance for the old Chudasama kingdom of Sorath—an area which corresponds roughly to the present-day Junagadh district. It is notable that they appear as pastoralists in the myths of Khodiyar. Though traditionally pastoralists, they are now farmers here, as are many in Amreli district and elsewhere. In Sorath, indeed, they form the closest approximation to a 'dominant caste',[7] and they are dominant, too, in a small pocket of the former Malia state, close to the Rann of Kutch. I came across nobody calling them Darbars, however.

Ahirs are found, also, in the Deccan and in northern and eastern India. In Saurashtra, no Gujars are found, but in Rajasthan, Gujar and Ahir informants tell me that these are only two names for the same caste.[8] According to Enthoven, the Ahir of Kutch and Kathiawar 'differ in many respects from those of the Deccan districts'. Such a vast community is, of course, subdivided. Enthoven identified five endogamous divisions in Saurashtra and Kutch, of whom the Macchua and the Sorathia have their settlements respectively in north-eastern and in south-western Saurashtra. The subdivisions interdine, except for the Sorathias, 'who are held in disgrace because they once betrayed their chief, Rao Navghan of Junagadh, to the emperor of Delhi' (1920, 17). I have not come across any reference to this betrayal elsewhere.

There are many theories about their origins; probably they were early immigrants. Enthoven was certainly of this view (op. cit., 23), as is Westphal-Hellbosch (1968, 1974, 1976). But we note Enthoven's remarks on subsequent sanskritization and integration of the Ahirs or Abhiras. In process of time, they must have,

> like many other tribes, become Hinduised and accepted Krishna worship. And as a community of occupation and religion is often thought to indicate community of origin, the Abhiras, who, like the original Indian *Gopas*, had become Krishna worshippers and were, like them, pursuing pastoral occupations, must naturally have been looked upon as coming from the same stock and soon incorporated with the *Gopas* into one community. (Enthoven 1920, 22-3)

Thus, the earliest of the present pastoral communities of western India, they are at first identified with Khandesh. They spread into Kathiawar, where they were later displaced from some areas by the Kathis (op. cit., 23-4). If Enthoven is right in believing that Ahirs founded some of the first 'clan monarchies', they were later displaced from dominance by Rajputs, except in Sorath and some minor pockets. There, as noted, their position under the Chudasamas parallelled that of the Mers in former Porbandar state. In the zamindari system of Muslim Junagadh, no rural caste could remain truly dominant, yet Ahirs are still headmen of villages there, even when outnumbered by Kanbis. In Enthoven's time, most Ahirs were settled (1920, 25), and he describes them as 'the least nomadic and predatory' of the pastoral castes (op. cit., 23).

Some informants claim that Ahirs rank below Kanbis, but the opposite seems to be generally true. Such was the case in Lathi, near the border of Bhavnagar and Amreli district, where the headman was an Ahir, in spite of Gohil Rajputs being the ancient Darbars of Lathi state. They are placed, then, near the middle of the caste hierarchy. Enthoven (1920, 26) gives a list of castes who interdine with Ahirs, consisting of 'Parajia Brahmans, Rajputs, Rabaris, Anja Kanbis, Charans, Bhats, Parajia Sutars, Hajams, Ojha Kumbhars, Malis, Atits, Darjis, Luhars and Ravals'.

Though fourteen castes are mentioned, this is clearly yet another enumeration of the ter tansali. Parajia Brahmins, who serve and dine with Ahirs, 'are looked upon as a degraded class' (op. cit., 25). This view, one assumes, is prevalent among other, high-ranking, Brahmins.

Ahirs of Saurashtra, like those in Kutch, speak a peculiar dialect.[9] In Enthoven's time, they were non-vegetarians and used alcohol 'in moderation', though these habits were seen as 'degrading' by the Ahirs of Kutch (op. cit., 26). But there are many Vallabhacharyas among the Ahirs, who are vegetarians; and the caste has certainly been influenced by modern trends in this direction.

Ahirs share their traditionally low age of marriage with the other pastoral castes. Married between 8 and 15, children were betrothed at 'any age'. Ahir marriages used to take place on one day of the year, fixed for each 'division', but varying somewhat between them. This day fell in the usual marriage season of these parts, April to May.[10] The low marriage age is still a reality, though usually glossed as a 'betrothal' in the presence of the authorities. Though group marriages are no longer common usage, the reference to them is significant, since we also find such marriages among the Bharwads and the Rabaris.[11]

Krishna is important to caste identity, but it is not obvious how the image of Krishna the herdsman is combined with the Vallabhacharyas' devotion to Krishna the child. Nor is it clear what role Krishna plays in the religious life of those who do not belong to the sect.[12] It is evident, however, that their link to the God provides the caste with its emblematic identity towards outsiders. It is in this connection it is said that the women of the caste wear black in mourning for Krishna.

THE RABARIS

The Rabaris remain the most traditional of the pastoral castes of Saurashtra, as well as enjoying the highest position among them. They are traditionally camel-keepers; and as Raikas they are known from princely Rajasthan, keeping camels for state transport or military purposes. Their annual fair at Pushkar has become a tourist attraction. Non-vegetarian by tradition, they eat not only with the ter tansali but also with Muslims. Enthoven (1922, 258) gives another list of the thirteen castes: Ahir, Charan, Bharwad, Raval, Parajia (Brahmins), Sutars, Kanbis, Kumbhars, Valands, and Sais, as well as Rajput. They are a relatively large caste,[13] ranking above the Bharwad, though they are not seen as the equals of the Ahir.[14] Nor do they share in the sacred status of the Charan. In Saurashtra, they are concentrated in peripheral areas: the Gir forest, the Barda hills, the saline plains towards the Rann north of Dhrangadhra.

The Rabaris are clearly immigrants. Enthoven believed they came from Marwar and Sindh, noting that they went regularly on pilgrimage to the Goddess Hinglaj in Baluchistan (1922, 252). Westphal-Hellbosch also stresses their relation to Hinglaj, and sees Marwar as their country of origin. This is where their greatest concentration is still found (1974, 40, 311-12). In one of their myths, we find a recurrent theme:

> The Rabaris of Cutch had their home in Jhalra Patan, in the time of Alla-ud-din Khilji. In one of his expeditions to Rajputana, Alla-ud-din heard of the extraordinary beauty of a Rabari girl of that place and wanted to marry her. The Rabaris craved a short respite to consider the matter, giving their bards as hostages. They then secretly left the place, and wandering west came to Nagar Summa in Sind, where a Sumra prince was ruling. He gave them shelter. Soon after, about the year AD 1315 the Sumra power in Sind was crushed by the Muhammadans. The Rabaris then took refuge with the Sammas and went with them to Cutch, supplying them with milk from their herds of camels and cows. But they never forgot their former patrons, the Sumras, and to this day, the women do not colour their ivory bangles but keep them white as a sign of mourning. (Enthoven 1922, 253-4)

They are still in Kutch, where some of them still hold land, and may well have come there with the Sammas around AD 1320 (ibid.). The story underlines protection of women against illicit male desire; this is the kingpin around which a whole tradition is organized. We recognize it from our treatment of Rajput culture (above; Carrin and Tambs-Lyche 1993), and shall have occasion to return to it again.

A minor point is the use of bards as hostages, well known in the context of Charan or Barot bards to Rajputs. Other, lower-caste bards—such as the Mir genealogists of Kutch Rabaris (Westphal-Hellbosch 1974; 36)—are not, to my knowledge, elsewhere referred to as standing surety in this way. The story claims aristocratic status for the Rabaris, for only aristocrats might have such bards. In fact, Saurashtra and Rajasthan Rabaris had, and still have, Barots as their bards (op. cit.).

Such aspirations are not evident from etymologies given for their caste name. Rabari is usually glossed as 'those who live outside'. There exist a number of other names, of which the Rajasthani 'Raika' is the best known, while the term 'Bhopa'—'spirit medium'—relates to the many Rabaris who serve as mediums of the goddess (Enthoven 1922; 252).

Sambal is unanimously acknowledged as the ancestor of the Rabaris. He was created by Shiva to take care of a celestial camel, and married to an Apsara.[15] Sambal was forbidden to speak to his wife, 'on pain of separation' (ibid; Westphal-Hellbosch 1974). Thus the Rabaris are also called 'Mogha'—'mute'. Their important goddess Momai Mata is similarly known as the 'mute goddess'. This aspect of their myth may be compared to some origin myths of the Charan.

Sambal had a son and four daughters; as he now had a large family, Shiva asked him to move from heaven and live outside—thus the name Rabari, which Enthoven sees as an obvious pun (op. cit., 253). Sambal's daughters all married Rajputs, their husbands as well as their descendants becoming Rabaris. We have already met this device of approximating one's caste to Rajput status, in the case of the Kathis. Like them, the Rabaris gave shelter to the Rajputs, in this case at the time of Parashurama's destruction of the Kshatriyas. There are several local versions of this myth (Westphal-Hellbosch 1974). Another myth explains that the Rabaris, originally Rajputs, 'went outside' the caste by marrying Apsaras (Enthoven 1922, 253).

From such myths Westphal-Hellbosch tries to sketch out Rabari ethnohistory. A thousand years ago, she concludes, the Rabaris moved south to escape the Muslim rulers of Sindh. Under Charan influence they became worshippers of the goddess, and even her mediums and temple-servants in parts of Kutch and Saurashtra. In Gujarat and Rajasthan, the cult of rider-heroes is equally or even more important among them.[16] She notes, and wonders at, the unexplained importance of the caste assemblies at Pushkar and Sirohi (Westphal-Hellbosch 1974; 303-4).

Their settlement in Saurashtra was among their latest. Westphal-Hellbosch puts their arrival there around AD 1100-1400 (op. cit., 41), more or less contemporary with that of the Rajputs. The Rabaris continued to wander east of and around the Great Rann, in the border area between Islam and Hinduism. Here they were protected by, and sometimes assisted, the Parmar and Rathod Rajputs, but generally continued their move towards the south. In the Barda Hills, they combined with the Hun or Hon.[17] Apart from Porbandar state, they seem generally to have kept aloof from the power struggles of Saurashtra (Westphal-Hellbosch 1974, 304).

Where a large group of Rabaris settled within the territory of an established state, they had to appoint a spokesman responsible to government. This prevented the otherwise strong tendency to split into minor groups. In Kutch they thus came to form a strong, localized, element of the population. In Saurashtra, the Barda Hills and Gir Forest groups have built a certain degree of localized political organization. In Marwar, however, their forms of organization remained loose (op. cit., 306-8). The headman (Sinai) has little political authority, but caste councils are important in settling disputes, says Enthoven (1922, 253).

RABARI-PEASANT RELATIONS

In Marwar, Rabaris began to settle down around a hundred years ago. This hardly happened in Saurashtra, until the settlement schemes of 1953 (Westphal-Hellbosch 1974, 308-9). While government policy tends toward settling all nomads, Saurashtran Rabaris have been reluctant to accept such schemes. They differ significantly from Bharwads in their stress on maintaining the traditional way of life.

This does not mean that Rabaris have no relations to settled groups. Trivedi mentions the symbiotic practices between the Mer and their Rabari neighbours in Porbandar district, where Rabari settlements are found alongside Mer villages:

> The Rabari are herdsmen and cattle breeders found concentrated in the interior of the Barda Hills. However, there is at least one or two families of Rabaris spread out in most Mer villages. A cluster of Rabari mud-huts, with yards full of sheep and goats, is a noteworthy characteristic of a Mer village. A Rabari habitation in a large village, is known as a *rabari khedo*, generally situated a furlong away from the village. The Rabaris generally tend sheep and goats rather than cows or buffaloes, but some of them from villages also work on Mer farms as labourers. They subsist on selling milk, clarified butter/ (*ghee*), dung-cakes, and firewood; they earn money, besides, by penning their flocks in fields for manure. The cattle herd of a Mer village is always entrusted to a Rabari, who practices animal husbandry on payment of cash and kind. (Trivedi 1961, 19)

The latter adaptation, in Saurashtra, is generally associated with Bharwads; wandering Rabaris often find themselves excluded from villages where Bharwads occupy this niche. Few long-distance nomads traverse this area. Rabaris from Kutch, can reach their dry season pastures to the south-east only by way of central Gujarat.

Enthoven mentions the practice of penning the flocks in the field, providing manure for money, for central Gujarat. Today, however, nomads are happy to have the grazing, and I had no hint that they were paid for the manure. The pressure on grazing, there, has increased greatly, since modern irrigation provides for crops which ripen in January or February, as the Rabaris pass by. The market for manure has expanded, too, but it is needed at a different time and bought from others.

As a whole, then, pastoral Rabaris are facing a very difficult situation, their grazing niche contracting year by year. In Rajasthan, many have settled in villages and towns, rather like the Bharwads in Saurashtra; they keep animals and sell their produce in the market. But apart from the Mer area, few Saurashtra Rabaris are found in this situation. More typical is a watchman at the old administrative centre of Dhrangadhra state, now used as offices by the present authorities. He is one of several Rabaris who have left the surrounding villages, due to the deterioration of grazing conditions. His job is typical of urban Rabaris, who have a reputation for courage. I have not come across any Rabari in the urban milk business, controlled by Bharwads.

RABARIS IN THE FOREST

In the Gir Forest and in the interior of the Barda Hills, the Rabaris live separated from farmers. Symbiotic practices are absent here, or can only be practised sporadically (Westphal-Hellbosch 1974). I visited one such settlement—a small *nes* or hamlet—in the Gir Forest. It is one of several such hamlets, where the herdsmen lead a precarious existence; they have repeatedly been chased by the forest officials, who blame their cattle for the gradual decay of the forest.

Their way of life in the forest is traditional, and they have kept the ban on selling milk, which has disappeared among Rabaris of the Barda Hills (Westphal-Hellbosch 1974, 20, 136, 177). Their location in the forest would, at any rate, make such sale difficult; Bharwads are much closer to the market. This may be relevant for the persistence of this custom elsewhere, too. Rabaris sell wool and ghee; all such market transactions are wholly in the hands of the women. Unlike Bharwads, Rabaris seem to avoid close contact with the settled people, and remain far more conservative in cultural terms. This is certainly not due to a lack of mobility. The Gir woman who invited us to see her settlement and offered us buttermilk, came from Rajasthan.

In spite of the obvious poverty of the *nes*, a new family, related by marriage to the present settlers, had just arrived. As we asked about living conditions, an old man just pointed at the river, and the rather obviously, to our eyes, decaying forest. There was grazing and water. Conditions were good, compared to the dry plains of Saurashtra.

RABARI WOMEN

As usual with Rabaris, the women served as spokesmen of the community. Common opinion, in Saurashtra, is that Rabari women are shrewd and intelligent, while the men are stupid and dull. Enthoven (1922, 257) is fully supported here by my observations, while Westphal-Hellbosch holds it as general for pastoralists of the area. 'Merchants', she writes, fear the pastoralist women, 'who insist with a stubbornness and a persistence which wear down the resistance (of the merchants).... Anyway, it is generally acknowledged that the women keep the pastoralists free of debt, in notable contrast to the often heavily indebted peasants' (Westphal-Hellbosch 1974, 30-1).

Typically, the women speak for the men, not only when selling their produce, but also when shopping. In the radio shop of a Dhrangadhra friend, a couple arrived; the woman asked to see a radio. Being shown several, she at once tried to bargain. My friend maintained his fixed price; radios are not sold at a discount. But the woman was not daunted, and when she left, we were sure she had not given up. 'Hopeless', said my friend, a Lohana. Explaining his meagre profit margin, he sighed. 'Was that woman a Rabari?' I asked. 'Of course', he answered. 'They always do that.'

If the settled people are impressed by the women, they make fun of the men, who 'have to ask the women for pocket money, which is only sparingly given to them; many a man can even today hardly offer himself a cup of tea at the market or in town' (Westphal-Hellbosch; ibid.).

This still seems true, and, as is Westphal-Hellbosch's next remark (ibid.), fully representative of my own impressions, that 'it was often the women who decided, by signs or words, whether the men could give information or not, and often enough they let go of all politeness and refused the men their speech, only to take over themselves. Not seldom with the remark, that the men were too stupid to answer...'.

Why such 'female dominance' in a patrilineal, pastoralist community? Moreover, this is the rule among pastoral castes of the area. One obvious answer is that, as the men are busy with the herding, it is the women who deal with marketing and with relations to other communities in general. Parallels may be found among some communities of fishermen in Europe (e.g. Brögger 1989). But the story of Sambal, forbidden to speak to his wives, or the Khodiyar myth relating to Naughan's adoptive sister Jasal, whose husband is unable to defend her honour, indicate that the idea of female strength vs. male weakness runs more deeply. The male/female distinction among the pastoralists is, indeed, conceived of very differently from that of the Rajputs.

For Rabaris, lack of male fierceness cannot be an explanation. In the Barda Hills, Rabaris were partly free from tax due to their service, as preferred soldiers, of the Jethwa rajas of Porbandar (Enthoven 1922, 257-8). Westphal-Hellbosch adds that the Rabari, like the Mer, placed a *tikka* of blood on the forehead of the Porbandar kings (1974, 133).

RABARI KINSHIP

Rabaris have six endogamous subdivisions in Saurashtra, which mostly carry Rajput names. According to Enthoven, marriage with MoBrDa is allowed, with the MoSiDa prohibited. Traditionally, polygamy and sequential polyandry was allowed (1922, 255-6). As will be seen, there are definite similarities to the kinship system of the Charan.

Westphal-Hellbosch, however, refers to preferential marriage with the family of the grooms' mother, but stresses that MoBrDa is considered too close for marriage. But for the Sorathia of Barda Hills at least, the matrilateral preference is seldom followed in practice. Rather, partners are sought from any lineage in the neighbourhood—provided that the Hindu tradition of avoiding relationships for seven generations in the father's line and five generations in that of the mother is respected (Westphal-Hellbosch 1974, 152). The latter statement rather precludes any 'matrilateral preference' unless it refers only to the mothers 'clan' in a very general sense. It might, of course, have been made explicitly to conform with 'sanskritic' norms.

Considering the 'matrilateral preference' and the ban on marriage with the MoSiDa, we are led to wonder whether the Rabari pattern is not simply, like among so many Gujarat castes, hypergamous. Thus a main reason for continuing marriages between the same two exogamous groups would be their stable rank relationship. The MoSiDa, of course, would belong to a group of roughly similar rank to that of her husband, since women of the same group have married into both.

Like Bharwads, and Ahirs formerly, Rabaris have group marriages, held during their great festivals or melas:

Normally there is in the assembly somebody who knows in which family a son or a daughter remains unbetrothed, a condition seen as unsatisfactory by all. Without any interest of his own he then asks the father of the boy, if he would not give the daughter of so-and-so to his son. It is remarkable that here, as in the ensuing deliberations, the talks are initiated and begun by men, whereas at other times the custom is, with the Sorathia, too, that the women betroth their children to each other. (Westphal-Hellbosch 1974; 152)

I just missed the Mela at Jellore in 1991, but local Rabaris told me that a large number of marriages had been contracted there that year.

RABARI RELIGION: THEIR SEMI-SACRED STATUS

We have noted the ambiguous relationship existing between Maldharis and the settled people. This ambiguity in social terms, however, goes with a certain respect and admiration on the part of the latter, which sometimes give the pastoralists a particular ritual status:

There are many occasions, such as fairs and calendar festivals, when Rabaris and Mers participate in each other's celebrations. For instance, when the Mers celebrate *Bhim agiaras* in May–June, the Rabaris also propitiate their goddess, Mamai Mata, and the people of both castes gather together at the villages of Visavada, Balej, and Odadar, all situated on the coast. On this occasion, the Mers and Rabaris visit each other's shrines of worship, and pay homage. The Rabari medium-man of Mamai Mata predicts the time of the rains, something every Mer is eager to know. Moreover, the Mers aspire to get the favour of this goddess for the well-being of their cattle. (Trivedi 1961, 19-20)

The admission to Mamai (Momai)'s temple is, indeed, a privilege. I once tried for hours to impress the Rabaris of Loj—a coastal village near Mangrol—to let me see the 'dumb' Goddess. At length they allowed me a glimpse of her, but against the dark background I could see very little. It was clear, however, that the caste Goddess of the Rabaris is not accessible to just anybody.

That she should be seen, by the Mers, as protectress of cattle is hardly surprising. But her association with the rains is interesting; does she possess powers over which Mer deities have no control? It would seem that the herdsmen, and by implication their Goddess, are assimilated by the Mer to that domain of supernatural powers which, opposed to village and civilization, corresponds to 'nature' in the categories of many anthropologists. This hypothesis is strengthened by other observations made by Trivedi. In effect, the Mers invite the Rabaris to a special rice dinner, 'probably a means of propitiating the dumb goddess, because it is the Rabaris who understand her language and can communicate messages' (Trivedi 1961, 20).

For certain purposes, then, Rabaris act as intermediaries between Mers and sacred powers, in the kind of non-Brahmin priesthood more often practised by lower-caste 'priests' such as Jogis or Atits. Their link to the sacred powers is even clearer when we consider Holi:

> Not only this, but the (Mer) highlanders light their Holi (bonfire) after that of the Rabaris at the Kanmera *nes* in the Barda Hills, because they believe that the Rabari Holi is lit and attended by the spirits of the great religious souls of Vedic and Puranic times. This belief makes the Holi of the Rabaris sacred; so much so, that people from distant villages watch from higher spots for a glimpse of the *nes* Holi to light their own. (ibid.)

In spite of these associations and of their frequent role as spirit mediums, the Rabaris are not seen as sacred like the Charan. But they certainly are a source of excitement, messengers from the 'jangal', and symbols of the freedom of movement denied to the peasant or even to his landlord. That the Rabaris themselves appreciate their way of life, is apparent in their reluctance to descend to the humdrum ways of life of the settled people. Their conservatism, in short, seems the expression not of a stigma but of pride.

THE BHARWADS

Bharwads traditionally herd sheep or goats, and were the lowest among the pastoral castes. This ranking is sometimes reversed by settled people, who regard them as more 'civilized' than the Rabari. They are also the most urbanized group, and monopolize the niche of milk merchants. They have proved capable of adapting to present-day changes, and tend, at least in Saurashtra, to rise in the hierarchy.

While they are shepherds above all, some Bharwads keep cows. A few are agriculturalists or labourers. Unlike Rabaris, they are never buffalo- or camel-herders. The association of the term Bharwad with the herding of sheep and goats is clear enough for a group of South Gujarati Ahirs to call themselves 'Bharwad by occupation' (Westphal-Hellbosch 1976; 12-13). They are rather a small group: Westphal-Hellbosch puts their present population at around 100,000 (1976; 22). The division of the Bharwad caste into Motabhai and Nanabhai is discussed by Westphal-Hellbosch and need not detain us here. The Nanabhai are strongly represented in Bhavnagar district (and in Surat), while the Motabhai dominate in most of Saurashtra.

Generally, the Bharwad caste is rather loosely organized. The inherited office of chief of the Jhalawar Bharwads, at Dhrangadhra, was disintegrating in the early seventies (Westphal-Hellbosch 1976; 43). Only on the outskirts of the Gir Forest was there a tighter form of organization (op.cit., 36). This consisted of 150 villages or quarters of Bharwads, organized in a similar way to the confederation of Jhalawar. Here, the Patel still settled disputes (op. cit., 47-8). Bharwads here are generally village-based.

When migrating, Bharwads prefer to move in family groups, finding it easier to adapt in small units to restricted space. This, of course, denies them any real political influence. The peasants

> ... are glad to see them come, but equally glad to see them leave; for conflicts with them are relatively quick to develop.... The relationship between settled people and the migratory groups is always a little tense, even if they are in contact for only a short time. The migrants do not take the protection of available fruits of the field too seriously, such is at least a common accusation of the farmers. The result is conflicts with and the ensuing departure of the Bharwads, who presently fear nothing more than conflicts with local officials.... (Westphal-Hellbosch 1976, 37)

It is interesting that one Bharwad claimed for his own community the right to place the *tikka* on the forehead of the Porbandar kings (op. cit., 20). As we have seen, this privilege belongs to the Mer and possibly the Rabari. This example of 'inclusion', however, again underlines the strong feeling of community among the pastoral castes.

Typically, Bharwads keep their sheep and goats on the outskirts of villages, grazing them by day and driving them home at night. They are paid in grain or cash for grazing their flocks in the field of farmers, who receive the manure. Between November and June many move in search of pasture; the rest of the year they inhabit hamlets or the outskirts of villages. These wanderings take them generally to eastern Saurashtra or the mainland; but some move towards the Gir Forest or other areas (see also Westphal-Hellbosch 1976, 35).

Westphal-Hellbosch adds that the earth of their pens, mingled as it becomes with dung, is a saleable and popular product (1976, 32). I have myself seen Bharwads herding their goats in barren fields, where fodder supplied by the farmer was spread out. This all indicates that the market value of manure and manuring remained important, and that it was perhaps still growing, as of 1991. When Bharwads live among settled people as milk producers, their way of life is quite similar to Rabaris in the same social position. But they do not share the specialized pastoral adaptations of the Barda Hills or the Gir forest (Westphal-Hellbosch 1976).

MYTHICAL LINKS TO OTHER CASTES

The origin of the Bharwad caste is obscure, but most seem to agree that they came from Thara Jampur or Thara in Banaskantha, where there is a Krishna temple of particular importance to them. According to legend it was here, in AD 961, that they were able to shelter Rajputs from nine different clans, seeking refuge from the Muslims. Protection was granted in return for intermarriage, so the descendants of these Rajputs became Bharwads. To this legendary occasion Bharwads ascribe the origins of their tradition of group marriage (Westphal-Hellbosch 1976, 18-19). One notes the similarity to the Rabari story.

One of Westphal-Hellbosch's informants claimed that the Ahir, Rabari and Bharwad came together to Thaṛa under Krishna's leadership. There the three communities parted (op. cit., 20). The Bharwad of south-western Saurashtra passed by Chotila (near Rajkot), from where, says Westphal-Hellbosch, their ethnohistory can no longer be traced.

According to another story, Bharwads are of the same stock as the Mer.[18] They also claim to have come from Mathura with Krishna (Enthoven 1920, 122). On the one hand, says Westphal-Hellbosch, they claim to be the protegés

> ... or even the creation of Krishna; on the other hand there are myths of origin which connect them with the Charan, Rabari and Ahir, since all four (often, with the deletion of the Ahir, three) groups are said to be the creation of Parvati, Shiva's consort. Even when the Bharwad see themselves as the creations of Parvati, however, they claim that they wandered together with Krishna, under his protection, form Gokal near Mathura to Dwarka. Since Krishna is descended from Vishnu, and the Bharwads even today are seen as the devotees of Krishna, they should really belong to the followers of Vishnu. But in their religious praxis they are particularly enthusiastic followers of the Mata cults and devotees of Shiva. (1976, 14)

The myths of origin of the Bharwad, Rabari and Charan, when referring to Parvati, are clearly versions of the same myth. These mythical links express a concern with the closeness of the culture and interests of the groups. The term *Daghlabhai* (brother of the blanket) is a living expression of solidarity among pastoralists. This consciousness of community is one reason for considering them an 'estate'.

Westphal-Hellbosch also gives a myth of origin concerning only the Bharwad. Here, Krishna occupies the central role:

In (Mathura) Lord Krishna made three small rolls of dirt, which he burnt at the fire. Thereafter he made them into three figures of herdsmen..... These ... were the ancestors of the Bharwads.

Krishna had many wives, but ... gave them all away, except three. He wanted to marry these to the three herdsmen.... but they were reluctant to take wives from Krishna, whom they regarded as their father. So Krishna gave away these wives, too. When Krishna then commanded the herdsmen to milk his cows, they refused ... they would only milk and herd cattle again, when they had been given wives. At last Krishna took them to a temple and bade two of them place themselves back to back and to circle the temple in opposite directions. As they met again, one of them had become a woman. Krishna bade these two marry. When the third complained that he, too, needed a wife, Krishna told him that... he should have a part in the wife of his older brother. Therefore the Bharwad women had several men and even today the younger brother marries the widow of the older. (1976, 15)

BHARWAD KINSHIP

The institution of levirate referred to here still exists (Enthoven 1920, 121; Westphal-Hellbosch 1976, 52). There are few kinship-based restrictions on marriage, says Westphal-Hellbosch, though 'there was a tendency to marry specific or more distant relatives on the mother's side' (1976, 51). Clearly, there is a parallel to the Rabari here. But such a tendency was not general. The most distinctive custom of the Bharwads, however, is their collective marriages. This form should not be confused with the group marriages among the Rabari, where there are 'a hundred individual marriages, with individual marriage poles ... and an individual ritual led, for each of the families, by one Brahmin. Among the Bharwads, however, there is only one marriage pole and only one religious ceremony, which bind all the couples together even if there are more than a hundred of them' (Westphal-Hellbosch 1976, 54).

Such collective marriages are known to have existed among the Kavda Kanbis; whatever their origins, they have now been given up by some Bharwad groups. It is certain that they were formerly celebrated at long intervals.[19] 'But', says Westphal-Hellbosch, 'since there are ... no restrictions on marriage age',

and none are supposed to have existed, no age classes were formed. At a collective wedding the Bharwads try to marry everybody who is still free. This goes so far that pregnant mothers promise each other their unborn children and stand in for them at the marriage ceremony. Only if the children turn out to be of the same sex does this marriage ... become invalid. That the actual establishment of the couple in married life is another matter, is of course obvious. (1976, 55)

Westphal-Hellbosch claims economic reasons for this custom; in earlier times a single, rich Bharwad paid for the whole affair. The area used for the ceremony can later be used only for pasture. Such collective marriages, taking place between February and May, must first be accepted by the goddess, she says, without specifying the Mata in question (1976, 52).

But the Goddess Bhavani is carved on the marriage pillar; 'While it is being planted', says Enthoven, 'the women drink large quantities of milk and butter which so excites them that they become frantic, singing lucky songs, breaking down hedges and spoiling the crops' (1920, 121). Moreover, the eunuchs of the Goddess Bahucharaji—known as Pavayas—play an important role.[20] Bahucharaji is yet another deified Charani. According to Forbes, she cut both her breasts in *traga*[21] as her party was attacked by Kolis. Thus she became a goddess (Forbes 1878, 426).

Not all Bharwad marriages are 'group-marriages' in this sense. I was present at the sending-off ceremony of a young groom in Bhavnagar; he was going to his bride in Surat, a child of seven. Unhappily, I did not get to know the bride-price, but there was certainly no question of dowry. Instead, people spoke of bride-prices ranging from 5000 to 15000 rupees (in 1974). Unlike pastoral peoples elsewhere, Indian herdsmen seem for a long time to have paid their bride-price in cash.

The sending-off ceremony, for which the groom wore a sword, was basically a dinner party to which some 150 guests of different castes came. The master of ceremonies, as well as the cook, were Patidars (Kanbis), thus making the food acceptable to most castes. There was one or two Rajputs and Lohanas among the guests, the highest castes present; there was no Brahmin or Bania. Thus, most guests were members of the thirteen castes, and there was little segregation. Still, the Bharwads tended to form a core group, sitting together, and Patidars, as well as the Lohana and Rajput, were treated as honoured guests. Thus in spite of the general commensal solidarity of the thirteen castes, a Patidar was brought in to cook. Bharwads are, after all, seen as the lowest of the pastoral castes. It was, indeed, deemed unlikely that any Brahmin would be willing to assist, even as a cook.

'Rabaris', said one Bharwad woman, 'come from the right side of Krishna's body, while Bharwads come from the left side.' And she added: 'The *real* Rabaris are very honest and upright; they never cheat anybody. Bharwads are not that good—and so have lost some status.' The statement is apt, for while Bharwads are the most pragmatic and businesslike of pastoral communities, one often hears them paying respect to Rabaris as the bearers of the real pastoral tradition.

'BHARWADS ARE BHOOTS'

Like all pastoralists of the area, the ritual status of Bharwads is ambiguous:

> Almost all classes of villagers talk of Bharvads as Bhuts, that is, evil spirits. The Bharvads do not quarrel with the name. We are Bhuts, they say. If a villager is asked why are Bharvads Bhuts, he answers: they are so stupid. Their wildness, their sudden and weird appearance among their sheep, a small heap of blankets rising into a huge figure, give point to the nickname. Their fitfulness is also uncanny, suddenly bursting from stolid dullness to frantic rushings and the oddest shouts, yells and calls. Moreover, they are unclean, seldom bathing, seldom washing their blanket clothes. Finally, they are sin-laden or *papi*, selling their sheep to be slain. The Bharvads admit their sinfulness. 'So evil are we, our Brahmins cannot support the burden of our guilt. Of our Audich Brahmins all are gone except one, and she is a childless widow....' (Enthoven 1920, 119-20)

Westphal-Hellbosch (1976, 13) makes similar comments: 'As a wanderer in the desert a Bharwad is conversant with the 'Bhuts', the terrible spirits of the wilderness, or is himself a Bhut. This conception the Bharwad takes quite lightly or even accepts it.'

We see clearly, here, the ambiguity with which settled people see the pastoralists. The Bharwads are *bhoots*; the Rabari semi-sacred; and the Charan, as we shall see, are properly sacred. There can be little doubt that one source of this sacredness is the liminal nature of the pastoral adaptation, midway between civilization and wilderness.

URBAN PASTORALISM

It was among the Bharwads in South Gujarat that Salzman found the urban adaptations referred to above. Rajkot has a very large population of Bharwads on its outskirts, scattered over many small hutments.

When Westphal-Hellbosch wrote, town-wide caste organization was only sporadic (1976, 46-7); but since then a considerable amount of caste organization has formed even on a regional level. It is difficult to get a clear picture of this organization without a more specialized study, but it seems clear that there is little continuity with any older pattern.

In Bhavnagar, I visited one of the households practising what we may call 'urban pastoralism'. They owned a small compound, where they had built their own hut of some 8 by 5 metres, of two rooms; they were busy adding an extension. This, the wife told me, they would let to other Bharwads, for some 40 rupees a month. It was she who kept the conversation going and answered all questions—as is so often the case among pastoralists. They also owned a small pucca bungalow, with two separate quarters—which they rented to other Bharwads. They had bought their land on moving here from a nearby village; now they had four milch cows, a couple of heifers, and two small calves. The heifers were to be sold; the calves were raised for later sale; and from the cows they sold milk in qualities of one rupee and two rupees a litre.[22] The two qualities of milk may be seen as another product of Bharwad enterprise. Some people told me bluntly that the half-price milk is half water. Shrewdly, the woman asked me if I could see any difference between her two bangles. One, she explained, was worth 700 rupees; the other, six rupees only. She concluded that no thief would know the difference either.

Shrewdness, certainly, is called for to make a success out of 'urban pastoralism', where most of the fodder has to be bought in the market.

BHARWAD ENTREPRENEURS

Thus it is Bharwad entrepreneurs who have opened milk-shops in the cities. One such businessman told me how his father had decided to give up herding in the sixties; now his four sons had three such shops between them, in three different towns.

I met this man when my motor cycle had developed some trouble and I was stranded on the road. Another bike—a Yezdi (Jawa) like my own, stopped. But this bike was special. It was customized with special handlebars, a very large headlight, a Japanese carburettor, and a host of other 'goodies'; a highly personal mode of transport. The fellow himself wore a white cap and sun-glasses, appearing, in the drab Indian countryside, like a vision out of 'Easy Rider'. I came to realize how the bike had become the new status symbol among Maldharis; my friend here was but an example. In no time he put my bike right and invited me to follow; then he showed me his shop.

While somewhat fanciful, Enthoven's rendering of the settled people's stereotype of Bharwads remains basically true. As for the Bharwad self-image, his impressions represent one aspect only. Perhaps the customized motor cycle of my friend represents the modern version of the other side of this image. Riding his bike he recalls the Hell's Angels—a highly modernized bhoot.

The image that the Bharwad has of himself is also one where he emerges from the stigma attached to his traditional position to become the most energetic and effective of pastoralists.

PASTORALISTS: THE PRESENT CRISIS

The process of sedentarization has, we have seen, gone on for centuries. When a ruler offered land to nomads, it was seldom refused. But such settlement often served only as a base for annual migrations. Typically, recent attempts at settling the pastoralists, undertaken by the present government, have met with little success. During recent years, however, especially in Rajasthan, worsening ecological conditions have led herdsmen to settle on the outskirts of villages, often where, originally, famine relief was offered to them. The conditions for pastoral adaptations, then, have grown worse, at least during the present century, and particularly in later years. Several factors are involved here. First, there is a general deterioration of vegetation in Saurashtra. In the twenties, several forest areas were still fit for hunting tiger or deer. Only the Gir forest is now left, and that too is in plain decay.

Forest reserves were protected by the princes, who monopolized hunting. Present authorities have not been as effective as their predecessors in protecting the forest. Meanwhile agriculture is expanding, due to population increase as well as advances in irrigation. Farmers grow new winter crops in fields formerly left barren for the use of pastoralists. Irrigation has also contributed to a sinking ground water level, and deterioration of surrounding lands.[23] Nomads, then, are threatened by drought in the dry season, and a lack of village pastures during summer. The pastoral niche, between fields and desert, is decreasing in capacity. In Rajasthan many Ahirs or Gujars were forced to settle during the crisis year of 1988, and have become part of the village poor, subsisting on temporary labour and their few remaining animals.[24] Elsewhere, as in Saurashtra, there is a trend towards sheep and goats replacing the larger animals.

The Rabaris, whether camel or cow herders, cling to their traditional adaptation. If leaving pastoralism, they tend to take jobs in town; quite a few are employed as watchmen or guards.

During the crisis of 1990-1, the plight of the cowherds and their animals provoked political debate in Gujarat. In spite of widespread attempts—by the state as well as local authorities—to provide for them en route from Kutch to south Gujarat, the BJP opposition accused the state government (Congress) of letting 3000 cows die. The government maintained that the real number was 300; but in a state where cow-protection is a political slogan, the situation was grave.[25] This debate brought the pastoralists firmly into the political picture in Gujarat. Yet the voices raised in their support were not their own but those of their political advocates; in Gujarat, the BJP has lost no occasion to criticize the government. As a whole, the nomadic pastoralists suffer from the lack of a political representation.

The Bharwads, however, are becoming steadily better organized. The contrast between the present time, and that of Westphal-Hellbosch's study in the early seventies is striking. But the many caste councils and more or less local committees have not yet combined to form a strong political voice.[26] As noted above, Bharwads, in contrast to Rabaris, have been willing and able to adapt to change. They are exploiting the growing market for milk and milk products in town; and their other traditional activity, making and selling blankets from the wool of their sheep, seems to be expanding. They have also been able to exploit a secondary result of irrigation and intensified agriculture: the increasing demand for manure.

Why are Bharwads better able than the nomadic Rabaris to exploit this expanding niche? The answer may lie in the flexibility of Bharwad organization. A small flock of sheep and goats, herded by a couple of men, is able to use one field at a time, even if small, and can easily shift to the next village whenever there is a demand there. Rabaris, travelling with a hundred cows or more, need large areas. Their negotiating position is critical; the cows may become too feeble to walk or even die if grazing is not available quickly and in quantity. For them, the need to negotiate may itself be new. In north Gujarat they used to have standing agreements with villages (not individual farmers) which they visited every year.[27]

The present crisis is serious; but does not affect the different pastoralist adaptations and communities equally. While there is a danger that long-range nomadism may disappear from western India, the semi-settled and settled 'milkmen' have been able to benefit from new possibilities. Their main opponent is not the ecological crisis but the expansion of government dairies.

The Bharwad entrepreneur, who with his brothers owns three milk shops, made this clear when asked why they had no shop in Rajkot: 'The dairy there is too powerful', he said. Yet even there, a Kanbi who had made his career as a *halwai*, producer and dealer of sweets, explained part of his success in terms of quality; 'I buy my milk directly from the Bharwads', he explained.

THE PASTORALIST ESTATE

Pastoralists, then, are seen by informants as a separate and well-defined category of people, known as Maldharis. They themselves accept the categorization, and stress their solidarity through the concept of Daghlabhai, 'brothers of the blanket'. Their myths see them as 'brothers', created by Parvati to guard their respective animals, or construe other 'kinship' links among them. When referring to Krishna, Bharwads see themselves as coming from the 'left side' of Krishna's body, while Rabaris came from the 'right side'. Here, they exclude Charans and Ahirs; but the latter have long ceased to be pastoralists, the former have no links to Krishna. The fluctuating membership of the Maldhari category rather underlines their strong identification with the adaptation; when Charans and Ahirs are included, the talk is of origins and traditions, rather than current occupations.

The category Maldhari thus alludes both to the pastoral adaptation, assuming a certain commonality of interest, and to a cultural tradition, spoken of with pride, which goes beyond present occupational divisions. As a culture-bearing element, as well as an 'interest group', Maldharis are clearly a separate 'estate' in traditional Kathiawar society. While the presence of Ahirs in this context is a matter of history, that of Charans has a very different character. For if few Charans remain pastoralists, they remain the vanguard of the cultural tradition with which Maldharis identify. As such they form an integrative element in the traditional social order, as we shall see in the next chapter.

NOTES

1. Leshnik and Sontheimer (1975) contains several useful articles on Indian pastoralists. For north-western India, see Westphal-Hellbosch (1974; 1976), and Tambs-Lyche (1992a).
2. We note here the description of this relationship by Pocock (1972) for the mainland. To my informants, pastoralists were certainly romantic, as well as primitive and a little frightening. The allusion to 'gypsies', frequently made, is to the romantic gypsy of folklore, not to the stigmatized minority of modern Europe.
3. Some aspects of the Gir Charan community are described in Westphal-Hellbosch (1976). Berwick has studied the Gir Maldharis from a medical viewpoint, in the context of a wider ecological study; see S.Berwick (1976). I visited a community of Gir Rabaris in 1991.
4. Since 1974 I have visited several such communities, and one early description is found in Tambs-Lyche (1975). Examples from south Gujarat are found in Salzman 1990.
5. No one denies, in Saurashtra, that pastoral communities are 'castes', but the word 'tribe' lingers on, and any attempt to integrate peasants and pastoralists into a common hierarchy seems to group the pastoralists as a separate 'sub-order'. Thus while acknowledging rank differences between pastoralist castes, they are often compared globally to peasants. Traditional informants tend to group them above Kanbis, while modern-minded people place them below. Nobody places them below Kolis, however. If statements were integrated statistically, Rabaris might end up between Kanbis and Rajputs, and Bharwads between Kanbis and Kolis, in a traditional ranking. But such integration would deny the ambiguity of the informants' presentation of the case.
6. Westphal-Hellbosch (1974) gives the story of the settlement of Rabaris in Kutch. She also comments on settlement attempts of the fifties and sixties.
7. See my discussion of this theme in Ch. IV.
8. This statement from Gujar informants in northern Marwar is supported by Inder Dan Detha of Borunda. In Bengal, I talked to several 'Goalas' who insisted on being true Ahirs.
9. This was true of the headman of Lathi. Enthoven, noting that the *Kavyadarsha* ascribes Apabhramsa, containing 'far greater corruptions than any other prakrit' to the Abhiras, concludes that Ahirs have non-Aryan origins. The term Ahirani, used for the dialect of Khandesh, lends credence to his view that Ahirs once had their own language (1920, 24).
10. The traditional Kathiawadi dance *dandia ras*, associated with the goddess festival at Navratri, was performed on these occasions (Enthoven 1920, 25). It has become a celebrated part of Gujarati folklore, and is danced on Navratri in places like London and Coventry. College youth, of all castes, perform it at festival time in Saurashtra. Its relation to the goddess is shown by the Garba and Garbi songs, sung be the dancers and mostly dedicated to her. It is clear that the dance is commonly ascribed to pastoral tradition. It is danced in circles of men and women respectively, with sticks which are struck against each other in the manner of swords.
11. It seems that pastoralists of the region share a need to concentrate their marriages

at certain prescribed dates. It seems obvious, too, that this is a practical solution in such dispersed communities. As will be seen, the modes of group marriage differ in content, and it is therefore reasonable to assume that the similarities are due to the pastoral adaptation.

12. There are other Krishnaite sects, among the pastoralists, apart from the Vallabhacharyas. But I was not able to find out much about them, except that they, apparently, do not concentrate on devotion to Balakrishna the child, but to his grown-up aspects, notably as herdsman. The literature, too, is silent on this point, and Francoise Mallison, whose research has dealt with Krishnaism in Gujarat, is as eager as I am to find out more about these sects.
13. In 1901 there were 108,715 Rabaris in Bombay Presidency, many of them in Saurashtra (Enthoven 1922, 252). Westphal-Hellbosch describes their geographical distribution, assuming a total of 415,000 by 1931 for all states, and about half a million today (1974, 41-2). Of the Sorathia Rabari, she estimates about 1000 households each in the Barda Hills and in the Gir Forest, the latter numbering some 10,000 to 12,000 people. The population of the two groups, taken together, should then come to 20-25,000, but there are quite a few Rabaris outside these two areas, notably around Dhrangadhra.
14. This ranking, reported by Enthoven, refers to Ahirs as settled farmers.
15. An Apsara is a celestial woman, invariably young and beautiful. In other contexts, Apsara like the Valkyries of German and Nordic mythology, are present at the battlefield to take the fallen heroes directly to heaven (*svarga*). This aspect of the Apsaras does not seem to be connected to their role in the origin myths of pastoral castes.
16. These cults are certainly important in linking other castes to the Rajputs. Most such rider-heroes are Rajputs. Westphal-Hellbosch comments briefly on these cults (1974, 168-9; 1976, 77-8). I have not much material on them.
17. Their Mer neighbours have been identified with the Huns (Enthoven 1921).
18. 'The Bharvads are of the same caste as the Mehers, to whom Krishna's foster father Nand Meher belonged' (Enthoven 1920, 122). The Meher are usually identified with the Mer. While the connection cannot be ruled out *a priori*, the physical traits of Bharwads, as given by Enthoven, would make them very different from the Mer. The 'heavy build and coarseness' he refers to is hardly obvious to the observer, however: to me they resemble other pastoralists in being slim and relatively tall. True, they are supposed to have less 'noble' features than Rabaris or Charans, but it is hard to say whether rank or physical stereotype comes first.
19. Baines saw them as a Scythian custom (1912, 103), noting that group marriages took place every 10, 15 and 20 years. Campbell has 'once in a generation'; Enthoven 12, 15 and 25 years (Westphal-Hellbosch 1976, 54-5).
20. The role of these eunuchs at Bharwad marriages is described by Westphal-Hellbosch (1976, 58-61). There is little serious study of these eunuchs, but a beginning has been made by H.G. Patel (1983; 1988). Enthoven, writing about the Goddess Bahucharaji, tells the story of their origin as follows. Propitiated by the childless king of Champaner, Baria, Bahucharaji gave him a son, Jeto, who was impotent. Baria decided that he should serve the Goddess. In a dream, Bahucharaji commanded Jeto to castrate himself and to wear women's clothes. He therefore became the first *hijara* or *Pavaya* (1922, 227-8).

21. *Traga* is demonstrative self-immolation or suicide by a Charan, bringing supernatural sanctions on his or her opponent. More about this institution in the following chapter.
22. All prices as of 1974.
23. The problem has been treated in an unpublished paper by H.G. Patel, for the 1988 International Conference of the Anthropological and Ethnological Sciences in Zagreb. I do not have access to this paper, cited as above in Brox (1992). Brox gives a brief resumé of it.
24. Beyond own observations, I rely here on discussions with Inder Dan Detha, of Borunda, Rajasthan (1990).
25. Beyond my own observations I rely here on Ahmedabad and Rajkot newspaper reports.
26. Sources here include newspaper reports from Rajkot, and interviews with Kharwabhai Rathadiya, a Bharwad who has become technical officer in the Rajkot dairy, and is involved in Bharwad politics. The reference to Westphal-Hellbosch is to her 1976 volume.
27. Westphal-Hellbosch's reference to such agreements are vague, and I rely here on the information of H.G. Patel, Reader in Sociology at Saurashtra University, Rajkot, who originally comes from north Gujarat.

CHAPTER VII

The Charans: Mediators between Divine and Secular Power

THE CHARANS

The Charan or bardic caste is a small but diversified community. Families of the old court bards may still be large landowners; not a few have become intellectuals, but some are still herdsmen, notably in Saurashtra. There, most traditional of pastoralists, they specialize in buffaloes, and in the Gir Forest they were still practising the ancient rite of buffalo sacrifice as late as the early seventies. Yet I have also met Charans living on the outskirts of towns, selling their milk products, and generally sharing the niche of some Bharwads. Within this adaptation, however, they remain a very small minority.

Enthoven sees all Charans, whether bards or pastoralists, as belonging to the same community. Different subdivisions speak Gujarati, Kacchi, Ahiri, or Marwari, but their bardic literature is in their own particular language, Dingala,[1] closer to Kathiawadi and Rajasthani than to Gujarati (1920, 274-5). It is significant in this context that the son of a suburban Maldhari family, when asked if he knew Pingala (prosody),[2] recited for me in the best traditional style, and in the Dingala language. He was a boy of ten or twelve. Thus even among Charan 'milkmen' today, the bardic tradition is alive. Similarly, when I visited a Charan friend he had another visitor, from his wife's family; for our pleasure, this relative recited some traditional poetry. The profession of bards may be dead, but the tradition lives on.

The Charans are perhaps the most critical community for our analysis, combining in a single caste the occupations of pastoralists and bards, the latter function going far beyond the composition of poetry. They were central to the traditional religious and political system. Yet the Charans are the smallest of the pastoralist castes dealt with here.[3] They were found all over Gujarat except Surat district, as well as in Kutch, Saurashtra, and even in Sindh (Enthoven 1920, 271). Charans, like Rajputs, were traditionally non-vegetarian. Today, even Charans have converted to the Swaminarayana sect, becoming vegetarians. The relative of my friend, in spite of his knowledge of the bardic tradition, was one of them.

Today, there are three main areas of Charan settlement in Saurashtra. One is on the west coast, the second in and around the Gir Forest, and the third around the Nal lake, bordering the mainland. The western group belongs to the Tumbel, the Gir forest group to the Sorathia Charans. The Tumbel claim to have come from Kutch with Jam Raval, the founder of Navanagar (Jamnagar) state.

The Charans are known as pastoralists and bards; but these were not their only occupations. Some held grants to land or even whole villages, while a tradition has it that in the eighth century they were given the whole of Kutch (Tod 1829, I, 84). The Charan who then came to Kutch may have fled from the Arab conquerors of Sindh. It is mainly in Marwar that we find Charan landlords today. Other Charans were peasants, traders and moneylenders, some served the princely states as soldiers, while some, at least formerly, made their living demanding gifts at feasts and marriages (Enthoven 1920, 283). Most of the Charans, especially those of the Kutchela subdivision, remained pastoralists when Enthoven wrote, but with this occupation were associated two others, cattle-dealers and pack-carriers. This latter speciality might develop into caravan trade. The pastoralists migrated from October to March, in groups of about twenty men.

Some such Charans got very rich. Inder Dan Detha's grandfather, from Borunda in Marwar, once took 3000 cows on migration. This was in the time of the First World War. On such occasions they not only grazed their animals and sold ghee, but traded in livestock. But then the Dethas were landholders, too.

Associated with trade were the Charans acting as guards to travellers and caravans (Enthoven 1920, 284). Linked, again, with the role as guards was that of standing financial security. In the two latter roles, the Charan's weapon was his threat to mutilate or kill himself. Self-mutilation or suicide were both known as traga. We shall return to this theme, but we note here that such deeds were commemorated by *palios* in the case of suicide—in complete parallel to the heroic deaths of warriors or satis.

Today, only the pastoral Charans remain in their traditional occupation. We may add that the rich Charans of Marwar, once feudal landlords, are still living well on their lands. But the role of court poet has gone with the princes, and caravan trade disappeared between the two world wars. However, some Charans maintain their traditional role as poets and genealogists, to this day, albeit at a reduced scale as their best patrons have lost their positions (Westphal-Hellbosch 1976, 122).

CHARAN BARDS AND GENEALOGISTS

The traditional role of the bard is rather well known; we shall analyse it as an element of Rajput polity and religion. But first we need a resume of the knowledge available on the bard.

The Maru Charan of Rajasthan were *the* bards of the Rajput kings, though Kutchela and Sorathia Charans also lay claim to such positions. The most prestigious role of the bard was to maintain the genealogy of the ruling house. Its importance can hardly be overstated, for kinship claims formed the main base of political legitimacy both among the Rajputs themselves and towards their subjects from other castes.

In all questions concerning descent, the genealogist was the recognized authority, and his importance was such that his person was held sacred. He was 'classed with "the cow and the Brahman" whose slaughter was forbidden to the Rajput', says Qanungo (1969, 40). In war everybody respected the Charan of their opponents, so that they were often employed as peace-makers (Westphal-Hellbosch 1976, 122-3). 'A single Charan', says Qanungo, 'rushing in between the ranks of fighting warriors sometimes stopped blood-shed.' 'If the exhortation of the well-wishing Charan went unheeded', she continues, 'he would kill himself with the katar in living faith that no Rajput would dare to cross the ban of a Charan's blood' (1969, 41). This is the classical use of the traga. It is taken by Westphal-Hellbosch to mean that such an action might forestall and prevent war (op. cit., 123).

The *dharna* (fast) constituted a parallel to the institution of traga; these were the means of pressure employed by Charans. Thus the Charan's 'weapon against the Rajput was only his moral force backed by superstition; namely, the threat to kill himself and thereby bring upon the obdurate Rajput the wrath of the gods' (Qanungo 1969, 40).

Moreover, the house of a Charan was similarly seen as a sacred refuge. In feuds 'both sides would send their women and children to the houses of the Charans', states Qanungo; thus 'the inviolability of the Charan's home saved the seed of the clan when its adults were killed in insane feuds' (op. cit., 40-41; also Westphal-Hellbosch, op. cit., 123). In Marwar, the villages given to Charans in *sansan* tenure were free not only of tax or tribute but, 'the paramount ruler's writ against fugitives from Justice did not operate in sansan territory (Ujwal n.d., 16). Qanungo further concludes that, in the local hierarchy of Rajasthan, 'The Charan's patriotism, courage and devotion earned for his community a precedence over all other castes inclusive of the Brahman in the customary law of the land' (Qanungo, op. cit., 41).

With all this, the Charan was sometimes seen as a beggar. Even the enthusiastic Qanungo finds it necessary to counter such attitudes (op. cit., 39). Westphal-Hellbosch also raises this problem (1976, 125-6), as does Enthoven (1920, 283). In such cases, the supernatural sanction released by self-sacrifice might be used for extortion of considerable sums. Enthoven cites a case where a royal marriage, in Bansvada in central India, was postponed to avoid extravagant demands made by a band of Charans, who threatened to sprinkle the marriage party with their blood from self-inflicted wounds (1920, 283n).

To Ujmal, they were the 'favourite' of Maha Shakti, the people chosen by Durga to come 'to the world's rescue when the situation demands' (n.d., 18-19). This is because the goddesses of the area are, almost all of them, deified Charanis. Qanungo accords them 'an intermediate position between the Brahman and the Rajput', adding that their character combines the characteristics of these two castes (1969, 39). In spite of their sacredness, Charans with a few exceptions on the mainland do not wear the sacred thread (Enthoven, op. cit., 280).

The dead are cremated, but those who made the pilgrimage to Hinglaj Mata (not accessible since 1947) were buried in a sitting position (op. cit., 283). Hinglaj, as we shall see, stands at the apex of a long line of Charan goddesses; sometimes she is herself seen as a deified Charani (Westphal-Hellbosch 1976).

PASTORAL CHARANS AND THE BUFFALO SACRIFICE

As for the Charan who remain pastoralists, Westphal-Hellbosch has made a brief study of them in Kutch and Saurashtra. The Charan living in the Gir Forest seem to be even more loosely organized than the Rabari of that area. They are recent arrivals, having come to the forest around the turn of the century. Generally each hamlet remains independent of the others, having its own Patel (headman) and its own Bhuva (spirit medium) (1976, 144-6). The role of the latter in the worship of Pithad Mata, the most important goddess of the Gir Charans, is interesting here.

Beside the usual goat sacrifice, buffalo sacrifices were performed for the Goddess. Her temple is in the house of the Bhuva, behind a partition. The Bhuva,[4] like other Charans of the area, is a buffalo herder and has no particular privileges in daily life. But when a perfect male calf is born to him, it is destined for sacrifice, if another is not already available. Such sacrificial buffaloes were allowed to graze freely everywhere, like those we meet in the myths of the Goddess Avad (mentioned later) and of Khodiyar. One night, however, the goddess will appear to the Bhuva in a dream and tell him that she wants a sacrifice. The proper day will be decided by a grain oracle,[5] and a tent roof will be erected. Here, the Goddess will be placed. At the appointed time, the buffalo appears, either of its own will or enticed by a herdsman. When the animal puts his head under the roof, she is ready to receive her sacrifice.

The animal is killed by two strokes of the sword; one by a Harijan (Westphal-Hellbosch does not specify further), the other by a Mahia Rajput. The latter also keeps the sacrificial sword. If the second stroke fails to part the head from the body, it is a bad omen, implying that the goddess refuses the sacrifice. The Bhuva catches the running blood of the animal on a plate, and drinks it; his sons then do the same. Other Charan mark their foreheads with a *tikka* of the blood. The Bhuva then begins to shake and to shout; the goddess has entered into him. Others now put questions to the goddess, and receive her answers through the possessed Bhuva.[6] When the trance ends, the ceremony is over (Westphal-Hellbosch 1976, 179-80).

Here we have in a relatively simple form, the buffalo sacrifice alluded to in the stories of Avad and of Khodiyar. Were Charans originally the 'priests' of the buffalo sacrifice? Data such as the above might indicate such a hypothesis, which certainly would help in explaining their peculiar position. But we have no other material to support the hypothesis, which therefore remains speculative.

THE MYTHICAL ORIGINS OF THE CASTE

Charans are also known by other names, of which we may mention Gadhavi, Barot and Mangan.[7] As various as the names of the Charan and their explanations are the stories of their origin. Probably the bardic profession is itself responsible for this proliferation.

One story, from Sindh, takes us back to the Goddess Sarasvati, the daughter of Brahma. Dancing and singing in praise of Shiva she dropped a flower from her mouth. This flower became a boy, whom Shiva employed to graze Nandi, his bullock. While out herding he found the clothes of some fairies bathing in the river. The boy took the clothes away, and ran to Shiva, followed by the fairies, who complained. Shiva asked Parvati to settle the dispute, and she ordered the clothes returned. But the boy refused unless one of the fairies agreed to be his wife. Thus he was married to Avari,[8] and their two sons are said to be the ancestors of the Charans (Enthoven 1920, 272-3) In a version given by Westphal-Hellbosch, Charan, son of Avari, marries Avad—the later Charan Goddess—daughter of the Naga[9] king (Westphal-Hellbosch 1976, 100-1).

Another myth of origin, from north Gujarat, states that Parvati made an idol from the dirt of her body.[10] Brought to life by Shiva, the idol became a man who was then employed by Shiva to tend four animals; a lion, a serpent, a cow and a goat. The lion attacked the cow, and the serpent attacked the lion, but the herdsman gave them some flesh from his arm, and they were appeased. Shiva recognized his talents by calling him Charan, 'grazier'. Charan found the clothes of some Naga girls, and the story above repeats itself. Married to one of them, he gets two sons and a daughter; his son Naga descends to earth to become ancestor of the Charans (Enthoven 1920, 273). In the offer of his flesh we may, of course, see a legitimation of the practice of traga.

Charan, then, in yet another version of the myth, was married to Avad. Here she is said to be the daughter of Shesh Nag, chief of the Nagas (serpents). In Kutch, where this version comes from, Charans address Ahirs as *Mama* (MoBr), since they are said to be descended from Ahi Nag, son of Shesh Nag. Karkotak Nag, another son, is said to be the ancestor of the Kathis (ibid.).[11]

The myth common in Saurashtra is again slightly different. Here, both the original Charan and his wife Avad were created by Parvati. They were married on the condition that if he spoke to her, she would leave him. They had three sons; Nara, Chauva and Chorado. When Avad was pregnant with the fourth child, she scolded her husband for the strange reason that he was milking a buffalo with the mouth of the vessel downwards.[12] As her husband responded 'she dropped the earthly body (in the womb) and left him' (Enthoven 1920, 273-4).

In the areas around the Great and Little Rann we find the legend already noted, of the creation, by Parvati, of the pastoral castes. This makes brothers of all the Daghlabhai. They are related through their father as created by the Goddess, as well as by their mothers, who were sisters. 'Relationships through the mother are often in Kutch given more importance than the kinship of male ancestors'[13] (Westphal-Hellbosch 1976, 100).

One obvious point that these myths have in common is their allusion to the pastoral origins of the caste. Enthoven regards these origins as obvious (1920, 274). But the Maru Charans have a separate myth relating to their function as royal bards:

> ... they were originally superhuman spirit-beings ranking with the other half-divine fame-spreaders the Siddhas, that is the knowing ones, and the Vidyadharis or female scientists, news agents, and god-messengers. In time, like certain other angelic classes, the Charans settled on earth, and became the bards of kings and chiefs. After Parshuram's dispersion of the Kshatris, the Charans accompanied them in their southward flight. In these troubled times, the Charans took charge of the supplies of the Kshatri forces, and so fell to their present position of cattle-breeders and grain-carriers.... (Enthoven 1920, 274)

Though all Charans lay claim to a function as royal bards as one of the peculiarities of their caste, others acknowledge that, in this respect, the Maru were the most firmly established (Westphal-Hellbosch 1976, 96). It was this group, too, which in the fifties published the journal *Charan Bandhu,* exclusively devoted to the affairs of the caste (ibid.). In this journal, several versions have appeared of the Charans' transformation from celestial to human beings. These versions agree in placing the godly ancestors of the Charans in the Sumeru mountains, with other celestials; due to over-population the Charans migrated to earth, establishing their first human home in the Himalayas. Here they were given the area of Telang by one king Prithu, who thus stands at the apical summit of their worldly history (Westphal-Hellbosch 1976, 96). Enthoven tells a similar story:

> Raja Prithu, king of Oudh, was at this time engaged in performing a sacrifice. He went to Shiva and implored him to be present at the sacrifice. Shiva ordered the two Charan lads to accompany the king, but they declined to do so unless the king made some provision for their livelihood. The king accordingly imposed a tax upon Khatris, payable to the Charans on every marriage or other solemn occasion. (Enthoven 1920, 273)

Here we may recall the story in which the Kumbhars of Anhilwada Pattan are made to pay a 'marriage tax' to the Charans (op. cit., 272).

King Prithu is normally seen as an incarnation of Vishnu, but opinions are divided as to his historical identity. Westphal-Hellbosch points out that several of the candidates lived too late to serve as the starting point of the real history of the Charans (1976, 97).

According to Westphal-Hellbosch, the Charan legends indicate a history of about one thousand years, which was spent in an area of constant Muslim incursions (tenth–thirteenth century). These incursions brought forth processes of ethnic changes which must have affected the Charan, as well as others. Any faithful account of the Charan during these and earlier times is complicated by the contradictions of the several myths and legends (1976; 104). Even so these dates make the formation of the Charan community contemporaneous with that of the Rajputs.

Tod, on his part, takes the caste back to AD 714. When

> ... the Pramar of Telung took sanctuary with Har, to the thirty-six tribes he made gifts of land. To Kehur he gave Kuttair, to Rae Puhar the coast of Sinde, to the heroes of the shell the forest lands. Ram Pramar of Telung, the Chukwa lord of Oojein, made the gift. He bestowed Delhi on the Tuars, and Puttun on the Chawuras; Sambhur on the Chohans, and Canouj on the Kamdhuj; Mar-des on the Parihar, Sorat on the Jadoo, the Dekhan on Jawula, and Cutch on the Charan. (Tod 1829, I, 77)

The Charan, then, are said to be the first of our pastoralist castes to come to Kutch. According to their tradition they came from the mythical, and unidentified, 'Telang' via Malwa to Saurashtra and Kutch (Westphal-Hellbosch, op. cit.). This would make them the first of the pastoralists in Saurashtra, too, with the probable exception of the Ahir. In these traditions the Charan trader Mavalji has a central role; but the different stories give varying dates for him, ranging from the eighth to the tenth century (Westphal-Hellbosch 1976, 105-11).

THE MYTH OF THE GODDESS AVAD

Apart from Mavalji, Ai (grandmother) Avad is the most important figure of Charan tradition. As noted, she is sometimes seen as an Apsara or as a Naga girl. Mostly, however, she is the central Charan goddess, and often spoken of simply as the Goddess of the caste (Westphal-Hellbosch 1976, 169). She is sometimes seen as a reincarnation of Hinglaj, but also, at other times, of the Avad mentioned in the origin myths. The later Avad, according to the legend, became a goddess even in life. Her legend has much in common with those of other Charani goddesses of the region, such as Khodiyar, who is often said to have been her sister:

> Avad was born on the 9th of Chaitra in the dark half of the month, Samvat 888 (AD 832). Her father Mammad or Mamadio belonged to the Mada group. He lived with his seven daughters in Vala, near Valabhi in Saurashtra. All the daughters remained unmarried, an early sign of their sacredness. During a famine Mammad drove his herd to Chalkhana in Sindh. With him went the daughters and the companions of his eldest daughter Avad. (Westphal-Hellbosch 1976, 160-70)

We are clearly talking about the same Mamoud Gadhavi, the father of the seven sisters, and his residence at Vala goes well with Khodiyar's birth at nearby Roisala. The dates, however, do not fit those of Khodiyar, and the migration to Sindh leads us rather to a parallel of the story of Jasal, Naughan's sister, according to which 'The seven daughters grew into such beauties that Umar Sumra wanted to marry them all ... Mammad went to Hamir and told him that his daughters, because of their sacredness, were seen by all Rajputs as sisters, i.e. women who could not in any circumstances be married' (ibid).

Umar Sumra is of course Hamir, the king of Sindh, whom we have met in Khodiyar's story; as a Rajput convert to Islam he used the name Hamir. As noted, he turns up in a number of myths, at different points of time. Mythically, he is always the same figure, the bad king thirsting after forbidden women. Jasal, an Ahir, was simply somebody else's wife; but here we meet what is effectively an incest taboo, between the daughters of Mammad and male Rajputs in general. It is not clear, however, whether this ritual sisterhood is a matter of caste, applying to all Charan women, or whether it is the unmarried, sacred status of these particular Charanis that makes them forbidden fruit.

In the Khodiyar story, we learned that the sacred status of the sisters precluded marriage, and we may be tempted to accept that sacred Charanis should remain chaste. We shall return to the matter below. In the meantime, we continue Avad's story:

> ... Hamir was burning with desire and threatened to use violence if he did not have his will within 40 days. Avad, too, went to Hamir to explain the circumstances to him, but with no success. Then the Goddess spoke through Avad to her father, who thereby learnt that the fall of Hamir through the agency of the Sammas was already destined. As Avad came before her father in the form of the Goddess, he had to believe her and to follow her advice. This was for the family to leave Sindh and to settle in the Temra Hills. (ibid.)

The parallel here, both to the story of Jasal and of how the Rabaris came to leave Sindh, is clear. The theme is a general one; marriage against the woman's will seems to stand, metonymically, for the breakdown of moral order or Dharma in general. In such cases, then, the goddess usually intervenes, though this element was lacking in the Rabari story. Whether she appears in a 'new' incarnation, as with Varudi helping Naughan to cross the Rann of Kutch, or, as here, incarnated in the very person threatened by abuse, her role may be seen as a re-enactment of the Puranic goddess' role in slaying the buffalo-demon to save the world for dharma. Indeed, we now meet the buffalo-demon in person, as Avad leads her family towards the Temra Hills:

On the way several things happened, which showed the sacred powers of Avad. First they met Bakha, a buffalo-demon, which Hamir Sumra kept as a future sacrifice to the Mother. Such sacrificial buffaloes had the right to graze wherever they liked. This buffalo was guarded by a Bhil, who did nothing to protect Avad and her family from the buffalo's attacks. Avad killed the buffalo and drank its blood, and thus came to thirst for the blood of the king. She sent the Bhil to Hamir to tell him what had happened and to predict his (Hamir's) death. (ibid.)

The parallel to Shiladitya's buffalo, killed by Khodiyar and her sisters, is clear but here the sacrificial buffalo is explicitly marked as a 'buffalo-demon', and the parallel to the Puranic Goddess—as Mahishasuramardini, killer of the buffalo-demon—is obvious.[14]

During sacrifice, the Goddess is indeed seen as 'drinking the blood' of the buffalo. But drinking the buffalo's blood, Avad comes to thirst for the blood of the king. The two are seen in parallel; the lascivious king brings to mind numerous Rakshasas of Indian mythology.[15] Is he himself a 'demon'? The allusion to drinking the king's blood would make of him a sacrifice, taking us all the way to the Frazerian theme of sacrificing the king.[16] But this may be taking the allusions too far.

The story now turns to the traditions of the 'lost river' of Sindh and Rajasthan, whose disappearance has turned the land into a desert.[17] But on yet another level, we are dealing with a quite different breach of dharma:

A second meeting she had with a Banjara,[18] who was leading a caravan of a lakh of oxen, loaded with sugar.[19] Hamir had forced the Banjara to pay a tax for each sack, even though normally no such payment was demanded from caravans. The Banjara was however headed for the Punjab, where he was now threatened by the sales tax. The meeting between Avad and the Banjara took place by (the river) Sutlej or Mita Mehran, which then flowed through Rajasthan. The Banjara had seen how Avad emptied the river of water by scooping from it three times with her hand. In this way her family could cross the river dryshod. The Banjara than told Avad his story and asked for her help. She told him to fill sand in the sacks of his oxen and to empty them at the source of the river. This altered the course of the Sutlej and laid barren the lands of Hamir Sumra. (ibid.)

The Goddess here continues to protect the moral order. The theme of the story is typical of Sindh and Rajasthan, and has only marginal relevance for Saurashtra. But clearly Avad, like Khodiyar and her incarnation Varudi, has special powers over water. Water, like blood, is indeed a female element, in the human body and elsewhere.[20]

The destruction of his country, however, is not punishment enough for the king, who continues his evil ways:

Avad spent some time in the Temra Hills, to look after her family. Then she went to Sindh, to avenge herself on Hamir Sûmra.... Hamir had confiscated all land belonging to the Charans, in the hope of forcing Mammad to give up his daughters in return for giving back the land. Under Avad's leadership the Charan of Sindh united themselves in a great Dharna (collective fast), and reinforcements came from all the neighbouring countries. As Hamir Sumra was showing no sign of giving in, Avad went to the Samma in Sammasatta Panjab and to the Bhatti of Jaisalmer. She knew that both Rajput houses were eager to have Sindh, both were ready to fight, and even more so when they heard that Avad would take part in the battle at the head of a lakh (100,000) goddesses. Avad killed Hamir Sumra, the Bhattis got Thar Parkar and the Sammas the rest of Hamir's lands. (Westphal-Hellbosch 1976, 169-70)

We see here an example of the dharna, which turns up frequently in myths and stories of the region. This mode of collective fast might sometimes be pursued to death; in all cases it was supposed to work, like traga, through the supernatural sanctions that it provoked. But as even this does not impress the king, military force is used, and we note that like some Rajput women, the sacred Charanis here take an active part in the battle. With the support of sacred as well as secular powers, Avad completes her revenge, and dharma is victorious.

Hamir is, of course, a Muslim. Historically, then, Avad stands for the struggle of Hindu Rajputs against Islam. Thus the stories about her are full of contradictions, as they refer to different waves of Muslim intruders. Usually her opponent is Hamir Sumra, who, however, turns up in accounts from widely different periods.

Thus on the one hand, Jam Lakhiar of the Sammas is often pictured as asking Avad for assistance; his reign is given as 883-9, in an unspecified calendar which could, however, refer to AD 827-33. But the historical Hamir Sumra, as far as we know, reigned around AD 1290, while the Sammas are supposed to have ruled Sindh from AD 1351 and at that time the Samma belonged to the Sunni sect of Islam. There are other Hamir Sumras before this, however, though their dates remain unspecified (op. cit., 111-12).

From all this it seems reasonably clear that there were Charans in Saurashtra by the ninth century (ibid.). The Khodiyar myth would take them one century further back. Avad led the Charans to Marwar, so by AD 1000 they inhabited roughly the same areas as today (Westphal-Hellbosch, ibid.). From then on we find several references to them.

THE GODDESS KARNI MATA

In his monograph on the Goddess Karni, Ujwal (n.d.) affirms that Avad is the incarnation of Hinglaj. He notes that the temple to the latter, at Las Bela in Baluchistan, was one of the original four Shaktapithas, where Shakti, having manifested herself to kill the buffalo-demon Mahishasura, established herself in the world (op. cit., 14). Karni is in her turn seen as an incarnation of Avad and of Hinglaj. She was born in BS 1444 (AD 1387-8) as the seventh daughter[21] of a Charan of the Kiniya clan, who had settled near the Jodhpur-Jaisalmer border. Her birth, he says, was the result of a pilgrimage to Hinglaj (op. cit., 17).

Karni, then, is important mainly in the Rajasthan, but she is also a major figure of Charan lore. Her first miracle appeared when her aunt, angry at another baby daughter, struck the child. The aunt's fingers were 'impaired'. It was understood that the child could 'do things' and so she became Karni—'the doer' (op. cit., 18). Still a child, she granted the boon of a son to the Brahmin Suwa (op. cit., 27) and performed other miracles.

Now, as we shall see later, all Charanis are 'potential goddesses'. The miracles serve to show that in Karni's case, the potential is realized; the cycle of Khodiyar myths likewise contain some early miracles, which I have not included here.[22]

More centrally for our purpose, Karni supported Rao Shekha of Pugal—to the west of Bikaner. When the chief came to pay her homage, she fed him and his following—140 persons—miraculously, as we have seen Varudi do for the army of Naughan. She then bestowed her boons, and in addition to being a 'sister' of the chief by definition—as a Charani to a Rajput—she tied *rakhi* for him, establishing a more specific sisterhood. Yet when he asks for immortality, she has to refuse him (op. cit., 28-34).

This refusal is interesting, for Karni is repeatedly stating the futility of the request. Humans are mortal, and granting immortality is not within the scope of the Goddess' functions. We are reminded of the observation of Kinsley, that as Maya the Goddess 'is the world, she is all this' (1986; 105).[23] Her role as creator, sustainer and destroyer of the world-illusion does not permit her to alter the fundamental rules of this world, even if she can work miracles within it.[24]

The reference to the brother-sister bond between male Rajputs and Charanis is much clearer here than in Avad's story. And that this incest taboo concerns even marriageble girls, may be indicated by the story of Karni's marriage. But as we shall see, the indication is hardly conclusive.

The parents of Karni are looking for a husband for her, but she herself announces her choice; she is to marry Depaji, of the Rohadiya clan, whom Ujmal identifies as an incarnation of Shiva. 'Only such an incarnation of Lord Shiva could have been considered for holding the hand of Karniji' he adds (op.cit., 35). The groom's clan was closely tied to the Rathods of Khed.[25]

The divinity of the husband mediates between the usually unmarried state of the sacred Charani and the ordinary status of the Charan wife. But we also learn that she refused to sleep with her husband. 'For the furtherance of his line, he would have to marry another girl' (Ujwal n.d., 41). To convince him, Karni appears in her divine form. He is convinced; he marries Karni's sister. The offspring of the second marriage still live in Deshnok, the location of Karniji's famous temple (ibid.).

We might be tempted to say that Karni remains a virgin. It is true, too, that while the Charani goddesses of western India may not all be unmarried, one never hears about them having children—except in the perplexing case of Shakti Mata of the Jhalas. But it is doubtful whether virginity as such is the point here. We should rather think in terms of untarnished sacred powers, where the subjection implicit in wifehood might be as destructive as marital cohabitation *per se*. In Karni's case, however, subjection is no problem, since her husband is construed not as an ordinary human being, but as an incarnation of Shiva, who is in any case the celestial consort of the goddess.

We may return, briefly, to Shakti Mata, whose powers seem intact even on marriage to a human husband. But, then, she is seen not as a deified woman but as a Goddess stooping to humanity. Yet she not only marries Harpal, but has children by him, who are the valiant, but utterly human, ancestors of the Jhala clan. At this point, then, we will only conclude that the question of virginity and sacredness, deified women or humanized goddesses, does not seem to allow for any simple conclusion.[25]

With the dowry received from Karni's father, her household has too many cows for the water available in the village; we learn that the water was apportioned according to the hereditary share of the village, regardless of the size of the herd. They leave the village, and come to the lands of Rao Kanha, where again there is conflict over water, this time with the chief himself. Ujwal stresses that in refusing water for Karni's herd, Kanha is guilty of cruelty to cows, as well as insulting a Charani. Rao Ridmal, the dispossessed brother of the chief, tries to intervene on Karni's behalf. She blesses him, and with her support, to make a long story short, he and his descendants found the kingdoms of Jodhpur and Bikaner (op. cit., 42-4ff.) He, then, exemplifies the figure which we have now met several times, of the morally good king whose success is ensured by the support of the goddess.

Kanha, however, tries to chase Karni from his lands, and as he continues his threats in spite of her warnings, a lion miraculously appears and kills him. The lion, the traditional mount of the Goddess Durga, is of course Karni herself. Kanha thus becomes a parallel to the ubiquitous Hamir Sumra; the immoral king destroyed by the goddess. Ridmal returns and takes over the throne (op. cit., 45-50). This establishes the link between his royal house and Karni Mata, who founds the village of Deshnok where her temple still stands.

Rao Ridmal proposes to call the village Deshoat ('shield of the land'), hoping that the seat of an incarnation of Shakti will forever protect his kingdom. But Karni replies:

> Kingdoms ... depend for protection on their masters. As Rajputs, he and his descendants should depend on their own might not counting upon anything more than blessings and divine grace which will be theirs so long as they fought for moral values. Neither this seat of Bhagwati nor blessings can save sinners from downfall. It will be improper, therefore, to call it Deshoat. Let it be called Deshnak (Nose of the land) and let it be as important for the prestige and honour of your kingdom as the nose is for an honourable man. (Ujwal, n.d., 50-1)

No clearer statement can be found of the relationship between the kingdom and its guardian, the Goddess. As we see here, she is above all the guardian of dharma, and the king only receives her support as long as he serves as its instrument.

THE SACREDNESS OF CHARAN WOMEN

Khodiyar, Varudi, Avad, Karni—these are but examples of the Goddess born into this world as women of the Charan caste. The traditions we have dealt with here stand witness to the idea, firmly entrenched in Saurashtra as in Rajasthan, that Charanis are potential goddesses. This leads us to ask how the human Charani is herself construed—and we may begin by noting her strong position with regard to men.

We have noted that this strong position of women is typical of the pastoralist castes. In the Charan hamlet in the Gir, says Westphal-Hellbosch, her access to information was due to the wife of the Patel. Once she had given the word, information was given freely (op. cit., 164-5). The wife of a Charan friend in Bhavnagar kept a strict purdah, as some rich or urban Charanis do. I was struck, therefore, by the privilege given to me when, visiting my friend's house, his wife served tea with her face uncovered. The way in which the room for male guests was secluded from her quarters left no doubt that her purdah was a case of exclusion by and not of her. The decision to show her face, too, was certainly hers. I was struck, too, by the demeanour of Inder Dan Detha's mother, a lady somewhat sceptical of the anthropologist friends of her son. When she met me, she bluntly asked my caste. I presented myself as a Bania, since my father's family once were merchants and shipowners. But I could not satisfy her as to my sub-caste, stating meekly that these were different in Norway. 'In what do they trade?' she asked, then, finding my identification all too imprecise. And, when I told her they used to trade in timber, she finished her questioning brusquely: 'What is the price of a log of timber in Norway?' I let go at that. This kind of self-confidence shows that the respect for the Charani is not solely a mythological matter, though this aspect remains important.[27] Westphal-Hellbosch remarks on the high position of the women:

> The reason for this is the belief of their community—and of other castes—that potentially every Charani can be an embodiment of the Goddess. The most important goddesses in Kutch, Saurashtra, Gujarat and Rajasthan are Charanis who have become sacred. Important migrations were led by women; thus

Hinglaj Mata led the Tumbel to Las Bela, Khodiyar Mata the Charan to Bhavnagar, and Avad Mata to Rajasthan. (1976, 164)

Thus the particular sacredness of the Charani must be distinguished from the generally strong position of her pastoralist sisters. As Trivedi puts it:

The Charan women are said to be potential *sati,* and therefore they are respected as sacred mothers or *Aii* (lit. grandmother), who on their tours, keep with them an iron trident (trishula), the symbol of Shakti. During the harvest season, they go about with a trident, conferring boons of plenty and prosperity. People seldom displease them for fear of a curse; contrariwise, they give them corn, money or other useful articles in order to get boons. (Trivedi 1961, 22)

The peculiarity, then, of the Charanis is that they are seen as controlling in life the kind of powers that a sati releases only at the time of death. It is a power, then, that all women intrinsically possess, though some more than others. Mewar Rajput women are sceptical of lower-caste women becoming satis; this of course does not refer to Charanis. Rajputs, indeed, were the arbiters of traditional society due to their dominance, and maybe Inder Dan Detha's remarks are of some significance:

Rajputs, being rulers, energetic fighters, needed some moral boost, and that boost used to come through the shakti; and so every Rajput clan had a Kuldevi which gave them their moral boost. Their poets, the Charans and Barots, were known as Shaktiputra. That is also why Charan women are considered as goddesses.

The Rajputs never trusted their own women. That is why they kept them in very strict purdah. They never regarded their own women as 'goddesses'.

We have seen that the Rajput woman, too, is certainly a source of shakti for her man. Yet may it not be, that the ultimate sources of shakti have to be beyond marriage, beyond the touch of man? Charan girls, we have heard, sometimes remained unmarried to retain their particular sacred status. This is at least the implication of Avad's story, where she and her sisters are said to be 'like sisters', i.e. unmarriageable, to all Rajputs. This, of course, is in spite of the frequent hypergamous marriage of lower-caste women to Rajput men. The unmarried, sacred Charani might be seen, like the kuldevi, as the arch-sister, giving men protection in the same (but infinitely greater) sense that a sister's protection is bestowed through the ubiquitous rite of *raksha-bandhan.*

We have seen how, for Rajputs, the sister is opposed to the wife; the latter, still bound to her natal clan, as dangerous as she is necessary for the clan's continued existence.

At the face of it, this view is confounded by the fact that Charanis retain, apparently, a large part of their powers even in marriage. But here we may be misled by Western ideas of 'virginity'.[28] The married woman is as capable of a sister's protection as the unmarried one, and moreover, the archetypal sati is, after all, a married woman.

CHARAN KINSHIP

Turning to kinship and marriage, we see that Charans resemble the other pastoral castes in this respect, particularly the Rabaris. They are, of course, patrilineal, and there are said to be 120 exogamous clans or lineages among them (Ujwal n.d., 35). Other sources give varying numbers, and few of them agree (Westphal-Hellbosch 1976, 137ff.) Enthoven only says that such clans are 'exceedingly numerous' (1921, 276ff). These, again, may have several sub-clans.

Enthoven gives six endogamous subdivisions: Gujar, Kutchela (from Kutch), Maru (from Marwar), Tumbel or Tumer (probably from Sind), Sorathia (from Saurashtra) and Suchia (Enthoven, op. cit.). Westphal-Hellbosch has made a thorough critique of Enthoven's statements, built on her own information as well as literature, and concludes that there are only 'three and a half' subdivisions, of which the Tumbel are the half. The three 'full' divisions are the Maru, the Sorathia, and the Kutchela, associated with Marwar, Sorath (south-western Saurashtra) and Kutch respectively (1976, 95, 137ff).

There are several explanations for the Tumbel being just a half division. It may be remembered that, in the Saurashtra version of one origin myth, Charan had three sons by Avad when he made the mistake of speaking to her. She then dropped the child in her womb, half-grown; this baby she put in a brass vessel and sent it off by the sea. He became the ancestor of the Tumbel, a half-division because he was only half-grown; in one version the vessel is found by the Samma chief on the coast of Makran, when he was on pilgrimage to Hinglaj Mata. The Tumbel insist strongly on their old ties to the Sammas, from which clan later sprang the Jadejas of Kutch and of north-western Saurashtra (Westphal-Hellbosch 1976, 148ff).

But there is a more sociological sense in which the Tumbel are only half a division. The other three groups distinguish between *bha* and *bhaneja* relatives, respectively 'brothers' and 'sister's sons'. The latter are actual or potential affines of the former. Thus they may marry mother's agnates as well as those of the grandmothers, though there are exceptions to this rule (Enthoven, op. cit.) The preferred marriage is with the MoBrDa. (Westphal-Hellbosch 1976, 152). This reminds us of the Rabari, and of the Bharwad in former times. But among the Charan each lineage is, on the local or regional level, classified as either *mama* or *bhaneja*. The latter give daughters to the former, who retain higher rank. Marriage is hypergamous, as for Rajputs and Patidars, but the classification of lineages into two groups makes for a moiety-like division of the endogamous groups, broken up only by the fact that marriage regions are loosely defined and therefore overlap.

The Tumbel, however, do not accept the *mama-bhaneja* division, and exogamous lineages intermarry freely. This apparently makes them 'half a division' only. They also practise marriage by exchange, which more or less dispenses with bride-price (Westphal-Hellbosch 1976, 139, 152).

The two Charans, I came to know well during my fieldwork, had, in fact, married their cousins, and regarded this as a common arrangement; in one of the cases, my friend had indeed been under some family pressure to do so. In both cases, too, visiting affines were a constant presence. This is rather different from the Patidar, where one is reluctant to visit the home of the married sister.

One reason for the difference may lie in the fact that Charans pay a bride-price, whereas the Patidars give dowries. The bride-price implies a reciprocity, whereby the daughter's family of marriage is constantly given gifts after marriage. Thus the visit of an affinal kinsman, especially the mother's brother, is a welcome event, not least among the children (Westphal-Hellbosch 1976, 153). This is more in tune with my observations than what the same author says later, that visits from the mother's family are few and far between, and highly hedged around with formalities (op. cit., 154).

Marriage among Charans appears thus as a close parallel to the MoBrDa marriage indicated for Rabaris, and said to have once existed among Bharwads. Like them, Charans marry asymmetrically (except for the Tumbel), and hypergamously; but unlike some other castes, including Rajputs, the wife's relatives are not openly treated as social inferiors. This point, too, has its parallel among other pastoral castes. Bharwads and Rabaris, of course, also traditionally paid a bride-price.

Thus in spite of the difference in rank between the lines of husband and wife, the latter has a stronger position than in many other communities of the region. Children were betrothed early, and the girl used to visit her future in-laws, sometimes for weeks; she thus knew them well, even before marriage. This is, of course, highly unusual in northern India. As the bride-price could be high, the groom might have to wait long before the marriage could be held. The ceremony was always held in the bride's village, and the full bride-price was usually not paid even then. Thus the bride would only accompany the groom to the boundary of his village, and then turn back to her own. Within a year, however, the outstanding part of the bride-price should be paid, and she should join him. But sometimes he was allowed another year to fulfill his obligations. The wife returns to her parents for the birth of her first child, and at all important festivals she visits them with her children (Westphal-Hellbösch 1976, 153-4). All this, of course, contributes to a relative equality between the families and to the strong position of women in the community.

According to Enthoven, however, Charans paid dowries, though a smaller payment was paid to the bride's father. Successive polyandry was then permitted but not obligatory (Enthoven, op. cit., 276-81).[29] This brings to mind the Bharwad arrangement, and underlines the close links to one or a few affinal lines. In spite of the similarity of their kinship organization to other pastoral castes, I have not found any reference to recent group marriage even among the pastoral Charans. But such references are found in myth, bringing us back to Mavalji, the figure who vies with Avad for pride of place in Charan lore. Mavalji stands at the apex of historical—as opposed to obviously mythical—Charan tradition. Mavalji was fabulously rich; some say he won his fortune by trade, others stress his magical powers. He is associated with Kutch, but his dates are a matter of dispute, ranging from the ninth to the twelfth century.

Central to the stories of Mavalji is the marriage of his daughters, which is often presented as a group marriage. In one version 140 marriages are indicated. Two other points are of interest here; Mavalji instituted the *mama-bhaneja* system, and one of his daughters married a Bhatti Rajput. (Westphal-Hellbosch 1976, 105-11). We shall meet this girl later, but by then she has become a Rajput orphan adopted by Mavalji.

THE MARRIAGE OF KARNI

I have not had occasion to witness a Charan marriage. The description that Ujwal offers of the marriage of Karni may perhaps serve, here, to indicate the traditional pattern.

As is customary the first reception was arranged at the boundary of the village. Meha with kinsmen and friends all riding bedecked camels or caparisoned horses awaited the bridegroom at the point where the Sathika-Suwap road entered the boundary of village Suwap. Music played, and Meha's drums kept time. All eyes were on the horizon looking for the marriage party. A hearty cheer went up when the much awaited group was first sighted. (Ujwal n.d., 39)

This is a scene familiar to us, local colour being added by the camels. But the familiarity is in its stress on the village and its boundaries. This is very far from the marriages of pastoralist Rabaris and Bharwads who in the group-marriage, mark no territory: as the Rabari fair or the chosen marriage-ground of Bharwads is neutral as far as the families are concerned.

The party was substantially smaller than expected. This naturally disheartened the receptionists. Dampened spirits were however revived when amongst the chanting of *mantras* by the Brahmans, singing by the Damamies,[30] *geet* recitation by the Motisars and Raos (Bhats),[31] Meha applied tilak on the forehead of his prospective son-in-law and heartily embraced Kelu.[32] Negs (customary gifts) were given to the Brahmans, Motisars, Raos, Rawats and Damamies as also to village servants like Suthars (carpenters), Luhars (Blacksmiths), Kumhars (Potters), Meghwals (messengers), etc. (op. cit.)

This is the scene we associate with a marriage of Rajputs or other dominant castes. We note that, in spite of the rivalry between Charans and Brahmins, which we shall discuss later, Brahmins are being employed in the marriage ceremony. With reference to 'centrality' in Raheja's sense (1988, 1989), we may note that two groups of 'servants' are remunerated by gifts here; those who take an active part in this sequence of the ceremony, such as Bhats and Brahmins, and the village servants in general. Brahmins are not singled out; they are included with the others. In the sequence that follows, we could have been present at a Rajput marriage, or that of another martial caste:

The two sides were only waiting for the reception rituals to be completed to jump on their mounts and race for the village. Each side endeavoured to beat the other—few holds being forbidden. Urging their mounts to breakneck speed and pulling riders of the other party from their mounts each was possessed by the desire to reach the destination ahead of others. Arriving at the village quadrangle they forgot all rivalry and warmly embraced their opponents. Wedding guests at this point parted company from the groom who rode towards the gate of Meha's house leaving his companions to enjoy the warm hospitality and sumptuous fare provided by Meha. (op. cit., 39-40)

This mock fight has no place, of course, in the group marriages of Bharwads or Rabaris. In short, the wedding ritual here is almost purely Rajput. The reception finishes, to the sound of ballads praising the grooms' ancestors, as he rides up to the bride's mother waiting at the main gate, the *thali* of ritual articles in her hands (op. cit., 40). Of the wedding ceremony proper, we only learn that it was 'solemnised in the prescribed *shastriya* way, and, one presumes, by Brahmin priests' (ibid.).

In short, then, we have here basically a Rajput marriage, though, as we have seen, the kinship system of which it is a part is close to the other pastoral castes. It is as if the most visible aspect of kinship, the marriage ceremony, has been adjusted to the aristocratic position of these Maru Charans, without greatly affecting the choice of partners and the underlying kinship structure. This is, of course, quite likely to have been the case.

CHARANS AND RAJPUTS: KINSHIP AND QUASI-KINSHIP

This in-between position between Darbars and Maldharis leads us to investigate the Rajput-Charan relation in terms of kinship, real or implied. Some precious material is found in Ujwal's work. We have heard that Karni's husband was considered an incarnation of Shiva. But his clan, the Rohadiya Barhats, has an intriguing history. Largest of all Charan clans, they were the hereditary bards of the Rathod Rajputs of Marwar.

The ancestress of this clan was one Jhima De, married to Bhati Budh of Tanot, a Rajput. Jhima was not a Charan by birth. She was an orphaned Rajput, who had been adopted by the great twelfth century bard Mavalji Varsada,[32] court poet to Lakha Phoolani of Kutch. (n.d., 35). This marriage was not universally accepted, because of the belief that Jhima had become a Charan by being adopted by Mawalji Varsada, and that the only way in which the marriage of a Rajput to a Charan can be taken out of the category of incest is by considering the boy adopted to another Charan thus converting the marriage into one between two Charans.' (op. cit., 36).

But Budh had not been so adopted, and so the marriage was considered 'anomalous'. Being adopted by a Charan, made the orphaned Rajput girl a 'sister' to all Rajputs, and a Rajput marrying her would, in this view, be committing incest.

This, then, is the confirmation we need that all Charanis, regardless of specific sacredness or married status, are 'sisters' to the Rajputs. But does this make 'brothers' of Charan men?

The couple's offspring seem to have been considered Rajputs, however. This is clear from the story of how their descendant became court poet of the Rathods of Marwar. According to Ujwal, the Rathod chief Dhuhar sought, in vain, the hand of a Solanki princess in marriage. But this offer of marriage alliance was turned down, and Dhuhar was told that 'the entrenched Rajput dynasties of the desert considered Rathods socially inferior and indeed not even Rajputs because they did not have, as is customary with Rajputs, their Charans' (op. cit., 36).

This was at the turn of the thirteenth century, and so we are right in the middle of the period when the traditional Rajput patterns were establishing themselves. This lends credence to the story. In fact, says Ujwal, Dhuhar was now told that establishing a proper relationship to a line of bards was 'more important than founding a kingdom', for anybody wanting to establish Rajput status (ibid.). Thus the Charan-Rajput relationship was itself seen as a necessary element in proper Rajputdom. But then, no unattached[34] Charan clan was available; clearly the demand for their services was rising. So, Ujwal tells us, 'recourse to the old practice of converting a Rajput into a Charan was one of the alternatives that could be thought of' (ibid.).

And at this point, Dhuhar's son Raepal heard of the story of Budh's and Jhima's marriage. Their grandson, Bhati Mangh, was invited to Khed, then capital of the Rathod chief, and forced or persuaded to become a Charan. In BS 1268 (AD 1211-12) he became the court bard—*polpat*—of the Rao of Khed. The name chosen for the clan is said to derive from Dingala *rohadana*, meaning detention or restraint (Ujwal n.d., 36-7).

This story of conversion from one caste to another does, of course, affect our idea of what a caste is. Ujwal holds that 'there is unexceptionable evidence of the fact that whenever and wherever an additional Charan clan was needed, the initial stock was very often furnished by the Rajputs. The majority of the present day Charan class, including the Kiniya clan in which Bhagwati Karniji was born, trace ancestry to Rajput stock' (n.d., 23-4).

This may or may not be historically correct. But the persistence of this tradition, underlining 'these ties of tradition and blood' may be an element in making Charan women the 'sisters' of Rajputs. I have asked, above, whether this makes 'brothers' of the men of these two castes. It is a question which cannot be answered conclusively.

The term *bhai*, brother, is used in western India in such an extended sense that even if we find Rajputs using it for their Charans, it proves nothing. A bhai may be a caste-fellow—Kanbis and Patidars use the term extensively in this sense, so that 'bhai' is affixed to the name of any other Patidar—Sunilbhai, Anilbhai, etc. But a bhai may also be a friend, and the word is often used as a term of address to underline amicality and informality, even when the other is a complete stranger. We must concentrate, therefore, on the relation that used to exist between the Rajput and the Charan. In Khodiyar's story, we have seen how the bard is construed as the close friend, rather than the servant, of the king. This is the cause of the jealousy of ministers and the rajpurohit. If the relation here is, surely, a later reconstruction, it is certainly true to the stereotype. As my colleague Dr Bapu Jhala, second son of the last ruler of Dhrangadhra, put it: 'Anthropologists have been possessed by the relation between the king and the Brahmin. But the Rajputs were not like that; they were much closer to their Charans'.[35]

And we have another royal testimony in Man Singh of Jodhpur, a contemporary of Aurangzeb, who wrote a poem in praise of Charans:

> The Charans excel the Rajput in four things
> namely brains, education, purity of heart and religious piety.
> The Charans, capable of discerning distinction
> describe it well, and thus, spread the fame of good kings around.
> They are very intelligent and illuminate the Court by their presence.
> Kings immensely relish their conversation;
> their impressive physique and handsome features
> give these poet-kings (Charans) a regal bearing
> and as such they do not look out of place among Kings.
> They keep the gathering in good humour and excel in good behaviour.
> These poets immortalise the valiant Rajputs and are themselves great warriors.
> Listen to *Maan*, and resent not, O! Kings, the Charans are verily invaluable.

(Ujwal n.d., 24-5).

Kings, then, valued their Charans, who vouched for their legitimacy in terms of kinship and sang their praise in poetry. They needed them, but feared them, for 'the Charan's tongue ... cut both ways, and cut deeper than the *katar* (broadsword) of a valiant foe. But for this eternal dread of satires and unsavoury reflections, the Charan as well as his counterpart in other climes, the minstrel and the chronicler—would have starved in the Middle Ages, whether of the East or of the West' (Qanungo 1969, 40).

The function of the bard was parallel to that of the goddess, his 'sister': he was the guardian of honour and, ultimately, of dharma. But while the Goddess was divinity itself and could do no wrong, the bard was only human, in spite of his sacredness. The scepticism that Westphal-Hellbosch notes regarding the qualities of the Charan was probably shared by many—even from the time of the ministers of Shiladitya, if myth is to be believed.

But such criticism only underlines his importance. It is certainly true, as Qanungo states, that 'the Charan and the Rajput in historical times are found inseparable like body and soul' (1969, 39). We have seen, too, that the institution of the bard rises with Rajputhood itself, in a period from at least the twelfth century onwards, just as it was to fade with the fall of the Rajput rulers from 1947 onwards.

NOTES

1. According to Tessitori, Dingala means 'irregular', 'not in accordance with standard poetry' or possibly 'vulgar'. The term was used in contrast to Pingala (below) which then indicated Braja Bhasa. The latter was, at the time, the poetic language of the Bhakta poets. It was, of course, derived from the dialect of Braj, near Mathura (cf. Tessitori 1914, 376). Qanungo adds, in this context: 'the Charan raised the dialect of the Desert to the dignity of the literary language of the court and aristocracy of Rajputana and outside, which later on developed into Rajasthani Dingal....' (1969, 49)
2. Pingala is, on the one hand, used for the language of poetry in Braj Bhasa (see note 1), but secondly, it seems, for prosody in a more general sense, thus including the poetry composed in the Dingala language. This explains why some informants regard Pingala and Dingala as one, for both words refer to traditional Charan poetry, composed according to certain rules (Pingala) in an idiom (Dingala) which now serves no other purpose.
3. They numbered only 32852 in 1901, with the usual shortage of females, in Bombay Presidency (Enthoven 1920, 271).
4. The term Bhuva usually means a spirit-medium of the goddess, and as such is common to all castes involved in traditional goddess worship. Here, he is closer

to being a sacrificial priest, but I have never come across the term used for a Brahmin.

5. Such grain oracles are common in the non-Brahmin cults of the region. I have mentioned such an oracle maintained by a Koli woman of Kankavati, near Dhrangadhra; she is also the Bhuva of Meldi Mata. It may be remembered that her oracle 'decides' by the even or uneven number of the grains in her hand. The oracle mentioned here may well be of a similar type.
6. The mode of questioning the medium here is likely to be similar to the one reported by Pocock from mainland Gujarat (1973, 45-6), but probably somewhat more ceremonious.
7. To the name *Charan*, Enthoven gives two etymologies; from *char-* (to graze), indicating their pastoral adaptation, and from *char-* (to spread), interpreted as those who 'spread the fame' of kings by their poetry. An interpretation of *Gadhavi* links it to *gadha* or fort, either as 'the owner of forts' or from a mythical reference to 'twenty forts' (*gadhavisa*). But Gadhavi is also a common term for headman, though there are yet other explanations. *Barot*, too, may be interpreted in various ways. *Bahurat*, 'much-speaking' is one; another is *Barahath*—'twelve kinds of obstinacy'. Further, we may consider it as a corruption of Sanskrit *varishth*, Enthoven sees them all as 'mere puns on the word Bahrot or Bhat, which means a bard and has been adopted from the Bhat section of the Rajputs and Marathas'. *Mangan* is a generic term for beggar, and may refer to wandering bards 'begging' food or payment in return for their art (Enthoven 1920, 271-2).
8. The names Avari and Avad are connected, and in some stories Avad is the wife of the first Charan. Probably the girls Enthoven calls 'fairies', are apsaras.
9. The Nagas are 'serpents' or 'serpent-spirits' (strictly speaking cobras). In one story Khodiyar and her sisters become Nagas. The connection between goddess-cults and serpents is certainly of importance but has been little studied, except for the case of the goddess Manasa in Bengal, herself a 'serpent'.
10. In other versions, she makes an 'idol'—or rather a doll—for each of the pastoral castes, together with their animals; camel, cow, buffalo and sheep or goat. The variations are considerable, but Bharwads and, as we have seen, Rabaris have the same myth. The best selection of such myths is in Westphal-Hellbosch (1974 and 1976).
11. Here, then, all pastoralists descend from Nagas. The logic of this relation between pastoralism and serpents is not clear, unless they are both associated with the *jangal* (wilderness).
12. I have no explanation for this strange move, unless it is another way to stress men's lack of intelligence compared to women.
13. Without entering into the question of a mythical, matrilineal past, I would certainly suggest that this stress on matrilateral kin must have some relationship to the strong position of women, already noted, and to the importance of alliance in the kinship system of both the Charan and the Rabari. A proper study of kinship among both castes is really an urgent task.
14. We remember that Shiladitya's bull is 'masked' in that myth as a fighting bull. The Goddess as Mahishasuramardini, the slayer of the buffalo-demon, in the context of buffalo sacrifice, appears most clearly in Biardeau (1976).
15. The most obvious example is, of course, Ravana in the Ramayana, who abducts Sita.

16. The sacrifice of the king being, of course, the main theme of *the Golden Bough* (Frazer 1916).
17. These myths otherwise tend to centre on the disappearance of the Vedic Saraswati river, supposed to have flowed through Rajasthan. There are, of course, a large number of dried-out riverbeds in Rajasthan, giving both occasion for, and some substance to, these myths. In Sindh, too, the course of the Indus has changed and a number of myths revolve around this theme.
18. The Banjaras were caravan traders, and may have been an occupational category rather than a 'caste'. Some of them, apparently, were Charans.
19. One of the main commodities of the Banjaras was, in fact, salt. As 'salt' and 'sugar' are both *mithu*, in Gujarati, I suspect Westphal-Hellbosch of a mistake in translation, and that the Banjara was in fact carrying salt.
20. Thus water and blood are seen as female components of the human body, elements coming from the mother, which the ascetic yogi should try to eliminate—cf. Parekh (1936, 15).
21. Here, again, we meet the theme of the seven sisters, a common theme in Indo-European folklore. In India, it turns up again and again in connection with the goddess, as with Khodiyar, Avad and Karni here. There are also said to be seven Kalis. To what extent the theme of the seven sisters is intrinsic to the mythology of the goddess, or whether it is an admixture to it of a folklore theme, is not clear to me.
22. In Khodiyar's case, these early miracles are often connected with the Nagas. In one story, Khodiyar is churning butter when her churning stick turns into a serpent. In another, she and her sisters become Nagas and are carried to the forest, in a basket, by their father. In the night they call him, asking him why they have to sleep in the forest. Thus they make their identity clear. It may be noted that Varudi, too, begins to work miracles when still a child.
23. In this view, the goddess is both the creator of the world and the creation itself. Thus her power over the visible world is absolute.
24. The point here does not seem to be that the goddess has no power to prolong life indefinitely, but that this would be inconsistent with the laws of the creation that is, in the last instance, herself. Humans, as part of creation, are mortal: to grant immortality would be to take them out of the realm of creation; what Shekha asks for is, effectively, to become a God.
25. The *polpats*—royal bards—of the Rathods were recruited from this clan. See below.
26. I have gone more fully into this question in a paper for the 13th European South Asia Conference at Toulouse, 1994 (forthcoming a).
27. In a forthcoming study, I endeavour to analyse more fully the ties between Charanis, the goddess, shakti and sati, all of which would seem to form a consistent body of ideas.
28. We have already touched on this theme. Another contribution of importance is Bouez (1991), where he interprets the sacredness of the goddess in terms of the incest taboo. His approach is close, then, to the conception of the sacred Charani as a 'sister', though he approaches the problem from a different angle and from Bengal material.
29. Enthoven gives other details: Child marriage was not practised in Kutch or Saurashtra, but polygamy was allowed in Enthoven's time. As for the Kanbis, the essential part of the marriage ceremony is the circumambulation of the sacred

fire. Four rounds are made. Widow remarriage was allowed for most groups at the time. For a widow, a bride-price to her parents was paid. Brahmins were employed at the marriage ceremony. Divorce, though rare, was allowed for Saurashtran Charans (1920, 276-81).

30. Damamies would seem to be the groups of women singers specially invited to sing at marriage.
31. These Bhats are, in some other contexts, seen as competitors of the Charans. Here, their role is complementary to them.
32. Kelu is the father of the groom.
33. This Mavalji is the same—or merges mythically with—the Mavalji already mentioned, who instituted the *Bha-Bhaneja* system. Thus while construed here as spurious, the Rohadiya clan is here seen as descended, but matrilaterally and by adoption, from the very person who, in other contexts, serves as a kind of apical ancestor of the Charans.
34. Thus the author implies that bards from one Charan clan could only attach themselves to rulers from a single, specified, Rajput clan. This is far from obvious from other sources, where itinerant bards visit kings and seem to be quite ready to enter their service. The latter sources may refer to a later period, but certainly we have still a lot to learn here.
35. Dr. Jhala has completed a substantial work on kinship and marriage among the Jhalas, which may soon be published. His view here reflects, of course, both his work and his position as member of an important royal house, but is also completely in tune with the tradition of Rajput studies starting with Tod.

CHAPTER VIII

The Brahmins of Saurashtra

THE PROBLEM OF THE BRAHMIN IN HINDU SOCIETY

No single category would seem to be more central for an analysis of Hindu society than the Brahmins. They are the main authors of the texts of Hinduism, and certainly their authorship lends to the sacred literature a certain bias. But then, this very bias is clearly an integral part of Hinduism itself. Did not early Western writers use the word 'Brahminism' for this all-Indian, 'sanskritic' aspect of Indian religion?[1] Perhaps this early usage was the better one, for while Brahmins stand, very largely, for similar values and rituals all over India, 'popular Hinduism', as studied by anthropologists, shows considerable variation.

It may be useful to consider Hinduism, as Srinivas does, as integrated from the top, by the 'sanskritizing' agency of Brahmins,[2] while accepting that popular religion may have different sources and various forms, and might not be particularly 'Hindu'. Thus the role of the Charan, in western India, indicates a specific regional pattern. Their relation to the goddess, and their position close to royalty, intrudes severely into the space occupied, elsewhere, by the Brahmin.[3]

Even Dumont, so often criticized for taking the Brahmin's point of view, stresses the dispersion of the Brahminical function from Vedic times onwards. Then, the Brahmin was a sacrificer; with the change from Vedic to Hindu religion, the replacement of sacrifice by other rites makes the Brahmin, above all, the incarnation of purity in society. This leads to segmentation of the brahminical function, and the temple priest is looked down upon by other Brahmins. Today, then, Brahmin groups are ranked according to the castes that they serve (1966, 97).[4]

These observations are highly pertinent to Saurashtra. Highest among Brahmins here are the Nagars, a caste of landowners and bureaucrats, who never serve others as priests[5] and whose only masters, in the realm of practical life, are the kings. The Guglis, hereditary priests to the temple of Dwarka, take a relatively inferior place among Brahmins, while other groups tend, as Dumont indicates, to take their position from the rank of their masters. And we may, like Raheja (1988, 1989) go further than Dumont here, and imply that most Brahmins are, first and foremost, the servants of others.

But with all this, something remains, making the Brahmin superior to other serving castes: this is what Dumont calls purity. And if Brahmins lack power, this is only the more consistent with his approach, where power and purity, the priestly function and the royal one are strictly separated (1966, 99-101, 351ff).

What becomes enigmatic, however, is the way in which the Charan's sacredness and the goddess' power relate directly to the royal function. This confounds the very distinction Dumont—and, in his view, the Brahmanas—make between status and power, priest and king. 'In its submission to priesthood, kingship participates in it', says Dumont (1966; 101), but the Rajput king partly avoids such submission by allying himself with the Charan. What place, then, remains for the priest?

Before turning to this question, however, let us look at some of the groups which make up the diverse category of Brahmins in Saurashtra.

DO BRAHMINS FORM AN ESTATE?

Brahmins in Saurashtra do not form a homogeneous group. Not only are there a large number of Brahmin castes, but these castes do not share, in any sense, a common position in the social division of labour, in spite of their acknowledged position in a rather abstract hierarchy. Here, as elsewhere, Brahmins of priestly caste do not work exclusively in the priestly function. This does not constitute a problem as we know from other parts of India that non-priest Brahmins may nevertheless share in the corporate rank of their caste-mates. But more seriously, we have to add to the members of these Brahmin castes two other, and rather different, categories of Brahmins.

First of these, and most famous of all Brahmin castes of Saurashtra, are the Nagars. Their function as ministers and bureaucrats in the princely states is well known; so much so, indeed, that it has overshadowed two other facts of importance. First, these state posts in no way constituted a caste monopoly; there were ministers who were Banias or slaves (Khawas). Secondly, beside these state positions, Nagars were landowners, though not everywhere to the same extent.

They were so especially in Junagadh where, as noted, they formed a class of urban landowners reminiscent of the situation in ancient India.

Thus Nagars differ fundamentally from the third group of Brahmins in Saurashtra, exemplified by the inhabitants of a village neighbouring Praj. When I asked my Praj friends to take me there, they refused; when I threatened to go there alone, they stressed the danger of these 'wild people'. I was told there was only one caste in the village, and when I compare these answers with other information, the conclusion seems clear: the neighbouring 'Brahmins' were really Kolis, engaged in a policy of sanskritization made possible by their relative geographical isolation but barely recognized by their neighbours. While the term 'Brahmin' was used,[6] the stereotypes invoked were certainly those about Kolis. Such communities may have little to do with 'real' Brahmins—except that cases of recent sanskritization are not rare. How many Brahmins in Saurashtra are of this type we do not know; to claim Brahminhood a low caste certainly depends on geographical and political distance to established and powerful Brahmin groups. The existence of such communities must deflate the prestige of the term 'Brahmin' in the eyes of others. They may be peripheral; their presence is certainly of no help in defining Brahmins as an 'estate'.

BRAHMIN CASTES OF SAURASHTRA

Who, then, are the Brahmins of Saurashtra? Enthoven (1920, 225-41) lists forty-eight Brahmin castes from Gujarat, twenty of them having less than a thousand members in the 1901 census. Three other castes are said to be 'very small'. Nine of the remaining castes are chiefly found in other parts of Gujarat. This leaves sixteen castes of some importance in Saurashtra: Auduchya (or Audich); Bhojak (or Maga); Garodas; Girnaras; Guglis; Mevadas; Modhs; Nagars; Paliwals; Parajias; Pushkarnas (or Pokarnas); Sachoras; Sarasvats; Shrigauds; Shrimalis and Tapodhans.

Of these 16 castes, the Garodas, Parajias and Tapodhans are held to be 'degraded' Brahmins, the Garodas serving the lowest castes, while the Parajias eat with their Ahir and Charan patrons. The Tapodhans, according to Enthoven, 'are guilty of the sin of using the offerings made to Mahadev' (op. cit., 241).

The Audich, Mevada, Modh, Pushkarna, Sachora, Shrigaud and Shrimali may be seen as typical, in that they all have members fulfilling priestly functions, while the range of other caste occupations is wide.

Of them, Sachora is a small caste, numbering only 1347 members in 1901. The Bhojak are the priests of the Jains, while the Pushkarna specialize in serving the Bhatias, and are Vallabhacharyas like their patrons. Shrimalis, too, are particularly the priests of the Banias.

While the Audich are by far the largest Brahmin caste of the region, Modhs were 'the commonest Brahmans ... employed for marriages and other ceremonies' in Enthoven's time (op.cit., 233). But their lowest division were wrestlers,[7] and Enthoven has a low opinion of the learning of Modh priests.[8] Of the Mevadas, Enthoven has little to say. Thus for this main group of Brahmins we shall concentrate on available information on the Shrimalis (including the Bhojaks) and the Audich.

The Girnaras and the Guglis are both related to traditional pilgrim centres. The Guglis, a small caste of 1025 members in 1901, are the priests of the Krishna temples at Bet Dwarka as well as at Dakor in mainland Gujarat. Others serve the Vallabhacharya Maharajas. The Girnaras, similarly, have the monopoly of officiating to pilgrims at Girnar and at Somnath Patan. They too are Vaishnavas. Beside their monopoly they are temple priests, beggars, traders, moneylenders, cooks and husbandmen, according to Enthoven (1920, 231).

The Nagars are treated separately later. Their position in Saurashtra society is quite unique, and they are considered distinct from all other Brahmin and non-Brahmin groups by informants.

The Paliwals are mostly traders and merchants.[9] The Sarasvats, for their part, were originally priests, but 'as time went on they accepted private or Government service; and at the present day there is not a single Sarasvat who is dependent for his livelihood on priesthood alone. While not giving up their right to be the priests of Brahma Kshatris, the Sarasvats, when need arises, engage other Brahmans as their substitutes to officiate at ceremonies' (Enthoven 1920, 240).

Let us now turn to some examples of these Brahmin castes to gain a fuller idea of the range of adaptations implied by the term.

THE SHRIMALI BRAHMINS

Shrimali Brahmins are named after the ancient city of Shrimal, now known as Bhinmal, near Mount Abu in present-day Rajasthan. They are the subject of an article by Natubhoy.

Shrimal was a city of importance; Natubhoy claims it was the capital of the Gujars from the sixth to the ninth century AD. In the *Shrimal Purana*, which is dated 'not earlier than the 13th century', its origin is ascribed to Vishnu himself, who married (Shri) Lakshmi, the daughter of the sage Bhrigu. He directed Vishwakarman, the sacred architect, to build the city and invited 45,000 'sons of Rishis' (i. e. Brahmins) to dwell there. These are said to have come from several places, some of them perhaps mythical, but it is notable that Prabhas (the town by the temple of Somnath in Saurashtra) is included. The myth thus explains the name of the Shrimali Brahmins as well as their adoption of Lakshmi as patron deity (Natubhoy 1905, 162-3).

A number of Shrimali Brahmins later embraced Jainism, and were known as Bhojaks, from *bhojan* or food. In Natubhoy's opinion, then, Jainism arrived in Marwar after the foundation of Shrimal. The story of the conversion of the Brahmin Gautam, mythical in content, is interpreted by Natubhoy as reflecting 'the struggle of the converts to the new faith of Jainism' (op. cit., 163-4).

Thus the majority of the Shrimali Banias 'adopted Jainism, [but] the Shrimali Brahmins continued to be their preceptors, and even to this day the marriage and death ceremonies are performed according to the Brahminical rites, though a movement is lately started to perform them according to the Jain rites' (op. cit., 164). Enthoven, certainly, treats the Bhojaks (for which he also gives the term Magas) as a separate caste, 'found in considerable numbers in Kathiawar and Kutch. They were originally Shrimali Brahmins who adopted the Jain faith for a living. They are called Bhojaks or eaters because they dine with the Osval Banias. Bhojaks act as priests to the Jains...' (1920, 229).

In AD 1146-7, according to the *Shrimal Purana*, the image of Mahalakshmi was removed from Shrimal and taken to Patan in north Gujarat, then capital of the Chaulukyas. Natubhoy feels the move was a result of the spread of Jainism in Mewar, even if it was a (Jain?) Bania who removed the image. He also thinks the Brahmin community left Shrimal for Patan at the same time (1905, 165). We may, of course, consider whether the migration of the image and its devotees was simply a case of moving from a decaying town to a rising centre of power.

In 1905, the Shrimali Brahmins were spread widely in Marwar, Kutch, Saurashtra and mainland Gujarat. In the latter area, Patan and Dholka are named as their main centres. Of the 17,398 in Bombay Presidency, 10,640 were living in Kathiawar at the time of the 1901 census (Natubhoy 1905, 165,186).

With the relative concentration in Saurashtra, there was also a greater tendency to divide the caste in endogamous sub-groups according to the Veda followed. There were fourteen exogamous divisions or gotras, all named after Vedic saints. Names used were those ending in Lal, Shankar or Das, as well as Oza, Trivedi, Dave, Vyas, and Joshi—the latter two particularly in Gujarat, Kathiawar and Kutch (op. cit., 166).

Natubhoy discusses the relationship between Kulin and Dhakad (inferior) sections of the caste, and the hypergamous marriages between them. He notes the problematic position of the hypergamous brides and the high dowries, which recall the similar marriages between Kulin and non-Kulin Brahmins of Bengal analysed by Inden (1976). But Natubhoy also notes the exchange of daughters between families, surely a non-Brahmin practice, though well established among such Gujarat castes as the Kanbi/Patidar (op. cit., 167-9; H.G. Patel 1961).[10]

Of a total of about 19,000 Shrimalis (1901 census) only about 200, or about two per cent of the males, followed a priestly occupation. These include caste members in the Kathiawar towns of Chuda, Dhrol and Jamnagar. 'Of the rest', Natubhoy writes, 'a few are employed in Native States or under Government, a large number are in service of private persons, mostly traders, while some in the Palanpur district, near the borders of Marwar, are engaged in cultivation' (op. cit., 169-70).

With the exception of the priests, then, most seem to have followed what today would be called white-collar occupations, serving the state or private firms. While undoubtedly holding a high rank in ritual terms, they did not themselves occupy powerful positions. In terms of estate categories, most Shrimalis would seem to belong, but in a serving capacity, to the same category as the merchants. Indeed, Natubhoy may have underestimated the importance of trade for the Shrimali Brahmins, an occupation which is associated with the caste by my informants. The Shrimalis today form an important section of the urban middle class, in business, the professions, and white-collar occupations. In the 1881 census, the Shrimalis were classed as cultivators. Natubhoy points to the fallacy of this classification, which we shall keep in mind when, below, we shall turn to the occupational classification of Brahmins (Natubhoy 1905,170). The reason for classing Shrimalis with cultivators, however, would be that they had some land, while Natubhoy's criticism implies that the land, like that of many urbanites in Saurashtra then and later, was farmed by others.

Natubhoy's views regarding the marriage rituals of Shrimalis are also of interest here. 'Though Shastras are said to be the authorities in this matter, family custom (*Kul Achar)* and feminine tradition *(Stri Achar)* or *(Doshi Shastra)* have largely influenced it. Some of the ceremonies are, no doubt, ... Shastric, but the others are illustrative of the usages and customs related to the occupations of the caste' (Natubhoy, op. cit., 172).

Generally, the Shrimali Brahmins are Shaivite by religion. As noted, however, Mahalakshmi is the caste goddess, or 'patron saint' as Natubhoy puts it. In addition, every gotra has its own goddess or kuldevi. But the way in which Natubhoy states the relationship between the gotra and its gods is worthy of note: 'Every Shrimali Brahmin', he says, has for his gotra, a goddess, a Shiva, a Ganesh, a Bhairav (form of Shiva), and a Yaksha (a follower of Kubera, the God of Wealth)'. Are we here given to understand that the forms of Shiva, Bhairav, etc., are in fact particular to each gotra? It seems so (Natubhoy 1905, 179).

Briefly, the impression of Shrimali Brahmins gained from Natubhoy is certainly that of a high-ranking Hindu caste, but in no way one which fully or prototypically expresses a Brahmin ideal. The incidence of exchange marriage, the character of the marriage ceremonies, all contribute to a picture of a caste which, though highly influenced by all-Indian brahminical ideas, retain a cultural particularity related to their regional origins. Unlike the Kulin Brahmins of Bengal (Inden 1976) they can hardly stand as a model of Brahmin culture.

THE AUDICH BRAHMINS

I have met several Audich Brahmins, some of whom bore the title of Rajghor (priests to kings)—probably the highest-ranking section of the caste, as they themselves saw it. One informant saw his caste as 'undoubtedly the most learned of Gujarat's Brahmins'. But it was not easy to get a clear picture of the caste from my informants. For a fuller description of this group, I shall have to rely on Enthoven.

The Audich are by far the largest group of Brahmins in Gujarat. At the time of the 1901 census, there were 178,254 of them. No numbers are given for Kathiawad, but as in Enthoven's time, the group is still found all over Gujarat. If we assume that there were between 20,000 and 45,000 in Kathiawar in 1901, we cannot be far off the mark.

Audichya sarv Rushiya—all Audich are seers—quotes Enthoven; their name he interprets as 'Northerner' (1920, 228-9). Their traditions date their arrival in Gujarat to the time of Mularaja of Anhilwada Patan (AD 961-6) who is said to have invited them to help with a sacrifice. Mularaja then offered them grants and presents, inviting them to stay.

> Some agreed, and others first refused till they were persuaded by the grant of a spot of special holiness at the mouth of the Mahi. Those who first agreed were a thousand strong and so became known as the Sahasra or Thousand Audichyas; those who first refused were, because they formed a band or *toli*, known as Tolakia Auduchyas. The Sahasras are again divided into Sihoras and Siddhapuras from the towns of Śihor near Bhavnagar in east Kathiawar and of Siddhpur near Mehsana in north Gujarat, which Mularaja is said to have bestowed on their ancestor. (op. cit., 228)

The occupations of Audich Brahmins cover a wide spectre. According to Enthoven, most live on alms, thus following a traditional Brahmin calling; but this should be modified by his remark that 'Many are particularly successful as exorcists, fortune-tellers and magicians' (ibid.). Thus not all alms-begging Audich are what we would understand by sanskritizing agents; rather, many seem to have catered to non-brahminical strands of folk culture.

Except for a few cultivators, whose geographical distribution is not stated, Enthoven points to typical Brahmin occupations: cooks, family or village priests, and the clerical professions. But we should add that some of these 'clerks' were in fact high-level bureaucrats in the princely administrations. One informant's father was the *karbari* of Gondal state, i.e. in charge of the state accounts.

Enthoven stresses the internal divisions in the caste, according to which castes are served. Thus in north Gujarat we find: 'Kanbi-gors who serve cultivators, Darji-gors who serve tailors, Gandhrap-gors who serve musicians, Hajam-gors who serve barbers, Koli-gors who serve Kolis, and Mochi-gors who serve shoemakers' (op. cit., 228-9). The mention of Brahmins serving shoemakers is surprising, since the latter are untouchables everywhere in Gujarat. The term Rajgor is not given by Enthoven; nor does he mention such high positions as current in the caste. The number of Audich in such positions would necessarily remain small, and they stand out as an exception; the communities mentioned here as otherwise served by the Audich are lower or medium castes. Enthoven does not mention whether similar divisions exist in Saurashtra.

Enthoven tells us nothing specific of the religion of the Audich, though, being a large caste for Brahmins, it is likely that they fall within his generalization that Gujarat Brahmins are Shaivite.[11] My Audich informants may, generally speaking, fit into this broad category, but they all seem to have their particular ideas on religion.

Thus one hotel-keeper is an ardent reader of the *Vayu Purana* and a follower of the recent revival of the Rama cult, both of which brings him closer to Vishnu than to Shiva, though he certainly belongs to no Vaishnavite sect. Claiming that the Audich are more learned in the Vedas than other Brahmins in the area, he implicitly claims the right to orient himself freely within the general range of 'sanskritic' Hinduism: being a Brahmin does not bind him to a specific cult but instead gives him the capacity to understand them all. This view is shared by many Brahmins at the present time, with no regard to their particular caste background. Here, the importance of Brahminhood is affirmed without having to rely on a tradition inherited within the caste.

Like Shrimali Brahmins, the Audich cover a wide range both in rank and social adaptation. They seem more often to have been priests than the Shrimalis—yet then, as now, they have been no match for the Shrimalis in rank. That several Audich subdivisions serve low castes as priests, must deflate the overall status of the caste. Their main position, however, is not as priests but as white-collar workers. They, too, are surely not the prototypical Brahmins of the Dumontian hierarchy, even if they have a share in the priestly function. Above all, they form part of the urban middle class.

THE NAGARS

Though relatively large for a Brahmin caste, the Nagars numbered only 21,617 in 1901, in Bombay Presidency as a whole (Enthoven 1920, 234). Their importance for understanding traditional Kathiawar in any case bears no relation to their numbers. This is due, not only of their prominent role as ministers and bureaucrats in the states, but also to their high social position—economically as well as ritually—and to their role as urban-based and absentee landowners in some areas. Nobody contests the rank of the Nagars; in Saurashtra, they are the highest caste, whether or not the suffix 'Brahmin' is added to the caste name.

Stevenson's classic work (1920) on Brahmin rites deals largely with the Nagars, but her approach does not inform us greatly on the caste as such. She seems to be the source of the reference, sometimes found, to a division between 'Nagar Brahmins' and 'Nagars', the implication being that the former are priests and the latter are not. Thus she stresses that no Nagar is a priest, while the Nagar Brahmins will serve only Nagars (op. cit., 42). In a note she adds, interestingly, that the Nagars are of higher rank than their Brahmin counterparts (ibid.). No such distinction was ever made to me in Saurashtra, where most Nagars stress that the caste has not been priests, except in a very distant past. There is no allusion, either, to separate 'priestly' and 'secular' branches of the caste.

Nagar tradition connects the name with Naga[12]—an interpretation rejected by Enthoven. He sees it as a place-name, probably of their original habitat, which he identifies with Ramnagar in Bareilly District, U.P (1920, 234-6). Other myths refer to Vadnagar, sometimes identified with Shrimal on the Gujarat-Rajasthan border, and some of the land grants of Vallabhi times explicitly mention this town. Among my informants, Nagar or otherwise, a popular rendering is simply as 'Town (*nagar*) Brahmins', an interpretation which is obvious but which, of course, proves nothing.

Amarji, author of the *Tarikh-i-Sorath* and himself a Nagar, refers repeatedly to Junagadh as 'nagar'. This town, originally known as Girinagar, was certainly the centre of the Nagar community in his day as it still is today. Whether Amarji used the name for the town to fit the caste or vice versa, we cannot, of course, know. He claims that they came to Junagadh with king Naughan, i.e. in the eleventh century AD (1882, 27). But sometimes one has the impression that Amarji refers, here, rather to the beginning of the Chudasama dynasty in the ninth century AD.

Enthoven, in tracing the Nagars to U.P., and noting that ten of the thirteen Sharmans mentioned below are common to Nagars and to the Kayasthas of Bengal, supposes a common origin for these two regionally important castes (op. cit., 235). We have, in fact, early mentions of 'Kayasthas' in Gujarat and Saurashtra, though no such group is found there today. It is true that only the priestly occupation of a small minority of Nagars set them apart from the Kayasthas in terms of the position they occupy in society. The similarity in their function as bureaucrats, ministers and urban landowners is quite striking.

A similar combination of landholding and high-ranking state service would seem to have characterized the position of Brahmins (possibly also Nagars) in Sindh during the early years of Muslim rule. It seems, indeed, as witnessed by the example of Junagadh, that Muslim rule was less inimical to the position of such a Brahmin community than the Rajput political system. Let us note in passing that the village of

Karimpur in the U.P., known to us through the writings of the Wisers (1936) as well as of Wadley (1975), owes its Brahmin dominance to the benevolence of its Muslim landlord—who, at the same instance, ousted the Rajputs from the village.

It has been held (Munshi 1954) that the Nagars emerged as a group under the Gurjara-Pratihara dynasty, sometimes seen as the first Rajput state, but I have argued that this is a case of what has sometimes been called proto-Rajput organization. Enthoven takes Nagar origins even further back, to the Vallabhi empire. Here I shall quote Enthoven at some length:

> The late Vallbhji Haridat Acharya of Rajkot was fortunate enough to find three MSS of the *pravaradhyay* of these Brahmans. One of these is nearly 200 years old and distinctly states that the *gotras, pravars,* etc., which are therein specified are those which were in existence before Samvat 1283, i.e. AD 1226. This MS. gives a list of thirteen *sharmans* which were in vogue amongst the Nagar Brahmans 700 years ago. They are (1) Datta, (2) Gupta, (3) Nand, (4) Ghosh, (5) Sharman, (6) Das, (7) Varman, (8) Nagadatta, (9) Trat, (10) Bhut, (11) Mitra, (12) Dev and (13) Bhav. To each of these *Sharmans* have been assigned two or more of the *gotras* that are at present prevalent among them. This list is not a fiction, but has a foundation in fact. For no less than three of these *Sharmans* have been traced in the copper-plate grants of the Valabhi kings who ruled over Kathiawar and North Gujarat from AD 509 to 766. They are Mitra, Trat and Datta, and are found appended to the names of Brahman grantees. That these Brahmans were Nagars is clearly proved by the fact that they are said to have originally belonged to Anandpur or Anartpur, which are both old names of Vadnagar. Again, the *gotras* mentioned of these Brahman grantees exactly agree with those assigned in the *pravaradhyay* to the three *Sharmans* just referred to. There cannot, therefore, be even the shadow of doubt as to these Brahmans being Nagar. And this shows that the Nagars make their first appearance in Kathiawar and Gujarat for the first time with the Valabhi kings in the sixth century AD. Now, these *Sharmans* cannot possibly be mere name endings. For in the first place they themselves always follow the name suffixes. Even now at the time of performing religious ceremonies, it is customary to say, e.g., Bhagwanlal Trat and Manishankar Gupta instead of mere Bhagwanlal and Manishankar. The *Sharmans* Trat and Gupta here follow the name suffixes *Lal* and *Shankar*. Secondly while name suffixes like *Lal* and *Shankar* pertain merely to individuals, each *Sharman* was and is the peculiar property of a certain separate group of individuals. There can, therefore, be no doubt that these *Sharmans* are clan indicators. (1920, 234-5)

The Nagars still rank with my informants as the most prestigious caste in Saurashtra, though their loss of position due to the disappearance of the states is also acknowledged. They, even more than the Rajputs, form the 'old aristocracy' of Saurashtra, especially as viewed from the towns.

The Nagars are divided into six endogamous subdivisions, and Stevenson underlines the strict ban on intermarriage among them (1920, 46-7). Of these, the Vadnagra hold the highest rank; their food is accepted by all others. They, on the other hand, do not interdine with them. It is among the Vadnagras that the few priests are found. It is they, too, that have provided most of the dewans or ministers of the states. They are named after the ancient city of Vadnagar, which, as we have seen, is one possible source of the caste name.

Of the other subdivisions, Chitrodas and Krashnoras are not found in Gujarat. Visnagras and Sathodras, who are moneylenders, landowners and public servants, are mainly found outside Saurashtra. The Prashnoras, on the other hand, are the archetypal *vaids* or ayurvedic doctors, and as such are important in Saurashtra where Jamnagar has one of the foremost Ayurvedic universities in India. Beside this important occupation, Prashnoras are 'readers of purans' (Enthoven 1920, 236-7).

Of all the Brahmin castes of Saurashtra, Nagars might be seen as the 'arch-brahmins'. This is not to say that they most closely resemble the poor but pious Brahmins of scriptural fame, nor that they are particularly known as priests. In spite of this, they and (-especially the Vadnagras) are the highest-ranking caste in the peninsula. Rather than from purity alone, this position seems to derive from a combination of attributes. They are learned—compare here the Modhs in Enthoven's estimation—and though this learning is not exclusively religious, it is universally acknowledged. Their Brahminhood, in spite of their often worldly occupation, is never in doubt. Their religion—they are followers of Shankaracharya—constitutes a highly philosophical and 'pure' version of Shaivism, far from the Shaktist interpretations of folk religion.

But finally, and perhaps most important, they are both rich and powerful—though their position has declined after independence. This position is still more marked in Junagadh than in the other cities of the peninsula, and their standing in this town and state seems to date from the time of the Chudasamas. Their history as urban landowners goes even further back, to the Vallabhi empire and its capital. We may also note that a Nagar is said, in the context of the Khodiyar myth, to have been the Rajpurohit (family priest) of the Vallabhi king.[13]

My hypothesis here is that the Nagars formed part of the class of urban landowners which seems to have dominated the Vallabhi empire—and other northern empires of the classical era. While Vallabhi fell, this position was re-established in Junagadh, as possibly in the other contemporary kingdoms supported by a 'king-tribe' alliance.[14] With the Muslim conquest of Junagadh, they seem to have shifted their allegiance to the new rulers.

In the states established by Rajputs on the base of 'feudalism from below', however, their position was limited by the emerging rural-based aristocracy. Thus, while the structure of urban landownership could, with relative ease, be fitted into the framework of the Islamic state, and survived in parallel with, or even transformed into, a system of zamindari landholding, the relative caste monopoly on jagir holdings in the Rajput states proper seems to be incompatible with the old position of the Nagars. While a symbiotic relationship could develop in relation to Muslim rulers, there was competition with dominant Rajputs.

All this implies that Nagars held a particular position in the 'proto-Rajput' states and in Junagadh, which transcended their importance as ministers and bureaucrats. In an analysis of these states, we have to include them in a particular 'estate' of urban landowners, which would merge or at least overlap with the position of merchants. In short, the Nagars form an element of continuity in the history of Saurashtra, from their settlement at Vallabhi to the annexation of Junagadh state by the Indian Union in 1947.

In later days, however, the interests of Nagars and merchants came to oppose each other, as Nagars became the firm allies of the princes while merchants became their opponents. But in Junagadh the merchants were relatively weak—it was never predominantly a trading city—and the Nagars consequently strong. For Junagadh, we must see the Nagars as an estate in themselves; though for Saurashtra as a whole they were rather the bureaucrats of the princes, allied to the Darbar estate.

PRIESTS OF PILGRIMAGE: THE GUGLI BRAHMINS

The Gugli Brahmins, hereditary *pandas* (pilgrimage priests) of Dwarka, form the subject of a recent article by Pocock (1981). We might expect, here, to find the priestly vocation in full flower; yet this seems hardly to be the case. Of the Gugli population of some 2000 at Dwarka, of whom about 600 are 'gainfully employed', only some 160 'derive all or part of their living from pandagiri' (caring for the pilgrims). Most of these combine their priestly work with other sources of income; one runs a taxi business, one a cloth-shop, while most have shops selling religious souvenirs (op. cit., 327-8).

The majority of the working caste members are quite secularly employed. Some are labourers, while a much larger number are clerks, or perform other white-collar work. Then there are a considerable number in business, ranging from tailor to moneylender. Quite a number are teachers or cooks (op. cit., 332-3). Thus if we look at the employment profile of the group in general, it differs little from several other Brahmin castes, such as the Audich. As Pocock puts it, it is 'a rather dull catalogue' (op. cit., 334).

Let us return, briefly, to the Guglis who actually engage in the traditional vocation of the caste. According to myth, they have served at Dwarka ever since the caste originated from the seed spilt by Brahma on illicitly catching a glimpse of Parvati as she was to be married to Shiva. 'When Brahma confessed his offence and begged pardon for it, Siva blessed the semen soaked sand and ordained that many great munis would arise from it who would be called Valkiliya because they were born of the sand, valuka, and they would be the first among high-souled Brahmans, learned in the vedas' (op. cit., 322).

Of this mass of Brahmins 505 were sent, at the instigation of Vishnu, to Dwarka to cater for pilgrims. Here they were to live as householders (*grahastha*). They protested that they would be spoilt by the gifts of kings, and begged to live as Brahmacharis or renouncers. But Vishnu told them that only householders can properly look after pilgrims; this would in no way reduce their sacred powers. Brahma wanted them to be considered sons of Shiva and himself, and Shiva granted them wisdom and scriptural knowledge, which would remain theirs as long as they refrained from adultery. 'For as long as they performed a special sacrifice they would be famous throughout the land' (ibid.).

Unhappily the early history of Dwarka remains a mystery to us. Krishna's city was destroyed by a flood, and, as Pocock puts it, 'it is very surprising that in the puranas it never receives the attention which Kashi or Gaya receives, nor is it accorded the status which they are assumed to have' (op. cit., 335). In 1212, according to myth, Krishna's image was removed from Dwarka to Dakor—or rather, Krishna himself got up and walked there, to join his devotee Bodano (op. cit., 327; Mallison 1990). Later, Dakor was developed into a main centre of the Vallabhacharya sect (Mallison 1983). Dwarka, however, also developed, and from the seventeenth century onwards appears as an important pilgrimage.

Among its important patrons were the Bhatias of Kutch and Jamnagar, whom we have already met.[15] They too were Vallabhacharyas; Pocock sees their wealth, earned in trade with Oman, Africa and the Gulf, as a major factor in the rise of Dwarka, whose prosperity 'appears to have reached its apogee in the last half of the nineteenth century' (op. cit., 326). The later decline of Dwarka, then, is seen to result from the withering away of the maritime trade dominated by Bhatias. This has led other Vallabhacharya temples to take Dwarka's role, while the rise of the Swaminarayana sect has further eroded its popularity among Vaishnavites (op. cit., 330).

Since each gotra of Guglis has a list of castes identified as their jajmans, some of them have fared better than others. But Pocock stresses that many prestigious castes figure in these lists in name only, and the priestly income depend largely on the lower castes. Thus for most pandas, their priestly income is very moderate indeed. It is the number and quality of the clientele which decides whether a particular family decides to stay in the traditional occupation. We may think that the sacred status of the work makes up for the meagre income. But, says Pocock,

> Apart from some two or three Guggali Brahmins who think of their work as a sacred vocation—'We make a great kalyana not only for all India but all mankind'— the great majority regard it simply as the job from which they get their living and one which they would happily relinquish should some more lucrative opportunity arise. The pervasive attitude is well exemplified by the head of one household who worked as an octroi inspector for the municipality. Seven of his eight children were at school, the eldest worked as a panda and was content to do so. His father said of him that he neither could nor would study but that if the other three sons were successful in their studies they should never depend on pandagiri. (Pocock, op. cit., 325)

This rather sad picture certainly does not fit the stereotype of the ideal Brahmin. True, we are dealing with a decaying centre of pilgrimage, which flourished a good hundred years ago; yet Pocock (op. cit., 335) feels there is 'no good reason to suppose that the Guggali population of Dvaraka was ever substantially greater or that a substantially greater proportion of it was ever dependent upon the pilgrim trade.' We should not be surprised at this, he says (op. cit.,

334) for 'the account accords pretty well with a general assumption that temple priests and the Brahmans of sacred centres are at best a pretty poor lot'.

Pocock's view of Dwarka is far removed from the impression one gets of some of the large south Indian temples. Certainly, when visiting Dwarka in 1979, I found no accommodation suitable for the modern, middle-class pilgrim; such rooms as could be found, were primitive indeed.[16]

This should not, of course, influence the religious mind; but in modern India it does affect the status of the pilgrimage. The scarcity of Western visitors is best indicated by the greeting of the first panda I met: 'Do you know professor Pocock?'

Pocock's view of the priestly vocation may be too negative or cynical, and Dwarka in decline may be a poor base for drawing more wide-ranging conclusions. But it does not help us in our search for the prestigious priestly Brahmin of classical texts and Dumontian sociology.

AGRICULTURAL BRAHMINS: SOME CONSIDERATIONS

In Gujarat as a whole, twelve of the forty-eight Brahmin castes are described by Enthoven as wholly or mostly cultivators or peasants (1920, 225-41). It should be noted that they range from such a case as the Anavil, a caste of great landlords in Surat district, to quite humble peasants. The category 'cultivator' therefore is not very informative. The Anavil (Van der Veen 1972) parallel the Nagars and some of the rich Brahmin trading classes in forming an urban or semi-urban 'aristocracy'. Their relatively ancient Brahmin status is not in doubt. On the other hand, sanskritization has sometimes created 'Brahmins' from groups of quite low origin. Some such cases are quite recent, and parallel the rise of the Mena Rajputs from tribal, or Mahia Rajputs from Koli, origins.[17]

The creation of Brahmin castes from other origins is not a new phenomenon. Enthoven cites several cases from the Puranas or the *Mahabharata* (1920, 214-15). More interestingly,

> in comparatively modern times, there are instances of the creation of certain classes of Brahmans. Thus in Partabgarh there is a legend current that the celebrated Oudh chieftain Manik Chand created Brahmans wholesale out of various Kurmis, Ahirs and Bhars. A similar case occurred in Fatehpur. In Unao, again, a story is told of Raja Tilok Chand, that one day while hunting he was very thirsty, and having no attendant he asked a Lodha, who was present there,

to fetch him some water, which he brought in his own drinking vessel. The Raja after drinking the water discovered that the owner of the vessel was a low-caste man, and so he asked him to call himself a Brahmin under the title of Pathak of Amtara, as he was watching the mango (am) trees. The title still remains with his descendants, who are acknowledged as Brahmans.... (1920, 215).

We cannot, of course, be sure of the historicity of such narratives. What they tell us is that the idea that Brahminhood might be created by man, not only by God, was relatively widespread. Such ideas may have been held mainly by lower castes, jealous of the Brahmins; but even so, our present knowledge of sanskritization processes leads us to believe that such stories may contain a grain of truth. Enthoven notes that classical sources—he mentions only Manu—hold that Brahmins degraded by marriage with low-caste women can again be elevated to Brahmin status after a certain number of generations. Enthoven concludes: 'The above remarks clearly show that a man who attained to a certain social and moral status was designated a Brahman ...' (op. cit., 215-16). Though the remark applies to ancient times, it may not be without relevance to more modern cases.

Looking at the present situation, we may fruitfully distinguish between three types of Brahmin 'cultivators'. First, there are the rich landowners such as the Anavil or Nagar. Nothing indicates that these castes were ever predominantly priests. Rather, as a rich, predominantly urban caste, they were among the prime subjects of the kingdom. Did they become Brahmins because of their position, or was the position accorded them because of their Brahminhood? As in the case of the Nagars, they may have kept both to the present day.

Even if we do not accept the theory of a common Nagar/Kayastha origin (Enthoven 1920, 235) it would seem that the Kayasthas of Bengal are a parallel case. Yet they never attained Brahmin status. Perhaps this should be explained with reference to the presence of important high-status priestly Brahmin elements in Bengal.

Whether Anavils have the same origins, we do not know; they may, as Enthoven believes, have been the earliest Brahmin settlers in Gujarat (op. cit., 225-6), or they may be a basically landowning caste who succeeded in attaining Brahmin status. In all these cases, the high ritual status is combined with power and economic position, making it difficult to decide whether rank or worldly power is primary in each case.

The second type are basically priestly castes, members of which have obtained land grants or taken to agriculture. These groups rank with small or middle peasants in socio-economic terms. They are seldom dominant in a village, though land grants to a whole village group may produce exceptions. Such is the case of the Brahmins of Karimpur in Uttar Pradesh (Wiser 1936; Wadley 1975). Landed Shrimali or Audich Brahmins may belong to this type. When they are rich, however, they approach the first type, for example through engaging in trade. More commonly, such Brahmins live dispersed among other cultivators, from whom they differ mainly in rank.

The third type is, I believe, largely a modern phenomenon. In peripheral villages, such as the one I mentioned in the introduction to this chapter, we find groups of peasants who were never rich enough, nor high enough in status, to attract any considerable number of service castes. Thus their settlements would remain hamlets,[18] though not necessarily small in size. Typically, in such areas as the Bhal on the coast of the Gulf of Cambay, they would be Koli settlements.

Under traditional rule, when caste was a matter of jurisdiction (at least ideally), such groups would remain bound by the view other castes had of them. Thus Kolis would remain Kolis, unless particularly favoured by authority, or unless determined political action made it possible for them to substantiate claims to Rajput status. Yet in the modern setting, where caste has no juridical value, their relative isolation would make it easy for them to claim higher status, and difficult for other castes to sanction such claims. Thus, as shown by the village close to Praj, their claim to be Brahmins might find superficial acceptance, but be shrugged off as insignificant.

BRAHMINS AS AN URBAN COMMUNITY

It is clear from the above that large numbers of Brahmins are engaged in occupations that are, essentially, urban. Apart from absentee landowners, traders and moneylenders would seem to be the most prestigious group. There are Brahmins in most white-collar occupations, and even in a few 'blue-collar' ones. For a considerable time, Brahmins must have furnished an important part of what we may call the tertiary sector, with its concentration in towns and cities.

Most such employment has no particular sacredness attached to it. But white-collar work remains ritually pure. In her study of economic activity in Mahuva, Pandit (1965) stresses that most people, but Brahmins in particular, try to find work in a 'merchant-like' occupation.

In the case of Brahmins, it may be wrong to read, as I did in my early work, into this statement respect for, and imitation of, the Banias. The merchants referred to may well have been Brahmins themselves.

Many Shrimali Brahmins are traders or industrialists, and Nagars have been traders and moneylenders as well as landowners and bureaucrats (e.g. Subramaniam 1991, 334-5). Among the important merchants of Surat during the eighteenth century, we find a number of Brahmins, of whom the most prominent was the Nagar A. N. Trivedi (Tarwady) (ibid.; Torri 1991, 52).

At a quite different level, the Guglis have, for quite some time, been engaged in local trade. We shall have to accept, in fact, that trade was one of the main occupations of several Brahmin groups, and that Brahmins were, in fact, the rivals of the Banias.

This conclusion is strengthened when looking at regions where the Bania element is weak or lacking. Thus in Maharashtra, trade and moneylending was largely in the hands of the Chitpavans and other Brahmin groups (Divekar 1984; Subramaniam 1992, 161-4). In Goa, the Gaudi Saraswati Brahmins became the main local Hindu merchant caste, competing with Gujarati Banias for the control of trade in Portuguese India (Pearson 1976). The same group, as migrants to south Kanara in Karnataka, have established themselves as the main trading community there.[19] Thus the role of Brahmins in Indian commerce is well documented. What is surprising for Gujarat is instead the strong competition they have suffered from the Banias.[20]

We have seen that urban society, with the Banias, is a continuous factor in Saurashtra since well before Rajput times. We may now add that at least some of the Brahmin groups, including of course the Nagars, have a very long history in urban, non-priestly occupations in the area.

THE BRAHMINS IN THE LARGER SOCIETY

This discussion underlines our earlier conclusions. While urban, landowning Brahmins may once have formed an estate singly or with other urban groups such as the merchants, they do so only locally in Saurashtra today. Urban Brahmins are important, but do not appear as a distinct estate from the Banias, at least in modern times.

Only the Nagars were influential in traditional society, but their role, in a pan-Indian view, is usually associated with the Kayasthas. Most Brahmin cultivators merge with the peasants from our point of view.

But what of Brahmins as priests? Certainly, in pilgrimage centres such as Dwarka or Prabhas Patan, they were important. But we have seen that the Guglis are far removed from the idealized view of such priests. They may stress that the status of their patrons does not affect the ranking of gotras within the caste (Pocock 1981, 333), but this is not the case for Brahmins in general.

Most of the priestly Brahmin castes derive their prestige from the people they serve. This is clear from the large number of 'degraded' Brahmin groups. Their fortunes and interests are tied to those of their jajmans; they are not set off, as a group, from them. This view, denying the Brahmins a place as a separate and identifiable force in Saurashtra politics, is shared by Spodek (1976, 23) who notes that, 'perhaps surprisingly, nowhere does the literature suggest that Brahmins as priests exerted special influence in public affairs. Brahmins and Nagars—often considered as a subcaste of Brahmins—did enter administrative services, but this was an alternative to priesthood rather than a fulfillment of it.'

Brahmins, then, were not a separate estate in Saurashtra. Divided by their functions, they form an addition to such estates as Darbars and Banias, from which the social structure of the region is constructed.

THE BRAHMIN AND THE CHARAN IN RELATION TO THE KING

Let us now turn to the priests employed in royal or dominant caste temples. The Rama priests of the latter seem to be treated very much as village servants, if the priest in Praj is typical. He certainly enjoyed some prestige, but apart from formalities, such as addressing him as 'Maharaj', he was not seen as an important person in the village.

What about royal temples? In the Rama temple opposite the city palace in Dhrangadhra, marked with the blazon of the state and once under royal patronage, priesthood may well have been prestigious. Yet nothing indicates that the ruler saw his priests as more than high-status functionaries, as they continue to be under public trusteeship.

To investigate the relevance of the Dumontian perspective for Saurashtra, then, we must turn to the Rajpurohit— the 'chaplain' of the ruler. No doubt, he was an important figure; but in the Charan he had a powerful rival for the king's attention, and it was the latter, rather than the priest, who played the main role in legitimating the king's position. Nor is there any doubt that the goddess, herself normally a Charani, was the central divinity on whom depended the fortunes of the kingdom and its king. Her cult did not depend on Brahmin priests. Where we find them in her service, they contribute to the prestige of the temple and the cult, but all important rituals of the goddess could be performed, in principle, by the devotee himself. The indispensible intermediary on certain occasions was the spirit medium (Bhuva), who was never a Brahmin.

Every Rajput ruler had a Charan, who might even follow him through the trials of outlawry. There is no doubt, from the literature, that the Charan was closer to the king than the Brahmin was. Yet the Rajpurohit was there, at the court of any chief of importance. The number and quality of Brahmins employed might vary. It was the successful ruler, well established in his castle, who employed several such men.

This may provide us with the clue to distinguishing the Brahmin's function from that of his bardic rival. The presence of the Brahmin did, I think, help to legitimate the ruler in the eyes of those who did not belong to the rural-based nexus of the 'thirteen castes', from which the king himself and his bard had come. Not least, of course, the Brahmin presence would be important for that portion of the urban population which was itself Brahmin. But even for Jains, who might be more partial to the presence of a Jain monk at the court, the Brahmin presence would underline the propriety of rule.

We must distinguish here between two possible bases of Brahmin legitimation of rule. One might see the Brahmin as representative of a 'community' of 'Hindus', but this would, I think, be spurious for ancient times. Rather, I would see the Brahmin as a neutral source of prestige in relation to the two most clearly defined estates: the Rajput-allied castes, whose saintly figure was the Charan, and the sectarian Banias, whose saints were Jain or Vaishnava monks.

The strength of this perspective lies in the ritual functions of the Brahmin. He is present at important life rituals both of Jains and Charans; in both cases, his sacred mantras are a source of prestige. Yet they are as external to the logic of the Charan's goddess worship as they are to the cult of the Tirthankaras.

The answer to the question: 'who legitimizes the Rajput king?' is therefore twofold; the Charan and the Brahmin do not perform the same task. The Charan makes the king a hero of the right blood; the Brahmin a king of the sanskritic type. Both take care of dharma, but it is the Charan goddess who rules the fortune of king and country; Rama and his priests give their polish to the accomplished fact.

While the employment of a Charan made the ruler a true Rajput, the legitimation of proper statehood needed the Brahmin. The role of the Brahmin at court, then, would seem to parallel the role of Rama in the king's pantheon. Together they helped taking the ruler out of the limiting frame of 'feudalism from below', to become a proper king in an all-Indian sense.

NOTES

1. For a recent discussion of this theme, see Inden (1990, 97ff.).
2. The term 'sanskritization' was coined by Srinivas (1952) to describe the spread of all-Indian, 'sanskritic' ideas and ritual through the agency of Brahmins all over the country. Later modifications of the concept led him, perhaps, to reify this process (1962, 1967).
3. I allude here to the place the Brahmin is given, as preceptor of the king, particularly in Dumont (1966, 351ff.).
4. Dumont's reference here is to the Panjab Census Report (1911, I; 310).
5. Nagars may have been priests in the past; the Rajpurohit of Shiladitya, in the myth of Khodiyar, is sometimes said to have been a Nagar. Nagars I have met stress that they never serve as priests for others, but that some Nagars thus serve other members of the caste.
6. These Brahmins actually claimed to be Paliwalas, like the merchant and landholding group that formed the base of the first Rathod chiefdom in Marwar. If so, they have certainly 'come down in the world'.
7. These wrestlers were known as Jethimals. I do not know to what extent their sport could be construed as a 'ritual'.
8. 'Modh Brahman officiating priests are usually quite ignorant, and repeat the mantras without any idea of their meaning' (Enthoven 1920, 233).
9. We have met the Paliwals in their original home at Pali, Rajasthan, where the Rathods started their rise to fame by protecting this group of traders. We have also met 'Paliwals' as the peasants inhabiting the village close to Praj. The fact that Enthoven sees Saurashtra Paliwals mainly as merchants does, perhaps, serve to strengthen my claim that this latter group are 'really' Kolis, who claim Brahmin status.
10. It may be remembered that the Tumbel Charan, too, practise exchange marriage.
11. 'All Gujarat Brahmans, except a few who belong to the Swaminarayan sect, are followers of Shiva. Their social and religious customs are chiefly ruled by the Mayukh, the Mitakshara and the Dharma and Nirnaya Sindhu. Of the sixteen Vedic *sanskars* or sacraments, Gujarat Brahmans observe only four at their proper time: *Simanta* or parting of the hair at pregnancy, *Upanayana* or thread girding, *Vivaha* or marriage, and *Svargarohana* or funeral ceremonies, literally 'heaven-climbing', some of the remaining being observed along with one or other of these, some being not performed at all' (Enthoven 1920, 224).
12. While Enthoven may be right in rejecting this etymology, the Nagars' assertion

that they are connected to Nagas is in itself interesting. In a sanskritic context, such an affirmation by a high Brahmin caste is surprising. But in view of the connections between the Nagas and the goddess, and the idea that pastoral castes, including Charans, descend from Nagas, a bond between Nagas and Nagars may have a significance which we cannot at present determine.

13. Even if this is a later interpolation, it shows that whoever made it saw the Nagars as possible incumbents of such posts.
14. Thus Amarji tells us that the Nagars were important landholders in Porbandar state. Few were left there during British times.
15. See Ch. III.
16. I actually occupied the only single room available. This was a bed with a door, to the effect that the door had to be opened to put my sandals under the bed.
17. See Village Monograph No. 8, or, for a brief resume, Tambs-Lyche (1992a, 262-7).
18. See Tambs-Lyche (1992a, 273-6), where I define the 'hamlet' as basically a single-caste community, without specialized village servants; this distinguishes it from the 'village'. The point here, specifically, is that even if the people of this village are 'Brahmins', nobody seems to be willing to serve them; this is equally the case with a community of a single, low caste, such as Kolis.
19. This observation from recent fieldwork in the area is supported by Pearson 1976, as well as Padikkal (1991), etc.
20. Indeed, Torri claims that Banias in eighteenth-century Surat was an occupational category covering all the trading communities. L.Subramaniam, on the other hand, uses the term Bania as I have done here, while stressing that several other communities were active in trade, including the Brahmins (both 1991).

CHAPTER IX

The Banias: The Merchant Estate

A TALE OF TWO WORLD VIEWS

Gandhi's grandfather is often held, incorrectly, to have been the only Bania to be Dewan in a Kathiawar state. While he was Dewan of Porbandar, and Ranmalji the ruler of Jamnagar, two Englishmen were murdered in the Barda Hills, which marked the boundary between the two states. Sharpe tells the story:

> A very stiff letter went from Rajkot to the Rana of Porbandar.... Gandhi sent word ... that the place of the murder was in Jamnagar, not part of the territory of ... Porbandar.... the Rana Sahib could not be held responsible.... The agency sent on the letter to Jamnagar; and the Jam had to pay 1600 silver kowries compensation. The wily Ranmalji promptly paid ... protesting on paper that as the Englishmen had not informed the Jam of their ... visit... he ought not to be held responsible .... Later on, when boundaries were being demarcated, Porbandar found that Gandhi's carelessness had cost Porbandar nearly the whole and certainly the half of Barda Hill; for the compensation paid by Jam Ranmalji, recorded in the agency books, was distinct evidence in favour of the claim of Jamnagar to Barda Hill. (1931, 17-18)

Sharpe, an admirer of Rajputs and no friend of the Congress, surely had her reasons to make old Gandhi seem foolish in 1931. Yet the story shows the contrast between the martial and the merchant ethos. The former sees territorial loss as proof of incompetence, while to Gandhi, the merchant, the cost of compensation and British disfavour were more important than staging a claim to every inch of available territory.

THE CALLING OF TRADE AND THE QUESTION OF ASCETICISM

How can we characterize this merchant ethos? Banias define themselves by *vepar* (trade), and often refer to, in strongly emotional terms, as a 'calling'. A young Bania who was doing 'service'—working for a salary—complained that 'to be in service is to be just like a slave. I must go where they tell me to go, and when they tell me to go.' Another young Bania likened 'service' to being a prisoner, while the first contrasted his situation with the ideal: 'We Banias mostly like to have our own business. That is the right kind of life.'

The ideal, then, is not simply what other castes call a 'merchant-like' occupation—a preference which may be identified with white-collar work (Pandit 1965). Independence is equally important; a Bania should work for his own account or that of his family. Most Banias I met in Saurashtra, did indeed work in their own (or their family's) business.

The preference for trade is matched by an aptitude for it. Why this particular aptitude? The answer must lie, not only in a set of distinctive values, but in a way of organizing social life (Timberg 1978, 17ff). We shall look more closely at both factors, which suit their adaptation as traders, but also sets them apart from other castes. Weber notes the 'ritual seclusion' of some of 'the great Hinduist merchant castes, particularly, for instance, the Bania, have been called the 'Jews of India' and in this negative sense, rightly so' (1958, 112).

Following the same logic, Fox states that profit

> ... signifies the introduction of economic rationality into a system which is based on the rationale of kinship and family. Whatever group undertakes business and the making of profit also accepts social ostracism and develops over time social traits which allow it to withstand the slings and arrows of its non-commercial neighbours (and victims), as well as traits which maximize the production of profit which is so socially disreputable. (1967, 313-14)

Fox writes from his experience of northern India. But in traditional Kathiawar, Banias were not social outcasts by any reasonable standard. They were not popular, some hate them even today, but there is no doubt about their high status. We are closer to what has been said about Gujarat, where folk tales 'were woven around '*shahsodagars*' or great businessmen, and merchants and traders occupied a place of honour in popular imagination. In many parts of India business and businessmen were looked down upon, but not so in Gujarat' (Tripathi and Mehta 1984, 153).

Weber's and Fox's observations rely upon a view of Indian society as originally and fundamentally agricultural, even 'feudal', so that merchants represent a minority intrusion. Weber wanted, of course, to show that Hinduism made Indians 'other-worldly' and unfit for the kind of entrepreneurial spirit he found among early Protestants in Europe (1930, 1958). But merchants may boast of a longer, continuous tradition, in Saurashtra and Gujarat, than the medieval, 'feudal' order of the Rajputs. Banias may be in a minority, their position criticized and even attacked by the rural elite, but by no means can they be seen as intruders. Our view of traditional society in Saurashtra must allow the merchant estate an integral part to play; its presence must colour our picture of the whole. As Timberg asserts, (1978, 33), 'The existence of the Marwaris, as large and successful commercial entrepreneurial groups within Hinduism, is an immediate challenge to the whole theory of Hindu unsuitability for entrepreneurship.'

Weber noted this exception; in the ascetic nature of Jainism he saw a parallel to Protestantism (1958, 199-201, 315). The Vallabhacharya sect was seen from another angle, as an attraction to already succesful traders (op. cit., 315). As Timberg notes, this difference seems less important in practice (1978, 35). His conclusions, based on Gillion's history of Ahmedabad (1969), are in accord with my own. While 'ostracism' of traders may explain their separation from other castes, their religions set them apart, and may well relate to their 'calling'. Does their 'calling', then, play the role it did for early Protestant groups? Nevaskar compares the Jains to the Quakers in the context of the 'spirit of capitalism'. Led by the monks and the principle of ahimsa,

> the Jain eventually became an urban dweller, usually a tradesman. Here his asceticism was, if anything, even more total than that of the Quaker. His honesty was proverbial. He worked diligently for religious reasons which drove him to seek moksha as his life's goal.
>
> Personal effects were limited; possessions beyond the necessary ones were considered to be detrimental to spiritual growth. Surplus wealth was invested wisely or channeled toward the upkeep of temples, the support of monks, care of animals, and for the social welfare of the needy and destitute. The more one earned, the greater was the capacity to channel one's wealth in the right direction. All this contributed toward earning merit....
>
> Like the Quakers, the Jains became bankers and moneylenders, and amassed immense wealth. This too was part of the calling ... the Jain layman had to earn more than what was required for his own support, since it was his sacred duty to support not only himself and the members of his family, but the order of monks and various charitable institutions. This he could do only by following his calling in a systematic, rational manner. Wealth was not to be squandered, but made the most of. (1971, 233-4)

Not all their neighbours, in Saurashtra, would attest to the 'proverbial honesty' of Jains, nor of other Banias. Their view is closer to that indicated by Fox; seeing wealth as the result of an intensive and not always morally defensible quest for profit. The rich merchants' houses or *havelis*, which include some of the finest examples of Gujarati wooden architecture, were tasteful and expensive examples of conspicuous consumption (Parmar 1988).

Asceticism may too readily be linked with the prohibition against meat, for Banias, within the limits of vegetarianism, eat very well indeed. They are excellent clients of the *halwai*. Markets in Gujarat are full of tasty snacks of every description, and the lack of alcohol is compensated by the universal presence of the *sherbetwallah*, whose products are among the best in India. Surely asceticism and vegetarianism are linked, in that carnal lust and worldly pleasures are seen as two sides of the same coin. But asceticism is, above all, related to the idea of non-violence. Indulgence in sweets, a non-violent and respectable matter, is not equated with a taste for spice, sex, alcohol and tobacco. Similarly, luxury does not exclude simplicity among Saurashtra Banias. Gandhi tells us that even just before his death, his father, the Dewan, always slept on a bare plank (Gandhi 1927, 16). Such examples abound, as if, in the midst of luxury, Banias try to find some salient symbolic expression of 'asceticism'.

Perhaps more to the point, S.C. Misra underlines the 'deep inclination' of Jains to 'use their wealth and their influence towards maintaining and reinforcing the cultural and religious ethos and its symbols ...'(1984, 48). While it is of ascetics that severe austerities are asked, 'for the laity too undertaking fasts and austerities was a virtue meriting public recognition'. And Misra stresses that both Shantidas Jhaveri—the founder of the line of Ahmedabad Nagarsheths—and Virji Vora, the famous merchant of Surat, 'followed their faith scrupulously, satisfying the demands of the orthodox' (op. cit., 49).

The sects of the Banias resemble Protestantism in their break with institutionalized religious hierarchy. Not only Jains, but other Banias too, have broken with brahminical domination. In supporting asceticism as a model for salvation, they see religion as an individual quest rather than a hierarchical organization for sacrifice and other ritual activity. This individualism extends to mundane activities, where Bania informants stress their high evaluation of independence. The parallels claimed by Nevaskar (1971) between the Jains and the Quakers, are not far to seek. Both Dumont (1960) and Heesterman (1985, 42) see, in the appearance of Buddhism and Jainism, a development towards individualism and universalism. Bania tradition relates explicitly to such values. But there is an important difference between these older, Indian traditions and European Protestantism, which is not adequately explained by Nevaskar.

The early Protestants in the West, such as the Quakers, had no religious specialists to carry the burden of asceticism for them. Indeed, their criticism of the monastery was fundamental, and an important part of Weber's analysis (1930) concerns, precisely the internalization of asceticism by the layman. The reform of his daily life resulted from the abolition of ascetic institutions. These had taken care of certain values on his behalf, now he himself became responsible for them. In the Indian case, the ascetic is a ritual specialist; the householder, while subscribing to the ascetic ideal, is not himself renouncing the material world. In this respect, Jains remain closer to Catholics than to Protestants. Symbolic expressions of 'simplicity', contrasting rather surprisingly with their surroundings, show the support of the rich Bania for ascetic ideals, without detaching him from the world, where his involvement is mainly regulated by the norms of non-violence. This leads him to keep apart, traditionally, from those exercising power in society. Such segregation between Banias and Darbars was a prominent feature of traditional society in Kathiawar.

It is only with Swami Narayana's *Shikshapatri* (Sahajanand Swami 1968), in the first half of the nineteenth century, that we find, in Saurashtra, ethics and capitalist values truly comparable to the one demonstrated by Weber.

What is more important, then, is that money can be spent, without limit, to gain religious merit and contribute to the attainment of *moksha*. Such positive evaluation of wealth produces a motivation for business, but not a 'Protestant ethic'. Catholic businessmen have left indelible marks in the religious monuments of southern Europe—the religious use of wealth is clearly anterior to the reformation.

THE MERCHANT-RULER OPPOSITION

And here we must return to the opposition between merchants and rulers, which is reflected in the regional discourse on relative rank. Banias are Vaishyas, members of the third varna, and rank below the Darbars—who are Kshatriyas—in the varna scheme. Yet a number of writers have spoken of this rank order as being 'reversed' in mainland

Gujarat.[1] In Saurashtra, the situation is more ambiguous, like the one Chauhan found in a village of Mewar, where Banias are called Mahajans.

> ... competing claims for a status ... are advanced by the Mahajans on the following grounds: (they)... are non-violent, the Rajputs are traditionally associated with violence; the *Mahajans* abstain from the use of liquor and meat and the Rajputs make them a part of their life at the time of rituals; the capacity of the *Mahajan* to advance this claim in the post-feudal society appear to be greater. (1967, 86-7)

Such rivalry between the two groups is typical of Saurashtra, and underlines the cultural distance between merchants and warriors.[2] This distance is visually rather obvious. Both communities may have large dwellings, bordering on mansions; but while Darbar houses are plain-looking, almost severe in places, the mansions of Banias are much more ornate, and distinguished by galleries of carved woodwork.

This traditional style is found on the mainland, and recalls Turkish or Iranian town-houses (Pramar 1988). They tend to look generally alike all over Saurashtra. Darbar houses, in contrast, vary considerably between the regions. In Praj they are built of large stone blocks with few or no windows on ground level, and rather small windows farther up. While not fortresses in any sense, and in any case defended by the village walls, they would be difficult to enter by force. Bania houses, rather, indicate conspicuous consumption and their cultural continuity with the mainland. In many parts of Saurashtra, the wooden galleries are not only foreign to the local style; the wood, too, would have to be brought from far away, being very scarce in Saurashtra.

Dress, too, distinguishes a Bania from other castes. While the Darbars and their allied castes wear the same form of male dress, a pattern of buttonless shirt and trousers with tight legs and wide waists, Banias tend to wear a frock and a long dhoti. A turban is the headgear of darbars and their allies; Banias wear caps, the 'Nehru cap' of boat shape being the most common. Thus, while it takes a local person or an expert to distinguish between the 'Rajput-allied' castes, the Banias stand out everywhere when wearing their traditional dress.

As for women, the distinction is blurred by the introduction of the sari, once typical of Bania women, among other groups. It has replaced the traditional skirt-and-scarf set among well-to-do women of many castes. But many poor or traditional women stick to traditional dress, including Rajput women and those of the Rajput-allied castes. And the better-off among the latter are seldom seen outside the house, since they tend to keep purdah, in varying degrees. The absence of purdah is in fact the most noticeable characteristic of Bania women in Saurashtra.

The mainland connection is conspicuous in language. While some trading castes[3] speak a variant of the Kathiawadi dialect, most Banias speak more or less standard Gujarati. While the martial and administrative communities in Saurashtra used to write in standard Devanagari letters, Banias have long used the Gujarati script. It may well be true that the merchants' 'shorthand' has been refined into the Gujarati letters. The first important publications in the script came, it would seem, from the Parsi trading community in Bombay.

THE MEANING OF 'NON-VIOLENCE'

We have seen that 'asceticism' among Banias does not preclude conspicuous consumption. We must consider, rather, two other material requirements of asceticism: food and sexuality, closely connected in the Indian context.

For all Banias, meat—the epitome of 'hot' food—is strictly forbidden. Meat is hardly part of the daily diet in Saurashtra; I have not visited a single home where meat was served. In the seventies, vegetarianism was spreading fast, and meat was expensive and difficult to obtain, even in town. But the difference in diet between Banias and others extends well beyond vegetarianism. Westerners expecting 'hot' Indian food would be surprised to eat with Jains. The restrictions on hot food are certainly stronger with Jains than with anybody else (except renouncers), but the style of cooking is rather similar whether the Bania in question is Jain, Vallabhacharya or Swaminarayana.

The trend toward vegetarianism may have been reversed in the eighties. In Rajkot, non-vegetarian restaurants have multiplied. Until recently, they were few and discreetly located usually on the first floor, and divided into secluded cubicles so that customers could eat unseen. Now, several such restaurants are of the open-plan type, and the guests are visible even from the street. Meat-eating used to be stigmatized; now it has become an open affair, at least in Rajkot.

Names like 'Muslim lodge' or 'Rajput lodge' are still typical of such places, indicating the clientele expected. Dining out was very popular with the Praj Muslims and in 1974 I went to Bhavnagar with them to eat meat. Eating meat together had definite symbolic value, expressing Muslim identity. It is not irrelevant to the infrequent occurrence of such meals, and the quality of meat in the seventies, that we all got sick.

The negative and positive aspects of eating meat are well put by Gandhi, who once did so, as a young boy. His friend told him:

> We are weak people because we do not eat meat. The English are able to rule over us, because they are meat-eaters. You know how hardy I am, and how great a runner too. It is because I am a meat-eater (Gandhi 1927, 12).

and Gandhi was, he says, beaten; it grew on him that

> ... meat-eating was good, that it would make me strong and daring, and that, if the whole country took to meat-eating, the English could be overcome. (ibid.)

But the result was disappointing; young Gandhi got sick and never touched meat again.

We see that the idea of meat giving strength is related to the concept of shakti . To fight the English one must tap their source of strength; to control the formless powers of the universe one must eat like the demons (Van den Hoek 1978). 'Hot' food must be taken by those who need the qualities inherent in it but avoided, equally, by those who wish to stay apart from *himsa* or violence. As meat is scarce in Saurashtra, the degree of 'hot' or 'cool' food can generally be inferred from its taste. Traditional peasants and Darbars take with most meals a large *rotlo*—a flat bread made from bajra—with a helping of extremely 'hot' sauce. Such a sauce is hot both in the cosmological and the culinary sense, while Banias use spice very moderately. The extreme in abstention from spicy or even tasty food is represented by Swaminarayana monks, whose food is dipped in lukewarm water after cooking. This is supposed to kill any effect the food might have in raising worldly desires. It also kills all taste. During the three days I lived at their monastery in Bombay, the process was wholly succesful in both ways.

While sexual activity itself may sometimes be associated with violence (e.g. Nandy 1973), we have seen that the power of shakti is necessary for those who depend on their capacity for violence. For non-violence, on the other hand, one must keep away not only from sex, but also from other manifestations of shakti. Thus 'hot' food is good for the warrior, while the merchant as well as the monk should stick to 'cool' food.

'Hot' food is taken not only by humans, but also by the goddess, while liquor, opium and tobacco—all 'hot' substances—are also offered to her. Abstention from alcohol is as central to non-violence as abstention from sex, and a traditional Bania is never seen smoking tobacco, much less opium. This, of course, does not deter Banias from trading in these substances.

Smoking is very popular in Saurashtra, and Darbar men as well as peasants and herdsmen smoke both the bidi and the *hookhli* (a small clay pipe). The water-pipe or hookah is seen at the Rajput *chora* (men's house) as an important form of traditional sociability. Even older women from these groups might still be seen smoking a *hookhli* in the seventies, though this was frowned upon and today seems to have disappeared, except among the lowest castes. On the other hand, a young Bania friend was typical of his caste in enjoying a cigarette, but—'Never tell my father!'. Drinking, on the other hand, is not common in Saurashtra, except with some of the lower castes.[4]

Non-violence is therefore not just an ideology but a whole way of life, opposing Banias to others but most explicitly to Darbars. With these contrasts, and their opposition to rulers, how did Banias relate to the state, and to kingship? We have noted the views of Merutunga, the Jain monk, regarding the ideal ruler. But what about more recent times?

MERCHANTS AND THE STATE: THE SIXTEENTH CENTURY

The distance maintained by the trading community from the power-holders is shown by Pearson (1976) for sixteenth-century Gujarat. He does not use the term 'estate', but his conception of the place of merchants in society comes close to Weber's ideas. The merchant estate consisted of a number of communities, Hindu, Jain and Muslim.[5] Among merchants dealing in overseas trade, however, Hindus and Jains 'outranked' Muslims, or, as Tome Pires put it: 'There is no doubt that these people (the non-Muslims) have the cream of the trade'.[6]

> In the economy of Gujarat as a whole there is no doubt that the dominant group in all trade matters was the *vanias*, if only because of their numerical predominance.... In fact the *vanias* were a rather diverse group. They were by *varna vaisya*, and so traditionally were allowed to lend money.[7] They were, and are, preeminently traders and merchants. There were traditionally forty-one divisions among the group in Gujarat, but these divisions were usually not based on occupational characteristics as was the case with other *vaisyas*. Many of these forty-one divisions in turn had Jain sections, some of the forty-one in fact being dominated by Jains. The Hindu sections were called *meshri*; during

the period under discussion most of them became converted to the Vallabhacarya sect of *vaishnavism*.[8] The Jain sections were called *shravak*. Inter-dining between Hindu and Jain sections was common, but marriage was severely restricted even within the forty-one divisions. (Pearson 1976, 26)

These restrictions on marriage have been relaxed somewhat in later days, but otherwise what Pearson says remains true.

The sixteenth century opened with the entry of a completely new factor in Gujarat's trade. This was the attempt of the Portuguese to control the Indian Ocean trade, of which Gujarat was by far the most important centre. The Portuguese had been welcomed at first, but as soon as they tried to monopolize the Red Sea trade and to introduce their system of trading licenses (*cartazes*), they were met by resistance. Gujarati merchants armed their ships to beat off Portuguese patrols, and they succeeded for a while in mobilizing the sultans of Gujarat in their defence. This period of conflict is well described by Pearson (1976).

Gujarati resistance to Portuguese control virtually ceased in the 1530s as indigenous merchants accommodated themselves to the Portuguese licensing system (op. cit., 92-3). Portuguese control of Gujarati trade, however, aimed largely at patrolling the entrance to the Gulf of Cambay. As noted, the rise of Jamnagar may have been partly due to its being outside the area of Portuguese control. It would be useful to know more about Kathiawar traders at the time, but no information is available.

The acceptance of Portuguese control became 'deeply ingrained' among Gujarati traders, especially after the Portuguese attacks on Gujarat in 1529-34 (op. cit., 94-5). Since their revenues depended on Gujarati merchants, the Portuguese to some extent adjusted themselves to the demands of the latter, who became 'something of an elite economic group in Portuguese India'. Gujarati traders and Portuguese authorities co-operated in making the 'Portuguese' system of trade work (op. cit., 104-5). Indeed, Gujarati money largely financed the private trade of the Portuguese, though not their administration (op. cit., 110).[9]

One reason for this was the restricted opportunities that Gujarati merchants had for investment, says Pearson. They lent money for trade as also to the Gujarat state and the Mughal administration—but they did not invest in agricultural land (Pearson 1976, 109). This underlines the distinction between the merchant estate and the nobility, which, we have seen, was not yet clear at the time of Vallabhi. Thus, as power was 'ruralized' during the middle ages, so the merchants, apparently, were divorced from landowning, with important political implications.

Faced with the Portuguese challenge, the merchants and the political elite reacted quite differently. The merchants often acted independently of their rulers in coming to terms with the Portuguese. After the latter's raids of 1614, for example, the merchants offered Jahangir full payment for goods seized by the Portuguese, in order to restore peaceful trading conditions. 'For Gujarati merchants', says Pearson, 'war, no matter for what reason, was to be avoided or ignored if at all possible' (op. cit., p.120). Merchants in Kathiawar were probably no different, even if they were not averse to finance the rulers' military establishments. Gujarat's merchants, indeed, later showed similar independence in dealing with the British and the Dutch (121-2).

Migration as a means of protest by merchants is known from the mainland,[10] and seems to have been a common practice in Kathiawar (Spodek 1976). Merchants were prepared to support a ruler, but equally ready and able to pose their own conditions. Thus, as Pearson puts it, merchants and rulers were

> two almost autonomous groups, responding in different ways to common demands from the outside, and negotiating with each other when necessary. There are two strands, which need to be carefully delineated; a large degree of autonomy for the merchants when the interests of the state are not involved; and the existence of connections between the groups, which were used on the relatively few occasions when contact was necessary. (1976, 123)

As we have seen, this distance is quite visible at the local level. But Chauhan also points to a symbiotic rather than competitive pattern, resulting from the place of merchants within the state system:

> In the state of Jodhpur, the *Oswal Mahajans* are divided into two groups: the *Mahajan* (meaning those in Govt. services) and the business group. The former are considered higher in status and a type of hypergamy exists among them. In Mewar some of the *Mahajans* who served the king added the suffix 'Singh' (like Rajputs—HTL) to their names, took over the style of dress and the household etiquette from the royal court, and thereby accepted the Rajput ruler's model as worth emulating. Even with regard to their origin, the *Mahajan* would like to claim a *Kshattriya* descent. These factors lead to a situation whereby the claims on the part of the *Vaishya Varna* to a higher status than the *Kshattriya* get diluted. (1967, 87)

We have earlier mentioned such state-merchant ties in the Chalukya empire. In Saurashtra, several Banias served as ministers (Dewans) in the states, just as they did in Rajasthan; in spite of Sharpe's remarks, Gandhi's grandfather was no exception.

How can we reconcile these two elements—the distance and relative independence of the merchant community, and their sometimes active collaboration with the state? The answer must lie in the need of the princes for finance; and it is obvious that even when close, the prince–moneylender relationship contained an element of opposition. The state needed the merchants. They, in turn, could hardly exist without the minimum of orderly conditions that the state tried to maintain. But interdependence need not lead us to suppose a harmonious relationship between Darbars and Banias in general.

One important intermediary in state-merchant relations was the shroff, who was in control of the state coffers. According to Pearson, citing the Walker of Bowland papers, many shroffs were Nagar Brahmins. Other Nagars were rich merchants and/or landowners. The shroff was evidently responsible for much of the state's dealings with merchants.

The fiscal situation underlines the considerable autonomy of merchants in Mughal India, for the taxes they paid were low. While agricultural tax usually amounted to at least a third of the income, merchants paid between 2.5 and 5 per cent only, mainly as customs. Pearson notes that taxes and customs from merchants were always paid by their chiefs,[11] acting as intermediaries between the merchant community and a rather remote state apparatus (Pearson 1976, 130-1). This remoteness made the merchants of Gujarat considerably more autonomous than members of contemporary European guilds. 'The state', says Pearson finally, did not 'consider it to be of any concern to itself if Gujarat's merchants wanted to pay extra taxes to the Portuguese, and sail under their direction....This autonomy is why the state let the merchants respond to the Portuguese as they did ...' (op. cit., 131-2).

S.C. Misra accepts this view, talking of an 'enclave system' (1984, 45). But Gopal, criticizing Pearson, stresses that even Virji Vora of Surat, India's greatest trader of the seventeenth century, was harassed by the Mughal authorities (1975, 240). Gopal's view is that the coming of the Europeans created a situation where only the richest and most powerful of Indian traders could survive; others went bankrupt or were reduced to a very secondary status (op. cit., 111 and *passim*). To arrive at his conclusion, however, he rather evades the question of the guild.

THE ORGANIZATION OF THE MERCHANT ESTATE

For most other writers, the guild is indeed an important feature of merchant organization in the history of Gujarat. We have discussed early evidence of guilds among its traders; from the beginning of Mughal times, their existence is well documented. By 1573, when Akbar conquered Gujarat, 'the guild system had consolidated itself and had become a prominent feature of the urban setting.' Under the Mughals, guilds proliferated, and they and their chiefs are often mentioned in official documents (S. Mehta 1984, 174-5).

As in Europe, the guild represented the collectivity of a craft or trade. Its organization differed from place to place, but always seem to have taken the form of committees or councils formed by the family firms. One common term for such a council was the Mahajan ('great people'), which in Rajasthan means simply a merchant. But in Gujarat, it usually meant a body

> ... representing a group of people engaged in the same commercial occupation, a governing council with an elected or occasionally hereditary headman. Sometimes *mahajan* meant simply a body governing all the *vania* merchants in a town, but it also applied more generally to 'any assembled or collective body of merchants' regardless of creed or *jati* .... The *mahajan* was ordinarily concerned solely with commercial matters, regulating such matters as prices, adjudicating disputes within the occupational group, and representing its members in disputes with other *mahajans.* Religious and social matters were outside its province, these being, as in other parts of India, handled by caste or *jati panchayats.* (Pearson 1976, 123)[12]

Pearson qualifies this generalization in several ways. Thus only relatively large towns had Mahajans in this formal sense. In small towns commercial matters were handled by the jati panchayats of the merchants. Secondly, artisans had similar regulatory bodies, but they were called *panch.* While the head of a Mahajan was called a Sheth, the panch was headed by a Patel. Finally, in large towns such as Ahmadabad (see also Doshi 1974)—as was certainly the case in Bhavnagar—the term Mahajan was also used for a city-wide body, 'on which sat representatives of all the occupational *mahajans* and sometimes some of the *patels* as well. It regulated general commercial activities in the city, such as rates of exchange and discount, and holidays' (Pearson op. cit., 123-4).[13]

These councils were headed by an 'elected' official—in practice the office seems often to have been inherited[14]—known, in these two cities, as the Nagarsheth ('chief of the town'). Here, Mahajan was the term used for the assembly of the chiefs of the guilds. These 'town committees' were not without influence, though they never became the 'town government', far less the 'free trading cities', that we know from European history (Spodek 1976, 11-13, 18-22).

The Nagarsheth acted as intermediary between the merchant community and the state. But while the two parties might negotiate as separate entities, there were important economic links between them. The state borrowed from merchants, as noted, but there were also instances, in Mughal India, of merchants borrowing from the state. Nobles, and sometimes the ruler himself, might engage in trade, often as shipowners, on whose ships merchants in turn rented space for their goods (Pearson 1976, 129). Both in Saurashtra and Gujarat, merchants might become Dewans.

By the beginning of the eighteenth century, the institution of the Nagarsheth—the head of all the town's guilds—was fully developed, and in that unstable century, when Ahmadabad had to cope with the raids of the Marathas, it played an important role in maintaining a semblance of order in the city (S. Mehta 1984, 175, Tripathi and Mehta 1984, 160).[15]

The importance of this institution may have been, to some extent, particular to Gujarat. Dasgupta even doubts that such institutions ever transcended caste organization (1984, 35-6). But their existence in Gujarat is well documented, certainly for the Mughal period and after.[16] As Pearson notes, the commercial class—or merchant estate—was ethnically very heterogeneous in Gujarat. This was not always the case in India. Elsewhere caste and commercial interest might coincide, and the composition of the merchant estate in Gujarat may have been an important factor in making the guild a cross-caste organization.

Merchants were more important in Gujarat, which has been a centre of trade for as far back as we can go. Pearson assumes that merchant organization in Gujarat remained basically the same for 'at least the past two millennia' (Pearson 1976, 124). This view is not easy to document, but is certainly shared by others.[17]

At a later date, too, the guilds acted as semi-autonomous units in dealings with the state. In Ahmedabad, the head of a guild acted not only as a spokesman for the members, he was also 'an intermediary between his community and the state', and it was through him that taxes and customs were paid. The government 'allowed complete autonomy to Mahajans in commercial matters' (S. Mehta 1984, 177).

THE ORGANIZATION OF TRADE

In the analyses of merchant organization, credit and information are primary considerations. Timberg notes, of the Marwaris in British times, 'The *organization* of credit produced networks of contacts, 'resource groups', all over the country which could be used for the selling and purchasing of the goods traded in the ports. Foreign firms naturally found themselves dependent on merchants with such networks' (1978, 37). He further quotes Pavlov to the same effect:

> In the rural economy of colonial India, such a system was based on the financial and commercial organization of the trading and money-lending castes whose members formed a complicated hierarchy starting from the petty village trader and moneylender up to the big city merchant and banker. The castes were firmly held together by credit arrangements that had developed between caste members. The trading and moneylending groups constituting the Marwari community were best suited to meet the needs of British capital, not only because they formed the largest organization of traders and moneylenders—apart from the Gujarati Banias—but also because the Marwari bankers were already established in almost every town in North India.... (Pavlov 1955, 143-8, cited by Timberg 1978, 37-8)

The same writer notes that the British lacked similar knowledge and networks of their own, making them dependent on their Indian contacts (op. cit., 139, cited in Timberg, 38). Nevaskar stresses the tight network of business relations among Jains, and relates it to the fact that they shared a common meeting house, the *Upasraya*, which he sees as the counterpart of the Quaker meeting-house (1971, 220). The *Upasraya* is the Jain lecture hall, found in all urban settlements of importance. Here, says Nevaskar, 'the Jain layman was taught what was expected of him in daily conduct, including his business practices. Because he was concerned with the problem of ultimate liberation and was anxious to have the guidance of the elders in the community, no Jain could afford to ignore the Upasraya. This served as a confessional for the Jain layman' (1971, 218).

These remarks indicate an area of study as fascinating as it is inaccessible to the outsider. Business networks are notoriously difficult to study, for obvious reasons. It may be clear why the role of the guild, in relation to caste, is also difficult to ascertain. But in Gujarati parlance, the guild, whether referred to as *shreni, shresti* or *mahajan*, is never confused with caste. It may well be that certain guilds were effectively constituted by members of a single caste. Even then it was guilds, and not castes, that were represented in the 'town committees' or 'guild assemblies' of the more important trading cities.

TEMPLE COMMITTEES AND THE SECTS

Temple organization in Saurashtra, as in the rest of India, varies widely, but the temples of merchants are invariably governed by a 'temple committee'. This assembly may or may not be identical to the 'layman's committee' administering the affairs of the local branch of the sect, whether Jain, Vallabhacharya or Swaminarayana. In the latter case, the two committees are one. The chairmanship of a temple committee and/or a laymen's committee is quite an important office, and the contest for such office, and for power within the guild and mahajan, constitute much of the internal politics of the Bania communities.

While such politics may be based on kinship alliances, and important posts monopolized by certain families, kinship is not a determining factor to structure the system, as it is for Rajput lineages.

The committee form of organization is as typical of the sects to which Saurashtra Banias belong, as it is typical of some of the Christian sects once associated with the 'Protestant ethic' and the 'spirit of capitalism' (Weber 1930). Unlike trade or residential organizations, such sects must be called voluntary organizations. While members may be born into them, it is possible both to leave them and to join other sects. We have already seen that such sects are associated with the Banias, but I think we can see now that they are in fact an expression of a particular 'Bania way of doing things', in short, of Bania culture. The typical features, then, of Bania social organization in Saurashtra and Gujarat are not very different from that found in a number of European cities in the late medieval age. I found much to remind me, here, of my native city of Bergen in Norway, a traditional port and trading centre once run more or less by the guilds.

The 'committee form of organization' seems to be typical of merchant committees almost everywhere. Such organization demands a capacity for compromise rather than conflict, for mutual benefit rather than honour. The sects fit this pattern perfectly. They offer an administrative and political structure very close to that of the guild, an opportunity for power and prestige outside the territorial political system as dominated by the Darbars, and, a chance to combine worldly pursuits with sanctity. Thus, in Jain temples, we find plaques stating that a particular statue, or the renovation of the temple in a certain year, was donated by this or that merchant. Similarly, when the Swaminarayana temple in London was opened, a long list of all contributors was read publicly, with a statement, too, of the sum donated; beginning with the largest sums. At Patidar weddings, a similar public reading and presentation of all gifts—their value precisely stated—may be held, and two witnesses note it all down. I believe this is originally a Bania practice.

We see, then, that the organization of the sects to which merchants belong is closely related to other features of their social organization. They, too, are largely run, on the local level, by committees of laymen. Moreover, within this framework, the stress is on individual devotion, and the relationship between members, at least relative to the Indian context, is egalitarian.

THE MERCHANT WARDS

Beside the caste, sect and guild there are other units of social organization. In Ahmedabad and elsewhere, there are *pols* or inter-familial dwelling units which we may call 'wards'.[18] Doshi's study of the pol in Ahmedabad is sufficiently extensive. He stresses its one-caste nature, which seems to hold good for Bhavnagar wards also.

The pol is ruled by a committee consisting of the heads of member families, which may levy a pol tax for purposes of common interest. Ahmedabad pols, like the Bhavnagar *vads*, are traditionally sited round a common courtyard and can be closed at night by a gate. The pol thus catered for the safety as well as the residential well-being of its inhabitants (Pramar 1988). According to Vakhatchant, the pol organization dates from the fifteenth century (cited by S. Mehta 1984, 174).

Mehta stresses the patron-client relationships that formed the basis of pol organization. The 'one-caste' pol included servants of the caste. Otherwise, each pol was strictly a single-caste dwelling unit (ibid.) S.C. Misra has stressed how 'the insecurity of the 18th century converted these pols into defensive bulwarks' (1984, 45, also 1981).

Pols are not exclusive to merchants, but they and similar forms of ward committee organization are clearly an urban phenomenon. Thus, if we take it as a general institution in the larger Saurashtra towns (with the exception of modern Rajkot, a post-independence town formation)—as I believe it was—then most Banias must have lived within such pols. 'The relationship between the guild system and pol federation was intimate indeed', says Mehta of Ahmedabad, 'This facilitated united action on the part of various communities' (1984, 175).

WOMEN AND MARRIAGE AMONG BANIAS

The relatively liberal attitude to jati, among Banias, cannot be understood apart from the relatively 'free' position of women. This is obvious in daily life; Bania women do not show the dignified reserve of Rajputnis, nor the assertiveness of the pastoralist women. Young girls, today, speak freely to young men, even to foreigners, and merchant matrons show no obvious signs of purdah.

Banias are, of course, 'non-violent'; and there are implications here for the relation between men and women.[19] While Rajput women are neither meek nor submissive, actual use of physical violence is basically a male monopoly. It is the man who has to prove himself through fighting. As we have seen, the strength necessary for this purpose, shakti, is a power inherent only in women. The woman is the man's shakti. Thus the male-female dichotomy is in itself, emically speaking, a prerequisite for being a proper Darbar of either sex. Business is rather a different matter. Shakti is a concept known and accepted even by Jains. Perhaps we may think that shakti is also necessary for being a good businessman, but I never heard such a claim, which would probably seem far-fetched to most informants.

S. Gupta points to the difference between Shaivite and Vaishnavite conceptions of shakti. In contrast to the former, which we have dealt with elsewhere, shakti in Vaishnavism 'has no autonomous power' She is 'almost never' seen alone or 'in a terrifying form' (Gupta 1992, 195). While Maya or Shakti is, in the Shaivite or Tantric framework, the very power that manifests as the world (op. cit., 208, Tambs-Lyche 1994b), Vishnu himself incarnates in the world, taking over the goddess' role.

Even if Shakti, as Lakshmi, is still seen as the personification of Vishnu's power, she effectively becomes the God's loving wife (Gupta 1992, 209). The model of the *pativrata*—the ideal wife—thus becomes the only role open to the Vaishnavite woman (Gupta 1992, Mallison 1979). Nevaskar notes the divided opinion among Jain scholars in this matter,[20] but his conclusion seems to parallel the Vaishnavite view. This lack of reification of specific female powers in a sense makes for greater equality of the sexes. Business is a matter of the mind; you must be shrewd rather than strong. While I have heard men of merchant caste claim that a woman's mental capacity is not equal to that of a man, nobody denies the existence of female shrewdness. While women doing business on their own are highly unusual in Saurashtra, there would seem to be nothing inherently impossible in it. All agree that Maldhari women have 'a mind for business'; in short, the capacity for business is not related to gender in the same way as the capacity for waging war.

Women of the Bania estate are not the 'bearers of shakti' to their men in the same way as Darbar women. A Bania woman's curse would in no way be comparable to that of a woman of bardic caste. Women of Bania castes are not feared. In short, they are not sacré in Durkheim's sense, at least not to the extent of bardic or Darbar women. Thus it may at one time have been fashionable to keep purdah among Banias, but today this would be highly unusual, at least in Saurashtra. Nevaskar holds that purdah was very rarely adopted by Jains (1971, 185).

Today's stereotype of the Bania woman is the very opposite of that implied by purdah; they are seen as 'very advanced'. The informant (neither a Patidar nor a Bania) who said, of Patidar girls, 'they will sleep with anyone', might as well have talked about Bania women.[21] This is of course untrue, but refers to the fact that Bania girls are more visible and approachable in public than those of, notably, the Darbar castes. Such openness has been beneficial to education; Bania families readily send girls to university. Among women in Saurashtra today, those from the Bania estate are among the best educated.

Banias marry comparatively late: as one informant put it, they 'mostly marry at twenty-five, the girls at twenty. If a boy has not married and is well past twenty-five, he may not get a good choice of girls. So people will advise him, that, he should really marry now....' Similarly, Nevaskar notes that the Jain bride 'must be younger than the bridegroom ... in ancient times, it was believed that the progeny of a couple where the girl was sixteen years old and the boy was twenty-five was bound to be very strong' (1971, 181). Even if Saurashtra Banias are today open to the possibility that boy and girl may know each other before marriage, the actual choice remains a matter for parents to decide. Nevaskar stresses that it is the father of the bride who searches for a suitable groom (ibid.).[22]

MARRIAGE AND THE FAMILY FIRM

For an explanation, we must turn to the specific function of marriage among Banias. Marriage decisions are, it seems, commonly taken with an eye to business relations as well as to other criteria for suitability. And business remains a male domain among Banias. Bania marriages are invariably dowry marriages; among Jains 'the bride is always a gift to the bridegroom' (Nevaskar 1971, 180). Dowries may be quite high. As so often in India today, Banias claim that dowries are constantly increasing, not only in absolute terms but also relative to income. Still, they claim, dowries are not as high as those reported from the Charottar Patidar (Pocock 1972, Tambs-Lyche 1980a, 42-3). The informant mentioned further commented, 'it is not common to give cash as part of the dowry. If the bridegroom asks for cash, the girl's father will think: Why is he interested in cash—he will not be properly interested in the girl. So mostly, they will refuse him. But it may happen that the girl's father wants to give some cash.'

This would be, he says, to set up the son-in-law in business; a link often used in developing the 'family firm'.

Since the dowry represents a large sum of money it is apparently not at all uncommon to use it for this purpose. Among Saurashtra Banias—as elsewhere in India—business is conducted, to a very great extent, in the form of the 'family firm' (Benedict 1968, Timberg 1978, 128-9). Marriages become one link in the family firm structure. Such a structure differs from other ways of linking enterprises, in that the connections between them are not traceable as juridical relationships between firms, only as reciprocal obligations or expectations between kinsmen.

A businessman operating within this structure does not establish a branch of his own business in another town; he sends his son or nephew to establish a separate business there, or indeed, his son-in-law. The senior partner, who provided the capital, may 'control' the new business, but only because the junior partner has an obligation to him. The 'old man' has not lent the money, he has given it, once and for all, as anticipated inheritance to his son or as dowry to his son-in-law. The sanctions working on the junior partner, therefore, are not legal. They are instead expressed through the network of family, caste and guild. An established position in such a network makes a man worthy of credit, as well as of trust in general. Without such a position, a businessman would be in a very difficult situation indeed (Timberg 1978, 128-9).

Thus a monopoly of each different trade is established, not by firms or individuals, but by subcaste groups among Banias, and by guilds. One instance of an outsider breaking into such trade may be noted. This was a grain merchant in one of the larger towns, established by an Ahir family. This caste is not within the 'merchant estate' and has little business tradition. The brothers running the firm explained to me, however, that their being of a farming caste inspired confidence among the farmers—especially their Ahir caste-fellows—and that some of their most important business connections followed this caste link.

This may be helped by the fact that there are quite a few Ahirs in the transport business running lorries—another important business connection. For credit, however, one would expect them to depend more on banks than firms run by members of a merchant caste. One wonders whether such a non-Bania entrepreneurship in this the most traditional field of Bania business might have been at all possible in earlier times.

Since business depends heavily on kinship and caste connections, marriage alliances are of considerable importance. Such relations, while not immune to conflict and certainly not to competition, are not antagonistic in the way that Rajput alliances may be. The family firm may extend into an empire, but such empires tend to become network agglomerations rather than clans. There is nothing to indicate conflict between man and wife, as representatives of their respective clans, such as we have observed within the Rajput polity. Rather, among Banias, in-laws are one of several possible links of alliance. But non-kin may also form lasting business relationships, and nothing, of course, excludes such alliance within the patrilineage.

While honour for a Rajput or Darbar is intimately connected with conflict and its corollaries, a businessman is dishonoured only by avoidable bankruptcy, by ineptitude, or by dishonesty in his dealings. Such disasters are best avoided by collaboration and compromise.

CLASS AND COMMUNITY AMONG TRADERS

There has been considerable debate concerning the terms 'community' and 'class' when dealing with Indian merchants. Both terms may well be applicable; one does not exclude the other. Thus in a purely economic analysis, Indian merchants are as much a class as those of any other society. Conversely, the idea that only Indian merchants are divided into 'communities' is, I think, not tenable, at least if we look at the matter historically.

Weber's Protestant sects were not a capitalist class; they were, in that time, quite distinguishable communities within it. So, clearly, were the Jews, in most Western countries. The Patidars I studied in London around 1970 were such a community (Tambs-Lyche 1980), largely successful in their commercial enterprise. Modern capitalism, however, creates cross-community links that may lead the older community organization of trade to fade into the background. As Tripathi and Mehta rightly argue, this may well be true in India, too (1984, 151ff). For traditional Saurashtra, however, the separate communities of traders remain important.

This follows logically from the structure of the family firm and the networks of which it is a part. Nothing, of course, precludes business connections between members of one 'community' and another. But the need to control information and credit indicates a correlation between a specific trade and a particular community, and such a correlation seems to have existed in traditional Saurashtra, as it still partly does.

Banks, too, have often sprung from specific business communities (e.g. Guha 1984, 130-2, for the Parsis of Bombay). But in Saurashtra, rulers often founded state banks: these made it difficult for a particular community to dominate local banking.

OTHER TRADING COMMUNITIES

Trade in Gujarat and Saurashtra has sometimes been identified with the Banias, without much qualification. It is necessary, therefore, to stress that this caste-cluster was not alone in doing commerce; there were other, sometimes important, communities of traders, which are never identified, locally, with the Banias. The Lohanas, for example, who have a stronger representation in the rural areas than Banias, are often included among the 'thirteen castes'. Traditionally, they never resembled Banias, and were until recently often non-vegetarian. The Bhatias of Jamnagar are not usually considered Banias, either, and then there are the Muslim trading communities, among whom the Khojas, Voras and Memons are the most prominent (Tirmizi 1984, 63-6).

The Charan, we have seen, were caravan traders, sometimes difficult to distinguish from the category of Banjaras (Westphal-Hellbosch 1976, 161-2). Finally, Nagar Brahmins have sometimes been important as bankers, and other Brahmin communities, too, have taken part in trade. Indeed, Pocock attributes some of the decline of the Gugli Brahmins to the increasing competition, in the last century, from the Lohanas (Pocock 1981, 327).

And yet the cultural image of the trader is, in Saurashtra, bound up with the Bania category, which seems, after all, to have formed the core of the traders. Thus when speaking of the merchant estate, I am concentrate on the Banias and their particular forms of culture and organization, while asking the reader to bear in mind that this category never monopolized trade completely. I see them as the cultural model of the trader, as well as the most important element of the commercial population when viewed as an interest group.

THE BANIA CLUSTER OF TRADING COMMUNITIES: CASTE AND SECT

We have thus seen that the commercial class has many communities, several outside the Bania category, whereas in cultural terms this class, as a source of inspiration and emulation, is largely identified with the Banias. When Patidars have, in modern times, become traders, it is to the Banias they turn for their cultural model. Banias in the strict sense, then, are a category of people who may be seen as belonging to one or a number of castes depending on the classification used. Regionally, all Banias are said to be Vaishyas. But if we look at the most prestigious of all Bania groups, the Oswals—who are Jains—we find that they claim Kshatriya origins. So do the Bhatias (Enthoven 1920, Tripathi and Mehta 1984, 156).

As I have hinted above, the classification of Banias into jatis in the strict sense of endogamous group is not easy. Enthoven mentions forty castes of Gujarati Banias (1922, 413); Pearson forty-one, certainly the same classification. But at present endogamy does not seem to be very strict, and I am not at all sure that intermarriage between jatis is a modern phenomenon. Enthoven puts it a little less bluntly than I have done here. He says, 'All the main divisions with their Visa and Dasa sub-divisions and local sections generally eat together but do not intermarry. The close connection between the Meshri and Shravak [Hindu and Jain—HTL] sections of these various Bania groups is a good instance of the greater strength of the social than the religious nexus in Gujarat.'

Jati names may be related to specific trades, and in such cases the dividing line between jati and guild becomes blurred. Sectarian affiliations, similarly, cut across jati and guild.

Srinivas has referred to the 'criss-crossing' of sect and caste in Gujarat. While this may not hold good for other estates in Saurashtra, or needs to be modified to suit the facts, it is eminently true of Banias. Thus members of the same caste may belong to the Jain community, or to the Vallabhacharya or Swaminarayana sects. Marriage across these religious dividing-lines is quite common. While sons generally tend to take the religion of their father, other choices are possible.

Generally, however, these changes are all in the same direction: Jains become Hindus, while I never heard of Hindus converting to Jainism. In the same way, conversions away from the Swaminarayana sect are few and far between. But this tendency—for the Jains to become Vallabhacharyas and for the latter to become Swaminarayanas—is not, it seems, the result of any structural prerequisite. Rather, it seems to represent the differential dynamism of the three religious communities.

Nevertheless, the direction of change is surprising in the Indian context. If we look at the distribution of sects by caste among Banias, we should expect a change in the opposite direction. It is among lower Bania castes, such as the Bhowsars (cloth-printers), that Swaminarayanas seem to be most strongly represented. Sonis (goldsmiths), on the other hand, who are rich and highly respected, number only a few Swaminarayanas but many Jains. The Oswals, perhaps the most prestigious of all Bania communities, are wholly Jain (Enthoven 1922, 414).

In general, Vallabhacharyas and Jains tend to look down upon the Swaminarayanas as 'upstarts' or '*nouveau-riches*'. While this reflects the distribution of sect membership among the various Bania castes, it certainly does not help us to understand what, in this context, becomes a 'downward' religious conversion.

Clearly, any hierarchical value ascribed to sect membership does not seem to influence the choice of marriage partners. Here we must rather look for arrangements of 'business alliances'. Even caste does not seem to form a strong barrier to intermarriage among Banias. Here, indeed, is one part of the caste system where cross-caste marriages have become more common, and what is more, it is highly doubtful to what extent non-Banias recognize such marriages as cutting across a true caste barrier.

In short, while one may assign differential rank to the numerous Bania castes, they do not seem to constitute an ordered hierarchy. Rather, it seems, among Banias a number of factors—the standing of the caste, of the family, of the family firm, differential adherence to the cluster of non-violent norms and values common to Banias—contribute to the standing of a potential marriage partner. I am here deliberately using Pocock's term 'standing' as opposed to 'status' or 'rank' (Pocock 1972).

Some jatis, then, are related to specific trades among Banias; others are not. Moreover, with historical changes in business conditions, new trades have been added while others have disappeared. Owners of factories are found in most Bania castes; such cases may or may not be connected to the original trade. Even so, caste seems to remain a factor in creating a closed network of business relations in a particular trade. Real monopoly of a trade, such as may have existed historically, is obviously difficult to defend today. Caste is not an obvious factor in getting a loan for investment, neither in the banks nor through the Gujarat Small Industries Corporation.

THE VALLABHACHARYAS

The Vallabhacharya sect, beside the Jains, has for a long time dominated Bania religion in Gujarat. Vallabhacharya himself lived at the turn of the fifteenth to the sixteenth century. He was a travelling scholar and we know that he came to Gujarat and preached there. His son Vitthalnath also came to Gujarat, and it was he who was largely responsible for institutionalizing the sect and developing its doctrine.[23] This process continued to the middle of the sixteenth century.

In 1492, Vallabhacharya was on pilgrimage to Braj near Mathura, where he found a particular image of Krishna, worshipped by the local cowherds. He '*recognizes* in this image a manifestation of Krishna in the form of Shri Natha ji' (Clementin-Ojha 1990: 123). The seventeenth-century text used by the sect to document the manifestation, starts, naturally enough, with the miraculous appearance of this image (ibid.; Vaudeville 1980).[24] The miracle becomes the foundation stone for the sect, whose worship consists essentially in taking care of the image as if it was exactly what it appears to be: Krishna as a small child. But before we describe the teachings and practices of the sect, let us note an important event in the history of Shri Nathaji.

In 1669, Aurangzeb ordered the destruction of Hindu temples within his domain. The priests of Shri Nathaji's temple, therefore, brought the image along with them, and fled to Rajasthan. In Jodhpur, they found the raja absent and his administrators unwilling to give the Emperor cause for complaint by keeping the image. 'In desperation', the chief priest 'sent an emissary to Maharana Raj Singh (of Mewar) requesting asylum for the exiled god in his state. Raj Singh gladly undertook to do so...' (S.R. Sharma 1971, 29).

But then the god manifested his own will; near Siah, the chariot transporting the image became stuck and could not be moved. 'Happily this was taken to imply that the god did not wish to proceed any further' (ibid.), and this is where the 'holiest shrine of the Vaishnavas in western and central India' (op. cit., 30), remains to this day. The king of Mewar had thus added another element to his position as head of the senior Rajput house. He had bought himself a place in the hearts of what was becoming an important merchant and moneylending community, which now rivalled the established Jains. This role of protectors of Shri Nathaji remained with the Mewar royal house to the end.

This event brought the ritual centre of the sect close to the borders of Gujarat. Contrary to what Toothi says,[25] it would seem that the sect had already gained a strong foothold in Gujarat by this time, for by 1625, Dakor in central Gujarat was already being remodelled into a Vallabhacharya centre of pilgrimage (Mallison 1983, 248). This major temple was reformed by one of the sect's early maharajas, Harirayji. The first of these leaders were the seven grandsons of Vallabhacharya by Vitthalnath; all later maharajas belong to his male line of descent. Dakorji, the image at Dakor, is no other than Ranchodji, the *murti* of Krishna who walked here from Dwarka to save his devotee, Bodano, the trouble of pilgrimage (Mallison 1990, Pocock 1973, 107).

Shri Nathaji and Ranchodji are manifestations of the personal god, Krishna, who relates to the devotee as an individual. He, in his turn, should look after the God with loving care. This view does not deny the good things in life. Vallabhacharya 'insisted on the enjoyment of life, and decried all hardship, bodily pain and self-torture of any sort' (Thoothi 1935, 92). 'Whatever you like', says a contemporary Maharaja, 'whatever temperament you have ... just with a little sense of the divinity of the idol, you can divert all your tendencies and temperament towards the idol and then you will be divine. Whatever attracts you...just try to sublimate it at the level of God' (Brent 1972, 198). And of the sexual themes of Vallabhite painting: 'We don't have the notion that God is always omnipotent and omniscient and we are always sinful. We sometimes have a sexual relationship with God.... We can have all sorts of relationships with God so we don't think in the terms that you (i.e. westerners) are thinking—that there is nothing but sex (in these paintings). We see there is everything.'

Vallabhacharyas I met, agree with him. 'You have to dedicate everything to God.' Here, we need not go into the cosmology of the sect. Outside his own following, Vallabhacharua is not very highly regarded as a philosopher. Though he follows some of Ramanujacharya's ideas, he declares himself a monist.[26] In practice, the emphasis is on service to the Lord, offering him all good things in life, whether food, clothing, painting, music, or poetry.

Unlike the early Protestants (Weber 1930), the Swaminarayanas (Pocock 1973, Richards 1984), and possibly the Jains (Nevaskar 1971), the appeal of the Vallabhacharya sect to merchants lies not in puritanism, nor in a duty to save or invest. Rather, the sect offers ample opportunity for conspicuous consumption (Veblen 1934, Thoothi 1935). This has made the sect contribute greatly to the development of arts and crafts in Gujarat.[27] Their stress on conspicuous consumption must have made the Vallabhacharya sect attractive to a group which, confronted with religious hierarchy and power, could only assert itself by spending lavishly. Thus Thoothi asserts that 'the sect naturally attracted the well-to-do from among the merchant and farmer population of Bhatias, Banias, Lohanas and Kanbis' (1935, 92). The power and influence of the sect seems to have expanded greatly during the eighteenth century, to reach an apogee in the eighteen-fifties.

THE FIELD OF TRADE AND THE NATURE OF BANIA CULTURE

If it is difficult to build a single model of the 'kinship-political' field of the Rajput state, it is even harder to produce such a model for the proper dynamics of the Bania 'business and family' field. Business communities are not, generally speaking, as well studied by anthropologists or historians as martial landowners.[28]

Yet some elements for such a model are clear. As the segmentary organization and the politics of conquering and holding land are central factors in the Rajput kinship-political field, so the family firm must be central to the model of the field of Bania commercial life. The firm is the central unit, with the family, of Bania social organization, and larger kin networks may be seen as an aggregate of such firms. But Bania social organization depends also on a number of inter-firm and inter-family frameworks, which form a contiguity of organizational patterns throughout what might be called the Bania 'life-world'. S.C. Misra has nicely sketched the elements in this contiguous pattern. According to him, the medieval merchant lived within several

> distinct but interlinked worlds; the primary entity in this complex was the family—the extended joint family with its innumerable obligations—a syndrome which furnished him with one of his major life-goals. Next in order were the social obligations due to the caste and to the faith; merit in this world and salvation in the other was to be gained by fulfilling these obligations, not in a routine fashion but with zeal and enthusiasm. This was the private and semi-public world, marked off from outside intrusion but obviously not free from internal tension and rivalry.
>
> Related but distinct was the world of the market, the polis. it was in this world that the merchant made money, came in contact with strangers and with powers that were. It was a world of relatively formed mores in large internal markets like Ahmedabad, a world in which a certain degree of stability had been secured. It was, however, a world of frenetic, cut-throat competition and rivalry in cities like Surat where short-term gains were sought and the principal actors in the drama admitted no rules. These related worlds were, thus, formed of several overlapping 'associations'. Primary among them was the immediate dimension of the extended family, kinship and marriage which furnished basic affiliations; next was the obligations to caste and faith.
>
> Distinct but related was the *mahajan* which in Gujarat implied a professional/ occupational body, usually but not necessarily a monocaste one. As a rule, most trades were followed by distinct castes, known by these occupational appellations; however, castes were not rigid but relatively fluid bodies sometimes with varying compositions. Closely bound up with the caste association and the mahajan was the residential pol organization, usually but not always overlapping. (1984, 45-6)

This sums up nicely the organizational levels involved in the field of business, and the relations between them. But it does not provide us with the 'proper dynamics' needed to simulate the field. What were the rules of the game in this merchant world?

The land available for conquest, in a given region, is necessarily limited. Political ascendancy means the fall of someone else. While competition in a given market might be seen in the same way, merchants in Saurashtra, and I believe elsewhere, do not generally see it thus. Rather, success or failure is related to individual capabilities in dealing with the vagaries of 'trade', not, primarily, with specific opponents. Banias see honour and dishonour as related to what we may call a non-zero-sum game rather than the zero-sum variety. In other words, when business is good, everybody stands to gain by it;

when times are bad, everybody loses. Thus the guilds and town-wide councils worked to regulate competition, while trying to improve conditions of trade for the members as a collective. Alliances between rulers, on the other hand, were mainly temporary and directed towards a particular opponent.

While the competitive spirit is certainly strong, a capacity for compromise and collaboration is an integral part of merchant culture. Business conditions demand such a capacity. Conflict, to a Rajput, may be sought or avoided, but it always offers an opportunity for proving oneself a 'real' Rajput or Darbar. Courage can be demonstrated. Conflict for a businessman, on the other hand, may quite literally be unaffordable, and courage is demonstrated not in conflict, but by discovering new and profitable transactions. Courage and shrewdness, in fact, tend to merge in the world of business.

The most striking difference between Darbar and Bania culture, then, is their different attitudes to violence. For the Darbar, violence can be avoided only be resorting to cowardice. For the Bania, violence represents a disruption of the order of things. Peace of the realm is usually best for business.

We recall the point made earlier that it is dangerous to jump the cinema queue in which Rajputs stand, but that Banias would gloss over the episode to avoid conflict. The stereotypical Bania is somebody who not only avoids violence, but is afraid of it. Innumerable stories tell of Banias imploring robbers to take their belongings, but spare their life and family. A Rajput, in the same situation, should fight unto death. 'Cowardly' is the expression often used about Banias. Such statements cannot, of course, be tested, but are certainly typical of the ideas people in Saurashtra have of Darbars and Banias.

One important implication of this difference is, as we have seen, religion. Even as Banias are divided between different sects, with considerable differences between them in relation to theology, all these sects give the doctrine of non-violence a central place.

What, then is the concept which parallels 'power' in the merchant universe? On one level, it is certainly money. But how is the activity of making money conceived? An interesting Bania name may be mentioned in this context, Kamdar. 'Dar' in this context is related to the verb for 'to hold, to own'—as in Darbar, Patidar, Zamindar, etc. Kam is work. Literally, then, the Kamdar is the owner or the holder of work. It is hardly necessary to recall how the nascent bourgeoisie, in Europe, saw themselves as the working sector of the population, in opposition to priests and aristocrats. Thus Oza (1946), referring to 'the working sectors of the population', means not the workers but the bourgeoisie. This term had a clear address to those who 'did not work'—the Darbars and their Nagar bureaucrats. For Oza, these 'working sectors' ought to direct developments in Saurashtra when independence, then a certainty, came. And so it happened; post-independence Saurashtra was indeed dominated by the bourgeoisie, led by the Banias and numerous (non-priestly) Brahmins, for a long time.

The opposition between Darbar and Kamdar, between the owners of land and the 'owners of work', is a major theme of this study. I hope to have shown how this opposition goes beyond mere politics to widely opposed values on a much more general level, values relating to gender and sex, to war and peace, to individual behaviour and to social organization, to morals and, both implicitly and explicitly, to religion.

NOTES

1. This is a recurrent theme in the literature on Gujarat. See, for example, Thoothi (1934), Munshi (1954), Shah and Shroff (1958), Pocock (1972), Tambs-Lyche (1982), etc.
2. See Spodek (1974, 1976) and Tambs-Lyche (1976, 1982, 1992a).
3. Some of these are not included with the Banias in local terminology, some like the Bhatias are included sometimes but by no means always.
4. Saurashtra forms part of Gujarat state, where the use of alcohol is prohibited. This is obviously related to the dominance of merchant cultural values in the state.
5. The great merchants at the ports of Gujarat were either Hindus, Jains or Muslims originating from outside Gujarat but now resident there. The local Muslim converts were apparently of lesser importance, with the partial exception of the *voras* and the *khojahs.* Most of these 'foreign' Muslims were resident in Gujarat, with their own houses there, and so were in fact subjects of Gujarat, whatever their country of birth, which could be Turkey, Egypt, Arabia, or Persia. Some, however, were only itinerant, being domiciled in such places as Alexandria, Damascus, Persia, Syria and Afghanistan (Pearson 1976, 25).
6. Tome Pires is among the main Portuguese sources for this period. The passage here is cited from Pearson (1976, 26).
7. Brahmins and Kshatriyas were theoretically barred from taking interest, but this seems to have been of little practical importance, at least for Brahmins, many of whom engaged in such activity. Note that Pearson here uses the term Bania in the sense we have used here, as a category of castes, not as a broad occupational term like Torri (1991) does.
8. Pearson is here referring to the sixteenth and seventeenth centuries. See below.

9. This should be seen in contrast to the British East India Company, which came to depend heavily on Gujarati finance (e.g. Subramaniam 1992).
10. When the merchants of Surat felt threatened by the intolerant policies of Aurangzeb, 8,000 heads of merchant families left the city, and went to Broach. They sent a petition to the emperor, and, having received a conciliatory answer, returned to Surat (op. cit., 122).
11. Thus the Nagarsheths; see pp. 236-7.
12. Singh and Rajshirke (1992) discuss several types of merchant councils in Surat at the end of the eighteenth century. The terms used are all different from those used by Pearson. Without entering more fully into the matter, their work certainly attests to the proliferation of councils or committees among merchants of the area.
13. Spodek (1976, 21) gives 'guild' and 'mahajan' as synonyms, but my understanding of the organization as it worked in Bhavnagar is that the two were distinct.
14. Thus in Bhavnagar a certain family—of Brahmins from Maharashtra, incidentally—were known as the family of the Nagarsheths, while the office in Ahmadabad, too, seems to have run in the family (S. Mehta 1984).
15. In 1725, there were 53 guilds in Ahmedabad (Tripathi and Mehta 1984, 159).
16. See e.g. Nurul Hasan (23), S.C. Misra (44, 46), Tripathi and Mehta (158-60, 166) and S. Mehta (173-83), all in Tripathi (ed) (1984), for discussion on several aspects of guilds and Mahajans in Gujarat.
17. V.D. Divekar cites V.K. Rajwade for the existence of Sheths and Mahajans in Maharashtra in Yadava times, while he himself maintains the continuity of such institutions at least from the thirteenth century onwards (1984, 88-9). He seems to support the idea that they have had a continuous existence since ancient times.
18. See Doshi 1974 for the pol of Ahmedabad; Surat has its *mohallas*; while in Bhavnagar such units are called *para*.
19. Pritish Nandy notes that there seems to be an association between violence and sex in Indian poetry (Nandy 1973). Certainly, the doctrine of non-violence puts a premium on sexual abstention. This is well known from Gandhi's writings, but there is no reason to suppose that such a connection is exclusively Gandhian.
20. Nevaskar cites the opinions of Acharya Somadeva, 'who felt that women are neither good nor bad; they are "like the cream of milk, the source of poison as well as nectar" and have "neither any innate merit nor blemish, but become like their husbands, as rivers assume the character of the ocean in which they merge themselves"(from Sangave 1959, 179 quoted by Nevaskar 1971, 184).
21. See, for this point, Pocock (1972), Shah and Shroff (1958) and Tambs-Lyche (1982).
22. Among Charans, it is the boy's mother who initiates such a search—and among the pastoral castes women seem to be acting for their children of both sexes. As for Rajputs, the last Rani of Jaipur makes it clear that it was her mother who opposed her marriage to the 'playboy' prince of the state. Her father, the ruler of Cooch Behar, had no say in the matter but tried to console his wife and daughter (Gayatri Devi and Rau 1983).
23. Thoothi gives his dates as 1478 to 1521 (1935, 92); Brent 1479 to 1531 (1972, 170). His travels in Gujarat are attested by Pocock (1973, 108), Thoothi (1935, 92) and Mallison (1983, 245), who also describes the work of Vitthalnath in Gujarat (see also Pocock, op. cit.).

24. Here the Vallabhas differ fundamentally from *advaita* philosophy; for the image is neither a symbol nor an incarnation: it is the manifestation of Krishna himself. It is 'really the form which God himself has chosen' (Clementin-Ojha 1990, 125). Thus it implies the idea of a personal god, a god with a will, essentially different from the abstract Brahman of *advaita*.
25. According to him, by the end of the seventeenth century no sect had been firmly established in Gujarat (1935, 92).
26. Vallabhacharya uses the term *shuddhadvaita*—pure non-dualism—to distinguish his philosophy from Ramanujacharya's *vishishtadvaita*—modified non-dualism. Ramanuja's 'modification' of *advaita* consists largely in recognizing a personal God, who cannot be nameless or quality-less in the sense of the Brahman of Shankaracharya, the founder of *advaita*. But while Ramanuja stresses the imperfection of certain aspects of creation in relation to those inspired directly by God, the Vallabhacharyas stress that any quality in the created world depends on how it is made to relate to the godhead, thus, when dedicated to God everything becomes pure. It is in thus modifying the opposition between God and the world that Vallabhacharya claims to re-establish monism.
27. Thoothi (1935, 217-22, 337-42, 346-7) devotes a large part of his work to the various influences the sect has had on Gujarati culture.
28. There are several recent monographs on Indian businessmen (e.g. Nevaskar 1971, Timberg 1978) as well as of Indian city life (e.g. for Gujarat, Desai 1964, Pandit 1965, Doshi 1974) but nobody has tried to construct a systematic model along lines similar lines to Fox's analysis of the Rajput political system.

CHAPTER X

The King
Integration Through Power

THE PROBLEM OF KINGSHIP

It will be clear by now that in traditional Kathiawar, the king, rather than the Brahmin, is the central figure. We have seen the Rajput king emerge gradually from the chief or clan head, as a primus inter pares.

In this context, we have stressed the importance of the bard and the relative absence of the Brahmin in the constitution of kingship. These two factors are closely related to the role of the goddess. She does not need priests, we have argued; when Brahmins are attached to her, they are not essential to her worship. She, however, is represented on earth through the Charan women, seen as her incarnations. They, rather than the priestly caste, serve as the intermediaries between goddess and king. The bardic men are equally necessary to king, as genealogists legitimizing his descent, and as poets celebrating his deeds.

All this is clearly at variance with Dumont's view of Indian kingship (1966, 351-75), where king and Brahmin form an indissoluble structural pair. For Weber, too, the Brahmin legitimized the king's power. Neither does our analysis fit Hocart's view of the Indian ruler as a sacred king (1927).

We have treated the king as a secular agent, and we have seen that the goddess provides him with the necessary force to fill this role. Without the goddess at his side, he cannot win a war. But she also presides over a moral dimension will desert an immoral king. Not only does she guard the honour of women, she also expects the king to do it on her behalf. Yet the king relates to the goddess as any other devotee would do; it is the strength of his devotion that gains for him her favours. Ritual in itself is of no avail. Thus we are brought to conclude, like Galey (1989) that though the king is not a 'sacred king', there are dimensions of kingship that go beyond the secular domain.

Having come this far, we cannot avoid a discussion of kingship on a more ideal level. To understand kingship in traditional Kathiawar, we shall have to relate it to the literature on Hindu kingship in general. As the literature shows, the interpretations of Indian kingship have repercussions even for the understanding of present-day politics in India.

THE THREE FUNCTIONS: KING AND PRIEST

Dumezil consecrated a great deal of his work to exploring what he calls the 'tripartite ideology' (1968, 15) of the Indo-European peoples. To him, the Indian varnas were built on the three functions he had thus identified: magic and juridical sovereignty, physical force—in particular related to war—and peaceful abundance and prosperity. The three functions correspond to the Brahmin, Kshatriya and Vaishya varnas respectively (op. cit., 16). But he stresses that the ideology is not necessarily accompanied by a triple division of society, which 'might be ... only an ideal, and at the same time, a way of analysing, of interpreting, the forces which made the world and the life of men possible' (op. cit., 15, my translation).

Dumezil here stresses the cultural rather than social character of the tripartite division.[1] Thus we may expect, among the Indo-European peoples, different ways of fulfilling the functions and of distinguishing between the people performing them. As for Vedic India, there is little doubt about the division between the first two functions, even if the presence of hereditary caste distinctions between Brahmins and Kshatriyas is sometimes doubted.

The relation between the two is, however, much clearer in the Brahmanas, written in the period between the Vedas and the classical age. It was on the *Satapatha Brahmana* that Hocart based his treatise on kingship, in which he stressed the religious functions of the king (1927). For him, the sacred origin of the king was general to kingship, but his reading and interpretation of the text differs considerably from that of modern writers. Dumont stresses precisely the division between priestly and royal functions, as setting India apart from other early empires such as Egypt, Sumer or China:

> The king depend on priests for the religious functions, he can not himself perform the sacrifice for his kingdom, he cannot be his own sacrificer, he instead puts 'in front' of himself a priest, the purohita, and so he loses the ritual preeminence to the priests, guarding for himself power only. (1966, 356, my translation)

Thus while the God-kings of the ancient Middle East[2] combined the first two functions, Indian kings did not. For Dumont, this leads to nothing less than the secularization of power in India. While the Brahmin takes care of dharma—the cosmic and moral order—the king and the Kshatriya are resposible for *artha,* which Dumont sees as essentially individualistic; in the pursuit of 'interest' or 'gain' the king operates in a competitive, rather than hierarchical, mode (op. cit., 356-7 and 365ff).

Heesterman, writing on the basis of the same texts, puts his point differently:

> ... in the Christian as well as the Islamic world both spiritual authority and temporal power have to be realized in a single sphere of society. India on the other hand recognize a second, independent human sphere, namely the renunciatory life that turns its back on the social world.... In the Indian case the two forces do not compete for priority within one single sphere ... the spiritual one simply opts out, leaving the other to cope for itself as best it can. (1978, 5)

The main difference here, as Heesterman points out, is his identification of the renouncer and the Brahmin, where Dumont views the two as 'opposite' (op. cit., 5n). Both writers, however, stress the complete separation of the priestly from the royal function by the time the Satapatha Brahmana was written.

THE CONUNDRUM OF AUTHORITY

While Dumont sticks to a structural view of Indian kingship, Heesterman gives an account of historical changes in the ritual of the king's installation. Through the changes, however, runs a 'conundrum': this is 'the problem of ultimate authority and it is insoluble'. The problem relates to a 'lack of consistent theory in the texts' (1978, 1), but in essence it is general, not Indian; 'the ... king-brahmin "model" is the formula that Indian civilization has developed to handle this general problem' (op. cit., 5).

The problem relates to the sources of authority. For Hocart (1927), the sacredness of the king provides absolute and transcendent authority, but other writers, such as Altekar (1949) and Ghoshal (1959), have stressed how the Indian king receives his authority from the people, the community.

To Dumont, the latter view is incompatible with the hierarchical world view; he therefore ascribes it to the influence of Jainism and

Buddhism, with their stress on renunciation and—implicitly—individualism (1966, 362-4).[3] Heesterman interprets the opposition between these two views as evidence of the 'conundrum', rather precisely envisaged, but never adequately solved, in the texts (op. cit., 1-9). The real problem is that 'the king has to belong to the community, but at the same time he must be foreign to it so as to guarantee his authority' (op. cit., 9). It is this dilemma that the installation ritual has to solve.[4]

To do so, it uses a basic paradigm: the opposition between the settled agricultural community (*grama*) and the forest *(aranya)* (ibid.) We have seen how the myth of Khodiyar employs a similar dichotomy. Stressing the complementary nature of this opposition, Heesterman continues: 'the king must belong to the grama, but his authority must be based in the alien sphere of aranya'.[5] There is abundant evidence, he says, that the king has a special relationship to the forest, related to his transcendent authority (op. cit., 10).

Thus, in the *rajasuya*—the investiture ceremony as given in the *Satapatha Brahmana* and elsewhere—the unction and enthronement of the king are separated by the chariot drive, a symbolic war expedition (op. cit., 11).[6] Heesterman gives further examples of how the ritual takes the king to the forest only to return to the village; this is repeated at several levels of the ceremony. The cycle is, in principle, endless. Later versions of the rite 'cut the cycle in different places, but it is still the same cycle ...' (op. cit., 12).

Further, the *danda* (staff), which stands for the king's 'capacity to punish' in defence of dharma, is originally the attribute of the warrior's life abroad: 'Authority and its symbol are situated outside the community. They can only be put into contact with the community by means of the alternating cycle' (op. cit., 13-14).

The ritual cycle of the installation rite, concludes Heesterman, far from offering a solution to the conundrum of authority, is 'wrought with constant risk and the threat of a violent breakdown'. A reform was needed, and it came. The endless cycle is cut up into 'single rectilinear stretches of rites with clear-cut beginnings and ends ... the purpose was to break out of the endless cycle by establishing a new conception of the transcendent, and therefore of authority' (op. cit., 15).

By breaking the cycle, the reform opened the way to free

> authority and made it unassailably transcendent. However, the price ... was ... a heavy one. Authority was still located outside the community in *aranya*, but by breaking the cycle that connected *grama* and *aranya* it was irretrievably cut

off from the social world. Absolute, transcendent authority could therefore not benefit society's premier agent, the king. It became instead vested in the Veda ... society and its king was barred from its operation.

This, then, leads to the classical king-Brahmin formula, where the 'king's access to esoteric knowledge and ultimate authority based on it was irrevocably cut off' (op. cit., 17).

Heesterman does not attempt to date these changes, though implicitly he is referring to the late Vedic to pre-classical period, when the relevant Brahmanas were composed. He does, however, identify what he sees as the social changes leading to the reform. As long as settled agricultural

communities were relatively limited in number and restricted in their resources, while wide expanses were left open, the alternation of settled life as against nomadic raiding and transhuming expeditions to supplement meagre resources may have been a reasonably effective proposition. However, with the growth and spread of settled agriculture a different type of organization and a new conception of authority will have been needed. (op. cit., 15)

This transformation cannot have taken place at the same time all over India; nor can we exclude reversions of the evolutionary process. In commenting upon the myth of Khodiyar, we concluded that the countryside of Vallabhi was as yet far from settled; the empty space was filled in by the pastoral communities of which Khodiyar herself was a representative. In that myth, the Brahmin and the bard represent divergent views of kingship; the bard binds the king to a 'tribal' community, the Brahmin to a transcendent source of authority. We are, here, talking not of demography as such, but of representations of society. In a sense, then, it is as if the fall of Vallabhi produces a reversion towards a conception of society and kingship that recalls the period antedating the reform to which Heesterman refers.

We may assume that the Brahmana texts were available and known to, say, the *purohita* of king Shiladitya. But the ritual cycle that had been cut at an earlier date was now, perhaps, in need of restoration, to integrate the new rural groups with the kingdom.

MEDIEVAL TEXTS ON KINGSHIP

Vallabhi fell at the dawn of the age of 'minor Puranas',[7] whose end coincides with the establishment of the medieval, Rajput order in western India. These texts brought new visions of kingship. But the view of the king which emerges from the Vishnudharmottara Purana, compiled between AD 700-800 in northern India (Inden 1978, 39), differs substantially from the Rajput institution.

Inden, commenting on this Purana, notes the binary structure of the installation ritual, whose first half takes the

> king-to-be out of the kingdom and infuses him, by means of a bath, with ... royal authority, thereby centralizing it in him. The second and complementary part ... returns him as a king to his kingdom where he in turn infuses the various constituents of the community with transvalued forms of the very things by which he himself was symbolically bathed; as a result, authority again becomes decentralized. (1978, 29)

Thus again, transcendent authority, rooted outside, is opposed to its 'decentralization', where it is shared with the community. But the symbols of kingship are now transformed into ever more abstract and metaphorical forms. In fact, we are getting closer to 'divine kingship' than in perhaps any other Indian text.

Mayer, comparing princely accession ceremonies in recent times, finds the two elements of the ritual still present. But in his prime Rajput case—Bikaner—the affusion or bath is a minor affair, allotted less than half an hour in the proceedings. That this part of the ritual—which 'infuses' sacredness—is especially weak in Rajput ceremony, is indicated by the contrast to the ritual at Baroda, where the Maratha Gaekwars lay much greater stress on it (1991, 767-9).

The king of the *Vishnudharmottara Purana* is said to be 'the husband' and 'lord' (*vallabha, pati*) of the land and these two are regarded as the 'father' *(pita)* and mother *(mata)* of the people, their children *(praja)* (op. cit., 30). This implies the subordination of the latter to 'the king and the land',

> while at the next level, the treatment of the earth or land as the wife and 'halfbody' of the king implies her subordination to and incorporation in the king, her husband and lord. Like husband and wife, the king and earth were to act as a single, corporate entity, guided by him, in producing good offspring and good crops. Every spring, for example, the earth's menstruation was to be celebrated and the king was to perform a ceremonial plowing (sexual intercourse) and sow seeds in (impregnate) her plowed field (womb).... (ibid.)

This relationship might, of course, be re-interpreted in Shakta terms; then the king would be the consort of the land rather than vice versa. The goddess, representing the land, would take pride of place.

Inden's reading, surely the correct brahminical one, corresponds to a Shaiva—or here Vaishnava—view. A Shakta reading does, however, bring us very close to the message of the Khodiyar myth.

Inden further stresses that the familial image of the king is not followed by indications of relationships among the people; these are 'virtually absent'. They are 'children of the king and the earth, but they are not brothers and sisters to each other...' (op. cit., 31). But quasi-kinship among the people was an important part of myth in traditional Kathiawar, where the dominant group were ideally junior kinsmen of the king, and the tikka ceremony identified certain 'tribal' populations as fictive kin of the ruler. Here the Rajput landlords, as well as the ruler, were *mata-pita*—'father-and-mother'—to the lower castes. In our Rajput world there was more stress on relationship among the people, and less on the king as metonymically representing the whole, than in the Vishnudharmottara Purana.

Inden stresses precisely this symbolic primacy of the king. He is, on behalf of the people, their 'sacrificer (*yajamana)*, executing a variety of ritual acts through the agency of the *purohita* or priest...' and the people receive the benefits of these sacrifices (1978, 31). Such may have been the role of king Shiladitya; but if so it is this very primacy of the king that the Khodiyar myth opposes. Jains and Muslims did not share this view either. We are dealing, here, with ideology. The king may, purportedly, have sacrificed on behalf of all; in Saurashtra at least, everybody did not accept this view.

This is not to say that such sacrifices were not important. An element of it is certainly present in such great rituals as the sacrifice at Bhuj, which Swami Narayana opposed so strongly. But by that time it had become as much a spectacle, showing the power and prestige of the sacrificer in attracting prestigious Brahmins and spending large amounts of money, as a ritual in which the people shared. Even more precisely; it was a ritual in which certain sectors of the people shared, to the relative exclusion of others. Yet we should be prepared here, for important variations within the medieval constitution of the Indian state.

Inden points to some of the medieval developments, such as the king's choice and establishment of an *istadevata*, a practice which gradually became more common during the period. This fits the Rajput pattern, but the lineage goddess, so central to their system, is missing. It is true that, in our area, the term istadevata was sometimes used for this deity, so the 'chosen deity' was, in a sense, inherited. The deity established by Inden's king is strategically placed in the city or palace, but ours is often in the 'wilderness' like Khodiyar; such places are hardly strategic except for the presence of the goddess.

In short, the puranic text stresses the active, independent stance of the king, while the Rajput king was more closely bound to pre-existing patterns. The king of the *Vishnudharmottara Purana* is, in effect, a God, partly descended from Vishnu himself; Lakshmi or Shri, Vishnu's wife, was also the consort of the king, and obviously connected with the land (Inden, op. cit., 31). We are, after all, talking of a purana dedicated to Vishnu, while most kings of western India were Shaivite. And the Vaishnavite kingdom—of which Orissa may be taken as the medieval archetype (Eschmann, Kulke and Tripathi 1978)—developed, precisely, the idea of the god-king to a far greater extent than the Rajput kingdoms did.

The Vaishnavite king of the purana, like the Rajputs, claimed descent from sun and moon, as well as being 'made up from the eight guardian deities of the quarters' (Inden 1978, 32). But in our area, all Rajputs, not only the king, were the descendants of sun and moon, and, moreover, the bards shared in this descent. This made them 'sacred' only in a very wide sense. It would be more precise to say that through the *Agnikula* myth (Tod 1829, 71) the principle of descent was deified; thereby the king might be closer to 'divine sources of power' than his kin, but he was not a divine king (Mayer 1991, 767). The importance of legitimacy through birth, for Rajputs, can hardly be overemphasized.

To make the contrast clear, let us have Inden explain what is meant by the divinity of the king in the puranic context:

> The divinity of the Hindu king ... has nothing to do with 'divine right' or 'absolutism' ..., but with a view, very different from the ... European one, about the nature of the world...and the place of the king in it.
>
> The life of the Hindu cosmos, ... is cyclical ... the fact that the Cosmic Man generates the units of this world out of his own body ... is of great significance, for it means that although the supreme god is transcendent ... he is also immanent: that is, all units in the cosmos belong to one single order of things.
>
> The place of the king in this cosmic scheme was crucial. Within the non-dualistically conceived order of the universe, the king was the immanent and microcosmic form of the transcendent, macrocosmic Purusa. Just as the body of Purusa was the macrocosmic symbol of unity and order and of power, prosperity and well-being for the cosmos as a whole, so, the king was the symbol of these things for his kingdom, conceived of as a microcosm of the

world as a whole. It would be wrong, however, to argue that the king was 'merely' a symbol here.... (1978, 32)

Indeed, this would surely be wrong in relation to Orissa. But keeping in mind the relative ease with which kings were replaced by murder; the actual position of the king in court, where he was at first surrounded by powerful vassals, then by ministers; always having to deal with the political role of the queen—in the Rajput states, the identification with Purusha had become largely a token. This is not to state that Rajput kings had no divinity; but it seems to have played a minor role in their case. Mayer, drawing on material from a number of princely states, concludes that 'to acknowledge a degree of sacredness seems to meet the situation' (1991, 777).

Yet when Inden states that, 'if the king acted correctly, he brought about the well-being of his land and people, his dependent wife and children' (op. cit., 33), we recognize the pattern. When he continues, 'in cosmic terms, his purpose was to regenerate and reintegrate the units which, having been emitted by the Cosmic Man, tended to disperse in all directions, into a single solitary and prosperous role', then we may agree to the implications of the formula on a sociological level, without fully recognizing, for our Rajput states, its cosmic base.

The *Vishnudharmottara Purana* presents an idealized picture not only of the king, but equally of his kingdom. The king, as *axis mundi*, is conceptually at its centre, where his capital should be located. His realm is seen as a large square; forts are to be built at its four corners. The capital itself is divided into 81 squares, the temple to the king's deity in the middle—and so on (Inden 1978, 33). It is trite to note that no real kingdom fits this sacred topography. Of course, such ideal representations might serve to guide the organization of the kingdom, but we need expect no closer approximation to the ideal on the ritual than on the practical or topographical level.

'The first of the imperial dynasties' says Inden, raising

> ... either Visnu or Siva (or Surya, the sun) to the status of supreme deity (*paramesvara, mahesvara*) equivalent to Cosmic Man, and relegate the Buddha to a secondary position, are the short-lived Karkota dynasty of Kashmir, the Gurjara-Pratihara at Kanjakubja in Northern India, the Rastrakuta in the Deccan, and the Pallava in south India. This change takes place in the eighth century and is marked by the building of the first monumental Hindu temples. (1978, 39)

Of these, only the Gurjara-Pratiharas were close to Saurashtra.[8]

Here, the Vallabhi empire was close to its end. But it was not replaced by the type of empire Inden refers to; it was followed by much smaller states built on the tribe-king alliance. Even when the Chalukyas ruled Gujarat, Saurashtra remained relatively independent. We must conclude that the type of empire Inden refers to, identifying the king with 'cosmic man', was never established in Saurashtra.

THE KING AS A GIFT-GIVER

In 1676-7 the ruler of Mewar, Maharana Raj Singh, performed the consecration of a large dam, the Rajsamund, and the resulting Rajsagar lake. Some of the elements of Inden's account turn up during this ritual, but they relate to each other rather differently from in his analysis of them (S.R. Sharma 1971, Tambs-Lyche 1993). The dam was almost three kilometres long. An enormous undertaking for the time and place, the ritual had to be in tune with the scale of the work. It may be analysed as consisting of three separate sequences.

One, largely secular, emphasizes the king as gift-giver: its high point was the weighing of the Maharana and several other notables against gold, the amount to be distributed as charity. Viewed as a spectacle, this was certainly the culmination of the ritual.

The second sequence, employing twenty-six Brahmin priests, is based on the *Matsya Purana*. The propitiation of Varuna—referred to as lord of the ocean—takes the central role; but he is also equated with the sum of the gods (Sharma, op. cit., 52). 'Whenever [the king] floods the world by showering down streams of wealth, the king is said to become Varuna' cites Inden from the *Vishnudharmottara Purana* (1978, 34). Here, surely, the sacrificer identifies himself with the sacrifice, and thereby with the God. This second sequence 'takes the king out of the community', while in the first he places himself over and above his people.

In the third sequence, we find the king praying to several deities—including his kuldevi—without mediation of the priests. He also walks around the lake and is greeted by his people; with a number of selected ladies he carries water from the lake; he transforms the lake into a 'real ocean' by furnishing it with precious stones (the submarine equivalent of the heavenly bodies), with fish, and with alligators.[9] In this third sequence, then, the king is acting on behalf of the community as its member.

Royal authority thus has a double base, as in Inden's and

Heesterman's analyses. But the third element is significant, for it is the king's role as gift-giver that integrates the ritual from a political viewpoint, and encompasses the other elements in terms of the ritual as a spectacle.[10] The Brahmin's role is to underpin this sequence, while the king's action as a member of the community lead up to it.

Let us now turn again to the Jain monk from Wadhwan, Merutunga.[11] We have seen how he argues for the superiority of the Jain king. But what is the Hindu king like?

Bhoja, the Hindu ruler of Malwa, is contrasted here with the Jain ruler of Gujarat, Bhima. The greatest attribute of Bhoja, Merutunga tells us, is 'his generous gifts to suppliants, especially to those who exhibit poetical talents. Poetical talent is the basis for determining the amount of charity and reward' (Arai 1978, 92-3). Bhija is desirous of fame and glory, evidently to an extent seen as exaggerated by Merutunga. Vedic scholars are excluded from his favour. (op. cit., 94). This does not indicate a court dominated by the Brahmin purohit; nor does Merutunga, apparently, hint at any tendency for the Hindu ruler to identify himself with God—surely an obvious theme for criticism if there had been any basis for it. As a whole, we are reminded not of the puranic ruler, but of the Rajput king.

Merutunga does not mention the Charan. But in tune with Jaina stress on achievement rather than ascription, he talks of poetical talent; not of bardic castes. Thus there is no reason for surprise here, especially as the *Bhoja-prabandha,* a Hindu eulogy of the same king, states: 'acquiring fame (*kirti* or *yasas*) is the most important goal for a king and generous gifts to the deserving is the means for it' (Arai, op. cit., 95).

In other words, the virtues of the king are just those commemorated and advertised by the Charan. The stress on gift-giving is entirely in tune with the conclusions we draw from our analysis of the ceremony referred to from seventeenth-century Mewar, where it eclipses the Brahmanic content of the ritual. We may add that Charans are among those most favoured with gifts on that occasion, and a large number of older grants to them are confirmed and honoured. No grants to Brahmins are noted in that context (S.R. Sharma 1971, 54).

Mayer's informants, too, stress the king's generosity, in contrast to present-day representatives of the state (1991, 782). The king, at the apex of the hierarchy, clearly had to conform to the rule that superior position implies the giving of gifts to inferiors.

RAJPUT KINGSHIP IN TRADITIONAL KATHIAWAR

Our discussion of the medieval kingdoms of Kathiawar, and, to a great extent, Rajasthan, leads us to conclude that they do not seem to have evolved from the reforms concurrent with the *Vishnudharmottara Purana* (Inden 1978). Rather, they succeeded, in a less settled and more peripheral area of India, to kingdoms prior in form to those changes. They developed, as we have seen, from 'tribal' forms of leadership founded on the segmentary lineage, through an intermediate period of king-tribe alliance.

The bardic institution is intrinsic to this form of kingship and evolved along with it, while the economics for expanding chiefdoms into kingdoms was provided by control of trade and traders.[12] Brahmins do not figure to the same extent. In Mewar, it is true, the kings were seen as but dewans of the god Eklingji, a form of Shiva, and the high priest of the god's temple thus had to invest the king with his royal honours (S.R. Sharma 1971, 17, Stern 1973). But this pattern seems to have been specific to Mewar, and there is no trace of a similar role for Brahmins in Porbandar or in Junagadh. In the latter case, the Goddess Khodiyar, from an entirely different angle, was the 'king-maker'.

Common to these early kingdoms is the king-tribe alliance, with the Bhils in Mewar, the Ahirs in Junagadh, and the Mers in Porbandar. Such alliances are replaced, in later kingdoms, by the king's membership of the dominant caste.

In all these kingdoms, however, some use was made of Brahmins. In the consecration of the Rajsagar lake of Mewar, we have seen how they serve to place the king above the community. This the Charan's eulogies could not achieve, since the king's mythical descent was shared by his caste. Thus at a certain point, Brahmins must have been important in making the chief a true king.

The necessary means for effecting this transition came from the control of trade. The merchant, in effect, pays for the military strength necessary to protect his trade. Here, too, the Charan has a role, as protector of caravans and as the living hostage in guarantee of loans. But just as the Charan's role in trade diminishes with hired armies and bankers' guarantees, so the ritual protection he offers to the king is gradually replaced by Brahmins. At the beginning of our period, he emerges as a poet and genealogist; at its end, these are his main remaining roles. Yet the Brahmins, like the soldiers, remain hirelings in Saurashtra; priesthood never becomes an estate in its own right.

In general, then, kingship and the state, in traditional Kathiawar, is characterized by the mélange of tribal and state elements which turns up so often in literature on Rajputs. Viewed state by state, region by region, the image of instability disappears and instead we see clear geographic and historic patterns. The main nodes of the political system—states such as Junagadh, Porbandar, later Jamnagar and finally Bhavnagar—show, in fact, a high degree of historical continuity. Junagadh and Porbandar, indeed, rival the oldest European states for the temporal span of their existence. These nodes owe their position to their strategic locations in military terms (Junagadh), or else to their facilities for trade—the other three are all ports.

Between these nodes, we find at one level minor centres of relative persistence, at the next 'buffer zones' where political instability has been the rule. The typical example of the letter is, of course, the Kathi area of central Saurashtra. Thus traditional Kathiawar had ample room for the dichotomy of the settled and the wild, of city and jungle, which—to a much greater extent—had come to disappear from the plains of northern India.

The coming of the railways upset this old order. Rajkot, in what used to be the peripheral area in the middle of the peninsula, now became an important centre of communications. But before the periphery became the centre, the central position of the periphery strengthened the continued interdependence of state and tribal forms of organization. This interdependence, leaving room for several stages of state formation at one and the same time, provided the background for the competition between Brahmin and Charan as ritual agents of the king.

The integration of Europe into strong nation-states, as opposed to the continued existence of the tribal stage in Rajput areas, is usually explained by the processes of state integration, viewed as it were from the top. But the present study invites an alternative view: is it rather the persistence of grassroots organization on the level of tribe and caste, in the Indian context, which produces the difference? I shall not pursue the question here, but turn instead to the role of the goddess, providing power—shakti— to chief and king alike.

THE GODDESS AND THE KING

The relationship between king and goddess has been shown in the context of Hindu Junagadh, and in other, scattered examples. Whether the goddess adopts the king, or, like the Gohils, the king adopts the goddess, is of minor importance; in traditional Kathiawar, as among the Meena of Rajasthan (Jain 1973), no temporal power is possible without the goddess.

We must distinguish here between the legitimizing function, for which Brahmin and Charan compete, and the function of the goddess. Shakti is the essence of political and military power; legitimacy is only its secondary effect. Thus among Charans, the women, becoming goddesses, provide power, while the men concentrate on legitimizing the king.[13] Devotion to the goddess does not set the king apart from other men. She may be of transcendent nature,[14] but she does not confer transcendence on the king. Her miracles are hers alone; they may be performed for the king but never by him. In his relation to the Goddess, then, the king remains primus inter pares.

This is even more so because she is the king's kuldevi, shared with other members of his clan. When, as in such classical Rajput states as those of the Jhalas and Jadejas, the clan is also the dominant caste in much of the realm, there is certainly little exclusivity to her worship. But this was so even in the Gohil dominions, where Khodiyar was a popular goddess available to all, and popular with all the castes of the 'feudal' establishment—almost everybody except the Banias and the Muslims. She would bestow her blessings on any one of these devotees, as well as on the king.

But the king needs to be the most powerful among men, and it is this power that the goddess provides, allowing the king to hold the central position in what, for ancient India, Heesterman describes as a situation where membership

> of the polity... is not primarily defined by residence in a specific well-defined territory, but rather the reverse: differential rights in a territory arise from personal ties of kinship and dependency. Outsiders may be admitted, even welcomed, but their admittance has to be legitimized in terms of personalities and even kinship. The state, then, is based on a network of personal relations in which rights in the soil are subsumed. This means that power and authority are situated at the cross-roads, so to say, of the personal relations which make up the polity. Power is dispersed. If there is a king, he can only be the living balance of these relationships and their opposing pulls and pushes, which tie him down and prevent his acting on his own. His authority does not transcend the community by divine right or otherwise. At best he is a primus inter pares. In this respect, cooperation with the brahmin imposes itself. (1985, 143)

This passage shows Heesterman's rejection of Kautilya's model of the state as a centralized and bureaucratic entity (1985, 121-40). It is, in fact, of Kautilya's king that he writes here: since the Mauryas are seen as the apogee of centralized power in ancient India,[15] is it not even more true of our Rajput kings?

Heesterman also rejects co-operation with the Brahmin as a solution to the king's dilemma, as we have seen. Royal power can not be made transcendent by one who, in his view, leaves the matters of this world behind.[16] The contempt with which our Khodiyar myth views the purohit reflects a similar view: the Brahmin paid by the king is not a 'real' Brahmin, but a corrupted one.

The control of trade provides the resources the king needs to free himself from the web of relations indicated by Heesterman, but implicates him in new sets of relations that may themselves become problematic. The goddess helps him deal with this and other problems.

Even in ancient India, the position of women in this web of relations was problematic. This is stressed by Heesterman, who says of woman, that she 'has to remain an element of insecurity between the two lineages which, through her, establish or maintain connubium' (1985, 135). We have already discussed this problem regarding the queen's role in politics. The dilemma is particularly salient in Rajput kinship, where the woman never completely gives up membership in her own lineage. In fact, next to battle, the marital bed was probably the greatest danger to the Rajput king.

But the queen is a source of the king's shakti, as well as the means to perpetuate his lineage and kingdom. As the ultimate source of shakti and sons the Goddess replicate the queen's role, but does so without marriage alliance. As a Charani, she is like a sister to the king; like a sister she protects him, but has powers to perpetuate the patriline that no human sister can have. Thus the goddess strengthens the patrilineal principle and reduces, on an ideological level, the ambivalence inherent in the reproduction of the royal line.

The king is not married only to the queen. Both in classical texts (Inden 1978) and in popular tradition, he is the husband of his country (Jain 1975). The kuldevi again replicates this relation; as the 'country-and-people' (*janapada*) is the material source of the king's power, so the Goddess is its spiritual source. Shakti stands for both these aspects of power. Mayer (1982, 1985) adds a beautiful explication—by a Rajput ruler himself—of the 'throne' (*gaddi*) as another source of power. The marriage idiom is again repeated; the relationship between king and throne is likened to that between man and wife. Finally, Heesterman shows how relationships centering on the king are ordered by pairs (1985, 145), recalling that ubiquitous idiom, marriage, standing for alliance and social integration. This reflects on the very conception of kingship: 'The sacrality or divinity of the king resides in his connectiveness' (op. cit., 151).

Thus the Goddess, representing the integrity of the royal lineage as well as the fruits of alliance in the form of fertility, becomes the perfect symbol of what the king is supposed to achieve, and by implication the obvious source of the power to succeed.

THE GODDESS' PEOPLE

The position of the goddess in the Rajput states is related, then, to the problems of legitimacy and power in a context where no state divinity—such as that of Jagannath at Puri (Eschmann, Kulke and Tripathi 1978)—is found. Since she does not need Brahmins, their position in the Rajput state is weaker than where they serve as intermediaries to a state deity. Instead, they compete, in western India, with the Charan. What, then, is the relation of the bardic caste to the constitution of Rajput kingship?

First, of course, the Charan is the king's genealogist. As presented by him, the Rajput lineage has a sacred source, which underlines the king's status as a Kshatriya. This does not, however, differentiate him from other Kshatriyas, of his own or other clans. It is caste and lineage that become sacred, and over this sacred entity the Kuldevi, herself a Charani, presides. The Charan, then, may be seen as the mouthpiece of the clan as well as of his 'sister', the Goddess. Like her, he represents the patrilineal principle; generally it is only the descent of males that is specified in his genealogies, except when important marriages are involved. The genealogy, in fact, may be seen as representing an ideology of patriliny which is stricter than that of political practice, where marriage alliances play an important part (Stern 1973).

It may be as a personification of the lineage that the Charan becomes 'son of the Goddess' (***deviputra***). But the link between the Charani and the lineage principle is even stronger, since she may herself become a goddess. The Charan caste, as a whole, may also be seen to 'incarnate' the lineage principle. We have seen how even the ordinary Charani has a larger share than other women in the powers of the Goddess.[17] These powers are intimately connected with fertility. In a strictly patrilinear society such as that of the Rajputs it is only natural that fertility and continuation of the lineage, fraught as it is with dangerous marriage alliances and the ambiguity of women in the system, should be sacralized.

POWER, LAND AND LINEAGE

We have cited Heesterman's remark that 'differential rights in territory arise from personal links of kinship and dependency'. The regions of traditional Kathiawar, in effect, carry the names of those who held them: Jhalawar, Gohilwar, and indeed Kathiawar, which at one time meant that central part of the peninsula over which Kathis held sway.

Land rights in traditional Kathiawar were based on kinship and personal grants—the latter predominant in the Muslim state of Junagadh. Basically, all land rights were of this kind; in the medieval period there were few examples of 'private ownership' as distinct from politically granted land rights. It is true that the land held by Nagar Brahmins around Junagadh was of a different nature, but such rights, too, would surely need political confirmation if they were to prevail during the medieval period. When disputes over land arose, claimants seem always to have referred to the deeds or grants of earlier rulers.[18]

Similarly, the term Darbar denoted equally the holder of land and of power, referring as it did to a member of a dominant caste, to a chief or king, or even to the assembly of the latter. Land rights and power were basically one and the same but rights to land derived from power and not vice versa.

Power, lineage and landholding, then, constituted a network of relations in which the king or chief occupied the centre. And, just as the king was bound by these links to a large number of people, so they were, directly or indirectly, bound to him. The logic that kept the king from becoming a true sovereign, also kept even the smallest landholder within the system. The pattern was hierarchical but endlessly and often ambiguously graduated.

It is no wonder, then, that when the decision of the battlefield was ruled out by Pax Britannica, kings and chiefs were constantly harassing the British about questions of precedence; the number of guns to be fired in salute, the seating arrangements at the 1911 Durbar in Delhi, and so on.[19] Though a rank order of Rajput clans existed, as witnessed by hypergamy, this order was neither unchanging nor unambiguous (Stern 1973).

In short, for those engaged in the 'game' of power and land, status was over time achieved rather than ascribed. While the claims to rank bear witness to the hierarchical principle as an ideal for reference, real ranking was a matter of endless competition. Hierarchy could only serve as a language of argument. Bids for power and rank, in traditional Kathiawar, did not lead to a synchronization of claim and reality, of rank and power. Arguments, like force, were but different pieces in the same game.

NOTES

1. Thus, in Rome, at the earliest period the first two functions were combined, as they are in early Scandinavian myths (Dumezil 1968, 264-6 and 271ff). Likewise, the *flamina major* of Rome, though priests, are not 'homologous' to Brahmins (op. cit., 15).
2. These were, of course, not Indo-European.
3. Dumont seems to be guilty of circular argument here.
4. We have already noted that Rajput kings always seem to pose as conquerors, coming to the society from the outside.
5. Heesterman notes, here, that when dharma—personified as a god—reveals himself to Yudhisthira (Mahabharata 3, 314)—he does so in the forest.
6. Heesterman specifies: 'The king has to shoot arrows in the direction of a *ksatriya* posted at the far end of the chariot course. According to one version this seemingly harmless rite even appears as a ritualized cattle raid' (1978, 11).
7. *c.* AD 700-1200. Inden calls this the 'early medieval period' (1978, 29). Dating and classification of Puranas is, in fact, often a difficult matter, which I leave to the specialists. O'Flaherty, for example, divides them into three groups: Early (300 BC to AD 500), Middle (AD 500 to 1000) and later, to AD 1500 (1980, 11). We deal here with her middle period.
8. Inden, indeed, is asking the question of the incidence of the *abhiseka* ceremonies, particularly as referred to in the Vishnudharmottara Purana, during the following period. Though an inscription of the Sakas is found at nearby Cambay this does not refer directly to this form of the ceremony. In general, the bias of the influence of this Purana towards northern and eastern India seems to be apparent in his discussion of the theme (Inden 1978, 39-40).
9. The latter, incidentally, doubted by Sharma.
10. Indeed, at the enthronement ceremony in Bikaner, the ascending ruler is addressed as Annadata—'giver of grain' (Mayer 1991).
11. We are referring, here, to the *Prabandhacintamani* of *c.* AD 1304.
12. Further support for this thesis, from south Gujarat, in Hardiman (1987, 86ff).
13. I here use Weber's dichotomy between power and legitimation, the latter converting power into authority (e.g. Weber 1948). But it will also be seen how gender, in the two Charan roles, parallels the opposition between the goddess and her male consort in a wide range of Indian contexts.
14. This is in itself debatable, since the goddess is identified with Maya and with Prakriti—with this very material world, not with the other.

15. Such is certainly the view of Basham (1969, 79-136).
16. Heesterman says: 'Ironically, the king who has succesfully enticed the brahmin to serve him only obtains an empty husk, for the brahmin then loses his special quality that was the reason to engage him and becomes equal to a ksatriya. The truth is that the ideal brahmin should cultivate the Veda and its ritual by himself, in himself and for himself. The ideal brahmin, like the ideal sacrificer, is a renouncer. Only in this way can the hard-won view of the transcendent that was gained out of the violence of the ancient sacrificial battle be saved from corruption by the world's powers and conflicts. The sacrificial battle for the transcendent is over, leaving world power without authority, transcendent authority without power, and ruling out priesthood as a mediator' (1985, 155).
17. See Ch. VII above; also Westphal-Hellbosch (1976, 167ff) and Trivedi (1961, 22).
18. We may note that the publication of the *Vir Vinod*, a history of Udaipur state by Shyamal Das, printed in 1887, was stopped by the Maharana. 'In claims about jagirs', says S.R. Sharma, 'the claimants started citing it as their authority for the claims they preferred. If they could prove from the narration in the *Vir Vinod* that an ancestor of theirs was present in a particular battle, they could press their claim for a grant which they claimed had been made to their family for fighting heroically in that battle' (1971, 8). We have every reason to suppose that a similar logic obtained in Saurashtra.
19. A brief analysis of such ceremonial relations between the rulers and the paramount power is found in Haynes (1990, 487-90). The voluminous correspondence regarding such matters in the former India Office Library, London, might provide for a study perhaps not entirely lacking in humour.

CHAPTER XI

Kathiawar to Saurashtra Moving toward Modernity

DEVELOPMENT: INDIGENOUS OR COLONIAL?

The years 1806-7 saw British suzerainty established over the peninsula, with the settlement effected by Colonel Walker. It might be natural to see this event as the watershed between the traditional and modern ages. The relative peace which followed marks an important change, but I wish to stress instead the dynamism that existed within the traditional system.

It is of little use to ask what might have happened if the British had not come. Yet we should avoid seeing the indigenous political system, as it continued to function under the British, as simply a reflection of colonial policies.[1] If Bengal is the part of India most thoroughly colonized, then Rajasthan and Saurashtra may be the regions least influenced by colonialism.

The eighteenth century saw an absorption of the smaller chiefdoms by their larger neighbours. But this trend towards integration into larger units though clearly visible, this was not a simple one-way process. The situation in the peninsula, before 1807, was very unsettled indeed. Wars and raids were frequent. Though the three large states and some others did enjoy a measure of political stability, there were also small chiefdoms emerging. While states tended to last once they had crossed a certain threshold, chiefdoms might disintegrate. Ownership of villages changed incessantly, and there were no clear boundaries between states, chiefdoms and more or less 'tribal' areas; rather we see a continuous process of transformations, from lineage-based 'tribal' polity through chiefdom to state.

We left Navanagar (Jamnagar) at the stage of becoming a real state. In the growth of modernity, however, Bhavnagar state was leading the peninsula. Its growth shows the indigenous system capable of renewing itself. Developing from the patterns described,[2] the state grows through a new awareness of the relation between economic and political factors, which is an important element in modernity.

FROM CHIEFDOM TO STATE: BHAVNAGAR

We left the chiefdom at Bhavsinhji's accession, in 1703. He and his successors expanded its area considerably, and completed the transition from chiefdom to state. In the wake of Mughal decline, expansion was possible in the eighteenth century; from 1807 frontiers were effectively frozen by Colonel Walker's settlement.

Bhavsinhji was to make the most of these opportunities, but his was no easy task. The Marathas, taking advantage of the crumbling Mughal empire, were raiding Saurashtra for tribute. During the first of these raids, in 1722-3, they sacked Sihor. Finding his capital too vulnerable to attack, Bhavsinhji removed his administration to Wadwa, then founded Bhavnagar just across the creek from Wadwa. While strategic considerations were no doubt important in his choice of the site, Bhavsinhji 'was not without plans to raise it to a port which would divert at least a share of the commerce which normally went to Surat and Cambay' (BDG, 62). Considering the establishment of Navanagar by Jam Raval, we here see history repeating itself.

But the new port was surrounded by competitors. To the north, Cambay was held by Momin Khan, while Gogha, just south of Bhavnagar, was held by Sher Babi Khan. Bhavsinhji's approach was novel for the area in relying on diplomacy rather than force. He allied himself with Sohrab Khan, the last Mughal governor in effective control of Surat. Bhavsinhji allowed Surat merchants duty-free passage at Bhavnagar in return for similar rights for his subjects at Surat. In addition, Surat got a percentage of the sea custom revenues of Bhavnagar, and they were to co-operate in suppressing piracy along the Saurashtra coast (BDG, 62).

The effects of this statesmanlike manoeuvre were not immediate, for Sohrab Khan was expelled form Surat, and then killed by the Mughal governor at Ahmedabad (ibid.). Gogha, which had also been granted to Sohrab Khan, reverted to Sher Babi in 1738, and Bhavsinhji's policies suffered a setback. But he renewed his alliance with Surat through the Sidi admiral of the Mughal fleet, now in effective power there,[3] who received a quarter of the sea revenues of Bhavnagar. When the British occupied Surat in 1759, they succeeded to the admiral's share (BDG; 63).

Alliance with the British remained a factor in Bhavnagar's policies until the next century. The Marathas had taken Ahmedabad in 1758, and Bhavnagar's friendship with the British was important in withstanding Maratha expansion. By 1764, when Bhavsinhji died, Bhavnagar was considerably strengthened. There had been some territorial expansion too, particularly to the south. It was during this period that village Praj became a part of Bhavnagar territory (BDG, 63; see above, p. 97ff).

Akheraji, Bhavsinhji's son, continued the same policy. In his reign (1764-72) the Marathas were still the main threat to Bhavnagar's independence, while Cambay and Junagadh were his most important rivals for power locally. Akheraji allied himself with the Marathas, helping them take Gogha from Cambay; for this assistance he received a remission of certain tributes, as well as Bhavnagar's own duties in *inam*. Thus, while he remained tributary to the Peshwa in name, these duties, estimated at 3000-4000 rupees annually, remained with him (BDG, 63).

Akheraji's friendship with the British was honoured; in their treaty with Cambay in 1771, they stipulated that Cambay should not disturb Bhavnagar's trade. In alliance with the British, the Baria Kolis to the south were suppressed, becoming subject to Rajput dominance for the first time. Talaja, taken by the British-Bhavnagari alliance, was offered to Akheraji by the British, but he refused, not wishing to extend his dominions beyond the Shatrunjaya river. Talaja was therefore given to Cambay, who held it as a feudatory of the British (BDG, 64). This point is interesting, for it was unusual for a Rajput ruler to refuse a conquest in this way. It seems that Akheraji had rather modern ideas of administration and statesmanship, not wishing to be the nominal head of a territory he could not control or administer efficiently with available resources.

State building started by Bhavsinhji, was consolidated and strengthened in Akheraji's time. The port, with its trade, had begun to extend its dominion to the hinterland.[4]

CONSOLIDATION AND EXPANSION

It was under Akheraji's successor Wakhatsinhji (1772-1816) that Bhavnagar became one of the three major powers in Saurashtra, ranking with Junagadh and Jamnagar (BDG, 64-5). Territorial expansion took two main directions. To the west, Wakhtsinhji gained control over large tracts of land from the Kathis. To the south, he gained Talaja and Mahuva. The boundaries established during his rule were, generally speaking, those that remained with the state till its final dissolution.

Talaja was bought from Cambay in 1780, as the Nawab of Cambay found the outlying province impossible to control.[5] The Nawab's deputy resisted the sale, but Bhavnagar gained control with relative ease. Through British mediation the Nawab was paid 75000 rupees for the transfer of the district to Bhavnagar (BDG, 65). Such a large sum could not have been raised without the help of the Bhavnagari merchant community. The ruler's ability to raise the money may be seen as proof of the transition from chiefdom to state proper.

Mahuva had become an independent principality when the power of the Mughals collapsed. Its rulers, the Kharadia Sipahis,[6] however, lost their chiefdom to the Kathi chief Misri Khatia. Thus Bhavnagar was faced by Kathis in the south as well as in the west. Misri's nephew Hamir had been given Waghnagar and had conquered Jhanjhmer; he started to raid villages in Talaja. Wakhtsinhji countered by attacking and conquering Jhanjhmer, driving Hamir before him to the temple of Gopnath on the shores of the Gulf of Cambay. Here the temple guardian intervened; Hamir kept his villages on the condition that he ceased to raid Bhavnagar territory (BDG, 66). When Hamir's uncle Jaso, the ruler of Mahuva, seized a Bhavnagari ship, Wakhtsinhji was given occasion to march on Mahuva. The pretext of putting down piracy was, no doubt, instrumental in appeasing the British.

For this expedition, Wakhtsinhji was able to muster a force of 15,000 men; Bhavnagar was no longer a petty principality but a state with a sizable army. No longer were kinsmen of the ruler the main element in its military strength; we must assume that the majority of these men were in the regular pay of the ruler. The battle for Mahuva was a hard struggle, raging for six days. In the end, however, the Bhavnagar army was victorious. Jaso fled but was returned to Wakhtsinhji by the local ruler with whom he had sought refuge. This battle took place in 1784 (BDG, 66-7).

Jaso, like so many displaced Saurashtrian rulers, became an outlaw and raided his former territories. He was helped by Hamir of Waghnagar. Thus Waghnagar was again attacked and taken by Wakhtsinhji's *jamadar* of Mahuva. He was helped by the Ahirs of Bhanwad and the Rajula Behlims. Hamir now became an outlaw himself (BDG, 67).

The Khasia Kathis of the south, who had expanded into a regional power when the Mughals withdrew, had been crushed by Wakhtsinhji. If they had hoped to develop Mahuva as a port competing with Bhavnagar, that hope was now gone. These wars, and the suppression of Koli 'pirates' along the coast, made the port of Bhavnagar free from piracy in home waters. Trade grew, and Bhavnagar prospered.

The British seem to have taken a sympathetic view of Wakhtsinhji's aspirations. While he fought the Khasias, Wakhtsinhji wrote to them of his efforts to 'suppress piracy'; at the same time, he asked for assistance against Junagadh, if that power should intervene. The British, congratulating him on his success against the 'pirates', did not, however, commit themselves with regard to Junagadh (BDG, 67)

But it was not Wakhtsinhji's southern acquisitions which led to confrontation with Junagadh. He also extended his dominions westwards. Here, too, the losers were the Kathis, whose small chiefdoms formed what we may call a 'buffer zone' in central Saurashtra, surrounded by the established powers of Junagadh in the west, Jamnagar in the north, and the emerging power of Bhavnagar in the south-east. It was their particular bad luck that Bhavnagar was backed by the British. In raiding territories often conquered from them by Bhavnagar only a few years before, they earned a notoriety in British eyes that was to brand them as a 'criminal caste' for most of the British period. 'The last quarter of the eighteenth century', the Gazetteer says, 'thus marked the prolonged attempt of the host of Kathi tribes to break through the forces which threatened them in an effort which virtually ended with the settlements made by Col. Walker' (BDG, 65).

Junagadh, too, had its quarrels with the Kathis, but was certainly not interested in seeing a rather chaotic aggregation of small chiefdoms replaced by the domination of a rival power. The struggle for domination over central Saurashtra between Junagadh and Bhavnagar forms the background to Wakhtsinhji's excursions against the Kathis. Both Junagadh and Jamnagar had already taken a good bite into what had been Kathi territory. The Kathi chiefdoms differed from the Rajput and Muslim powers around them in that they—generally speaking—never completed the transition from chiefdom to state.[7] The Kathis never developed their caste domination of villages into the 'feudalism' typical of Rajput chiefdoms, nor anything like the bureaucratically-based 'feudalism' of Muslim states. Yet, as we have seen in Chital, they might form viable states when able to control trade.

BHAVNAGAR VS. JUNAGADH: THE SHOWDOWN

Junagadh at this time, was a typical example of a Muslim state. It was ruled by its great Dewan Amarji. He was a formidable statesman of the area. The basis of his state, however, differed from that of Bhavnagar and Jamnagar in several ways. Junagadh had been the administrative centre of the peninsula under the Mughals, becoming independent as a result of the decay of their empire.

Throughout history, it had been a fortress and a garrison town, its great fort Uparkot unique in Saurashtra. Almost impregnable, the 'ancient castle' ruled the surrounding countryside by the intermediary of zamindars, the 'semi-feudal tax-collecting bureaucrats' familiar from the Mughal empire. Kinship between the ruler and the zamindars was of minor importance. The latter in turn controlled their villages from a separate fortress manned by hired soldiers. The contrast to the walled villages designed for 'collective defence' of the Rajput areas is most marked, a reminder even today of the different social inheritance of Muslim and Rajput-dominated areas.

The organization of the Junagadh state made it formidable one when Rajput kings were but the first among their chiefs and the loyalty of their 'vasals' in constant doubt. However, with the advanced Rajput rulers controlling trade revenues to pay their own armies, Junagadh's advantage became less obvious. Junagadh was a real state, and no petty chiefdom; yet it seems to have been less adapted than Bhavnagar to take advantage of the developments of the eighteenth century. The lack of a commercial orientation may explain why Junagadh never sought an alliance with the British, though its location farther from British interests may also have been important.

Wakhtsinhji's expansion westwards stemmed from the threat that the Kathis represented to the smaller, outlying Gohil states, his junior kinsmen. Lathi and other such chiefs asked for his protection; he was also appealed to by the Chudasamas of Bhal—distant descendants of the old Hindu kings of Junagadh (BDG, 66). A succession dispute in the Kathi chiefdom of Kundla gave Wakhtsinhji his chance. One pretender sought his protection, promising his share of Kundla in return. Marching against Kundla, Wakhtsinhji found that Junagadh supported two of the other pretenders. He thought it wiser to retreat, to avoid war with Junagadh (BDG, 67).

In 1784, however, Junagadh was weakened by the strife following the murder of Dewan Amarji. Trusting to his friendship with the

British, Wakhtsinhji again marched against Kundla in 1790. He now had the use of good artillery. Though other Kathi chiefs joined in the defence of Kundla, Wakhtsinhji's force won the battle. The Kathis were joined by a small Junagadh contingent, but Wakhtsinhji conquered several petty chiefdoms, in spite of Junagadh's support. Again, the Kathis tried to put up a united front, but Wakhtsinhji, supported by his collateral clans and by the junior Gohil states of Vala and Lathi, as well as the Gowalia Kathis, was victorious. The artillery was again used to good effect. Gadhada, Botad, Chital and Salda were occupied, sparing only Babra, which was mortgaged to the Marathas of Baroda. Wakhtsinhji then took Jasdan, and now held most of the former Kathi territory. Hamir Khasia Kathi, the outlawed chief from the south, was now conciliated with some villages (BDG, 67-9).

It would seem that Wakhtsinhji could now rest on his laurels; he reduced his forces to cut expenses. This was the chance of Unadji Gohil of Palitana, his junior kinsman, to win back some land lost to Visoji when Sihor was capital of the senior state. In fact, Palitana's forces were now in a majority. But they were defeated, in 1794 (BDG, 69-70).

Bhavnagar had now gained most of the area it was to retain in British times. It had become the third major power in the peninsula, and had shown itself able to take on Junagadh if necessary. But there was unrest in the Kathi areas, and in 1795 the Marathas from Baroda came to collect tribute. They marched on Bhavnagar but withdrew after a three-day battle. Palitana again saw a chance and attacked Sihor. Bhavnagar retaliated by attacking Palitana; though the force withdrew when the Palitana forces returned, the aggression had been checked, and the attack on Palitana itself was a humiliation to its ruler. Bhavnagar now emerged as the most powerful state in Saurashtra (BDG, 70). This development caused major concern in Junagadh, where, under Hamid Khan, the period of unrest was now over. The Nawab got his chance when the chief of Rajula, now tributary to Bhavnagar, promised Hamid his share if he could expel the Bhavnagar troops. The Nawab attacked and drove them out, but Bhavnagar then managed to take Rajula back.

The showdown between Bhavnagar and Junagadh, which had to come sooner or later, was now in full swing. Allied with the Khachar, Khuman and Wala Kathis—who all had grudges against Bhavnagar—the Nawab attacked. Kundla and Rajula fell to the allies, who then proceeded to attack Bhavnagar itself. They were driven back, but then

Jiaji Jethwa, a kinsman of the Rana of Porbandar, and brother-in-law of Wakhtsinhji, proposed a peace whereby Bhavnagar retained its territorial gains, but agreed to pay Zor-Talabi tribute to Junagadh. This peace, accepted by both parties, left Bhavnagar's real strength untouched but acknowledged Junagadh as the superior power. The Kathis, once again, seem to have been the real losers (BDG, 71).

Wakhtsinhji's expansive policies had strained his resources severely; what Bhavnagar now needed was peace. By restoring Chital, one of the most important Kathi chiefdoms, to Kumbha Wala, he broke the Kathi alliance. Other Kathi chiefdoms, too, were restored, including Gadhada,[8] to which we shall return later (BDG, 71-2). Throughout these wars, Wakhtsinhji had relied on a modern army of mercenaries—Sindhis, Belims and Arabs[9]—supplemented, however, by a militia of his *bhayats*. His excellent artillery, which must have been financed by Bhavnagar's merchant community, played an important role in his success. Some years later Tod was proudly shown the ruler's small navy (1971, 263). Thus Bhavnagar at war in the later part of the eighteeenth century was a full-grown state, retaining but reminiscences of the chiefdom it had been when it was founded in 1723. The successful development of the port was a cornerstone in laying the economic foundation for this growth.

The year 1800 saw the Peshwa withdraw from Ahmedabad, which came under the Gaekwad of Baroda. By the treaty of Bassein in 1802 the British effectively replaced the Marathas as the paramount power in Gujarat. The Gaekwad was still a troublesome neighbour, however. The tribute-collecting force that Baroda sent against Bhavnagar was repulsed in 1804, but in 1805 Bhavnagar had to pay the tribute (BDG, 72).

In 1800 Wakhtsinhji made a pilgrimage to Dwarka to express his respect for Shri Krishna. This move may have strengthened his relations with the merchant community. In 1806, he drank the 'red cup'—a symbol of peace and friendship—with Unadji of Palitana, his kinsman and former rival. Jadeja Kumbhaji of Gondal, married to Wakhtsinhji's daughter, acted as go-between. If kinship had lost its place in the constitution of the state, marriage alliances between ruling houses remained important.

The year 1807 brought Walker's settlement, and a degree of peace. British paramountcy, putting an end to the Maratha incursions, had come to stay (BDG, 72-3).

PARALLEL DEVELOPMENTS: THE GREAT DEWAN AMARJI

In the trend towards modernization, in the eighteenth century, Bhavnagar had forceful rivals. We have seen Junagadh in decline; but it had earlier reached its apex, as a Muslim state, under its great Dewan Amarji. Jamnagar, too, was ruled by its minister, Meraman Khawas, during this period, known as the age of the great Dewans. Wilberforce-Bell writes, 'In the latter half of the eighteenth century ... three remarkable men arose in Saurashtra, and its history during those years is almost entirely bound up with their lives ...' (1916, 135).

Wakhatsinhji of Bhavnagar was one of them. The two others were ministers or Dewans, and this in itself was new; never before had the effective control of a state, in Saurashtra, been in bureaucratic hands. We see here clear evidence of the increasing administrative burden of the state, as we see it in Europe a century earlier, in the age of Colbert. But none of the ministers showed the foresight, in mercantile and civil affairs, of the Bhavnagar ruler. Though administrators by position, Dewan Amarji and Meraman Khawas were mainly modernized warlords.

Amarji was born about 1742, of a Nagar family in Mangrol. At the age of eighteen he went to Junagadh to seek service with the Nawab, Mahabat Khan. He came at a critical moment. The army, which consisted of 'Arab' mercenaries, was in full revolt, demanding their pay.[10] Amarji was told that if he could oust them from the Wageswari gate,[11] which they held, he might be offered a commission by the Nawab.

Amarji accepted the challenge and went to Porbandar, where he found an Arab *jamadar* willing to come along with his men and attack the gate. But when they reached Junagadh, the Nawab, wary now of such soldiers, refused them admission. They attacked the gate from outside—no easy task—and were successful; the rebels surrendered to Amarji on being promised half their pay claims. This action gained him a 'high place' in the service of the Nawab (Wilberforce-Bell 1916, 136). This story shows that, in the eighteenth century at least, there was indeed a 'military labour market' (Kolff 1990) in Saurashtra.

Amarji's next task was to capture Veraval from Sheikh Mian of Mangrol; he was now directing the state's military affairs. The town was carried by surprise attack, using sea-borne troops. Amarji then marched against the Sheikh himself, and beat him (op. cit., 138-9). He went on to forestall an attempt at usurpation of the Nawab's position by his uncle, and to rout a robber's nest in the Gir Forest. His personal courage in such actions gained him a great reputation. Then, strategically, Amarji removed a vassal from his jagir on the Porbandar frontier, fearing he would be unable to hold it, and gave him land in a less dangerous area. In the attack on the vassal's fort, we first hear of Amarji mining his way to enter, a technique he was to use repeatedly.

He took an active part in the joint British-Bhavnagari attack on Talaja and was wounded; then marched against the Mianas of Malia,[12] at the north-east of the peninsula, and the Rabaris of Babriawad, in the far south.[13] By such peace-keeping moves well outside Junagadh territory, Amarji was in effect staging a claim to overlordship in the peninsula.

Amarji's success made the Nawab anxious, and the fear was nurtured by Kumbhoji, the Jadeja ruler of neighbouring Gondal. Amarji was imprisoned for five months, and released only on paying a heavy fine, while his son Raghunathji was kept hostage. The minister retired to Jetpur, a Kathi state, for a while (Wilberforce-Bell 1916, 139-42).

But the Nawab suffered heavy losses against Sheikh Mian of Mangrol, now reasserting himself, and found himself unable to do without his capable minister. He recalled Amarji in 1774. The latter had just been offered the dewanship of Kutch; we now see the 'labour market' for ministers establishing itself. Amarji, always faithful to Junagadh, returned to the Nawab's service, and Sheikh Mian submitted to the overlordship of that ruler. Amarji next conquered Sutrapada for Junagadh. He was now invited by his colleague in Jamnagar, Meraman Khawas, to help in subduing the Vagher pirates of Okhamandal. Amarji mined the walls of their fort, and the expedition was a success (op. cit., 142-3).

But news came that Mahabat Khan had died; the minister hastened home to seat Hamed Khan, the son of Mahabat, on the throne, in 1775. The new Nawab was only eight years old, and his mother soon found supporters for a rebellion against Amarji. The rebels occupied Vanthali and sought assistance from the Marathas, who were in the peninsula on a tribute-collection campaign (op. cit., 143).

The triangle of ruler, *zenana* and minister was, indeed, to play a major role in palace politics in this century, replacing the conflict between the ruler and his *bhayats* which had characterized an earlier period. We shall soon see parallel examples from Jamnagar.

Amarji marched against the Marathas, who abstained from further involvement, and then captured Wanthali. But next year the Marathas were back, and Amarji had to fight them until a settlement was reached by the intervention of Kumbhoji of Gondal and the Kathi ruler of Jetpur. Amarji's fight against the Marathas differed from that of other Saurashtra states, for Junagadh was rivalling the Maratha claims to overlordship in the peninsula. This claim, indeed, seems to have been a cornerstone of Amarji's policies. Thus he even went outside Kathiawar, helping the ruler of Morvi to subdue two villages in the Vagad, in Kutch—on another 'peace-keeping' expedition, which gained him 'many valuable presents as a peace-offering from the Rao of Kutch' (op. cit., 144).

There was war again with the Marathas in 1777, when Amarji destroyed their fort at Amreli, while next year, their general decided to remit the tribute claimed due to them. In 1779, too, the Marathas desisted from attacking Junagadh territory. Amarji's designs seemed to be crowned with success (op. cit., 145).

In 1778 Sultanji, the Jethwa chief, had built a fort on Navanagar's boundary, provoking Meraman Khawas to attack. The Jethwa applied to Amarji, who helped him, and the two Dewans drew up an agreement by which Navanagar desisted from further attack, and the fort was demolished (ibid.). Sultanji had, however, gathered a large force of mercenaries, who created trouble in the Barda Hills on Navanagar's borders. Amarji took upon himself to subdue them, and Sultanji had to accept his involvement (op. cit., 145-6). Again, we see how the Junagadh minister tried to play the role of paramount to the surrounding rulers. They, in turn, reacted, and Sultanji joined Kumbhoji of Gondal, while they found the support of Meraman Khawas. In 1782 the allies attacked. Amarji was successful against Meraman, who managed to implicate the Marathas, but they soon withdrew. The allies retreated; Sultanji's territory was laid waste, and Meraman sued for peace to co-operate with Amarji against the Jethwas. Gondal was, however, left untouched, as Amarji departed for Jhalawad to collect tribute.

This move, clearly intended to assert Junagadh's claims on overlordship in the penisula, was Amarji's bane. Hamed Khan, the young Nawab of Junagadh, had long been suspicious of his powerful Dewan. Now he went to Gondal, where the wily Kumbhoji did everything to strengthen his suspicion, and offered the Nawab three lakh Navanagar Koris to kill his Dewan. Amarji was murdered on 6 March 1984[14] (op. cit., 147). As Wilberforce-Bell points out, there is no reason to suspect that Amarji was ever disloyal to the Nawabs. He had made Junagadh the most powerful state in Kathiawar, and came close to having its claim to overlordship recognized in the peninsula. He was a great strategist and an innovator in the military field, as his well-remembered mining operations indicate.

But he never seems to have worked systematically to develop the economic base of his state, as the Bhavnagar ruler did. After his death, therefore, Junagadh could match Bhavnagar only in military terms; and when peace came with the nineteenth century, the state and city were poor and devastated from the exertions war had imposed upon them.[15]

MERAMAN KHAWAS: THE SLAVE MINISTER

Meraman had served the Jhala state of Halwad before he came to Navanagar, accompanying Bai Jawuba on her marriage to the Jam Lakhaji (Wilberforce-Bell 1916, 136-7). He soon dominated the Jam completely, and in 1756 the queen rebelled, trying to overthrow the minister. Meraman's brother was killed, but Meraman got together such followers 'as he could find, stormed ... the palace, slew or captured the guards, and took Bai Jawuba prisoner. He placed her under a guard and in secure retreat, and assumed complete charge of the administration of Navanagar with very little opposition' (op. cit., 137).

Here, then, we see another example of the triangular struggle for power between chief, minister and zenana. Lakhaji died in 1768, succeeded by his infant son Jasaji. The young Jam was kept in confinement untill Meraman's death in 1800 (ibid.).

Meraman soon got to prove his mettle in foreign policy and war, for the Rao of Kutch declared his intention to invade Navanagar unless he was handsomely paid. When the Rao attacked, however, he was beaten, and lost Balambha, his only enclave in Saurashtra, to the Jam. The rebellious Halaji, who had been responsible for the murder of Jam Tamachi in 1743, found his fort taken and was himself shot in the neck. Meraman's power caused Bai Jawuba, the queen mother, to go to her natal clan in Dhrangadhra, where she plotted against Meraman; however, he induced her to return only to have her murdered (op.cit., 149-50). Thus ended this triangular intrigue where the minister and the zenana fought for power over the ruling chief.

In 1774, Meraman invited Amarji to help subdue the Vaghers. While this co-operation stressed Junagadh's peninsular sphere of interest, the immediate advantage was, of course, to Navanagar, whose trade was disturbed by the pirates. In 1778, Meraman came to an understanding with Junagadh regarding the Jethwa's fort and frontiers. After signing the treaty, Meraman invited Amarji to celebrate at Khambhalia: it is said that he wanted to poison him. Amarji excused himself, however. In 1783, Meraman joined the alliance against Junagadh; when beaten, he instead joined in ravaging Sultanji's lands. When Amarji was murdered, however, Meraman sheltered members of his family (op. cit., 150).

Meraman was now free to improve the military strength of his state. The fortifications at Navanagar were greatly improved. Then, in 1792, he launched an expansive campaign against the Kathis, reaching as far as Jasdan, close to Bhavnagar's borders. Like Wakhtsinhji, he thought it wise to restore some territory to its former chiefs, but the sphere of Navanagar's influence was nevertheless considerably enlarged.

In 1794 the cadet Jadeja states, feeling that Meraman had become too powerful, united to restore Jam Jasaji to his rightful powers. Rajkot, Gondal, Dhrol and Khirasara marched against Navanagar, but Jaswantsinhji of Dhrangadhra, perhaps surprisingly, came to the aid of Meraman. This is probably the last example of cadet states trying to influence the affairs of their senior state, a throw-back to earlier times. While on this campaign, Meraman mediated between Junagadh and Bhavnagar. But now there was another attack from Kutch, led by its Dewan Fateh Mahomed, at the head of nearly thirty-five thousand men. They thus joined the other Jadeja states against Navanagar. Bhawan Khawas, Meraman's brother, led the forces against them, but was about to be defeated when Raghunathji, Amarji's son, now serving Navanagar, saved the situation. Yet at the next battle Bhawan was beaten and the Kutch forces though stayed by the Dharangadhra troops, ravaged the country. In Navanagar, Meraman was well entrenched; the town was not attacked, and he still controlled the young Jam. The latter mounted a plot, but all who took part in it, had their ears and nose cut off at Meraman's orders (op. cit., 151-4). Meraman's situation would have been desperate had he not bought the assistance of the Marathas, who laid Rajkot and Gondal waste. The Kutch forces withdrew.

In 1795, Meraman again marched against the Vaghers, probably to secure his flank against Kutch and to suppress piracy. In 1797 the Jam and his brother managed to escape, and recruited an Arab force to rebel against Meraman. Soldiers were clearly available, now, to those who could pay for them. The attempt failed, for the night they should have entered the city to free the Jam a rainstorm broke, the rivers were flooded and the rescuers were unable to cross. The Jam was virtually imprisoned, though later left under strict guard.

Both that year and the next, Fateh Mahomed attacked from Kutch, but in 1797 Meraman obtained support from Junagadh, Bantwa and Mangrol, and the invaders turned back. The next year, they sacked Navanagar, but again withdrew. In 1799, Meraman was trying to suppress supporters of the Jam in the Barda Hills. When Kutch attacked again, Meraman bought the support of the Marathas, by paying their full tribute claims. Then, however, he made peace with Fateh Mahomed, which greatly angered the Marathas, who felt they were being trifled with (op. cit., 154-6). Meraman now obtained hereditary rights to three villages for his retirement, but never enjoyed them as he died in AD 1800 (op. cit., 157).

Meraman was, no doubt, a skilful political tactician. He had to be, sandwiched as he was between the ambitious schemes of Amarji and Fateh Mahomed, another ambitious Dewan. But as far as we know, he made no attempt to build an economic foundation for military expansion, though his expeditions against the Vagher indicate that he wanted to protect Jamnagar's trade. Neither was he a military man of Amarji's stature. And unlike Amarji, it is not obvious that he had particular ambitions for his state beyond gaining power for himself. The three great men of Saurashtra's eighteenth century, then, are not really alike. Controlling state apparatus and armies superior to those of their predecessors, they do represent a stage in the bureaucratization of the state, but for the rest are very different.

Meraman is modern only in being a minister and in his skilful manipulation of power. Amarji adds to this a vision of Saurashtra united under the Nawabs, and certainly demonstrates statesmanship. But his means of reaching these goals remain those of the Mughal period. Only the Bhavnagar rulers point towards modernity in carefully constructing the economic base for their military and political ambitions.

The rules of the political game had now changed. Court politics were no longer a matter of kinship; the army and the minister were key players in it. The role of the former, as an unruly element, we have seen particularly in Junagadh. We have also seen how 'Kasbatis', 'Sidis', and other mercenaries could set up their own states. The threat of unpaid soldiers was a real one. As for the minister, he now becomes party to a triangle with the chief himself and the zenana, while the bhayats—

the junior kinsmen of the chief—recede in the background. With them goes the kinship base of the state; bureaucracy and the military establishment have become its main elements.

Finally, the three main powers were expanding at the cost of the smaller chiefdoms. Had the British come later, the number of political units in the peninsula would have been substantially reduced.

COLONEL WALKER'S SETTLEMENT

At the end of the eighteenth century this centralization was far from complete. In the 'buffer zones' between Jamnagar, Junagadh, and Bhavnagar, a large number of smaller states and chiefdoms remained.

Even so, the Kathi chiefdoms were being absorbed by the end of the eighteenth century. Rulers of small states felt threatened. This was their main object in appealing to the British. Such appeals came from Sataji—the brother of the Jam of Navanagar, who had established a small chiefdom—from the ruler of Morvi, close to the much larger state of Dhrangadhra, and from the three Kathi chiefs of Chital, Jetpur and Kundla. (Wilberforce-Bell 1916, 178).

The British saved such states from extinction. As many as 202 'states' or political units were recognized by them, ranging from single villages with a couple of hundred inhabitants to the large states of Bhavnagar, Junagadh and Navanagar.[16] This extreme fragmentation was due to the agreements concluded by Colonel Walker. When he had finished, in 1807, the network of treaties to bind Kathiawar into British suzerainty, 153 'states' had signed. By 1924, there were 225 in the Western India States Agency, including some states on the mainland. While some minor estates were not included in the original treaties, there was some increase.

Walker's definition of political units in Saurashtra differed from that applied, later, in Rajasthan. Any hereditary chief was seen, by Walker and his successors, as a 'ruler' in his own right. Many of these 'states' would have been no more than 'estates' to Tod, who dealt with minor estates only through the ruler of which their chief was a vassal. Tod wanted to avoid fragmentation. But in Saurashtra, British policy conserved the inherited status of even the most petty chief, preventing his decline into 'yeoman-peasant'. Such petty 'rulers' were chiefs in little but name, but chiefs they remained, unlike their counterparts in much of mainland Gujarat (Pocock 1972; cf. Fox 1971, 117-23).

One reason for Walker's approach lay in the alliance with Baroda. The British wanted to safeguard the interest of their ally, but also to put an end to the tribute-collecting expeditions that had so often ravaged the country. It was not in the interest of the allies to leave too many intermediary stages in the chain of offices set-up for purposes of revenue collection. In fact, only Junagadh remained between the local chiefs and the Gaekwad.

Had Walker's settlement come later, or been made according to Tod's policies, the smaller chiefdoms would have ceased to exist, their rulers landlords within a larger state formation. The settlement halted an ongoing process of state-formation in Saurashtra. But while the larger states might have been capable of approaching modernity on their own, the periphery had not ceased to be rebellious. Even under British dominance, such opposition continued, though on a smaller scale.

KATHI OPPOSITION

We have seen that many Kathis continued to live outside the larger states in their petty chiefdoms, and how their political excursions—or raids—into adjacent territory earned them the dubious distinction of becoming a 'criminal caste' in British eyes.

Shortly after Meraman's death, Wajsur Khachar of Jasdan came to Navanagar to congratulate the Jam, Jasaji, on the assumption of power. He gave the Jam a horse, a gift normally fit for a chief, but the Jam did not like it. He returned the horse, which Wajsur gave to a Charan. The Jam saw this as an insult, and prepared to attack Jasdan; Wajsur retaliated by raiding Navanagar territory. When the Jam attacked, however, Wajsur had to flee to Limbdi, then to Bhavnagar, while the Navanagar forces burnt his town and plundered the surrounding country. Wajsur got his chiefdom back, but had to pay a heavy fine to the Jam (Wilberforce-Bell 1916, 180-1).

Jasdan, important among Kathi states, was of course secured by the Walker settlements. But these did not end Kathi unrest. In 1820 the Khuman chiefs of Kundla plundered Bhavnagar territory, trying to regain some of their lost lands. Beaten by Bhavnagar's army, they fled to the Gir Forest, but disturbances continued until 1822, when the British intervened. Several important Kathi states were implicated, and Jetpur was placed under British administration. By 1824, things seemed to have settled down, the remaining Kathi outlaws retreating to the Gir. But during the 1825 famine they again broke forth, and it was only in 1829 that Bhavnagar and the British came to an agreement with them.

The period 1836-40 saw further instances of unrest among the Kathis, but since the involvement of British troops in 1822, these gradually became characterized as 'criminal' rather than 'political' incidents. The critical point here seem to be the settlement of 1824. The British had, in fact, captured the Kathi outlaws, but delivered them to Wajesinhji of Bhavnagar, as their 'crimes' had been carried out in his territories. Wilberforce-Bell says (1916, 201) that 'Negotiations were now opened with Wajesinhji, but no satisfactory arrangement could be achieved at, and finally the hostages took the captured Khumans with them and returned to their villages'.

Who was not satisfied? Wilberforce-Bell blames the outcome on the 'hesitation and vacillation on the part of Wajesinhji'. It seems that the British, delivering 'criminals' for punishment, found Wajesinhji negotiating terms with them, as if they were chiefs in their own right—which, indeed, they had been just a generation ago. Wajesinhji, on his part, must have felt that straight punishment would arrange nothing. In the end, the British view prevailed. The Kathis were labelled a 'criminal caste', though after 1840 they gave only minor trouble.

THE REBELLION OF THE WAGHERS

Even the segmentary lineage reasserted itself politically after 1807 in at least one instance. This was in 1857-8, during the 'mutiny' as it was then called, in the far north-western corner of Saurashtra.

The Waghers of Dwarka, Okha and the surrounding areas still have a reputation, in Saurashtra, as a freedom-loving people. Their position at the tip of the peninsula must have been ideal for piracy, an activity for which they are still notorious.[17] Under Colonel Walker's settlement their lands were held in fief from the Gaekwad. But they rebelled agaist him in 1820, and it was only in 1822 that the revolt could be put down, with British assistance (Dharaiya 1970, 118). Yet they remained 'seething with discontent and ... complaining ... against the mismanagement of their territories by the Gaikwar's officers. They ... resented the rule of the Gaikwar over the places once occupied by their forefathers and they were seeking the opportunity to end it.' (ibid.)

The opportunity came in 1857 when rumours of the revolt reached the Waghers. A meeting of representatives from the Wagher clans was held at Dransunwell[18] on 1 January 1858, to discuss the possibility of regaining their country from the Gaekwad's rule (Dharaiya 1970, 119). It seems clear that in this meeting of clan leaders we have a tribal form reasserting itself on the occasion of a weakening of state power. The revolt was succesful at first. The Waghers attacked and took the fort at the island of Bet outside Okha in March 1858, where they were joined by the remaining garrison. Leadership seems to have been informal; Rewa Manek, Ranmal Manek, Asha Manek and Deepa Manek were the main leaders.

The British attacked the fort, but had to retreat; on 2 April, when they attacked again, the Waghers retreated to Wasaya. Here, they held out until December. When the British left the Bet fort in the hands of the Gaekwad's forces, however, the Waghers attacked again, and re-occupied it. The Gaekwad sent his representatives to meet the Wagher leaders, but none of them was willing to talk. Instead, the Gaekwad's troops joined the rebellion. By July 1859 Dwarka and the Bet were again in the hands of the Waghers (Dharaiya 1970, 119-21).

The lineage organization had indeed reasserted itself. The Waghers occupying the Bet are said to have numbered 1500, with an additional 500 others, including the deserters from the Gaekwad's forces.

At this stage, an interesting thing happened. Jodha Manek was 'declared as the supreme head of the regions and his followers greeted him as the king of Okhamandal'. In this capacity he wrote to the Jam of Navanagar and the Rana of Porbandar inviting them to join in the struggle against Baroda and the British (Dharaiya 1970, 121).

Thus while the rebellion had been organized by the lineage heads, the Waghers must have felt that consolidation of their gains called for the formation of a more durable polity. Their attempts at establishing a state were not, however, to be crowned with success. The Gaekwad again appealed to the British, who attacked the Bet on 4 October, 1859, with about 1350 men. The Wagher force is said to have been smaller than this. The Wagher confederacy may not have been strong enough to keep a large, permanent force, though part of it was perhaps deployed elsewhere. The British took the fort but allowed the Waghers to evacuate it; they took their stand at Dwarka, which was only given up on 31 October. After that the Waghers were reduced to 'guerilla warfare', which they continued, however, until 1867 (op. cit., 122-30).

Jodha Manek became one of the most famous of Saurashtra's outlaws, he and others operating during the years 1860-7 mainly from the Gir Forest (ibid). Though state boundaries largely remained fixed during the nineteenth century, the situation was not yet completely peaceful. 'Tribal' polity was not dead; it had simply gone hiding in a period of relatively strong state control. The situation, now and earlier, is not far removed from the one shown by Barth for Kurdistan (1953, 9).

THE MAHIAS AND THE MIANAS

The Mena Rajputs came from Marwar; according to their tradition they established the village (later town) of Wankaner in north-eastern Saurashtra. They were apparently driven from there by the Jadejas and finally settled on the outskirts of Junagadh state.

One village there, Chichod, had been established by Parmar Rajputs in the sixteenth century, but only some Rabaris and Sandhis remained when the Mahias—as the Mena Rajputs came to be known—settled there in the early nineteenth century (Village Monograph No. 8, 2). They, even at this late period, represent the band of adventurers corresponding to stage one in Fox's model (1971, 69ff.). Such bands, then, continued to exist well after the establishment of a 'labour market' for professional soldiers. Like earlier such bands, they settled in the area of a declining state, as Junagadh had by now become (Tod 1971, 360-1).

They were evidently 'taxing' the surrounding periphery of larger states. Watson regards them as Kolis at this time (1884, 139; Village Monograph No. 8; 6). We hear of a revolt in 1867, when they sought refuge in the Gir hills. Then, in 1872, they tried to attack Junagadh itself

> with the idea of restoring the dynasty ... of the Chudasama Ras. In consequence ... they were ... deprived of their arms, with the result that they went into outlawry, and were with difficulty persuaded to return to their homes. Subsequently their holdings were demarcated and their rights defined, and they were ordered to pay a moderate assessment in lieu of military service, which they could no longer perform to the State. They refused positively to pay ..., and when their appeal to the government ... suffered rejection they deserted their villages in December A.D. 1882, and taking up a position on a hill in neutral territory, defied all attempts at mediation.... (Wilberforce-Bell 1916, 238-9)

It is remarkable that the memory of the Chudasamas could inspire such enthusiasm after four hundred years. If the adventurers of Fox's stage one reasserted themselves at such a late date, the result was now a foregone conclusion; a settlement was finally reached in 1888 (ibid.).

But even before this insurrection, and perhaps as one reason for it, the Mahias' hold on their village had been severely weakened by the immigration of Kanbis, supported by the neighbouring state of Gondal, which was extending its control over former Junagadh territory. By around 1860, the Kanbi population of Chichod equalled that of the Mahias (Village Monograph No. 8; Tambs-Lyche 1992a). Paradoxically, though the Mahias thus lost their dominant position, their heroism seem to have gained them the title of 'Rajputs', which had been far from clear earlier.

The story of the Mianas is quite different. At a time when larger states were acquiring regular armies, around 1730, the first chief of the minor state of Malia invited them to settle in the north of his territory, which bordered on the Rann of Kutch. The chief, Morji, wanted their aid to gain independence from his brother, the chief of Morvi (Watson 1884, 1966-7). The Mianas, however, remained entrenched in their inaccessible hamlets, 'pre-eminent for their depredations and their contempt of authority', until a concerted drive against outlawry by various states brought them to order in 1903 (Village Monograph No. 16, 10).

Thus, in Saurashtra, several stages of Fox's 'development cycle' co-existed at the time. As long as lineage politics were not influenced greatly by the dynamics of other fields, the state of flux was maintained. Lineage clusters became chiefdoms, but remained unstable. Stable statehood was achieved through the influence of two other fields: the relation to traders, and the dynamics of established state bureaucracy.

THE BIRTH OF THE SWAMINARAYANA SECT

In the midst of unrest an unknown sadhu arrived at the ashram of Ramananda, at Loj, on the west coast of Saurashtra, in 1800. Ramananda was a follower of Ramanujacharya, of the *vishishtadvaita* school of Vaishnavism.[19] While staying among Ramanuja's disciples at Shri Rangam in the south he had a *darshan* of Krishna, and returned to Saurashtra to established his ashram. The new sadhu was a Vaishnava of the same school, and hagiographies describe his confrontations with shaktist monks of Bengal. He liked Ramananda's ashram and joined it.

The newcomer soon made his mark; around 1803, Ramananda called a meeting at Jetpur, announcing his decision to retire and let the recruit, known as Swami Sahajanand, take over leadership of his sect.

Though still small in relation to its later growth, the group had control of a few temples and quite a number of lay followers. The decision to appoint Sahajanand as the new leader was not universally popular, for the followers expected Muktanand, the right-hand man of Ramananda, to take over. But the latter had himself 'realised the greatness of Sahajanand' (Dave 1967, 34) and supported the new leader wholeheartedly.

Leadership of the sect was not an easy task, as Sahajanand met considerable opposition. Moreover, this was still an unsettled period in Kathiawar. 'Saurashtra was politically brought to pieces', says the saint's biographer Dave, 'as the small feudal chiefs were fighting among themselves'. 'The mood of the people was to grab anything they came across', he continues (1967, 37).

Neither Dave nor Parekh, an earlier biographer, mention Colonel Walker's settlements. These certainly helped change the situation, but their effect was not immediate. It was only in 1818-20 that the British took over the former Peshwa territories on the mainland, and began to control matters more effectively. Thus in 1812 there was civil war in Kutch; 136 villages were plundered and some 40,000 heads of cattle were carried off. In 1810, 1813 and 1825 there were famines; in 1814 an epidemic; and in 1819 an earthquake. None of these helped matters. Yet, 'in the first quarter of the nineteenth century British influence, military and political, gradually spread like a slow wave through greater Gujarat' (Williams 1984, 4).

Swami Sahajanand's ministry, then, coincided with the gradual establishment of British control. The meeting between Swami Narayana, as he was to be known, and Governor Malcolm, is fittingly displayed in many Swaminarayana temples. It illustrates two forces that worked side by side to pacify the area.

THE RISE OF THE SECT

Swami Narayana gained part of his fame by his capability of granting to people the vision of their deities in *samadhi* (trance). He thus demonstrated his yogic powers, and made quite an impression. But he also organized almshouses—an enterprise which was given up when these were attacked by sadhus of competing sects—and started work on repairing wells and tanks.

At the same time, the first written works of the new sect began to appear. The first of these, the Yama-Danda, 'is drawn as a warning to the people', but announces hope and freedom through 'the Master who has manifested himself'. Swami Narayana is here equalled with Krishna (Parekh 1936, 70). The position which the leader occupies almost from the start, is one of the most surprising features of the sect and its founder. The miracles wrought by him at this stage, remain a problem for his followers. Were they just an expression of yogic power, or do they reveal the saints' identity with the godhead? The so-called Yogijipanth, which split off from the original sect in the 1940s, are particularly eager to stress the last point.

The stress on the founder's yogic powers set the sect clearly apart from such rivals as the Vallabhacharyas. It recalls, rather, the Radha Swamis of upper India.[20] But the miracles appealed to the common people, giving the new sect a far wider range of recruits than the Vallabhacharyas, who had remained, basically, a sect supported by Banias. We must see the Swaminarayanas as a 'low-church', puritan movement winning new groups for Vaishnavism. This brought them into direct conflict and competition with the Shaktist religion of the area, centered on goddess worship.

It was against these cults, therefore, that Swaminarayana launched his main attack (Mallison 1974, 449; Williams 1984, 21). Animal sacrifice, meat-eating, use of alcohol and of opium, were common to all these popular cults. These practices were all inimical to the new sect; yet when Swaminarayana sources describe their opponents as 'left-handed' *(vama-marga)*, this is clearly an ideological denunciation of them, and ought not to be taken to describe the more extreme forms of tantricism, as Williams (op. cit.) seems to do.

But within Vaishnavism itself, the sect's opposition to the Vallabhacharyas is important. To Swami Narayana, the latter may not have been 'immoral' in the sense of the accusations of the later 'Maharaja Libel Case'.[21] But the luxurious life of their Maharajas and the liberal outlook of the members surely cannot have appealed to him. Within Vaishnavism, the Swaminarayanas continue even today to represent the puritanical extreme.

A CHARAN CONVERTED

Symbolic of the success of the sect against its main adversaries is the early conversion, in AD 1805, of the Charan Ladu Barot.[22] He was a court poet, both skilful and popular. Then he met the saint, and composed the following poem:

Blessed is this hour, blessed it is indeed;
I have seen Sahajananda, blessed is this hour.
Now no more can Lust or Anger or Covetousness trouble me.
The Master's Person has come and taken hold of my heart.
This is too great a thing to be known by human understanding;
It is found only by seeing the glance of the true Guru.
I have wandered all these aeons in the dark vale of millions of
births and deaths,
But now that I am united with the Lord, all my misery is at an end.
With the key of knowledge given to me by my Guru,
all the locks have been opened.
O, Ladu, seeing Sahajanand, thy eyes have found their desire.
(Parekh 1936, 72-3).

Ladu became a sadhu taking the name Brahmanand (Jhaveri 1978, 59) and this was the last poem written under his caste name. He became one of the great poets of the Satsang, as the sect came to be known. His songs describe the doings of his master, whom he identifies with Krishna (Parekh, op. cit., 73); his forte is moral instruction (Jhaveri, op.cit.).

The story goes that Ladu's conversion was planned by the Swami himself. Having won a rich reward for his poem in honour of the Prince Wajesinhjee of Bhavnagar, the Charan wanted to convert it into ornaments made by Hirjee and Sundarjee. These famous goldsmiths of Bhuj (in Kutch) were Swaminarayanas, and Ladu approached the Swami for a letter of recommendation. The Swami, on his part, wrote to his disciples. Hirjee was a poet, too, so, as the Swami put it, 'If an elephant gets stuck in the mud, it is only another elephant who can drag him out ... keep him, therefore, with you for six months feeding him at your expense and cast the mould....' As Parekh comments, the latter remark applies both to the ornament and to the poet's life, to be recast (1936, 145).

Another famous convert of this period was Magniram, a Shakta Brahmin and follower of the goddess Kali, famous for his supernatural powers. He travelled with a band of semi-military sadhus, exacting payment from religious and secular bodies. In Kathiawar he met Swami Narayana, who refused to pay. But when Magniram called the goddess to avenge this insult, she told him 'that neither she nor he could do anything against Sahajananda'. Impressed, Magniram offered his services to Swami Narayana, who bade him cut his long hair. He did so, and was ordained as the Swaminarayana Sadhu Advaitananda[23] (Parekh 1936, 74-5: see also Dave 1967, 63-5).

Here, then, is the conversion of the arch-enemy. Groups of fighting sadhus were rather common at the time, and they represented a formidable opposition to the sect. So much the better when the goddess herself comes forward; in admitting her incompetence she is, in fact, recognizing Swami Narayana as an incarnation of god. The victory is symbolized by the incident of the hair—the mark of the Shaivite and the Shakta monk. Vaishnavite monks shave their head.[24]

OPPOSITION TO THE SECT

Not all opponents gave up so easily: the conflict between Bhaktism and Shaktism is still strong in Saurashtra, today. So violent was the opposition that Swami Narayana moved under the protection of an armed guard,[25] though the sadhus of the sect went unarmed.[26]

We have seen, moreover, that the cult of Shakti was an integral part of the traditional political system. The Rajput rulers, therefore, in general opposed the new sect. But among the Kathis, recent victims of expansive wars by more powerful states,[27] the Swami found followers. The fact that they were the losers in the political game of the times may have led them to sympathize with the new, non-violent creed.

Swami Narayana took refuge with a Kathi chief, Dada Khachar of Gadhada, who became his disciple; and this little town in central Saurashtra became a centre of the sect.[28] The Swami stayed with Dada for more than twenty years. The family bore the brunt of expenses incurred through his many visitors. It is said that when the Swami asked the chief to build a dharmashala for his followers, Dada at once put his own quarters at their disposal. This, however, the Swami would not allow (Parekh 1936, 141).

The chief's sisters, too, became devotees, and taught the female visitors;[29] but there was opposition, too, to the Swami among the Khachars. Dada's uncle would have him killed, but Swami Narayana discovered the plot; he is said to have forgiven both assassin and instigator. Another story is more amusing. Dada was being shaved, when the Swami called; and so he appeared before the master half-shaved. Asked the reason, he replied: 'that can wait, but to obey your command is the most important thing...' Says Parekh, 'at the time ... a thing like this would not be done except under the gravest of emergencies.... an action of this kind was exceedingly undignified in the eyes of the world and also ceremoniously unclean' (1936, 142-3).

The episode demonstrates the regard the chief had for the saint;[30]

it invalidates the courtly context in favour of that of the devotee, and it does so through the symbol of hair, when a man's hair and—above all—his moustache was the very locus of dignity and honour.[31]

There is a whole cycle of stories in the Swaminarayana canon related to Dada Khachar, the Kathis and events in Gadhada. They are construed to show how followers gave up smoking and opium,[32] theft of cattle,[33] and use of personal ornaments.[34] The sect gained a strong following among Kathis, who formed the Swami's armed escort, given by Heber as two hundred horse and a number of armed men on foot. Meanwhile, his sadhus carried their preaching underground,[35] renouncing the distinctive marks of Vaishnava sadhus. Both strategies bear witness to the opposition encountered by the sect.[36]

THE GREAT SACRIFICE AT BHUJ

The opposition of Swami Narayana to the political order of the day is nowhere clearer than in this story, in which we may see the 'beginning of the end' of animal sacrifice in Saurashtra.

> Once while Swami Narayana was in Bhuj in the province of Cutch, the Prime minister there[37] was performing a big sacrifice.... Such bloody sacrifices seem to be very common in those days all over India, and they were usually performed by the Princes or big people such as Ministers etc. To do this was considered a meritorious act, and not to do it...as a sin of omission that might invite the wrath of gods on the kingdom or the people. The Brahmins took part in these, and hence the sacrifices got the sanction of the priestly class .... Sometimes learned Brahmins came from far off places such as Benares etc. ... and therefore to protest against such sacrifices was like throwing a challenge to the vested interests of both Princes and Brahmins...' (Parekh 1936, 100-1)

This, then, was the great buffalo sacrifice, underpinning the authority of the Rajput state. Swami Narayana is invited by the Dewan's brother Kuberjit; 'his very presence would add to the glory of the festival', says Dave. The disciples warn him not to go, fearing controversy. But he insists (1967, 55).

The Swami's line of argument, according to Parekh, was that

> the Vedas inculcated bloody sacrifices not for the sake of taking animal life, but to circumscribe the universal taking of such life by confining it only to these occasions with a view, however, to the complete abolition of it in the course of time ... the Vedas at their highest taught Ahimsa (Non-violence) ... these bloody sacrifices were only a stage on the way to the complete realization of the principle. He even said that those who performed such sacrifices were

acting against the teaching of the Shastras (Scriptures) and that they were no better than malecchas.... This was carrying the war into the enemy's camp, and it was no wonder that Sahajananda made many enemies. (Parekh 1936, 101-2)

The Swami arrived with his retinue; he was horrified to see the animals ready for sacrifice (Dave 1967, 56), and bluntly told Kuberjit:

'The Brahmins should not perform such sacrifices' where the animals are killed and offered to the sacrificial fire. Every sane man would condemn such acts which do not have any sanction of the scriptures. The objects to be offered into the sacrificial fire as prescribed by the Vedas are rice, curd and ghee. You should, therefore, release these beasts and break off this vile tradition ... fostered and supported only by the selfish brahmins to satisfy their own desires. (ibid.)

To this provocation, the brahmins retorted by telling Jagjivanram to defy the authority of Sahajanand, and the minister told him, 'There are thousands of learned Brahmins here much wiser than yourself, who have so far performed many sacrifices knowing full well that the Vedas have prescribed such offerings. You are invited here to witness this sacrifice and not to advise.'

'Yes', the Swami answered, 'but when I find that the Law of Dharma is violated, it is my duty to explain to you the truth.' Jagjivanram ordered the Swami and his followers to leave, which they did. But then, on the third day after the sacrifice,

... the King of Kutch summoned him and reprimanded him for insulting Sahajanand Swami who was acclaimed as a great divine personality. To the utter disregard of the King's caution, Jagjivanram and his brothers Ramachandra and Kuberjit revolted, and as a result they all were ordered to be executed by the King. Thus they met the fate for disregarding the Law of Dharma. (op. cit., 56-7)

The wheel has come full circle. In the myth of Khodiyar, the king's line is extinct from his failure to offer to the goddess her due, the buffalo sacrifice. Now the minister dies for preserving it. Dharma has, indeed, evolved, at least in the view of the Swaminarayana sect.

THE GROWTH OF THE SECT

From 1808 the sect began to perform large, 'bloodless' sacrifices. This created opposition among the Brahmins; the Peshwa's governor, at their instigation, tried to murder Swami Narayana by a plot. He was found out, however.

Gradually, the sacrifices were replaced by annual conventions, at Vadtal (on the mainland) and at Gadhada. These large gatherings were instrumental in creating the particular 'corps d'esprit' which is so conspicuous in the sect. Solidarity was spread across Gujarat through the establishment of contacts and friendship. The unity of all kinds of people before God, always a feature of the Bhakti sects, was emphasized by the variety of the recruits. Here they were 'drawn away from a world where their social and other limitations and disabilities were emphasized, and brought into a new world of fellowship and brotherhood, a world in which neither birth nor social position but only spiritual character counted.' (Parekh 1936, 111)

Caste restrictions were, in fact, never set aside, but the solidarity of sect membership cut across them and opened a way to recognition for people from even the lowest castes.

In the last decade of Swami Sahajanand's leadership a large number of temples were built, big and small. It is remarkable, for India, that they were built by the voluntary labour of laymen as well as sadhus of the sect. This, too, certainly built a spirit of solidarity and co-operation.

In 1825 the Swami met Bishop Heber.[38] Disappointed in his hope of finding a true monotheist, the prelate was clearly impressed by the sect's achievements, and the meeting helped to form a strong sympathy for the sect among the British. They saw in it an ally in the pacification of the country and in social and religious reform.[39] Thus the Swaminarayanas were active against sati and female infanticide. The meeting between Governor Malcolm and the Swami, shortly before the latter's death in 1830, cemented the alliance, and left the sect with powerful supporters as well as a considerable popular following.

PAX BRITANNICA

The campaigns against sati and female infanticide were important in the process transforming feudal Kathiawar into vegetarian, merchant-dominated Saurashtra. They hit precisely at the group which dominated traditional society: the Darbars. At the same time, the Swaminarayanas gradually undermined the cultural support of the dominant communities.

It was certainly not the British intention to destroy traditional patterns of authority. While attacking certain Rajput practices, they in effect propped up the rulers; the cessation of warfare made the rulers less dependent on traditional channels of political support. Thus, indirect rule in Saurashtra drove a wedge between the native ruler and the native ruled. It created a new class which was tied in style, interests, and geographical orientation outward toward the foreign rulers; conversely it severely weakened the ties between the princes and their own countrymen and 'subjects'. By elevating the urban-based princes and extending new opportunities to professionals and businessmen, the British widened the gaps between urban and rural societies, levels of political consciousness, and degrees of economic development. (Spodek 1976, 34)

Spodek divides the period from the eighteenth century to independence into three parts. The first lasted until the 'mutiny' of 1857-8; the second till the beginnings of the nationalist movement around 1920. The third period, when the Congress and its support grew steadily, lasted to 1947 (op. cit., 35).

The first period was mainly characterized by revenue-collection, protection of trades and peace-keeping. After 1857-8, when the states were loyal to the British, the paramount power took a greater interest in their affairs and development. Schools and roads were built under British direction from state revenues. The famous Rajkumar College[40] at Rajkot dates from 1870. Dispensaries run by vaids were opened. British pressure on the states to improve their administration led to considerable bureaucratic expansion. Rulers were expected to send administrative reports annually to Rajkot (Spodek 1976, 38-40).

According to Spodek, bureaucracy was extended primarily to serve British interests, and transport networks served mainly to link the princely capitals with the British at Rajkot civil station (ibid). The first railway in Kathiawar was built by Bhavnagar state, from its capital north to Wadhwan, on the main route from the mainland into the peninsula. Here it connected with the British-owned line from the mainland. It was begun in 1879, when the state also undertook, with the collaboration of Gondal, the construction of a line from Dhola to Dhoraji (Wilberforce-Bell 1915, 237). The lines linked these two progressive states to the mainland. Later extensions linked princely capitals to British territory—but also to each other.[41] Other lines were built for internal communication within the states.[42] Taken together, the lines certainly show the importance of communications with the mainland, but they also show each state's desire to tie its territories to the capital.

Meanwhile, the British built roads from princely revenues. Improved communications, helped by the suppression of piracy along the coast, caused a general growth in commercial activity.

TRADE AND BUREAUCRACY

Improved transport is probably the most important reason for the recent urbanization of Banias. There is no need, now, to stay permanently in the village to buy its products; the trader or his agent can easily go to the village, and the farmer may come to town. In Praj, quite a few Banias have moved to town recently, leaving their large houses almost, or completely, empty. Other traders have come to the village, retailers but not Banias. In Loj, a large village near Mangrol on the west coast, almost all the Banias have left their large mansions. Most smaller villages have no Banias left. The concentration of Banias in larger towns and cities, in short, is a general phenomenon.

British dominance in the nineteenth century put an end to the wars. But if peace was good for trade, it did not lead to regional integration. Rather, state enterprise increased in relation to private enterprise, as most states remained strongly mercantilistic (Oza 1946). State and private capitalism competed with each other within each state.

> By strengthening both the princes and the non-landed urban classes at the same time, the British increased the tensions within the capital cities as well as between them. As the opportunities for trade increased, pleasing the merchants, the princes imposed increasing restrictions on trade. The blockages in the inter-state transport system stung the merchants. The development of industries as state monopolies or as state supported monopolies, angered them still more. (Spodek 1976, 53)

The regional economy was marked by competition between states, and while some like Bhavnagar and Gondal adopted free trade principles, the smaller states were strongly protectionist. Lack of scope for 'free enterprise' became a main grudge of the traders in the next century and a main factor in their support for the independence movement (Oza, op.cit.).

Even so, states such as Bhavnagar developed steadily towards a degree of modernization and efficient administration comparable and sometimes superior to that of British India.[43] This has been attributed to state initiative and the role of the Dewans. One might even venture the thought that if the Dewans had 'really been given their head they might have tested out a 'Prussian' or 'Meiji' road to Indian development—with an authoritarian government, under skilled and forceful administrative command, leading the way ...' (Low 1978, 387).

Low concludes that such a development was hindered by the 'very nature' of traditional rule, by which he refers to its kinship base (op. cit., 379). Certain states however, most notably Bhavnagar, had largely outgrown these restrictions. But faced with the supremacy of the British, and of independent India later, these small states did not stand much of a chance.

British control had its limits. Copland points to the role of 'graft and intrigue' in maintaining local control: 'In Kathiawar ... the Nagars are the real political agents and our officers but puppets in their hands', said an article in the *Times of India* (1864). Thus, both in 1894 and in 1911 the British launched schemes to 'de-Brahminize' the administration of Kathiawar, without much success (Copland 1978, 282-3). Yet intrigue by the indigenous administration was met with interference by the British authorities (op. cit., 283-4; Jacob, 1872).

Wingate observed, in 1933, that in western India 'a Political agent is really not a Political Agent at all but a District Officer' (Copland, op. cit., 284). British influence over the states may have increased. Yet the Dewan of Rajkot, Durbar Virawala, was capable of out-maneuvering, during the Rajkot satyagraha of 1938-9, no less formidable opponents than Gandhi and Sardar Vallabhbhai Patel (Wood 1978).

TOWARDS INDEPENDENCE

The trends of the nineteenth century continued into the twentieth. The 'Viramgam cordon', a customs line barring the export of finished products from the peninsula to the mainland, was removed in 1917: its removal greatly helped trade and industry in the peninsula (Spodek 1976, 97). Traditional shipping experienced its last boom during the Second World War, due to the shortage of shipping facilities (Vaidya 1945).

Industrial development was considerable but unevenly distributed. Bhavnagar, in particular, out-distanced its rivals.[44] But the most intensive growth took place in Rajkot. A minor state and cadet to Jamnagar, its growth was partly due to the establishment of the civil station. From here, the British controlled affairs in the peninsula. But Rajkot also became central to the network of modern communications. Between 1911 and 1931 the population of Rajkot city grew by 69 per cent (Wood 1978, 244), and the phenomenal growth has continued ever since.

In 1890, Lakhajiraj succeeded, as a minor, to the throne. At the time of the 1911 darbar, he was twenty-six. His enlightened rule helped

Rajkot grow, and by 1931 the state's rate of literacy was the highest in the peninsula (26.7 per cent). No less than 18.21 per cent of the population belonged to traditional merchant castes, against 9.99 per cent in the Western States Agency as a whole. Conversely, the proportion of agricultural castes—Rajput, Kanbi, Koli—was relatively low. There were more Brahmins and less untouchables than the average for the agency (op. cit., 245-6).

Urbanization and development were well advanced. But Rajkot was above all remarkable for its experiments with popular participation in government. The Rajkot Praja Pratanidhi Sabha[45] was established in 1923. Its members were elected from six vocational groups; men and women aged twenty-one and over might vote if they owned land or a business. The Sabha represented a real step towards democracy, even if its proposals were only advisory. In 1929, however, two thirds of its 90 members[46] were Brahmins or from merchant castes. The Sabha was dominated by urban groups (op. cit., 247-9), in these years when the tension between them and the landed interests were on the increase (Spodek 1976, 50-9).

In general, the independence movement had few repercussions in the peninsula: its limited base became clear during the Rajkot satyagraha. The first 'nationalist' organization of Saurashtra, the Kathiawar Rajkiya Parishad, was founded in 1915 by Mansuklal Ravjibhai Mehta, a Jain goldsmith from Morvi successfully established in Bombay. Lakhajiraj let him hold the organization's first conference in Rajkot in 1921; Mehta was also his jeweller (Wood 1978, 251). The prince donated land for a National School, which became a centre for nationalist activities. These were, in general, concentrated in Rajkot and the British enclaves, as well as in Bombay, where large numbers of Banias and Brahmins had migrated due to the problems facing trade and commerce in the peninsula (Spodek, op. cit., 53-4; Wood, op. cit., 251). When Mehta died in 1924, the nationalists of Saurashtra split into four groups, all led by Brahmins or Banias. The movement retained its urban, high-caste base till independence (Wood, op. cit., 252).

Lakhaji, who died in 1930, had adjusted better to the new trends than any other ruler in Saurashtra. He created a state bank, but also a chamber of commerce, and tried to help merchants in matters of credit and exports. He introduced telephone, electricity, a tramway, and a textile mill (Spodek 1976, 99). But his successor Dharmendrasinhji got a bad name for 'womanizing' during his studies in Europe; one of his first acts on coming to power in 1931 was to abolish the Sabha. 'In fact, the prince had become so preoccupied with the pursuit of pleasure that his Dewan, Durbar Virawala, became the effective ruler' (Wood, op.cit., 250). He financed his spending by selling off new state monopolies, but, though 'the people of Rajkot grumbled at the iniquities of the palace', they did nothing until 1938 (ibid.). When the Congress decided to mount its campaign in Rajkot that year, these factors were undoubtedly important, but Gandhi's father had also been Dewan to Lakhajiraj's father, and Gandhi 'probably regarded Rajkot as his home' (op. cit., 256-7).

The Rajkot satyagraha failed to elicit response except from the urban population of Brahmins and Banias; Virawala managed to mobilize the peasants against it, and Muslims and Rajputs demonstrated against Gandhi's attempt to force a settlement on the state by fasting (Wood, op. cit., *passim*; 264-5).

The Limbdi satyagraha in 1939 also misfired. The peasants supported the ruler, and Banias living in villages were expelled from the state (Spodek 1976, 57-8). In effect, the opposition between rulers and merchants had reached a climax. Spodek writes, 'In the years immediately preceding independence, both of the antagonisms in the urban system had been rubbed raw. Mobile urbanites and landed princes confronted each other directly within the capital cities, and agitation for regional, horizontal integration directly opposed princely desires for territorial fragmentation into personal fiefs' (1976, 59).

And, during the repressive conditions of the Second World War, the princes, in their loyalty to the British, went against the nationalist politicians in their states, giving the latter 'the kind of kudos as political martyrs which the civil disobedience movements had already given to so many Congressmen in British India' (Low 1978, 384). Gandhi's strategies had made it possible for merchants to combine heroism with non-violence.

INDEPENDENCE AND THE END OF PRINCELY RULE

With the British gone, the Congress were the victors, and the position of the princes considerably weakened.[47] Saurashtra and Rajasthan were given an intermediate status for some years. They were not included in the new, language-based units but became federations of states under a Rajpramukh chosen from among the rulers. The transition may have been necessary. Nobody who talked to older Kathiawaris in the seventies could fail to note their pride in the achievements of 'their' state, the nostalgia for the princes, and for 'the good old days'.[48]

Jeffrey regards the settlements with the former rulers as 'generous' (1978, 25). Yet the change was dramatic. When Saurashtra became a state, elections—in 1952—gave an overwhelming victory to the Congress. Only four non-Congress members were elected; the government, led by the Nagar U.N. Dhebar, contained Brahmins and Banias only. Yet its main policies were for emancipation of the peasantry; full occupancy rights were granted almost immediately. But while left-wingers criticized these settlements as inadequate, the elections had been postponed due to right-wing insurgence. From 1949 to 1952, eighty to eighty-five persons were killed and a large loot taken by dacoits who, in the old Kathiawar tradition, reacted to the loss of their lands by going into outlawry. The insurgence, says Daniel Thorner, 'virtually amounted to a rebellion'. But it intimidated

> the potential beneficiaries of the land reforms among the peasantry. Some of the *Girasdars* perhaps dreamed of causing the downfall of the Saurashtra government ... and restoring the rule of the princes. The *girasdars*, however, overestimated their strength; when the Government arrested a prince's brother—who had been associated with India's most notorious dacoit, Bhupat—and later led him through the streets in chains, the rebellion collapsed. (Thorner 1956, 43)

Perhaps surprisingly, Bhupat was a younger brother of the ruler of Bhavnagar, long the most progressive of states. The houses of Palitana, Dhrol, Morvi, Limbdi and Jamnagar were all shown to be more or less implicated in the revolt (Spodek 1976, 77). The 'harmonious' integration of the peninsula into the Indian Union, then, was highly relative; Junagadh, of course, had tried to join Pakistan and was annexed.[49]

It is to be assumed that the crushing victory of the Congress stemmed directly from the defeat of the insurgents. While landlord interests continued to be active, the princely families of Saurashtra never again involved themselves in politics, unlike their colleagues in Rajasthan (Richter 1978, 352). From 1952 onwards, urban interests, led by what we have called the merchant estate, dominated Saurashtra for many years.

These years brought considerable economic development, but distribution remained conservative. While Saurashtra, in 1973-4, was among the richest regions of India, agricultural wages were among the lowest. The 'feudal' links between landowner and tenant were gone;

those who held sufficient land became capitalist farmers.[50] On the cultural level, these developments and 'merchantization' of Saurashtra, weakened the whole Rajput tradition (Tambs-Lyche 1982).

This greatly affected the position of the goddess, who no longer received animal sacrifice.[51] The Swaminarayana sect, bringing the non-violence of the merchants to a much wider sector of the population, became the strongest single factor in religious and cultural life. The wheel, then, had come full circle, returning to an urban-dominated society as in Vallabhi times.

NOTES

1. This point emerges strongly from R.W. Stern's analysis of relations between Jaipur and the British (1988).
2. The reader may refer to our earlier account of the establishment of the Gohil chiefdoms, for the traditional pattern from which Bhavnagar grew (Ch. III).
3. The Mughal navy was now independent of Delhi. Later, they withdrew from Surat to found the state of Janjira south of Bombay, which long held the enclave of Jafrabad in Southern Saurashtra. These 'Sea Lords' were Sidis, of African descent. Though seamen, they show the transition from soldier to ruler suggested by Kolff (1990).
4. In 1772 the state consisted of the districts Sihor, Gundi-ko-liak, Vartej, Umrala, Trapaj, Bhandaria and Dihor, as well as a portion of the Sarvaiya taluka of Bakhalkha and some villages in the Bhal (Watson 1910, 30).
5. This may show the wisdom of Akheraji's reticence in taking over Talaja.
6. The Sipahis ('Sepoys') were soldiering communities in Mughal times. Like many leaders of such communities, the ruler of Mahuva had risen to a chief in the times of Mughal decline. He is typical of the pattern suggested by Kolff (1990). It is perhaps indicative of their weak local base that they were so soon deplaced by a Kathi chief.
7. They (the Kathis) had the genius to forage, to raid, to plunder and the ability to weather through prolonged periods of stress and adversity. But they had little of the ability to organise, to plan a long-term campaign against a superior foe (BDG, 65).
8. Dada Khachar of Gadhada, who became the protector and devotee of Swami Narayana, is likely to have been the son or heir of the chief to whom Wakhtsinhji had restored Gadhada.
9. All these are well-known Muslim 'soldiering' communities. The strong presence of 'Arabs' at Bhavnagar is noted by Tod, who visited it in 1821. He was particularly surprised at the presence of Arab musicians in the party sent to welcome him at Ghogha (1971, 261).
10. A Muslim state, which had broken away from the Mughal empire, Junagadh retained many features of the latter's organization. It was probably the first Kathiawar state to depend entirely on 'professional' soldiers. These were

troublesome, especially as state finances were sometimes insufficient to pay them. See also Kolff (1990).

11. This was, of course, the ancient and famous Uparkot.
12. We shall meet this unruly population later in the chapter.
13. This, too, seems to have been a 'law and order' operation. Babriawad had always been a 'periphery', largely outside the control of the larger states.
14. In fact, Amarji had returned to celebrate Holi. This festival, when roles are reversed and etiquette is put aside, has often proved an ideal occasion to assassinate prominent persons.
15. Tod clearly shows the contrast between Bhavnagar and Junagadh by 1821-2 (1971).
16. In 1896, Mehta and Mehta give their population as follows: Bhavnagar 467,282; Junagadh 387,499; and Navanagar 316,147. While Bhavnagar had a revenue of 35 lakhs, and the two other major states 24 lakhs each, the smallest 'state' paid an annual tribute of 12 rupees to the Crown. (Mehta and Mehta 1896; 487, 529, 557; Watson, 1884).
17. We have met Vagher pirates in the story of the merchant Maulana Mahmud Samarqandi—at the time of Mahmud Begada, who took Dwarka and the Bet in 1473. We have also seen Meraman Khawas fighting against them.
18. Dharaiya gives the names and villages of the leaders, which I have omitted here.
19. Ramanuja developed his ideas in opposition to Shankaracharya, whose Advaita philosophy sees the ultimate Brahman as identical with the soul of man as well as with an abstract, formless principle (Tuck 1986). The two are one; his philosophy is monistic. Ramanuja's stress on the personal character of the God made him 'modify' Shankara's advaita (Esnoul 1964). God and the soul are one, but both have a separate identity—leading his philosophy to be called 'modified monism' (*vishishtadvaita*).
20. A description of this sect and its current practice is found in Kakar (1982).
21. The Maharaja Libel Case was a great setback to the Vallabhacharya sect. Briefly, the reformer Karshandas Mulji wrote, in 1860, in his Bombay journal an article accusing the Maharajas of several immoral acts, of which the most shocking was the allegation that they were committing adultery with the wives and daughters of their devotees. In 1861, the Maharaja of Surat filed a case of libel, which came before the court in 1862. The verdict was 'certainly a moral victory' for Mulji, who also awarded costs'. Mulji's accusations were not proved, as he was the defendant, but widely believed among both Gujaratis and British (Pocock 1973; 118-20). Pocock's recent and concise rendering makes other sources seem obscure and biased to the modern reader (Mulji 1865; Malabari 1884; Thoothi 1935, 96ff).
22. Ladu Barot or Brahmanand lived from 1772 to 1849. Beside Dingala (Charani) and Gujarati he wrote in Hindi, using then the name Shriranga (Jhaveri 1978, 59).
23. The name alludes to his past as a Shaivite monk and, therefore, a follower of Advaita.
24. The opposition between Shaivite monks, who let hair and beard grow, and Vaishnavite ones, whose head are shaven, is clear. Dave implies that Magniram wore his long hair in a *jata*, i.e 'matted' into a knot. This distinguishes Shaivite monks from tantrics, who wear their hair loose. (cf. Leach, 1958).

25. These were Kathis, as we shall see p. 299.
26. The sadhus were supposed to adhere strictly to non-violence. (Parekh 1936, 78-9; Dave 1967, 98-9).
27. See the beginning of this chapter for Bhavnagar's and Jamnagar's expansion, as well as the Kathi response. See also Parekh (1936; 121-5) and Dave (1967, 77-82).
28. Dave calls it the 'Holy City'. He makes Dada Khachar a 'king' (1967, 77). The little town still has an important Swaminarayana temple.
29. Dave stresses only the devotion of these women (1967, 79-81), but Parekh states that they 'proved of very great help to the Satsang, especially in organizing the Woman's side of the fellowship (1936, 143). Parekh describes the sect before the schism between the older 'Acharyapanth' and the new 'Yogijipanth'. The latter, separating in the fourties to become by far the larger group, is more puritanical (Tambs-Lyche 1992, Williams 1984). Williams describes an attempt to create female ascetics within the sect; this led to another split, as the Yogijipanth, especially, refuses such a role for women.
30. See especially Parekh (1936, 141-3).
31. The moustache is a powerful symbol of manhood with Rajputs. To shave somebody's moustache when sleeping conveys ultimate disgrace. Tod notes that Albuquerque, sadly in need of money for his campaigns, was able to raise it by mortgaging his moustache! (1971, 260).
32. Mulu Khachar, a Kathi convert, was allowed to use tobacco and opium 'if he practised the five major vows'. But when he was seen with his hookah, people said he was no Swaminarayana. Thus he gave up smoking. Then at the convention of believers, everybody embraced each other, but nobody would embrace Mulu as they saw him taking opium. Finally Mulu gave up, saying 'I gave up smoking because of the criticism of the unbelievers and opium because of the criticism of the believers' (Parekh 1936, 124-5).
33. Sura Khachar, another Kathi devotee, was late for the lord's meeting. Asked why, he said: 'Maharaj! my two oxen were stolen yesterday'. The Swami inquired how he could then proceed with his ploughing. Sura reassured him: 'I have brought four (oxen) of others'. Dave clearly enjoys such a naive answer to the Swami's injunction against stealing (1967, 70).
34. Ladu Barot's conversion had not killed his vanity. His love for clothes and ornaments was criticized by Ladu Bai, one of Dadu Khachar's sisters, who made him see that beauty was an invitation to sin. Ladu immediately laid his ornamants before the Swami, and renounced the world, to become Brahmananda (Parekh 1936, 143-4).
35. Parekh says, 'not only did these renounce their caste, but they gave up their status as Sadhus also'. They were expected to go about incognito, while preaching in secret the tenets of the sect, and to be known as Paramahamsas. This arrangement was, of course, temporary (Parekh 1936, 81-98, Dave 1967, 46-54, Tambs-Lyche, 1992a; Williams, 1984).
36. Both Parekh and Dave describe this opposition dramatically, and there is never any doubt that Shaktas and Shaivites are the main opponents, i.e. followers of the Goddess. Nor are they in any doubt about the political opposition from the ruling Rajputs (Parekh 1936; 76-81, 100-5; Dave 1967; 39-40, 61-5, 55-60). See also Tambs-Lyche (1992a).

37. Jagjivanram is described here as Diwan of Kutch. Fateh Mahomed, who in 1813 invaded Navanagar, died soon after. Rao Rayadhanji died the same year. He was suceeded by Bharmalji, who was only fifteen years old. Mehta and Mehta tells us that 'the entire management of the state was entrusted to one Hussein Miyan, the son of Fatteh Mahmud'. A friend of the British, Hussein was opposed by his brother Ibrahim. According to this source, Jagjivan Meheta—most likely our Jagjivanram—was a 'trusted protegé' of Fateh Mahomed; he supported Hussein, and it was probably Ibrahim who had him and his family murdered, on 30 August, 1814 (1896, 357-8). The sectarian sources seem to have inflated Jagjivan's position somewhat.
38. Bishop Heber describes his meeting with the Swami (1846, II, 106-15). Williams (1984, 58-61) discusses it thoroughly, and Parekh (1936, 290-1) briefly.
39. See Williams (1984, 6-7), and Dave (1967, 120-1) for a sectarian view.
40. Rajkumar College, founded exclusively for the education of princes, remained dedicated to this purpose till the end of the British period. It remains a high-class institution even today, and its President continues to come from a royal family.
41. In 1886 Wankaner was linked with Wadhwan through a junction at Dolia, and in 1888 Veraval and Junagadh was linked to the Dhola-Dhoraji line through Jetalsar. 1889 saw the Dhoraji line extended to Porbandar, and the Wankaner line to Rajkot (op. cit., 244). In 1893 the line from Rajkot to Jetalsar was opened, linking Junagadh to Rajkot, but also, for example, Gondal to Wankaner. Dhrangadhra was connected to Wadhwan in 1898 (op. cit., 252-3). A line from Rajkot to Jamnagar and the port of Bedi was begun the year before (JDG, 324).
42. Sihor to Palitana (Bhavnagar state) 1910, Junagadh to Bilkha (Junagadh state) 1912, Wankaner to Morvi, Dhasa to Kundla and Vanthali to Bantwa (all before 1915), (Wilberforce-Bell 1916, 262-3); Jamnagar to Dwarka and Okha 1922 (JDG, 325). Only the latter was built by a private company—though Jamnagar and Baroda states were involved—all others were built and run by the State Railways of the respective states.
43. Compare also, for Baroda state, Hardiman 1978.
44. In 1936-7, Bhavnagar had 48 ginning factories, as against 31 in Junagadh and 15 in Jamnagar. Of cotton presses, the numbers were 10, 5 and 2 respectively. Of 8 modern textile mills 3, including the largest by far, was in Bhavnagar; Junagadh and Jamnagar had none. Though other states too, such as Porbandar and Morvi, saw considerable industrialisation, Bhavnagar was firmly in the lead (Trivedi 1939).
45. The name translates as 'Rajkot People's Representative Assembly' (Wood 1978, 247).
46. Wood has analysed the 1929 Sabha membership. By vocational group, 18 were from 'business', 44 'agriculturalists', 61 'labourers or artisans', 4 'priests', 2 'professionals', and 50 'other citizens'. The classification by caste is more enlightening; 20 Brahmins, 30 Banias (including Jains), 9 Lohana, 6 Muslims, 3 Rajputs, 12 Kanbis and 9 others (1978, 248).
47. Manor sees the princes as 'doomed' from the introduction of the Government of India act of 1935 (1978, 306). Other commentators are not so sure. A balanced discussion is found in Jeffrey's introduction to the volume (Jeffrey, ed. 1978).

48. The nostalgic memory of the princes, found in Saurashtra in 1973-4, has diminished since. There is, however, a renewed interest in them as 'Hindu' states. The earlier nostalgia parallels that described by Hardiman (1978) for Baroda state.
49. The accession of Junagadh to Pakistan and the subsequent military action has been described several times, for example, by Moraes (1956, 365-7).
50. Cash-cropping (groundnut, onion, tobacco) dominates, and much of the farming is on irrigated land. Thus the farmer is firmly tied to the market, and dependent on market trends. The last prices were by far the most important news in Praj in 1973-4, read out loud in the teashops. The reader was never short of a public.
51. The disappearance of animal sacrifice is truly metonymous of the cultural changes since independence. It forms the theme of Tambs-Lyche (1982).

Epilogue

'You should properly call it Kathiawar', said my Jhala landlord to me, in Rajkot, when I spoke about Saurashtra. And when I answered, 'Yes, we must not forget the battle of Bhuchar Mori', he was delighted. He certainly wanted to recall the Rajput past. An active BJP member, he was typical of the trend, as the eighties came to an end, of a return to precisely those traditions that thirty years of domination by the merchant estate had swept under the carpet.

Stickers appeared on scooters and trucks, proclaiming their owners' support for the Goddess. 'Jay Mataji', or 'Jay Khodiyar Ma', was to be read everywhere, while radios and loudspeakers chanted 'You are Rama, You are Sita'—the most popular song line from the televised *Ramayana*. The cassette shop of my friend in Dhrangadhra now had a wide choice of traditional songs; those to Khodiyar and other goddesses, but also cycles of heroic stories from Charan poetry. The cassettes were produced in Rajkot, where the small firms making them were experiencing a boom. As my friend said, they sell well these days, almost like film songs.

In Shakti Mata's temple, however, I heard not the traditional *garbo*-style songs, but devotional chants in the style of the bhakti tradition. These were new; the singer, an old man, had recently composed them. And at Khodiyar's temple, great changes have appeared in the past fifteen years. The old priests, descendants of those who had served at the time of Bhavnagar's rise to statehood, are now gone; the temple has become a public foundation and is run by a committee. The change did not come about without conflict for there was a court case. The committee has done great things for the temple, which has been extensively renovated. On the old platform where animals used to be sacrificed, they are now building a park for children, who can thus enjoy themselves while their parents are practising their devotion. It has to be said that everything is now clean and freshly painted.

People I spoke to said they come because Khodiyar is a famous goddess, but their visit now smacks heavily of tourism. The temple is becoming, to put it perhaps a little too strongly, a popular picnic spot. In fact, there are now tables and benches for the pilgrims, since the class of visitor who arrives in his own car does not like to eat on the ground.

Saurashtra, then, may return to Kathiawar in name, but the revived tradition differs considerably from the past it evokes, a 'past in the present' (Bloch 1977), for which history is but a loose reference. Still in the making, the new tradition does not form an integrated whole. Thus my Rajput host shares his enthusiasm for tradition and the BJP with my Brahmin guesthouse keeper in Dhrangadhra, who insists that pastoralists and other 'primitive' people know nothing of the Goddess. Her essence can only be understood by Brahmins, born with the intuition needed to understand the sacred texts. He may be proved right, for the singer to Shakti Mata, or Khodiyar's temple committee, are engaged in a 'rediscovery' of the pure, vegetarian Goddess. But is it of her, or her meat-eating predecessor, that the Maldhari is thinking when he fixes a sticker on his motorcycle? And how does the vegetarian Goddess fit into stories of martial Rajput exploits, which the heroes' descendants now listen to from their cassette recorders?

The inconsistencies in this new tradition may never be solved, but they did not keep Brahmins and 'backward castes' from celebrating together, in festive mood and their best (preferably yellow) clothes, the BJP's march towards Srinagar in 1992. When Rabaris suffered heavy loss of livestock due to drought that year, pastoralists and Brahmins united behind the BJP, blaming the death of an alleged 3000 cows on Congress. Contradictions may not preclude united action, but the unity masks differences which may well surface later, if the ideal Hindu state ever becomes a project for practical politics.

In this book, I have presented a different picture of the diverse traditions of Saurashtra, or of Kathiawar as the case may be. The Rajput tradition is the dominant streak, though opposed by the non-violent tradition of merchants, present before Rajputs came. Tradition is manifold; a storehouse from which any party may draw a selection to suit his purpose. As post-modernists like to stress, this makes the writer creator of his stories, and so, for them, a work like this is little different from a novel.

Perhaps my best defender is the Goddess herself. Creator of this world, indeed she is the world. Yet she is Maya, illusion: the world of appearances, which the social scientist observes, is but a manifestation of the really real. Maybe this is why traditional Indian thought evades the positivism which is the most obvious target of the post-modern thinkers. What we describe is Maya, as we ourselves are. This view parallels another, unfashionable these days, where human, social existence is both the basis for understanding and the limits of what can be understood; a Marxian world-view is not as far removed from that of the Goddess-worshippers as both parties, no doubt, might have liked. In short, post-modernism may be right in insisting that the object of our analysis and that analysis itself can only exist at the same epistemological level.

In the present work we are dealing with the creation of tradition through history, as well as its influence on those who, in the next instance, make history. We need not reify tradition; the actors themselves take care of that. Traditions are made and unmade by man, but in becoming tradition, the past is reified, and it is as such a *res* that it influences our further action.

Specifically, I have tried to show how Rajput tradition grew. When Naughan became king by the grace of the Goddess, no such tradition existed. Later, kingship comes to imply her grace, a tradition disappearing only when kings are no more. 'Rules of the game' between chief and vassals emerge gradually, as the game itself grows. The category of Rajput, originally a fighter, crystallizes into a caste, and norms of hypergamy appear, as the game gradually settles into a defense of acquired positions. Meanwhile, the bardic tradition is built by the Charans who are themselves its foremost product. For 'Rajputs' in the tenth to twelfth century tradition was still in the making; in the seventeenth it had become doxa, to borrow Bourdieu's term. By Tod's time, tradition had settled into a form which he recast, in the mould of his fascination with Scotland's feudal past. Of course Tod's version of Rajputdom is fiction. So was the bardic material on which he built. But the existence of fiction is a fact.

Similarly, we have seen how the continuity and growth of merchant tradition owes a great deal to Jain literature. This tradition, from which Gandhi borrowed so much, was no more or less a fiction than that of Tod. The sum of Bania and Darbar traditions does not exhaust traditional Kathiawar society, even if we add Maldharis and Kheduts. There are several Muslim traditions, those of artisans, of untouchables, and so on. But those we have treated here form a reasonable grid for understanding what kind of things Saurashtrians refer to in speaking of their society and its past.

Society, then, is not in itself an object, as Durkheim would have it. Yet I submit that tradition makes most of us, in daily life, think of it as such. As social scientists, we try to avoid reifications; as laymen, we readily employ them. We see society as the sum of traditions about it that we know. This book may read like history. Most of it is not; much of the mythical material is unlikely to have happened at all. The 'way through the waters' has the same epistemological status whether it brought Naughan across the Rann or Moses across the Red Sea. Yet in both cases, the existence of the myth is itself a significant historical fact.

What I study, then, is the process by which a certain referential object, 'traditional society', has found its form. I am looking for a social 'object', which must be studied through the references people make to it. Does this make me different from the novelist? At an existential level, emphatically no. The difference between the anthropologist and the novelist, as I see it, is in the rules of the game, albeit man-made and wilfully chosen. Once chosen, they should be followed; unlike the novelist, I have not invented stories, nor personalities. But I have cut the material to fit, a highly subjective process. Anthropology may indeed be no more than a literary genre; but it seems to be a productive one, since more and more anthropology is being written. Surely, the effect we want to achieve is a coherent picture of a certain society, in which the elements are arranged according to a defensible rendering of the social processes that bind them together—defensible in that the interpetration should relate meaningfully to how we have thought and interpreted social process till now. Anthropologists may never reach a real understanding of the societies they study but surely contribute to an effort at such understanding. Perhaps the effort is more important than the result, as human activity is more meaningful than the (reified) results it produces.

What understanding, then, does the present volume contribute to? I have wanted to give readers an idea of a tradition, now fast changing, and a society, already disappeared, that fascinates me. With its incessant wars, it is a society where I am happy not to have lived. But perhaps we may learn something from it, concerning other, more current, ideas about that object, society in general, our society—which we all try to shape in our own image?

First, it may be a system, but it is certainly an open one, in which conflict and contradiction are major generative forces. It is not 'the caste system' as an integrated whole, though the idea of this whole exists. Its integration, however, is not effected by Brahmin ideological dominance and its moral concomitants.

It is, I think, clear that the states of traditional Kathiawar were held together by the exercise of power. It is apt, therefore, that their primary deity should be the source and incarnation of power herself. As is usual where one value is central to the system, its negation is a constant presence too, in the shape of the non-violence of the merchant groups.

The Rajput states of Saurashtra were certainly Hindu, but the Goddess worship they maintained, and which maintained them, was very different from the 'Hinduism' with which the re-found Rama is credited. The king's morals are not those of his subjects. The Goddess provided the strength to rule a very diverse population, according to rules of conduct that, to an extent, guaranteed them a degree of moral independence. The Banias may have been disliked by the Rajputs; they were not asked to propitiate the Goddess. Certainly, the Goddess was a guardian of dharma, as our stories bear witness. But the Rajput states were not moral empires, torn as they were by internal strife and wars against their neighbours.

Secondly, whether the term 'feudalism' is applicable to India, or not, seems to me a matter of definitions. I have tried to show that the factors which underlie the growth of Rajputdom and of the Rajput states are essentially similar to parallel developments in the West, and probably elsewhere. Lyall opposed this view, I side with Tod; there is nothing in the constitution of the Rajput state to hinder its development towards modern statehood.

It could only become a real state, however, by tapping resources outside the kinship–political field, and control of agriculture was not enough. Only the control of trade and merchants made statehood possible. Once attained, its further development may have been hampered but not hindered by kinship; by the eighteenth century, the army and the bureaucracy had bypassed the kinship links in political importance.

What ultimately stopped the growth of Saurashtra's states was the overwhelming strength of British India, just as they had been hampered, earlier, by Mughal domination. Faced with independent India, they were, of course, doomed. Then, too, the Rajput tradition on which their legitimacy rested had become divorced from contemporary experience. Yet Bhavnagar was certainly better equipped for independence than say Nepal or Bhutan.

Thirdly, it will be clear to the reader that the Kathiawar rulers cannot be seen as 'sacred' kings in Hocart's sense of the term. I have argued, too, that Rajput kingship does not rely on Brahmin legitimation in the way that Dumont conceives of it. The ruler in Saurashtra was above all a warrior and a conqueror, and conquest in itself made for legitimacy. By descent, such legitimacy was prolonged in time, and by British times descent had become the primary factor. Both conquest and descent was communicated through the same channel, the genealogy and poetry of the Charan. It was his word, not that of the Brahmin, which built or destroyed a ruler's legitimacy. Power from the Goddess, legitimacy from her brothers: the position of the Charan is, indeed, the kingpin around which Rajput kingship turns. I have not been able to go as deeply into this complex of ideas and relationships as I would have liked. But I hope to have indicated some directions the investigation might take.

What, then, of the Brahmin? It is unjust to say he recedes into the background. But he does seem to enter the constitution of kingship at a point where the king has already become a chief. The Brahmin legitimizes kingship when its foundations have been laid. His function is less oriented towards the rural, 'feudal' order from which the chief has sprung, than to the wider, more complex society over which he gains sovereignty in taking control of the city.

The dream of moral empire is very much with us. In India, such dreams refer strongly to a tradition, a 'Hindu tradition', an object constantly recreated. I have wanted to show that traditional Kathiawar was a very different object from what the dreamers have in mind.

Bibliography

ADG: See under *District Gazetteers*.

Alsdorf, L. 1962, *Beiträge zur Geschichte von Vegetarismus und Rinderverährung in Indien*. Wiesbaden: F. Steiner.

Amarji, R. 1882, *Tarikh-i-Sorath*. Bombay: Education Society's Press.

Arai, T. 1978, Jaina Kingship as viewed in the Prabandhacintamani. In: J.F. Richards (ed.): *Kingship and Authority in South Asia*. Madison: University of Wisconsin.

Ardener, E. 1972, Belief and the Problem of Women. In: J. La Fontaine (ed.): *The Interpretation of Ritual*. London: Tavistock.

Asad, T. 1972, Market Model, Class Structure and Consent: A Reconsideration of Swat Political Organization. *Man*, (n.s.): 7: 74-94.

Babb, L.A. 1975, *The Divine Hierarchy: Popular Hinduism in Central India*. New York: Columbia University Press.

Baines, A. 1912, *Ethnography (Castes and Tribes)*. Strassburg: Trübner.

Banga, I. (ed.) 1992, *Ports and their Hinterland in India 1700-1950*. Delhi: Manohar.

Barth, F. 1953, *Principles of Social Organization in Southern Kurdistan*. Oslo: Universitetets Etnografiske Museum.

———. 1956, Ecological Relationships of Ethnic Groups in Swat, North Pakistan. *American Anthropologist*: 58: 1079-89.

———. 1959a, *Political Leadership among Swat Pathans*. London: Athlone.

———. 1959b, Segmentary opposition and the Theory of Games. *Journal of the Royal Anthropological Institute*: 89, Part 1.

———. 1964a, *Nomads of South Persia*. Oslo: Universitetsforlaget.

———. 1964b, Competition and Symbiosis in North East Baluchistan. *Folk*: 6,1: 15-22.

———. 1969, Introduction, in F. Barth (ed.): *Ethnic Groups and Boundaries*. Oslo: Scandinavian Universities Press.

———. 1983, *Sohar*. Baltimore: Johns Hopkins University Press.

Basham, A.L. 1967, *The Wonder That Was India*. Calcutta: Fontana. BDG: See under District Gazetteers.

Beck, B.E. 1972, *Peasant Society in Konku*. Vancouver: University of British Columbia Press.

Benedict, B. 1968, Family Firms and Economic Development. *Southwestern Journal of Anthropology*: 24: 1-19.

Bernier, F. 1916, *Travels in the Mogul Empire*. London: Oxford University Press.

Berreman, G.D. 1962, *Behind Many Masks*. Ithaca: Society for Applied Anthropology.

Berwick, S. 1976, The Gir Forest: An Endangered Ecosystem. *American Scientist*: 64: 28-40.

Béteille, A. 1965, *Caste, Class and Power*. Berkeley: University of California Press.

Biardeau, M. 1976, Le Sacrifice dans l'Hindouisme. In: M.Biardeau and C.Malamoud: *Le Sacrifice dans l'Inde Ancienne*. Paris: P.U.F.

Bloch, Marc 1975, *Feudal Society*. London: Routledge & Kegan Paul.

Bloch, Maurice 1977, The Past as the Present in the Present. *Man* (n.s.): 12: 278-92.

Bohannan, L. 1952, A Genealogical Charter. *Africa*: 22: 301-15.

———. 1958, Political Aspects of Tiv Social Organization. In: J. Middleton and D. Tait (eds), q.v.

Bouez, S. 1992, *La déesse apaisée*. Paris: Cahiers de l'Homme.

Brent, P. 1972, *Godmen of India*. Harmondsworth: Penguin.

Brox, O. 1992, The Common Property Theory: Epistemological Status and Analytical Utility. In: Grønhaug, Haaland and Henriksen (eds): *The Ecology of Choice and Symbol*. Bergen: Alma Mater.

Brögger, J. 1989, *Prebureaucratic Europeans: A Study of a Portuguese Fishing Community*. Trondheim: Norwegian Universities Press.

Burgess, J. 1882, *Introduction to Amarji 1882*, q.v.

———. 1971, *Report on the Antiquities of Kathiawad and Kacch* (first published 1876). Varanasi: Indological Book House.

Carrin, M. and H. Tambs-Lyche 1993, La vengeance des femmes dans ce monde et l'autre. *Cahiers de Littérature Orale*, 34: 47-75.

Carrin-Bouez, M. 1991, Un roi venu d'ailleurs... ou la conception santal du roi dans les contes. *Cahiers de Littérature Orale*, 29: 89-124.

Census of India 1911, *Punjab Census Report*, Vol. 1.

Chatterjee, A.K. 1978, *A Comprehensive History of Jainism*. Calcutta: KLM.

Chaube, J. 1975, *History of Gujarat Kingdom, 1458-1537*. Delhi: Munshiram Manoharlal.

Chaudhuri, K.N. 1985, *Trade and Civilization in the Indian Ocean*. Cambridge: Cambridge University Press.

Chauhan, B.R. 1967, *A Rajasthan Village*. Delhi: Vir Publishing House.

Clémentin-Ojha, C. 1990, *La divinité conquise*. Nanterre: Société d'Ethnologie.

Copland, I. 1978, The Other Guardians: Ideology and Performance in the Indian Political Service. In: Jeffrey (ed.), 1978, q.v.

Dave, H.T. 1967, *Life and Philosophy of Shree Swaminarayana*. Bochasan: Akshar Purushottam Sansthan.

Dasgupta, A. 1984, Indian Merchants in the Age of Partnership, 1500-1800.

In: Tripathi (ed.), q.v.

Desai, I.P. 1964, *Some Aspects of Family in Mahuva*. London: Asia.

Dharaiya, R.K. 1970, *Gujarat in 1857*. Ahmedabad: Gujarat University.

District Gazetteers. *Gazetteer of India 1961. Gujarat Census.*

———. Amreli district (abbreviation ADG)

———. Bhavnagar district (abbreviation BDG)

———. Jamnagar district (abbreviation JMG)

———. Junagadh district (abbreviation JDG)

———. Ahmedabad: Director of Census Operations.

Divekar, V.D. 1984, Business Elements and Business Class in Maharashtra: A Historical Analysis. In: Tripathi (ed.), q.v.

Doshi, H. 1974, *Traditional Neighbourhood in a Modern City*. New Delhi: Abhinav.

Dowson , J. 1982, *Hindu Mythology and Religion*. (Reprint): Calcutta: Rupa & Co.

Dumont, L. 1965, The Functional Equivalent of the Individual in Caste Society. *Contributions to Indian Sociology*: VII: 13-61.

———. 1966, *Homo Hierarchicus*. Paris: Gallimard.

———. 1971, Religion, Politics and Society in the Individualistic Universe. *Proceedings of the Royal Anhropological Society for 1970*. London.

———. 1983, *Essais sur l'individualisme: une perspective anthropologique sur l'idéologie moderne*. Paris: Esprit/Seuil.

Eck, D.L. 1991, Following Rama, Worshipping Shiva. In: D.L. Eck and F. Mallison (eds): *Devotion Divine*. Paris: Ecole Francaise d'Extrème-Orient.

Enthoven, R.E. 1920/ 1921/1922, *Tribes and Castes of Bombay, I-III*. (Reprint 1975: New Delhi: Cosmo).

Entwistle, A.W. and F. Mallison 1994, *Studies in South Asian Devotional Literature*. Delhi: Manohar.

Esnoul, A-M. 1964, *Ramanuja et la mystique vishnouite*. Paris: Seuil.

Evans-Pritchard, E.E. 1940, *The Nuer*. Oxford: Oxford University Press.

———. 1949, *The Sanusi of Cyrenaica*. Oxford: Oxford University Press.

Fischer, E. and H. Shah 1971, *Rural Craftsmen and their Work*. Ahmedabad: National Institute of Design.

Forbes, A.K. 1878, *Ras Mala. Hindu Annals of Western India*. (Reprint 1973: New Delhi, Heritage).

Fortes, M. and E.E. Evans-Pritchard 1940, *African Political Systems*. Oxford: Oxford University Press.

Fox, R.G. 1967, Family, Caste and Commerce in a North Indian Market

Town. *Economic Development and Cultural Change:* XV: 297-314.
———. 1971, *Kin, Clan, Raja, Rule: State-Hinterland Relations in Pre-industrial India.* Berkeley: University of California Press.
Frazer, J. 1916, *The Golden Bough.* London.
Fried, M.H. 1967, *The Evolution of Political Society.* New York: Random House.
Fruzzetti, L. 1990, *The Gift of a Virgin.* Delhi: Oxford University Press.
Fuller, C. 1990, Misconceiving the Grain Heap. In: J. Parry and M. Bloch (eds.): *Money and the Morality of Exchange.* Cambridge: Cambridge University Press.
Gadre, A.S. 1938, Buddhist Influence in Gujarat and Kathiawad. *Journal of the Gujarat Research Society,* 1,4: 61-70.
Galey, J-C. 1973, L'état et le lignage. *L'Homme*: XIII, 71-82.
———. 1989, Reconsidering Kingship in India: An Ethnological Perspective. In: J-C. Galey (ed.): *Kingship and the Kings.* History and Anthropology, No. 4. London: Harwood Academic Publishers.
Gandhi, M.K. 1927, *The Story of My Experiments with Truth.* Ahmedabad: Navajivan.
Ganshof, F.L. 1961, *Feudalism.* New York: Harper.
Gayatri Devi and S.S. Rau 1983, *A Princess Remembers: The Memoirs of the Maharani of Jaipur.* Ghaziabad: Vikas.
Ghaddavi, S. n.d., *Causes and Consequences of Conflict in a Saurashtra Village.* Bhavnagar: Cyclostyled.
Ghurye, G.S. 1962, *Gods and Men.* Bombay: Popular Prakashan.
Gillion, K.L. 1969, *Ahmedabad: A Study in Indian Urban History.* Berkeley: University of California Press.
Gopal, S. 1974, Merchants in Western India in the Sixteenth-Seventeenth Centuries. In: Sharma and Jha (eds.), q.v.
———. 1975, *Commerce and Crafts in Gujarat.* Delhi: People's Publishing House.
———. 1984, Jain Merchants in Eastern India under the Great Mughals. In: Tripathi (ed.), q.v.
Grönhaug, R. 1974, *Micro-Macro Relations: Social Organization in Antalya, Southern Turkey.* Bergen: Bergen Studies in Social Anthropology.
———. 1978, Scale as a Variable in the Analysis. In: F. Barth (ed.): *Scale and Social Organization.* Oslo: Universitetsforlaget.
Guha, A. 1984, More about the Parsi Sheths: Their Roots, Entrepreneurship, and Comprador Role,1650-1918. In: Tripathi (ed.), q.v.
Gupta, S. 1992, Women in the Saiva/Sakta Ethos. In: J. Leslie (ed.), q.v.
Gururaja Bhatt, P. 1975, *Studies in Tuluva History and Culture.* Manipal: published by the author.
Hardiman, D. 1978, Baroda: The Structure of a 'Progressive' State. In: R. Jeffrey (ed.), q.v.

Hardiman, D. 1981, *Peasant Nationalists of Gujarat Kheda District, 1917-34*. Delhi: Oxford University Press.

———. 1988, Class base of the Swaminarayana Sect. *Economic and Political Weekly,* Sept. 10.

Harlan, L. 1991, *Religion and Rajput Women. The Ethic of Protection in Contemporary Narratives.* Berkeley: University of California Press.

Haynes, E.S. 1990, Rajput Ceremonial Interactions as a Mirror of a Dying Indian State System,. 1820-1947. *Modern Asian Studies:* 24: 459-492.

Heber, R. 1846, *Narrative of a Journey through the Upper Provinces of India, 1824-25: I-III.* (First published 1828). London.

Heesterman, J.C. 1978, The Conundrum of the King's Authority. In: Richards (ed.), q.v.

———. 1985, *The Inner Conflict of Tradition.* Chicago: University of Chicago Press.

Hobsbawm, E. 1959, *Primitive Rebels.* Manchester: Manchester University Press.

Hocart, A.M. 1927, *Kingship.* Oxford: Oxford University Press.

Inden, R.B. 1976, *Marriage and Rank in Bengali Culture.* Delhi: Vikas.

———. 1978, Ritual, Authority and Cyclic Time in Hindu Kingship. In: Richards (ed.), q.v.

———. 1990, *Imagining India.* Oxford: Blackwell.

Irfan Habib 1974, The Social Distribution of Landed Property in Pre-British India. In: Sharma and Jha (eds.), q.v.

Jacob, W. Le Grand 1872, *Western India.* London: Henry S. King.

———. 1894, Historical, Geographical and Statistical Memoirs on the Province of Kathiawar.... In: *Selections from the Records of the Bombay Government,* n.s., No. XXXIX. Bombay: Central Government Press.

Jacobson, D. 1977, Flexibility in Central Indian Kinship and Residence, in K. David (ed.): *The New Wind.* The Hague: Mouton.

———. 1981, The Chaste Wife. In: S. Vatuk (ed.): *American Studies in the Anthropology of India.* Delhi: Manohar.

Jain, P.C. 1971, *Labour in Ancient India.* Delhi: Motilal Banarsidass.

———. 1976, *Socio-Economic Exploration of Medieval India.* Delhi: B.R. Publishing Corp.

Jain, R.K. 1975, Bundela Genealogy and Legends. In: J.H.M. Beattie and R.G.Lienhardt (eds.): *Studies in Social Anthropology,* Oxford: Clarendon.

Jeffrey, R. 1978, Introduction, In: R. Jeffrey (ed.), q.v.

Jeffrey, R. (ed). 1978, *People, Princes and Paramount Power. Society and Politics in the Indian States.* Delhi: Oxford University Press.

Jhaveri, M. 1978, *History of Gujarati Literature.* New Delhi: Sahitya Akademi.

JMG: see under: *District Gazetteers.*

Julien, S. 1857, *Mémoires sur les contrées orientales.* Paris: Imprimerie Imperiale.

Kakar, S. 1982, *Shamans, Mystics and Doctors*. New York: A Knopf.
Kennedy, M. 1908, *Criminal Classes in the Bombay Presidency*. Bombay: Government Central Press.
Kincaid, C.A. 1905, *The Outlaws of Kathiawar and Other Studies*. Bombay: Times of India Press.
Kinsley, D. 1986, *Hindu Goddesses*. Berkeley: University of California Press.
Kolff, D. 1990, *Naukar, Rajput, and Sepoy*. Cambridge: Cambridge University Press.
Kosambi, D.D. 1975, *An Introduction to the Study of Indian History*, Bombay: Popular Prakashan.
Kothari, R. and R. Maru 1961, Federating for Political Interests: the Kshatriyas of Gujarat. In: Kothari (ed.): *Caste in Indian Politics*. Delhi: Orient Longmans.
Kumar, R. 1965, *India and the Persian Gulf Region*. Bombay: Asia.
Kulke, H. and D. Rothermund 1986, *A History of India*. London: Croom Helm.
Lamb, H. 1959, The Indian Merchant. In: M. Singer (ed.): *Traditional India: Structure and Change*. Philadelphia: American Folklore Society.
Leach, E.R. 1954, *Political Systems of Highland Burma*. London: Athlone.
———. 1958 Magical Hair. *Journal of the Royal Anthropological Institute:* 88: 147-64.
Leshnik, L.S. and G.D. Sontheimer (eds.), 1986, *Pastoralists and Nomads in South Asia*. Wiesbaden: Harassowitz.
Leslie, J. 1992, Suttee or Sati? Victim or Victor? In: J. Leslie (ed.), q.v.
Leslie, J. (ed.) 1992, *Roles and Rituals for Hindu Women*. Delhi: Motilal Banarsidass.
Lobo, L. 1989, Koli Kshatriyas of North Gujarat. *Eastern Anthropologist*: 42: 171-192.
Low, D.A. 1978, Laissez-faire and Traditional Rulership in Princely India. In: R. Jeffrey (ed.), q.v.
MacMurdo, J. 1894, Report and Memoir of the Province of Kathiawar....In: *Selections from the Records of the Bombay Government (n.s.), XXXIX*. Bombay: Central Government Press.
Majumdar, A.K. 1956, *Chalukyas of Gujarat*. Bombay: Bharatiya Vidya Bhavan.
Malabari, B.M. 1884, *Gujarat and the Gujaratis*. Bombay: Education Society Press.
Malinowski, B. 1954, *Magic, Science and Religion*. New York: Doubleday Anchor.
Mallison, F. 1973, *L'épouse idéale. Le Sati-Gita de Muktananda*. Paris: Institut de Civilisation Indienne.
———. 1974, La secte des Svami-Narayana au Gujrat. *Journal Asiatique:* CCLXII: fasc. 3-4.

———. 1979, A Note on Holiness Allowed to Women: Pativrata and Sati. In: *Ludwig Sternbach Felicitation Volume,* Akhila Bharati Sanskrit Parishad, Lucknow .

———. 1980, Saint Sudama of Gujarat: Should the Holy be Wealthy? *Journal of the Oriental Institute* (Baroda): XXIX: 90-9.

———. 1983, Development of Early Krishnaism in Gujarat: Visnu, Ranchod, Krsna. In: M. Thiel-Horstmann (ed.): *Bhakti in Current Research.* Berlin: Dietrich Reimer Verlag.

———. 1991, Lorsque Ranachodaraya quitte Dwarka pour Dakor, ou comment Dvarakanatha prit la succession de Dankanatha. In: D.L. Eck and F. Mallison (eds.): *Devotion Divine.* Paris: Ecole Francaise d'Extrème-Orient.

———. 1994, Early Kṛṣna Bhakti in Gujarat: The Evidence of Old Gujarati Texts Recently Brought to Light. In: Entwistle and Mallison (eds.), q.v.

Manor, J. 1978, The demise of the Princely Order: A Reassessment. In: R. Jeffrey (ed.), q.v.

Maqbul Ahmad, S. 1978, *Indo-Arab Relations.* New Delhi: Indian Council for Cultural Relations.

Marriott, McKim 1968, Caste Ranking and Food Transactions: A Matrix Analysis. In: M. Singer and B. Cohn (eds.): *Structure and Change in Indian Society.* Chicago: Aldine.

———. 1976, Hindu Transactions: Diversity without Dualism. In: B. Kapferer (ed.): *Transaction and Meaning.* Philadelphia: ISHI.

———. 1989, Constructing an Indian Ethnosociology. *Contributions to Indian Sociology* (n.s.): 23: 1-39.

Marriott, McKim and R.B. Inden 1977, Towards an Ethnosociology of South Asian Caste Systems. In: K. David (ed.): *The New Wind.* The Hague: Mouton.

Mayer, A.C. 1958, The Dominant Caste in a Region of Central India. *Southwestern Journal of Anthropology:* 14: 407-27.

———. 1960, *Caste and Kinship in Central India.* London: Routledge & Kegan Paul.

Mayer, A. C. 1982, Perceptions of Princely Rule. In: T.N. Madan (ed.): *Way of Life.* New Delhi: Vikas.

———. 1985, The King's Two Thrones. *Man* (n.s.): 20: 205-21.

———. 1991, Rulership and Divinity: The Case of the Modern Hindu Prince and Beyond. *Modern Asian Studies*: 25: 765-90.

Mayne, H. 1921, *History of the Dhrangadhra State.* Calcutta: Thacker, Spink & Co.

Mehta, M.N. and M.N. Mehta 1896, *The Hind Rajasthan, or the Annals of the Native States of India, I-III.* Bhadarwa, Rewakantha: Amritlal G. Shah.

Mehta, R.R. 1978, *Shri Khodiyarmata Akhyan* (in Gujarati). Surat: Shri Harihara Pushtakalaya.

Mehta, S. 1984, The Mahajans and the Business Communities of Ahmedabad. In: Tripathi (ed.)., q.v.

Middleton, J. and D. Tait (eds): 1958, *Tribes Without Rulers.* London: Routledge & Kegan Paul.

Misra, S.C. 1964, *Muslim Communities in Gujarat.* Bombay: Asia.

———. 1981, Some Aspects of the Self-Administering Institutions in Medieval Indian Towns. In: J.S. Grewal and I. Banga (eds): *Studies in Urban History.* Amritsar.

———. 1984, The Medieval Trader and his Social World. In Tripathi (ed.) q.v.

Moraes, F. 1956, *Jawaharlal Nehru.* New York: Macmillan.

Mulji, K. 1865, (published anonymously) *History of the Maharajas, or Vallabhacharyas of Western India.* Bombay.

Munshi, K.M. 1954, *Gujarat and its Literature,* I-II. Bombay: Bharatiya Vidya Bhavan.

Nandy, P. (ed.) 1973, *Indian Poetry in English Today.* New Delhi: Sterling.

Natubhoy, T.M. 1905, Shrimali Brahmins. *The Journal of the Anthropological Society of Bombay,* VII, 162-90.

Nevaskar, B. 1971, *Capitalists without Capitalism. The Jains of India and the Quakers of the West.* Westport: Greenwood.

Newcomer, P.J. 1972, The Nuer are Dinka: An Essay on Origins and Environmental Determinism. *Man* (n.s.): 7: 5-11.

Njammasch, M. 1992a, Die Dorfgemeinde im Maitrakaraeich. *Beiträge des Südasien-Instituts,* Humboldt-Universität zu Berlin, 1: 1-49.

———. 1992b, Die Flur- und Besitzverhältnisse im Dorf Madasara auf Kathiawar im Jahre 675 n. Chr. *Beiträge des Südasien-Instituts:* 2: 27-68.

———. 1993, Freie Bauern und Pächter im frühmittelalterlichen Indien. *Beiträge des Südasien-Instituts:* 5: 1-61.

Nurul Hasan, S. 1984, Historian and the Business Communities. In: Tripathi (ed.), q.v.

O'Flaherty, W.D. 1973, *Asceticism and Eroticism in the Mythology of Siva.* Oxford: Oxford University Press.

———. 1980, *Women, Androgynes and Other Mythical Beasts.* Chicago: University of Chicago Press.

Olivelle, P. 1978, Ritual Suicide and the Rite of Renunciation. *Wiener Zeitschrift für die Kunde Südasiens:* XXI: 19-44.

Oza, K.C. 1946, *Reconstruction of Life and Polity in Kathiawar.* Rajkot: published by the author.

Padikkal, S. 1991, Some Moments in the History of the Kannada Novel, with Special Reference to Dakshina Kannada. In: *Perspectives on Dakshina Kannada and Kodagu.* Mangalore: Mangalore University.

Pandit, K.M. 1965, *Earning One's Livelihood in Mahuva*. London: Asia.
Parekh, M.C. 1936, *Sri Swami Narayana*. Rajkot: Sri Bhagwat Dharma Publishing House.
Parsons, T. 1936, *The Structure of Social Action*. Glencoe, Ill: Free Press.
Patel, H.G. 1961, Status and Prestige by Marriage among the Lewa Patidars of Five Villages in Mehsana District. M.A. Thesis, M.S. University of Baroda.
———. 1966a, Anawari—The System of Social Status Among the Lewa Patidars. *Journal of the Gujarat Research Society*: XXVII, 1-4.
———. 1966b, The Change in Structural Unit and Attitudes towards Marriage by Exchange. *Sociological Bulletin:* No. 2.
———. 1973, *The Change and Resistance in the Few Determinants of Caste-Status among the Lewa Patidar of Western India*. Bhavnagar: Cyclostyled.
———. 1983, The Hijada (Eunuch) Culture-Complex: Urgent Research Needs. *Bulletin No. 25 of the International Committee on Urgent Anthropological and Ethnological Research* (Vienna).
———. 1988a, Human Castration: A Study of Hijada (Eunuch) Community of Gujarat in India. *Man and Life*: 14, 3-4: 67-76.
———. 1988b, *Paper read at the XII International Congress of Anthropological and Ethnological Sciences, Symposium on 'Emerging Issues of Common Property Resources'*, Zagreb, July 25.
Pavlov, V.I. 1955, Ocherk Deyatel nosti Torgostev i Rostovshchikov v Kolonialnoi Indii. *Uchenye Zapiska Instituta Vostokovedenya:* XII: 99-149.
Pearson, M.N. 1976, *Merchants and Rulers in Gujarat*. Berkeley: University of California Press.
———. 1981, *Coastal Western India: Studies from Portuguese Records*. Delhi: Concept.
Pehrsson, R.N. 1966, *The Social Organization of the Marri Baluch*. Chicago: Aldine.
Peters, E. 1967, Some Structural Aspects of the Feud among the Camel-herding Bedouin of Cyrenaica. *Africa*, 37: 261-82.
Pocock, D.F. 1955, The Hypergamy of the Patidars. In: K.M. Kapadia (ed): *Ghurye Felicitation Volume*. Bombay: Popular Book Depot.
———. 1957a, Inclusion and Exclusion: Two Processes in the Caste System of Gujarat. *Southwestern Journal of Anthropology:* 13: 9-31.
———. 1957b, The Bases of Faction in Gujarat. *British Journal of Sociology:* 8: 295-306.
Pocock, D.F. 1972, *Kanbi and Patidar*. Oxford: Clarendon.
———. 1973, *Mind, Body and Wealth*. Oxford: Blackwell.
———. 1981, The Vocation and Avocations of the Guggali Brahmans of Dwarka. *Contributions to Indian Sociology*, (n.s.), 15: 321-36.
Pradhan, M.C. 1966, *The Political System of the Jats of Northern India*. London: Oxford University Press.

Pramar, V.S. 1988, *Haveli: Wooden Houses and Mansions of Gujarat.* Ahmedabad: Mapin Publishing Co.

Qanungo, K.R. 1969, *Studies in Rajput History.* New Delhi: S. Chand.

Radcliffe-Brown, A.R. 1952, *Structure and Function in Primitive Society.* 1952, London: Cohen & West.

Raheja , G.G. 1988, *The Poison in the Gift.* Chicago: University of Chicago Press.

———. 1989, Centrality, Mutuality and Hierarchy: Shifting Aspects of Caste Relationships in North India. *Contributions to Indian Sociology* (n.s.): 23, 1: 79-101.

Rajagopalachari, C. 1968, *Ramayana.* Bombay: Bharatiya Vidya Bhavan.

Ray, A. 1992, Cambay and its Hinterland: Early Eighteenth Century. In: I. Banga (ed.)., q.v.

Records of the Bombay Government (*Selections from...*). Vols XXXVII and XXXIX (new series). 1856, Bombay: Government Central Press.

Richards, J.F. (ed.) 1978, *Kingship and Authority in South Asia.* Madison: University of Wisconsin.

Richter, W.L. 1978, Traditional Rulers in Post-Traditional Societies: The Princes of India and Pakistan. In: Jeffrey (ed.), q.v.

Sahajanand Swami, Shree 1968, *Shikshapatri.* Bombay: Bharatiya Vidya Bhavan.

Sahlins, M.D. 1961, The Segmentary Lineage: An Organization for Predatory Expansion. *American Anthropologist*: 63: 322-45.

Saletore, B.A. 1938, *Medieval Jainism. With Special Reference to the Vijayanagara Empire.* Bombay: Karnataka Books.

Salzman, P.C. 1989, From Nomads to Dairymen: Two Gujarati Cases. *Nomadic Studies*: No. 2.

Sangave, V. A. 1959, *Jaina Community: A Social Survey.* Bombay: Popular Book Depot.

Shah, A.M. 1964, Political Systems of 19th Century Gujarat. *Enquiry:* 1: 83-95.

Shah, A.M. and I.P Desai 1988, *Division and Hierarchy. An Overview of Caste in Gujarat.* Delhi: Hindustan.

Shah, A.M. and R. Shroff 1958, The Vahivanca Barots of Gujarat. A Caste of Genealogists and Mythographers. *Journal of American Folklore:* 71: 247-76.

Shah, P.G. 1967, *Vimukta Jatis: Denotified Communities of Western India.* Bombay: Gujarat Research Society.

Sharma, B.N. 1972, *Social and Cultural History of Northern India, c. 1000-1200 A.D.* New Delhi: Abhinav.

Sharma, D. (ed) 1966, *Rajasthan through the Ages,* I-II. Bikaner: Rajasthan State Archives.

Sharma, G.D. 1977, *Rajput Polity.* Delhi: Manohar.

———. 1984, The Marwaris: Economic Foundations of an Indian Capitalist Class. In: Tripathi (ed.), q.v.

———. 1992, Ports of Gujarat in the Nineteenth Century: Trading Networks and Commercial Practices. In: Banga, (ed.), q.v.

Sharma, R.S. 1965, *Indian Feudalism, ca. 300-1200 A.D.* Calcutta: University of Calcutta.

Sharma, R.S. and V. Jha (eds): 1974, *Indian Society: Historical Probings.* Delhi: People's Publishing House.

Sharma, S.R. 1971, *Maharana Raj Singh and his Times.* Delhi: Motilal Banarsidass.

Sharpe, E. 1931, *Thakore Sahib Shri Sir Daulat Singh of Limbdi, Kathiawar.* London: Murray.

Sinha, S. 1967, Caste in India: Its Essential Pattern of Socio-Cultural Integration. In: A. de Reuck and J. Knight (eds): *Caste and Race: Comparative Approaches.* London: Churchill.

Singh, D. and A.B. Rajshirke 1992, The Merchant Communities in Surat: Trade, Trade Practices and Institutions in the late Eighteenth Century. In: Banga (ed.), q.v.

Singh, M.H. 1990, *The Castes of Marwar (first published 1894).* 2nd. edition. Jodhpur: Books Treasure.

Solanki, P. n.d., *Jay Khodiyar Akhyan* (in Gujarati). Ahmedabad: Mahavir Book Depot.

Sontheimer, G.D. 1993, *Pastoral Deities in Western India.* Delhi: Oxford University Press.

Sopher, D.E. 1975, Indian Pastoral Castes and Livestock Ecologies: A Geographic Analysis. In: Leshnik and Sontheimer (eds.), q.v.

Spodek, H. 1974, Rulers, Merchants and Other Groups in the City-States of Saurashtra, India. *Comparative Studies in Society and History,* XIV, 448-70.

———. 1976, *Urban-Rural Integration in Regional Development: A Case Study of Saurashtra, India.* Chicago: University of Chicago, Dept. of Geography.

Srinivas, M.N. 1952, *Religion and Society among the Coorgs.* Oxford: Oxford University Press.

———. 1953, Prospects of Sociological Research in Gujarat. Journal of the M.S. University of Baroda: 2: 21-37.

———. 1962, *Caste in Modern India and Other Essays.* Bombay: Asia.

———. 1967, *Social Change in Modern India.* Berkeley: University of California Press.

———. 1988, Foreword. In: *Shah and Desai, 1988,* q.v.

Stein, B. 1977, The Segmentary State in South Indian History. In: R.G. Fox (ed.), *Realm and Region in Traditional India.* New Delhi: Vikas.

Stern, H. 1973, Le pouvoir dans l'Inde traditionelle: territoire, caste et parenté. *L'Homme:* XIII: 50-70.

———. 1986, Le temple d'Eklingji et le royaume du Mewar (Rajasthan). In: L'Espace du temple II: *Purushartha*: 10: 15-30.

Stern, R.W. 1988, *The Cat and the Lion*. Leiden: Brill.

Subramaniam, L. 1991, The Eighteenth-Century Social Order in Surat: A Reply and an Excursus on the Riots of 1788 and 1795. *Modern Asian Studies:* 25, 2: 321-65.

———. 1992a, Western India in the Eighteenth Century: Ports, Inland Towns and States. In: Banga (ed.), q.v.

Tambs-Lyche, H. 1975, Indias befolkningsproblem sett nedefra. Samtiden, No. 4.

———. 1976a, Social Significance of Hinduism. In: *Papers of the Fifth European Conference on Modern South Asian Studies.* Leiden.

———. 1976b, *On the Nature of Ethnic Stereotypes.* Bergen: cyclostyled.

———. 1980a, *London Patidars.* London: Routledge and Kegan Paul.

———. 1980b, Gujarati Communities in Norway and Britain: Some Comparative Notes. *New Community:* VIII: 288-94:

———. 1982, The Merchantization of Saurashtra. *Journal of Social Science* (Dhaka): No. 16, 39-50.

———. 1991, Le roi et les enfants de la déesse. *Cahiers de Littérature Orale,* 29, 61-85.

———. 1992a, *Power and Devotion: Religion and Society in Saurashtra* (2 vols.). Bergen: University of Bergen.

———. 1992b, Heroes in the Hills, Power in the Plains: Patterns of Traditional Politics in Western South Asia. In: R. Grønhaug, G. Haaland and G. Henriksen (eds): *The Ecology of Choice and Symbol.* Bergen: Alma Mater: 121-38.

———. 1993, Flooding the World with Wealth. The Consecration Ritual of the Rajsagar Lake in Mewar. *Journal of the Oriental Institute* (Baroda): 40: 275-91.

———. 1994a, The Concept of Maya in the Vacanamrta of Swami Narayana. In: *Entwistle and Mallison* (eds), q.v. 192-209.

———. 1994b, The Region as Object of Discourse: An Example from India. *Social Science Information:* 33: 731-52.

———. 1995, Un défi mortel: le sacrifice de soi dans l'ouest de l'Inde. *Revue de l'Histoire des Religions,* ccxii.3, 327-50.

———. 1996, Une tradition orale face au post-modernisme. l'Exemple der bardes du Saurashtra. In C. Champion (ed.): *Traditions orales dans le monde indien.* Paris: Collection Puruṣartha, No. 18: 23-37.

———. forthcoming (a), Marriage and Affinity among Virgin Goddesses. In H. Tambs-Lyche (ed.): *The Feminine Sacred in South Asia.* Delhi: Manohar.

———. forthcoming (b), *Individual, Situation and Society in Saurashtra*. Delhi: Manohar.
Tessitori, A. 1914, A Scheme for the Bardic and Historical Survey of Rajputana. *Journal of the Asiatic Society of Bengal*, 373-410.
Thoothi, N.A. 1935, *The Vaishnavas of Gujarat*. Calcutta: Longmans, Green & Co.
Thorner, D. 1956, *The Agrarian Prospect in India*. Delhi: University Press.
Timberg, T.A. 1978, *The Marwaris. From Traders to Industrialists*. New Delhi: Vikas.
Tirmizi, S.A.I: 1984, Muslim Merchants of Medieval Gujarat. In: Tripathi (ed.), q.v.
Tod, J. 1829, *Annals and Antiquities of Rajasthan*, Vol. 1. (reprint 1950: London: Routledge & Kegan Paul).
———. 1884, *Annals and Antiquities of Rajasthan*, Vol. II. (first published 1832). Calcutta: Brojendra Lall Doss.
———. 1971, *Travels in Western India* (orig. publ. 1836 or 1837). Reprint: Delhi: Oriental.
Torri, M. 1991, Trapped inside the Colonial Order. The Hindu Bankers of Surat and their Business World during the Second Half of the Eighteenth Century. *Modern Asian Studies:* 25, 2: 367-401.
Tripathi, D (ed.)1984, *Business Communities of India*. Delhi: Manohar.
Tripathi, D. and M.J. Mehta 1984, Class Character of the Gujarati Business Community. In: Tripathi (ed.)., q.v.
Trivedi, A.B. 1939, Present Industries of Kathiawar. *Journal of the Gujarat Research Society:* 2: 26-72.
Trivedi, H.B. 1961, *The Mers of Saurashtra*. Baroda: M.S. University.
Tuck, D.R. 1986, *The Concept of Maya in Sankara and Radhakrishnan*. Delhi: Chanakya.
Ujwal, K.D.S. n.d. *Bhagwati Shri Karni Maharaj*. Ujlan (Marwar): published by the author.
Vaidya, K.B. 1945, *The Sailing Vessel Traffic on the West Coast of India and its future*. Bombay: Popular Book Depot.
Vakhatchand, M. 1851, *Amdavad na Itihas* (in Gujarati). Ahmedabad.
Van den Hoek, A.W. 1979, The Goddess of the Northern Gate. In: *Asie du Sud: Traditions et Changements*. Paris: CNRS.
Van der Veen, K. 1972, *I give Thee my Daughter*. Assen: v. Gorcum.
Vaudeville, C. 1980, The Govardhan Myth in Northern India. *Indo-Iranian Journal*: 22: 1-45.
Veblen, T. 1934, *The Theory of the Leisure Class*. New York: Modern Library.
Village Monographs: 1961 Census of Gujarat, (Census of India, vol. V, part VI). - no. 1: Pacchatardi.
———. - no. 8: Chichod.
———. - no. 16: Kajarda. Ahmedabad: Director of Census Operations.

Wadley, S.S. 1975, *Shakti: Power in the Conceptual Structure of Karimpur Religion.* Chicago: University of Chicago.

Watson, J.W. (ed.) 1884, *Gazetteer of the Bombay Presidency.* Vol. VIII: *Kathiawar.* Bombay: Government Central Press.

———. 1910, *Statistical Account of Bhavnagar.* Bombay.

Weber, M. 1930, *The Protestant Ethic and the Spirit of Capitalism.* London: Allen & Unwin.

———. 1948, *From Max Weber. Essays in Sociology and Political Science.* (H.H. Gerth and C. Wright Mills, eds). New York: Oxford University Press.

———. 1958, *The Religion of India.* New York: Free Press.

Weinberger-Thomas, C. 1990 Cendres d'immortalité: la crémation des veuves en Inde. *Archives de Sciences Sociales des Religions:* 67: 9-51.

Westphal-Hellbosch, S. and H. Westphal 1968, *Zum Geschichte und Kultur der Jat.* Berlin: Duncker und Humboldt.

———. 1974, *Hinduistische Viehzüchter im Nordwestlichen Indien, I: Die Rabari.* Berlin: Duncker und Humboldt.

———. 1976, *Hinduistische Viehzüchter im Nordwestlichen Indien, II: Die Bharwad und die Charan.* Berlin: Duncker und Humboldt.

Wilberforce-Bell, H. 1916, *A History of Kathiawad from the Earliest Times.* London: Heinemann.

Wilkins, W.J. 1975, *Hindu Mythology* (first published 1882). Reprint: Calcutta: Rupa & Co.

Williams, R.B. 1984, *A New Face of Hinduism: The Swaminarayan Religion.* Cambridge: Cambridge University Press.

Wiser, W.H. 1936, *The Hindu Jajmani System.* Lucknow: Lucknow Publishing House.

Wood, J. R. 1978, Indian Nationalism in the Princely Context: The Rajkot Satyagraha of 1938-39. In: Jeffrey (ed.), q.v.

Ziegler, N.P. 1973, *Action, Power and Service in Rajasthani Culture: A Social History of the Rajputs of Middle Period Rajasthan* Ph.D. dissertation, Dept. of History,University of Chicago.

Index